LOOKINGFLASH

LOOKINGFLASH
CLOTHING IN AOTEAROA NEW ZEALAND

Edited by Bronwyn Labrum, Fiona McKergow
and Stephanie Gibson

AUCKLAND UNIVERSITY PRESS

First published 2007

Auckland University Press
University of Auckland
Private Bag 92019
Auckland
New Zealand
www.auckland.ac.nz/aup

© the contributors, 2007

ISBN 978 1 86940 397 3

Publication is assisted by the History Group, Ministry for Culture and Heritage

National Library of New Zealand Cataloguing-in-Publication Data
Looking flash : clothing in Aotearoa New Zealand / edited by
Bronwyn Labrum, Fiona McKergow and Stephanie Gibson.
Includes bibliographical references and index.
ISBN 978-1-86940-397-3
1. Fashion—New Zealand—History. 2. Clothes and clothing—
New Zealand—History. I. Labrum, Bronwyn. II. McKergow,
Fiona, 1964- III. Gibson, Stephanie (Stephanie Dawn), 1967-
391.00993—dc 22

This book is copyright. Apart from fair dealing for the purpose of private study, research, criticism or review, as permitted under the Copyright Act, no part may be reproduced by any process without prior permission of the publisher.

Front cover image: Queen Elizabeth II and the Duke of Edinburgh chatting with champion shearers and brothers Godfrey (left) and Ivan Bowen during a Royal Command Performance in McLean Park, Napier, 1954. Photograph by Edward P. Christensen.
F 19828 ½ (AAQT 6538, 15/C/8), courtesy of Archives New Zealand Te Rua Mahara o te Kāwanatanga Wellington Office, National Publicity Studios Collection, and Alexander Turnbull Library, Wellington, New Zealand

Cover design: Athena Sommerfeld

Printed by Prinlink Ltd, Wellington

Contents

	Acknowledgements	vii
	Abbreviations	viii
1	Dressing History Up: Introduction *Bronwyn Labrum*	1
2	He Whatu Ariki, He Kura, He Waero: Chiefly Threads, Red and White *Patricia Te Arapo Wallace*	12
3	Unpicked for the Voyage? Heirloom Dresses in Colonial New Zealand *Rosanne Livingstone and Valerie Carson*	28
4	Kilts as Costumes: Identity, Resistance and Tradition *Katie Pickles*	41
5	Every Garment Tells a Story: Exploring Public Collections *David Butts*	59
6	'What are These, So Withered, and So Wild in their Attire?' Castaways' Clothing from the Auckland Islands *Jennifer Quérée*	76
7	Weaving a Journey: The Story of a Unique Cloak *Awhina Tamarapa*	94
8	Hand-Me-Downs and Respectability: Clothing and the Needy *Bronwyn Labrum*	112
9	'Just the Thing': Shopping for Clothes in Palmerston North *Fiona McKergow*	132
10	On the Beach: Or the 'Unbearable Scandal' of Shrinking Swimwear *Caroline Daley*	154
11	Dressing for War: Glamour and Duty in Women's Lives During the Second World War *Deborah Montgomerie*	168

12	Moving in Unison, Dressing in Uniform: Stepping Out in Style with Marching Teams *Charlotte Macdonald*	186
13	Engaging in Mischief: The Black Singlet in New Zealand Culture *Stephanie Gibson*	206
14	One Man's Fantasy: The Eden Hore Collection of High and Exotic Fashion Garments *Jane Malthus*	222

List of Contributors	242
Notes	245
Further Reading	276
Index	278

Acknowledgements

We gratefully acknowledge the support we have received from the many people and institutions who assisted us as we brought this lengthy project to completion. Our first debt is to the contributors, who were all working on multiple projects, for their patience, grace and good humour. Staff at many museums and libraries, particularly at the Alexander Turnbull Library, Archives New Zealand Te Rua Mahara o te Kāwanatanga, the Hawke's Bay Cultural Trust, Puke Ariki, Te Manawa, Te Papa and the Whanganui Regional Museum facilitated our documentary, image and object research. Portions of this book were presented at conferences and seminars: the reactions of audience members at the New Zealand Historical Association Conference (Auckland, 2005), the 5th Annual Textile Symposium (Wellington, 2006) and the Massey University Social Anthropology material culture seminar series (Palmerston North, 2006) were very useful. Bronwyn would like to thank her former colleagues in the History Department at the University of Waikato and present colleagues at Massey University Wellington for their interest and support. The School of Visual and Material Culture provided financial assistance. The wonderful members of her Wellington research group helped to keep her on track. Bronwyn Dalley and Conal McCarthy have been constant sources of wise advice and encouragement. Conal also made useful comments on the text. Fiona wishes to thank Robert McLachlan, who enabled us to have our regular Sunday editorial meetings uninterrupted, by looking after Helena and Willa and taking time off for Fiona to work on the book. His support is warmly appreciated. Stephanie is grateful for her Te Papa colleagues' advice and support and to her family and friends for their general good will and interest. We are also very indebted to Anna Rogers for her intelligent and professional editing; Pat Sargison for compiling the index; and Elizabeth Caffin, Anna Hodge, Annie Irving, Katrina Duncan, Christine O'Brien and Sam Elworthy at Auckland University Press for their care and skill.

Abbreviations

AJHR	*Appendix to the Journals of the House of Representatives*
ANZ	Archives New Zealand
ATL	Alexander Turnbull Library
AS	*Auckland Star*
DM	Dominion Museum
DNZB	*Dictionary of New Zealand Biography*
DT	*Daily Telegraph* (Napier)
EP	*Evening Post*
FS	*Feilding Star*
JPS	*Journal of the Polynesian Society*
NZL	*New Zealand Listener*
NZMA	New Zealand Marching Association
LT	*Lyttelton Times*
MES	*Manawatu Evening Standard*
MT	*Manawatu Times*
MP	Member of Parliament
NZD	*New Zealand Draper, Clothier and Boot Retailer*
NZJH	*New Zealand Journal of History*
NZH	*New Zealand Herald*
NZWW	*New Zealand Woman's Weekly*
ODT	*Otago Daily Times*
OW	*Otago Witness*
SST	*Sunday Star-Times*
ST	*Southland Times*
Te Papa	Museum of New Zealand Te Papa Tongarewa
WAAC	Women's Auxiliary Army Corps
WAAF	Women's Auxiliary Air Force
WRNZNS	Women's Royal New Zealand Naval Service
YWCA	Young Women's Christian Association

1. Dressing History Up: Introduction
Bronwyn Labrum

AROUND 1935 FRANCES HODGKINS WAS PUTTING THE FINISHING TOUCHES to her first self-portrait. Rather than putting her face in the picture, she chose instead to represent herself through her clothing. Hodgkins 'loved clothes, and given the necessary large income would have dressed in the height of fashion all her life'.[1] For a time during the First World War and the 1920s, she was employed as a designer at the Calico Printers Association, and was renowned for her sartorial 'Frenchiness'. She adored bold and colourful scarves and hats, especially berets.[2] In this painting, her fluid brush strokes reveal a red beret, scarves, shoe, handbag, belt and handkerchief, surrounding a mirror (Plate 1). Hodgkins blends the idea of objects from a still life with a 'revelation of femininity and a love of dressing up'.[3] There are elements of surrealism and symbolism, and 'of her dress sense, the signatures of her style'.[4] Her portrait is a literal embodiment of the common observation that we are what we wear.

It has taken time for many scholars to catch up with Hodgkins' acute insights. Until very recently, many thought that clothing and fashion were ephemeral and frivolous; neither fitting subjects for 'serious' research nor key themes in accounts of the past. Yet these attitudes have changed dramatically in the last two decades. Increasing numbers of writers are observing that clothing reveals as much as it may conceal. It has more than a practical function: it provides important evidence of personal identities and much broader social patterns and forces. Furthermore, although clothing practices are usually 'quotidian' by nature, the 'cultural work of dress' is profound.[5] This collection of essays demonstrates that what we wear and what has been worn provide immediate and often overlooked pathways into our history and culture.

As Lou Taylor has noted, the study of the history of clothing has often reflected the great divide between artefacts and the academy.[6] This separation originated in the artefact-based approaches within museums and personal collections. Specialist collectors were often more interested in the formal qualities of clothing as artefacts and perhaps less concerned with what they might say about the wearers and owners, or about larger social processes. Their inquiry followed a trajectory of collection, identification, conservation, display and interpretation.

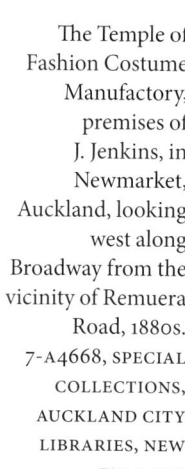

The Temple of Fashion Costume Manufactory, premises of J. Jenkins, in Newmarket, Auckland, looking west along Broadway from the vicinity of Remuera Road, 1880s. 7-A4668, SPECIAL COLLECTIONS, AUCKLAND CITY LIBRARIES, NEW ZEALAND

Usually quite independently, and much later, approaches based on social and economic history, material culture and cultural studies, developed on the other side of the divide amongst academic researchers. Taylor is aware that the investigation of clothing and textile history 'has long been full of tensions and strains which can be laid at the door of the subject itself. [It] attracts the passions of an extraordinarily wide group of specialists and enthusiasts.'[7]

In the last ten or so years, however, this division has been increasingly blurred and a more adventurous range of interdisciplinary approaches to clothing – rather than only 'dress' or the earlier 'costume history' – have resulted. These newer approaches draw on developments in consumption studies, material culture and the ubiquitous 'cultural studies'. For example, John Brewer has argued that it was 'high time' for 'big history' to 'address one of the special features of modern Western societies: not just industrialisation or economic growth, but the capacity to create and sustain a consumer economy, and the consumers to go with it'.[8] Clothing and textiles are a key part of that larger story. Researchers have since argued strenuously for the all-encompassing social embrace of material culture both in and outside of Western, industrialised societies. They argue that material objects matter because 'the meanings people give to objects, the whole process of acquisition, notions of taste, style, social competition, the emotional pleasure derived from material objects, and the symbolic product values . . . help us examine the shifts in intellectual feelings about the core relationships between humans, goods, and society'.[9]

Mr and Mrs Imrie, with their prized possessions, including a sewing machine, photographed in Wanganui by William James Harding, c.1869. G-8112-1/4, W. J. HARDING COLLECTION, ALEXANDER TURNBULL LIBRARY, WELLINGTON, NEW ZEALAND

In terms of studies of fashion and clothing, cultural studies have had, arguably, the bigger impact on this approach. This is particularly true of those investigations that focus on women and gender, stemming from feminist analyses. Drawing on backgrounds in sociology, cultural history and media studies, with training in the analysis of meaning, symbols, ideology and identity, these scholars were broadly interested in the 'social life' of clothing. Dress, behaviour and the construction of appearance, taste and distinction, social marginalisation and subcultures, all became the subjects of major studies.[10] However, there is a new fear among some researchers that attention has shifted from garments to text and theory. The artefact–academic divide seemed to have reappeared in a new form.[11] A new volume entitled *Clothing as Material Culture* aims to put an end to what it saw as 'a rather unnecessary if ancient antagonism'. The editors want to show how their collection of essays 'transcends and refuses this simplistic dualism'.[12] Their book proceeds on the understanding that:

the dissection of clothing into pattern, fibre, fabric, form and production is not opposed to, but part of, its consideration as an aspect of human and cosmological engagement. The sensual and the aesthetic – what cloth feels and looks like – is the source of its capacity to objectify myth, cosmology and also morality, power and values.[13]

At the same time as the scholarly field has been expanding and diversifying, there has been a growing general interest in all aspects of dress, fashion, design and culture. The number of tertiary courses in these areas, the increasing profile of New Zealand designers in the media and on the street, and the rise of blockbuster clothing exhibitions in museums are testament to this appetite. All these developments have contributed to more eclectic, more complex and more interesting historical studies of clothing internationally. Few studies in New Zealand range widely or reflect the burgeoning interest and new approaches. Hardly any general histories have 'dress' or 'clothing' as index entries, for example. Is it because for most of our history we have played to our national stereotype and been wary of 'looking flash', afraid of appearing too ostentatious or gaudy and therefore above ourselves? Designers have despaired of the 'Saturday morning feel' to our clothing and for a good part of our history we waited for the northern hemisphere to dictate fashions to us.[14] A recent account reiterates the assumption that we have always been a dowdy country: 'The wardrobes of this country were colonised by the sturdy and sensible clothes of our mostly British forebears, and any flair or individuality was overwhelmed by conformity and, in the case of men, a sea of grey sports coats.'[15] Overlooking the wide variety of fascinating contrary evidence provided in work like this, generalisations and unexamined notions remain. Despite the changes in interest and research agendas, most accounts to date are narrative histories of dress and exhibition catalogues focused on stylistic changes, or they treat dress and fashion as primarily feminine worlds.[16] Recent popular histories with a slightly wider ambit continue such breathless accounts with their 'I can't believe we wore that!' theme.[17]

As well as a comprehensive study of Māori clothing by Hirini (Sidney) Moko Mead, several published studies of specific aspects of clothing provide a useful counterpoint.[18] These include an account of the roles of Māori cloaks in social life by Amiria Henare; research about nineteenth-century clothing and dress reformers by Jane Malthus; clothing in southern Dunedin from 1890 to 1940 by Jane Malthus and Chris Brickell; 1940s and 1950s clothing by Fiona McKergow; Heather Nicholson's history of knitting; fashion, gender and modernity in the interwar period by Danielle Sprecher; Frazer Andrewes' account of post-war masculinity; and late twentieth-century style by Barbara Brookes. These studies constitute a new research agenda, mostly for the twentieth century, and reflect the wider questions raised in recent studies. These and other writers show that there are now a number of people researching clothing from a wide range of

Neighbours pinning dress patterns to fabric on the kitchen lino floor, photographed by John Pascoe, 1944.
F11741/4, J. PASCOE COLLECTION, ALEXANDER TURNBULL LIBRARY, WELLINGTON, NEW ZEALAND

institutions – museums, as well as universities, and independent scholars – and writing from a variety of perspectives.

This book aims to dress history up and to bring this exciting work to a broader audience. Not all the contributors we invited were able to write for us and inevitably there are absences in the book and gaps in the research that we present here. Those that immediately come to mind include fashionable men's clothing, children's dress, garments worn by Pacific Islanders and migrant groups, and the current generation of fashion designers and their international success.[19] Patricia Te Arapo Wallace opens the volume with her careful analysis of creativity and evolving style in Māori society before European colonisation. Resourcefully bringing together scattered evidence from a range of sources, she discusses the way Māori used what was to hand to devise everyday and fine clothing. She shows how mana (authority, control, influence, prestige or power) was an important part of dressing and that it applied not only to individuals but also to group endeavours, reflecting the wider organisation of society. Wallace argues that notions of style

Two male models in Auckland, 1956. SPARROW 6-1947B,
SPARROW INDUSTRIAL PICTURES LTD, AUCKLAND MUSEUM

A range of children's homemade clothing and elegant female daywear is evident in the waiting room at the Plunket Building, Waterloo, Lower Hutt, in the 1950s.
AALF 6112, BOX 3 23/1/11, ARCHIVES NEW ZEALAND TE RUA MAHARA O TE KĀWANATANGA, WELLINGTON OFFICE

and fashion were important in Māori society, providing a strong counterpoint to conventional Western histories of tastes and trends.

In their chapter on eighteenth-century heirloom dresses brought to colonial New Zealand, Rosanne Livingstone and Valerie Carson attempt to solve a long-standing puzzle. Using the rare examples of unpicked garments from the collection of the Museum of New Zealand Te Papa Tongarewa, they reveal the personal and familial significance of clothing to migrants and their descendants. As they literally piece their story together, the importance of recycling and reuse of clothing in a range of contexts becomes clear.

Kilts have been an influential mode of dress in our history. In her wide-ranging and provocative discussion, Katie Pickles takes a largely southern perspective on the different wearings of the kilt in New Zealand. After untangling the history of the modern kilt from its mythology, she demonstrates the convergence of national, international and trans-national influences on the way that kilts have been worn as costumes representing the politics of identity, resistance and tradition. Kilts have been worn by those upholding tradition and hegemony and those fomenting rebellion and resistance. As well as illustrating the strong presence of the Scots in New Zealand, she shows how this masculine form of attire has been appropriated by schoolgirls and gay men, among others, to underline the socially constructed nature of dress and the challenge to gender roles, sexuality and identity it can represent.

Much of the material evidence in this book relies on the initiative and foresight of museum curators and conservators. In highlighting the stories of his favourite garments at the Hawke's Bay Museum, David Butts demonstrates the way that collections provide many and varied kinds of evidence with which to construct histories of clothing, particularly articles associated with rites of passage and those handed down in families. He notes that the museum was slow to collect Pākehā (European New Zealand) clothing, unlike Māori garments, which were avidly collected by early colonists. Moreover, the focus from the later twentieth century has been on designer or special garments, rather than the local or everyday. The vagaries of institutional fortunes and the critical influence of individual staff predilections are a consistent theme.

As well as being part of celebrations and rites, clothing is also fundamental to the preservation of self and identity in extreme circumstances, as Jennifer Quérée demonstrates with her fascinating story of how sailors and others shipwrecked on the Auckland Islands in the mid-nineteenth and early twentieth centuries made sartorial provision when they lost everything. Drawing upon personal accounts of those involved and a series of remarkable photographs, she describes how existing sewing and tailoring skills were applied to sealskin, bone, wood and anything else to hand. Even in the most adverse circumstances, a concern for contemporary expectations and the fashions of the day remained important to those who feared being seen as wild and uncivilised.

'Castaway suits' ended up in a number of New Zealand museums, as did many fine examples of Māori weaving. Yet the documentation of taonga (treasures) is often much more sketchy, as Awhina Tamarapa's intriguing tale demonstrates. It focuses on the journey of a single cloak between maker, owner, dealer, and museum – a common trajectory for such garments. The technical knowledge that comes to light about the cloak, its history and wider social and cultural meaning, provides a deft illustration of the Māori curator's primary role: reconnecting taonga and people.

Most of the previous chapters have taken as their focus élite examples of clothing and particular types of garments. Bronwyn Labrum turns the spotlight on hand-me-downs, arguing that this is a necessary corrective to the typical histories we read. Ranging over the nineteenth and twentieth centuries, she discusses how clothes of the poor and the needy were often passed down through successive family members, distributed by charities, churches and members of the community or sold at second-hand clothes shops. What did this mean for those involved in the informal economy of clothing? Also powerfully conveyed are the difficulties of those living in institutions, where clothing provision was variable and garments might be part of the punishment.

No history of clothing would be complete without consideration of the changing nature of shopping. The rich material brought to light in Fiona McKergow's chapter on Manawatū retailing reveals a story at once highly local, yet also global in nature. Canvassing tailoring and dressmaking, ready-to-wear and home sewing supplies, she offers an engaging description of how buying and selling garments in Palmerston North's central square developed over the period from the 1870s to the 1920s, in terms of types of shops and merchandise and also sales techniques. The sensual and social pleasures of shopping are revealed in the habits of Emily Mildon, a wealthy farmer's wife, based on her surviving invoices. This chapter shows in illuminating detail how retailing involved the trade of ideas as much as goods.

The international dimension of retailing is echoed in Caroline Daley's racy account of shrinking bathing suits at the beach. Emphasising changing fabric technology, individual desires and pleasures, and global fashion trends, she highlights the importance to our twentieth-century clothing history of consumption, modernity and understandings of gender that challenged conventions. Disputing the received wisdom that New Zealand was a 'tight society', she shows how it was part of a wider world of fashion and scandal.

Fun and frivolity also infuse Deborah Montgomerie's account of wartime femininity, which argues against the drab and austere stereotype persistently attached to women's garments of this period. Using women's own words, she demonstrates how important it was to look good both for themselves and for men, to have access to consumer pleasures and to differentiate clearly the sexes. In her nuanced discussion of dance outfits, wedding dresses and uniforms, Montgomerie points out that women were not blind to the personal and cultural significance of dress.

Uniformity and its varied meanings are explored through a different set of clothing in Charlotte Macdonald's evocative chapter on marching uniforms. Arguing that these constitute a unique body culture in international terms, she analyses the origin, production and wearing of these outfits. She shows how girls' marching involved a unique transformation of military-style parade ground drill into a civilian, competitive display sport. Personal accounts and the material culture of marching, which illustrate the empowerment of young women, are placed within a wide context. The appeal of British royalty ceremonial, Cold War security issues and the uniforms' links to Scottish emblems, the military and other influences are all critical to her account.

Stephanie Gibson offers revealing insights into the cultural history of the black singlet, that archetypal New Zealand garment of the practical Kiwi male. She shows how it has become part of the fabric of our lives. Worn by a range of people including manual and rural workers, athletes and anti-authority figures, it has also appeared in comedy programmes, cartoons, artworks, on stamps, in memorials, on the street and the dance floor. Her chapter traverses pioneer mythology, the rural economy, national identity, gender roles and fashion, and forces us to think very differently about this humble item of clothing as it takes on a new lease of life in the twenty-first century.

Jane Malthus introduces us to one of the most singular characters in this book: Eden Hore, the farmer turned collector of *haute couture* 1970s fashion. Illustrating again the importance of collectors and collecting, and the evidence

'Otara, Auckland, 1981', photograph by Glenn Jowitt. 003175, MUSEUM OF NEW ZEALAND TE PAPA TONGAREWA AND GLEN JOWITT

they leave for historians, Hore's 'parallel fashion universe' of clothing reveals the colours, designs and fabrics of this period in all their glory. From sequins to suede, folkloric to glam themes, the designers who entered the premier fashion competitions of the day followed European couturiers rather than the increasing casualness and individuality of everyday fashion. Hore's collection represents some of New Zealand's best designers, who were becoming an endangered species during the 1980s. The survival of these outfits as a collection allows us to reflect on the multi-faceted and often unsettling nature of fashion.

Taken together, these essays highlight key themes, continuities and changes in clothing in New Zealand over at least three centuries. It is striking how, from earliest times, the environment and climate have conditioned the way we clothe ourselves, whether at work in the countryside, on the beach, in schoolrooms throughout the country or on remote island outposts. The military context of attire runs from kilts through wartime strictures to school uniforms and sporting contests. Uniformity, in the sense of order and control, but also of wanting to fit in, occurs in circumstances as various as the military, education, recreation and in provision for the poor and needy and the institutionalised. Contrary to the common view of globalisation as a late-twentieth-century phenomenon, these chapters illustrate the long-standing international dimension of what we have worn, whether it is the imported stock of fabrics and supplies at the local dressmaker or department store, the avidly read fashion magazines or the influence of different ethnic communities on local manifestations of transnational garments.

The way that black singlets were worn in completely new ways by the end of the twentieth century alerts us to the undeniable changes in our sartorial habits. The handcraft techniques and meanings associated with the valuable and magnificent garments of the colonial period, both Māori and Pākehā, are rarely used today. New Zealanders increasingly bought their clothes, rather than making them at home, reflecting wider changes in retailing and marketing. The importance of the growing diversity of New Zealand society in the later twentieth century, and especially challenges to gender roles and sexual norms, are evident both in second-hand clothing shops and on the dance floor. Conformity has given way to a greater acceptance of subcultures, at least in some areas and on some occasions – the street if not the school playground. *Looking Flash* demonstrates that the clothes we wear, even high-fashion garments meant for the élite, reveal the changing social, political and economic contexts in which we live.

This collection also tells a shifting story about the fate of various types of garments that found their way into museums as preservable material culture. For these writers conducting historical research, the survival of clothing is as important as the continued existence of texts and images. The way clothing is worn – shifting the angle of a hat, adding a bow, taking a garment out of its conventional context – is crucial to its interpretation and meaning. And drawing on oral histories, as many contributors do, adds a vivid dimension to their accounts.

Looking Flash does not attempt to be a study of New Zealand's national dress nor is it preoccupied with what makes New Zealand clothing distinctive, although there is plenty of evidence of local inflections and characteristics in these essays. That question awaits a different kind of study.[20] But we hope that we have opened the wardrobe of history, picked out some new hangers, shaken out the garments and held them up to the light.

2. He Whatu Ariki, He Kura, He Waero: Chiefly Threads, Red and White

Patricia Te Arapo Wallace

I te oranga o te tama a Kiripūia he kura, he waero.
In the lifetime of Kiripūia's son there were garments of red kākā feathers and garments of dogskin.[1]

LIKE THE CRIMSON AND ERMINE ROBES OF COURTLY EUROPEAN HISTORY, prestigious garments of red kākā feathers or white kurī (Māori dog) hair were once the stately mantles of important tribal leaders in traditional Māori communities. Kiripūia was such a chief, but sadly, his role and that of his son, their time and place in Māori history, have been long forgotten. In contrast, the resplendent cloaks are remembered. The prized kākahu kura was covered with rare red feathers, painstakingly intertwined in the weaving process; tassels of white kurī tail hair were attached to cover the entire surface of the valued kahu waero. According to Māori scholar Hirini Moko Mead, these chiefly garments belonged to a time of organised tribal society with higher standards of conduct; the opening quotation suggests a previous era of greatness, and this introductory pepeha (proverb) expresses regret that things are not what they used to be.[2] The decline of traditional forms of finery has continued to be observed in elements of Māori dress; although these highly esteemed historical garments can still be identified, other styles and materials have evolved and changed considerably over the ages.

An inclusive history of New Zealand clothing must take account of previous forms of Māori dress and attempt to uncover aspects of their diversity and symbolism. Although this is an area that has been underresearched, this chapter endeavours to look beyond the Classical Māori period (circa AD 1650–1800) as defined by Mead in early studies.[3] It reveals some of the less well-known types of clothing worn by Māori as it explores developments from the earliest evidence of bark cloth beaters until the time of the signing of the Treaty of Waitangi in 1840 between Māori chiefs and the British Crown. This chapter also demonstrates the versatile skills of the earlier garment makers, revealing that the range of traditional dress was more varied than is commonly realised, and through oral histories provides glimpses of an earlier Māori philosophy of dress. At the same time, rather than perpetuating an exclusively Western concept of 'fashion', this chapter reflects the universality of fashion as an inherent part of human social interaction and a means by which individuals of status and power have displayed their importance.[4]

Traditional Māori dress was the product of an ongoing process of discovery, experimentation and creativity. Far from being static, it evolved continuously from the practices associated with the Eastern Polynesian origins of the first settlers. Familiar techniques were applied and adapted to semi-familiar materials in Aotearoa. Functional and effective procedures were passed on through successive generations. These time-honoured habits led to a range of different garments. The wearing of customary Māori clothing continued into the nineteenth century, when the influence of Christianity, a cash economy, new ideas of status and different concepts of 'civilisation' combined to encourage Māori adoption of European colonial dress and a gradual ceding of the customs of their ancestors. Nonetheless, the status and concept of mana (authority, control, influence, prestige or power) attached to an impressive cloak has lingered in the perceptions of Māori and non-Māori alike. This was manifest in the gifting of such items between Māori and certain respected individual Pākehā (European New Zealanders) in the latter part of the nineteenth century. In the nineteenth and twentieth centuries the wearing of traditionally styled cloaks was generally restricted to Māori at marae and cultural events, but in the twenty-first century this practice is developing to reflect pride in cultural identity across a much broader public spectrum.

The natural degradation of organic textiles and the absence of a print culture mean that the evidence of customary Māori dress must be pieced together from alternative sources. Oral traditions supply the earliest information about chiefly appearance and the various garments that were worn in the distant past. Archaeological discoveries confirm these traditions and add further information. Material evidence that has been collected can be corroborated by the documentary and pictorial evidence of early explorers and settlers. Similarly, these early writings and drawings support elements of the older stories and explain the significance of certain ways of dressing. Collating these disparate sources enables a broader understanding of the diversity of customary Māori dress. Nonetheless, as with other cultures, the surviving evidence leads to a focus on garments of high-status individuals and the clothing of ordinary people is underrepresented.

A register of prestigious garments can be gained from oral histories that told of regional taniwha or legendary monsters which once prevailed upon local people. When such a taniwha was finally slaughtered, the contents of its abdomen often revealed each precious item it had swallowed. These invariably included weapons of pounamu (greenstone or nephrite), whalebone and hardwoods, ornaments of pounamu and sharks' teeth, as well as finely woven garments and kahu (cloaks or capes) of birdskins or feathers such as kahu kiwi, kākahu kura (red feathered), kahu toroa (albatross) or kahu kererū (wood pigeon).[5] They also included kahu kekeno (sealskin) and a wide variety of different styles of kahu kurī (dogskin cloaks). That such garments were recorded, along with desirable weapons and ornaments, indicates the high level of importance given to them in Māori society.[6] The history of Māori dress is, however, even more rich and complex than those storytellers realised.

The story begins with successful sea-voyaging waka (canoes), which prove that the early Polynesian settlers possessed a range of textile technology. Competent cordage and plaited weaving skills – the whiri and raranga of modern Māori – were essential to produce the anchor and fishing lines, ropes and sails necessary at sea. But the cooler, temperate climate of Aotearoa presented the newcomers with considerable clothing challenges. The new-found need for warm garments that could withstand cold rain had to be met from the diverse resources they discovered here. Besides the indigenous birdlife, and the Polynesian dog that they brought with them, there was an assortment of new and semi-familiar botanical species that might prove to be potential weaving materials. By trial and error, the newcomers learned how to make the most of these various plants. They modified the weaving skills of their ancestors and, from a range of resources, created a variety of innovative apparel.

One of the earliest experiments must have been attempts to reproduce the familiar barkcloth within Aotearoa. In some parts of their new land, early Māori settlers were able to establish the aute or paper mulberry tree (*Broussonetia papyrifera*), a traditional source of barkcloth worn in Polynesia. The discovery by archaeologists of wooden barkcloth beaters from North Auckland to Taranaki shows that there was once a widespread practice of producing aute cloth within Aotearoa.[7] Māori also experimented with indigenous trees and applied the same beating technique to strips of the ribbonwood and lacebark species (*Hoheria spp.*), producing a specifically New Zealand textile. However, although pieces of plain barkcloth have been recovered from archaeological sites, there is no evidence that Māori actually wore beaten barkcloth garments; the cloth was probably impractical for local purposes.[8] But barkcloth retained an element of high prestige within the cultural memory of Māori in Aotearoa. Thin white paper-like strips of barkcloth were recorded as items of hair adornment as recently as the late eighteenth century. Members of Captain James Cook's expeditions wrote about seeing fragments of the cloth worn as ear ornaments by chiefly Māori.[9]

The newcomers would have soon learned to use birdskins. Ngāi Tahu tradition tells of kākāpō skins being used for the girdles or kilts of young women. When a party of chiefs were travelling south in the early eighteenth century they claimed and named tracts of land to provide kākāpō for their daughters' clothing.[10] In 1769, on board Jean-François-Marie de Surville's vessel, *St Jean Baptiste*, his first lieutenant Guillaume Labé described the use of birdskins to create a frontal apron, or maro: 'some have the skin of a bird to cover their nudity, without passing underneath'.[11] He alluded to maro again when he recorded women 'drawing aside the birdskin which covers their nakedness'.[12] Birdskins were still being prepared for use in Queen Charlotte Sound during 1820, where members of the Russian Bellingshausen expedition recorded seeing a white birdskin stretched out to dry. However, the traditional technology used to preserve such skins is not fully known. Birdskin garments could be made in different ways. While entire skins might be worn as a maro, others were stitched together for larger items of clothing. During Louis-Isidore Duperrey's visit to the Bay of Islands aboard *La Coquille* in 1824, the use of kiwi skins was recorded. His naval surgeon and chronicler René Primavère Lesson noted that Māori hunted kiwi with dogs and made cloaks of them by sewing several skins together.[13]

Such stitching had a long history. Archaeological evidence of bone needles and awls found at the Wairau Bar in Marlborough indicates that Māori were sewing some several hundred years ago in the mid-twelfth century.[14] Although no evidence of moa skin garments has been discovered, it is highly probable that early Māori made use of this rich resource, given that they were already consuming the flesh of these large birds and using moa egg shells and bones. However, later evidence of weka skins being used for clothing *has* been recovered. In 1881 a schist cave burial site on the Strath Taieri plains, near Middlemarch, was found to contain some stitched weka skins that were probably once part of a garment. The pieces were clearly part of a carefully planned whole. Each of the five remaining brown weka skins had been cut into an approximately rectangular shape, then placed side by side with the wing holes in line, indicating some form of routine practice. The remnant was probably part of a patchwork type of cape or cloak, fashioned in a manner that would have emphasised the pattern created by feather colouring and texture, thereby suggesting an aesthetic intention. The seams were joined with a form of knotted blanket stitch on the inner side of the skins, and sewn with muka or whītau – both regional names for the fibre extracted from the blade of the harakeke (flax) plant (*Phormium tenax*). When these skins were initially examined, a fragment strip believed to be of moa skin was found covering one seam, although which side of the seam does not appear to be recorded.[15] Unfortunately, this has since been detached. It is possible that the design was originally highlighted with strips of moa skin, poignant remnants that might have provided tangible links with a remembered ancestor or a significant element of a bygone era.

Māori also stitched both dogskins and sealskins together. Despite references to kahu kekeno in oral traditions, Cook and other members of his expeditions did not see Māori making use of sealskin. However, in 1913, a piece of sealskin was found in an old burial cave in Te Kuiti. Although this was a single rectangular piece, there is evidence that it was once part of a stitched article. This is indicated by a double row of very fine holes around three of its sides – holes with the regularity and fineness of twin-needle machine sewing. As Māori have customarily wrapped cloaks and blankets about their bodies, it is very probable that this item was once part of a sealskin garment. Although this is the only material evidence of its type, it provides confirmation of the traditional stories.[16] It clearly establishes that Māori used sealskins, and that they had developed appropriate technology to work the skins into articles of clothing. This uniqueness suggests that at some point, a number of generations before Cook's arrival, seal numbers may have been depleted to such an extent that this resource ceased to be used. It is impossible to know why it was never revived when seal numbers increased, particularly as dogskins continued to be used. One possible explanation could be that by the time seals were more plentiful, sealskin garments had lost their status and dogskin cloaks were more favoured.

Dogskin cloaks were made in at least two different ways: one method used whole pelts; the other used tassels of dog hair or numerous narrow strips of skins on a woven base. Oral tradition suggests that the former method is the older. Te Rangi Hiroa (Sir Peter Buck) recorded that one was involved in an exchange for the *Aotea*, a recently completed sea-voyaging canoe which would eventually leave Rangiātea (identified as Ra'iatea, north-west of Tahiti) and journey to Aotearoa. The eponymous ancestral chief Turi gave a 'double' dogskin cloak to his father-in-law Toto.[17] This cloak was so important that the names of the dogs used in it were retained in the mythology of the migration: Potakatawhiti, Pukekowhatarangi, Whakapupahiakura, Matawaritehuia, Kākārikitawhiti, Mitimaiterangi, Nukuteapiapi and Mitimaiteparu.[18]

One double-sided dogskin cloak of this type is held at Puke Ariki, the regional museum at New Plymouth. Known locally as a huru kurī, it was constructed from eight full-sized pelts stitched together to create a rectangular shape.[19] Made around 1800–10 by Rawahotana, at Te Namu, Ōpunake, it used skins that had been obtained by his father. It was purchased for £4 from Whakataupoti, the son of Rawahotana, by W. H. Skinner at Parihaka in 1885. Skinner had the cloak photographed, as worn by Ramaka Te Amai, with the fur side outwards.[20] The pelts show that the colours of dogskins were varied – brown, black and white – and that all still retained the ears and tails of the animals. The seams have the appearance of a mock French seam. They were formed with a row of double running stitch, the kurī thong stitches about 1.5 centimetres apart, being worked through a single row of holes and passing through a total of four thicknesses of dogskin. On the inner side of the pelts the seams are ornamented; hanging strips of dogskin tipped with hair are inserted at intervals into the original seams. They show unmistakably that this was designed as a reversible garment. In Southland, remnants of dogskin garments suggest that they were less sophisticated in design. Pelts at the Otago Museum show a variety of colours, but no evidence remains of their original form. These items were not stitched like the Taranaki cloak but joined with a seam similar to that used for the local weka skins.

Huruhuru kurī (width: 1720 mm, length: 1450 mm). Obverse and reverse views. A79.966, PUKE ARIKI, NEW PLYMOUTH

Unlike the huru kurī of stitched pelts, kahu kurī cloaks had a firmly woven kaupapa (base) to which dog-hair tassels or narrow cut strips of dogskin were attached. The kaupapa was made of plied muka, using closely packed, very even single-paired twining – an extremely skilled and time-consuming weaving process. The surface was then ornamented with awe (attachments of white dog-hair tassels) or closely overlaid with narrow parallel strips of dogskin.

The most richly adorned cloaks decorated with white awe were known as kahu waero and were so densely covered with hair that the kaupapa could not be seen. These prestigious awe clusters were a visual statement of affluence and power. They were produced by a protracted and intricate process from the long bushy wool-like tail hair of white dogs.[21] Such dogs were highly valued by Māori. They were carefully tended and slept inside on clean mats to ensure that their luxuriant tails would be kept as white as possible. Their hair was regularly shaved and set aside for decorative purposes.[22] The shaving procedure, the preparation of the tassels and assemblage into clusters, and their subsequent attachment to the kaupapa, were all highly skilled techniques. The combination of exclusive materials with the time-consuming expertise required to produce one of these garments clearly established its owner as a high-ranking individual and explains why twentieth-century ethnologists reported that this was the most prized of all 'dogskin' cloaks.[23] A single example held in the Pitt Rivers Museum collection in Oxford is the only known extant specimen. Already old when it was collected during Cook's first voyage, it was probably no longer the epitome of style. It has lost a number of its awe attachments but this kahu waero remains an inspiring garment. The intricacy and variation of the construction of its awe attachments, the neatness and skill with which they are stitched to the kaupapa, the unique design and elegance of its dark contrasting tāniko border – all combine to provide a glimpse of exceptional eighteenth-century artistry. According to oral tradition, maro waero (a type of frontal apron) were also made with white dog hair. A similar version of the kahu waero, the māhiti or māwhiti, was made of the same

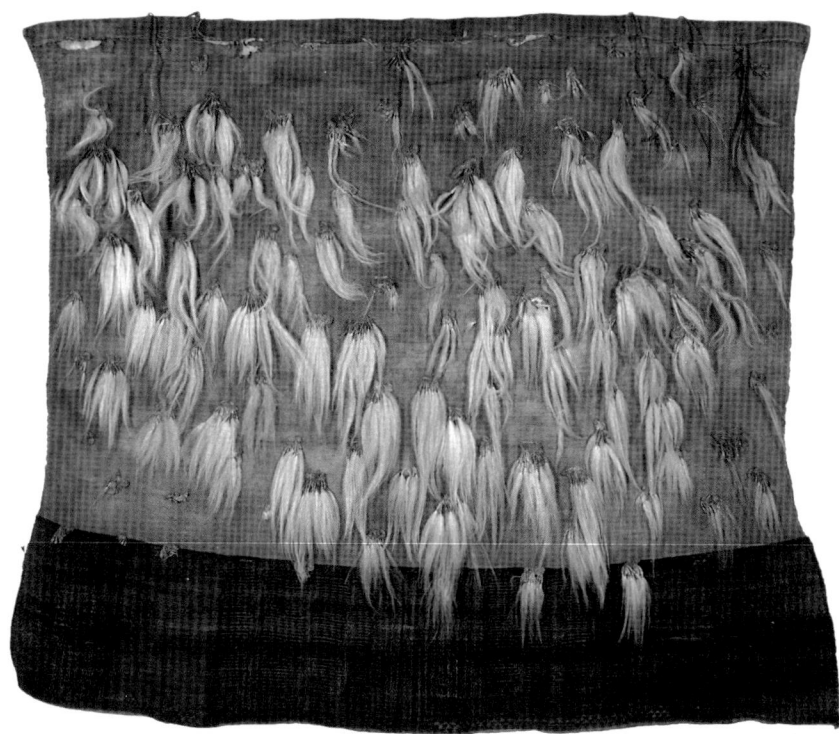

Kahu waero (width: 1300 mm, length: 1030 mm). This unique cloak was woven of flax (*Phormium tenax*) fibres and decorated with white awe (dog-hair tassels) and has an unusual dark rectilinear tāniko border. Collected by Joseph Banks during James Cook's first voyage to New Zealand (1769–70), this cloak entered the Pitt Rivers Museum collection in the 1880s, where its true provenance was recently rediscovered.
PHOTOGRAPH BY MALCOLM OSMAN, 2003. PRM 1886.21.19, PITT RIVERS MUSEUM, UNIVERSITY OF OXFORD

materials, but appeared to have less numerous or single tassels that were spaced further apart.[24]

The other forms of kahu kurī also required a woven kaupapa. Dogskins were cut into narrow strips with the hair generally running downwards. In another intensely laborious process the dogskin strips were overlaid and attached to the prepared kaupapa in neat straight rows. Parallel rows of strips were commonly laid vertically, overlapping sufficiently to appear continuous, and stitched with muka so that the overlaying hair concealed the lines of sewing. This caused the plain-coloured cloaks to look as if they were skins from large animals which some eighteenth-century voyagers such as Cook assumed to be from bears.[25] Once again, the time, materials and labour involved in creating these weighty and luxurious garments ensured that they were highly prestigious and owned only by those with high status and power.

The technique of attaching strips in this way may have developed to enable a few pelts to cover a larger area; at the same time, it enabled the growth of a new element of creativity. Rather than being restricted to the limited design created by nature on an animal's hide, variations began to appear, with the introduction of blocks of colours, striped borders and entire striped garments. Specific designs were identified by different names that apparently varied between iwi (tribes)

'A New Zealand Warrior in his Proper Dress, & Compleatly Armed, According to their Manner' (engraving by Thomas Chambers after Sydney Parkinson, published 1784). The cloak that inspired Parkinson's original drawing has not been found, but was almost certainly made of dogskin strips attached to the plain woven interior (seen in the engraving) to create a striking black and white pattern. To complete his appearance, the warrior has a knotted hairstyle with a chiefly heru (comb) and feathers in his hair, a whale-tooth ornament and bone flute at his neck, holds a tewhatewha in his hand and has a patu tucked into his belt. PUBL-0037-15, ALEXANDER TURNBULL LIBRARY, WELLINGTON, NEW ZEALAND from region to region. A tōpuni, for example, usually had a very dark or black body, with a white border framing the front edges and the neck. In the ihupuni colours were reversed – a white body with black framing the front edges and collar line. An awarua had vertical stripes in two colours (suggesting two rivers) flowing the length of the garment, while the puahi was described as having white skins, without hair. The possible variations offered by the overlaying technique were limited only by the different colours of dog pelts.

In regions remote from European influence, the designs of diverse dogskin garments continued to evolve in the early nineteenth century. During 1814–15, John Liddiard Nicholas observed the dress of a number of Northland chiefs from various warrior parties: 'the different coloured furs presenting an uncommonly curious appearance, from the strange devices they had conceived, in joining them together; some of them being cut in square patches, as white as snow, and others extending in long mottled streaks, while intermingled with these, were several spots all differing from each other in shape, colour and size'.[26] Although there are no known names for these garments of different designs, of patches, streaks or spots, the description provides evidence of continuing experimentation with the arrangement of colour and form. This is significant because this attire clearly indicates a lively cultural interest in fashion and style.

Over the centuries between the initial age of stitched garments made of entire bird-, seal- or dogskins, and the appearance of a variety of 'designer' kahu kurī, dexterous Māori weavers had developed and refined their skills to a high level. The traditional techniques of weft twining are found in many areas of the Pacific where they were used to create fish and eel traps. Adaptation of this technique to locally available materials ensured a variety of different garments suited to variable New Zealand weather conditions. In place of the familiar pandanus leaf, weavers experimented with harakeke leaves and discovered a range of species with differing textile properties. Some were best for the raranga form of plaited weaving, while others were easily stripped to extract the strong muka fibre. Some were better for softness, others for sheen. They discovered additional useful weaving plants that included tī kōuka (*Cordyline australis*), kiekie (*Freycinetia baueria*), pīngao (*Desmoschoenus spiralis*), tī toi (*Cordyline indivisa*), kuta (*Scirpus lacustris*) and tikumu (*Celmesia spectabilis/coriacea*), among others, and developed specific uses for them all.

Although woven Māori capes and cloaks were rectangular with only a modicum of shaping, weavers created styles with a diverse range of functional and decorative elements that might be incorporated in the manufacture or applied to the surface. They devised techniques that enabled the insertion of hukahuka (tag or thrum attachments) in the weft twining process. Such hukahuka could be introduced parallel to the warp, incorporated with one twist of the weft threads, then folded over and reanchored by a second twist. Alternatively, they could be inserted and further secured by successive rows of twining as they eventually became part of the garment's warp threads. Hukahuka could be either serviceable or decorative. Pākē (rain capes) were constructed with a variety of functional hukahuka, usually densely layered, like thatching, to allow moisture to run off. For even these most practical of garments their makers and wearers took pleasure in applying design and colour: some included patterns of dark dyed hukahuka, interspersed among the undyed.

Other varieties of hukahuka were purely ornamental: fine and reed-like, long or short, dyed or natural, or combinations of these. Designs could also be scraped onto strips of harakeke, dyed and dried in tube-like strips that rustled or swished when the garment moved. Two, and sometimes three, strands of muka fibre were plied to create cords called kārure, to make the tassels by which specific types of cloaks would become identified. Skilled artisans could create these cords in tight firm twists or loose springing coils. They could be naturally coloured or dyed in hues of russet, tan, chocolate or black. They might be plied in single colours and various combinations. Other complex tags and tassels were designed as composite fringes, devices to appeal not only to the eye, but also to the ear and the touch of the hand. Although waist garments such as maro and various types of wrapped kilts such as rāpaki (loincloths) were also twined and sometimes decorated, cloaks allowed the greatest variety of decoration. In addition to being ornamented with hukahuka, they might be designed with striped vertical warps or twined with contrasting weft fibres to create horizontal stripes. Sometimes the stripes were hidden in the interior of a garment with a dense outer surface, so that only the weaver and wearer knew of its inside appearance. There is no indication of any particular significance in this other than the creative pleasure of the weaver.

Other cloaks relied for their splendour on the colour, fineness and beauty of their fibre, the skilled precision of their weaving and their rich and intricate tāniko borders. Aronui, paepaeroa, parawai, kaitaka and pātea were the names of some of the finely woven garments made of the highest quality prepared whītau or muka, and differing from one another in details of their tāniko ornamentation. Garment names and styles varied within tribal regions, and although weft twining was found in many parts of the world, tāniko weaving was and is uniquely Māori. Some tāniko designs fall into pattern types that are named, but the symbolism behind the patterns is a specialised study.

Kākahu designs varied from the subtly restrained to the luxuriously conspicuous; historically, the most eye-catching were the white kahu waero and the red-feathered kākahu kura of the opening proverb. Feathered cloaks were an adaptation of the same basic huka attachment techniques, with pre-prepared clusters of feathers inserted during the twining process. Kiwi and kākāpō feathers were much admired, but red was considered a sacred colour throughout Polynesia and red plumes were the most prized ornaments of Māori before European contact. Thus kākahu kura were the most highly esteemed of feathered cloaks. The colours of kākā feathers varied from the rare predominantly red mutant birds that Māori called kākā kura, to glowing fiery reds or rich deep red-browns.[27] Those of the male South Island kākā subspecies (*Nestor meridionalis*) were more vivid in colour than the North Island *N. septentrionalis*. Similarly, feathers from under the wing were brighter in colour than those on other parts of the body.[28] The comparative rarity of red feathers in Aotearoa ensured that kākahu kura remained exclusive and few in number (Plate 2).

Indeed kākahu kura were so uncommon that individuals could be identified by their ownership of them. Tūhoe tradition tells of twin sisters who were killed in the forest by Tamango, the chief of Te Tini o Toi, at Otere Pā. When their half-brother Kahuki asked how he could recognise Tamango in battle, the answer was 'A red feather cloak.'[29] In the same way, the Ngāti Tūwharetoa warrior Te Kiore was identified by his red cloak in the last Tūhoe raid on Taupō. En route to Taupō, the Tūhoe tohunga Uhia had prophesied that they would achieve success following the death of a man who wore a red-feathered cloak. At Orona, Uhia held the Tūhoe forces from attacking until the red-cloaked figure of his dream had appeared and could be destroyed. Te Kiore was specifically targeted and his appearance was keenly awaited. When he was seen in an approaching canoe, Te Kiore's cloak marked him out, his demise was inevitable and Tūhoe had their victory.[30] As this story shows, as well as identifying individuals with mana, particularly distinctive garments might be known far beyond the immediate tribal boundaries of their owners.

Such important garments could even be named. Some 20 generations ago, the chief Taiwhakaea lived at the top of Maunganui on the south head of Tauranga Harbour. Taiwhakaea, who had a red-feathered cloak called Te Aho o Kuranui, was famous for his benevolence. Whenever he required provisions for a feast, he would spread out his magnificent cloak on the slope of the mountain so that his vassals living 20 miles (32 kilometres) away at Maketū would see it and immediately send great quantities of foodstuffs.

When Cook visited New Zealand on his three voyages in the eighteenth century, only a few chiefs were seen wearing kākahu kura. On the first voyage, Joseph Banks noted, 'Some there were who had their dresses ornamented with feathers, and one who had an entire dress of the red feathers of parrots', but these cloaks were not common.[31] Two feathered maro were also observed. In 1773, naturalist Johann Forster had purchased one from a group of Māori visiting Queen Charlotte Sound. He described it precisely: 'They sold us an apron made of their close-wrought cloth, covered with red feathers, faced with white dog-skin, and ornamented with pieces of the ear-shell, which is said to be worn by the women in their dances'.[32] Four years later, on Cook's third voyage, the ship's surgeon William Anderson reported a very similar garment: 'a few have small triangular aprons adorn'd with parrots feathers and bits of pearl shells, furnish'd with a double or treble set of cords to fasten it about them and cover certain parts'.[33]

That only a few such items were seen, and that Māori were prepared to trade them, suggests that maro kura (red-feathered aprons) were losing their prestige towards the end of the eighteenth century. An earlier oral tradition serves to demonstrate that Māori had their own ideas of fashionable trends. When the Ngāi Tahu chief Tamanuiaraki and his wife Rukutia hosted a visiting chief, Tutekorepunga, members of Tama's family wore white dog-tail-hair maro when performing to entertain their guests. However, when Tama saw the visiting whānau all wearing red maro for their responding performance, he felt outdone by them, and ashamed.[34]

The persistent refinement of weaving skills may explain why, for chiefs, being well dressed at significant gatherings became a fundamental element of Māori culture. Presenting a suitable appearance applied to both men and women and included attention to hairstyle and headdress. When the Ngāti Mahuta chief Kapu was caught at a disadvantage by a group of impromptu visitors, they failed to recognise the grimy worker and asked, 'Where is Kapu?' Seizing the chance to remain undetected, he offered to go and fetch the chief. He left the visitors and went to assemble his people, who waited while he washed, combed his hair and tied it on top of his head, then put on his huru kurī, before returning to meet the guests.[35]

Dressing well to convey rank and personal mana was also conventional practice. Just as today, how an individual appeared could affect how he or she was treated, and the appearance of rangatira (chiefs) reflected not only their own status but also that of their people. When the Tūranga chief Taharākau visited Tapuae of Te Reinga at Te Wairoa, he went to considerable lengths to ensure that he would be able to uphold his mana by means of a suitable appearance, demonstrating his rank and adding further prestige to the gathering. Taharākau travelled with his fellow chief Te Angiangi. The weather was fine and Te Angiangi set off wearing his best clothing. But Taharākau anticipated rain so, rather than wear his best garments, he wrapped them carefully and carried them with him. Sure enough, they were caught in a rain storm and were saturated. Just before they arrived at their destination, Taharākau changed into his superior clothing to show his hosts that he was a person of some consequence. In comparison, the drenched Te Angiangi presented a sorry figure, his cloak dripping and his feathers bedraggled. Meanwhile, their hosts had dressed up in preparation to greet the visitors. Tapuae had arranged his māhiti with its white dogtail-hair over his paepaeroa, while his wife, whose mana and status was higher than her husband's, awaited the travellers wearing her kahu kiwi around her shoulders and huia feathers adorning both sides of her head.[36]

The wearing of superior garments was also sometimes an essential factor in ensuring a successful outcome for major tribal enterprises. One such instance recorded in Ngāti Kahungungu tradition suggests that cultural rites may have been rendered more effective by dressing judiciously. On this occasion a fighting party was assembled at Te Mania, ready to move into battle. Before the warriors set off, the men stood waiting for their chief Tamaterangi to recite the ritual tohi (an intonation for the warriors), but he remained sitting silently and made no effort to move. Eventually, after a considerable delay, his younger brother Makoro asked him to stand and perform the rite over the war party. Tamaterangi replied, 'He ao te rangi ka ūhia ā mā te huruhuru te manu ka rere ai' (It requires clouds to clothe heaven and feathers to make a bird fly). Makoro immediately grasped his brother's meaning, and understood that Tamaterangi considered he did not have clothing befitting this important ceremony. Without further ado, Makoro took off his own fine cloak and placed it around Tamaterangi's shoulders. Appropriately robed, the chief stood up and the ceremony could proceed. Makoro later presented Tamaterangi with his own wife Hine-muturangi, as Tama's wife Hine-rangi was not a skilled weaver. When Māori claim, 'I am a descendant of Hine-muturangi', it means they are 'well heeled'; conversely, they describe themselves as 'a descendant of Hine-rangi' when their financial state is less desirable.[37]

In a similar vein, a tradition linked to the planting of kūmara on the East Coast implies that personal presentation was the key to a successful crop. According to the chief Pita Kapiti at Waiapu, men involved in the ceremonial planting of kūmara plots must be clothed in '"goodly garments". Such garments as the "pueru" or "tarahau" must not be worn, otherwise the kūmara might run to underground stems, or throw small tubers . . . . On the other hand such garments as the "aronui", "mahiti", "paepaeroa", "puhoro", or "patea" are suitable garments for planting a "mara tautane".'[38] The pueru was described as a coarsely woven garment of dressed flax, and the tarahau as a shaggy cloak of kiekie fibres, whereas the māhiti, aronui, paepaeroa, puhoro and pātea were different types of finely woven whītau garments with various forms of decoration.[39] The māra tautāne was a special part of the kūmara ground ritually set apart for the atua or spirits to secure their goodwill for the remainder of the crop. Dressing well was necessary to ensure auspicious conditions and the best possible outcome for the iwi.

The mana of high-status individuals became imbued in the items they owned, rendering them exclusive to that person and potentially dangerous for anyone else to touch or use. With respect to clothing, this allowed for some unusual extensions of tenure. Much as people today might reserve a space for themselves by placing a bag on a seat, or draping a towel over a deckchair, important Māori figures employed a similar practice. A headstrong young chief, Tāwhaki, left his father's Ngāti Awa lands and went to visit his mother's Ngā Pōtiki people of Tūhoe. As he came near, he met an old woman called Wharepapa, who gave him food and taught him about the Ngā Pōtiki methods of snaring kererū (wood pigeons). Tāwhaki killed the old woman and went on to the Kaiwata Range. There, he discovered a toromiro (miro) tree (*Podocarpus ferrugineus*) full of kererū caught in snares. Tawhaki hung his cloak on the tree as a tāpui or taumou – a sign that he marked the tree and its contents for himself. He went on to the village, sent the local people back to fetch 'his' birds and had them cooked for himself.[40] His Ngā Pōtiki birthright contributed to his mana and ensured that his will was obeyed; his cloak was an extension of himself.

Near Taranaki, a strong-willed chieftainess applied the same principle in a different situation. A niece of the Ngāti Toa chief Te Rauparaha, Rangi Topeora was one of the few women who signed the Treaty of Waitangi in 1840. Sometime around 1817 she was part of a Ngāti Toa party that had surrounded the pā of Tapui-nikau. She recognised one of the handsome defending chiefs as a previous paramour, Te Ratutonu, and devised a plan to rekindle their relationship. She persuaded her uncle to make use of a time-honoured custom in warfare, to call a person out of the besieged stronghold under safe conduct. Te Ratutonu responded, but a second woman, a well-known composer named Nekepapa, also had her eye on this fine-looking man. Determined not to be outdone, Topeora ran faster than Nekepapa and threw her tōpuni around the chief's shoulders, thus securing him for herself. Te Ratutonu remained Topeora's husband until he was killed a few years later near Waitotora.[41]

In 1840 Ruhia Pōrutu used her cloak to prevent a young boy from being killed. Ruhia grew up at Waiwhetū in Lower Hutt, but moved to Pipitea Pā in Thorndon, Wellington, after marrying Ihaia Pōrutu. Her father-in-law was a principal chief, Te Rira Pōrutu of Te Matehou, and a signatory to the Treaty of Waitangi at Port Nicholson. In the same year, a thirteen-year-old orphaned boy named Thomas McKenzie had arrived on board one of the early immigrant ships, the *Adelaide*. As local Māori were helping to build accommodation for the migrants, Te Rira saw young Thomas go into a newly constructed house near the pā. This was a very serious breach of tapu. Te Rira went to kill the boy, but Ruhia saved Thomas's life by throwing her cloak over him and claiming him as her own. From that time, Thomas was regarded as her son. Ruhia died in 1872, yet thirty-nine years later, at Thomas's funeral in 1911, Ruhia's cloak was draped over his coffin.[42] Ruhia Pōrutu's cloak, a fine example of an elegant kaitaka is now held at the Museum of New Zealand Te Papa Tongarewa (Plate 12). It is simple in style; its beauty emanates from the glossy whiteness of its fibre and the even tension of its weaving, all discerningly framed on three sides with beautiful tāniko borders.

Impressive kaitaka were certainly a feature of the spectacle at the signing of the Treaty of Waitangi. In discussions the day before, Māori participants were dressed in a variety of clothing, reflecting the numerous colonial influences that had begun to infiltrate their civilisation – the Protestant and Catholic missions, and the various traders and settlers. William Colenso recorded that some wore 'splendid-looking new woollen cloaks' in crimson, blue, brown and plaid that were probably of French manufacture, while some dressed in European apparel.[43] Others wore their customary dress (which Colenso did not describe further), but many rangatira wore traditional garments that indicated their high status and added mana to the occasion. Some of the leading chiefs wore awarua of vertical

Traditionally styled cloaks retained their importance in the twentieth century, adding mana to ceremonial occasions and becoming statements of identity, even when woven from introduced European materials. This was evident in the 1906 gathering at the Wood family residence in Palmerston North, after the post office clock tower chimes were started in honour of Kerei Te Panau, son of the revered Rangitāne chief Tāmati Te Panau. Seated in the centre, Kerei Te Panau wears a contemporary korowai made of candlewick yarns with single- and two-toned woollen hukahuka and looped borders. His wife Ereni Te Awe Awe is seated fourth from the right, wearing European clothes. Sitting beside Te Panau, the noted local body politician W. T. Wood wears a similar korowai, while his wife is dressed in a multi-coloured feather cloak. PG8, PALMERSTON NORTH CITY LIBRARY

black and white stripes. Here and there, the snowy white feathers of toroa or tākapu (gannet), or the elegant plumes of the kōtuku (white heron) contrasted with the dark hair of their wearers.

According to Colenso, the dress of one chief, Hakitara of the Te Rarawa tribe, stood out amongst the rest. Hakitara was a tall figure, wearing a very large, very beautiful, silky-looking white kaitaka with a deep, dark-coloured tāniko border woven in a zigzag and diamond design. Although the spacious tent that had been erected on the lawn at Waitangi had filled rapidly, Hakitara was positioned in a central area where an opening in the roof above him allowed the sunlight to stream like a spotlight onto his magnificent white garment – he was an eye-catching and impressive figure, standing out against those in the half-light around him.

Māori were equally capable of dressing down to emphasise their disdain for something. Another chief that day presented an intentionally unkempt appearance, as a means of reinforcing his verbal opposition to the treaty. Tareha was

Ngā Puhi, a chief of the Ngatirehia people, who lived near Kokorāreka in the Bay of Islands. He was a huge man, tall and well built, with a 'deep sepulchral' and imposing voice.[44] He spoke vehemently against Māori being ruled over, and told Governor William Hobson to go. He challenged the notion that Māori had need of foreign garments and foods. At the same time, Tareha made his opinion visually obvious by his clothing: 'a filthy piece of coarse old floor-matting, loosely tied round him, such as is used by the commonest Natives merely as a floor-mat under their bedding', while he brandished a bunch of dried fern-root on a string in his hand, as a reminder of the most traditional common food resource of the people.[45]

The signing of the Treaty of Waitangi marked a turning point for many traditional Māori ways and signalled the increasing influence of European mores and values. The ultimate adoption of European clothing by Māori is another important story, which requires its own separate telling. Despite this trend, customary Māori clothing has continued to evolve. Some technologies developed, then passed out of use as newer projects required different expertise. The kurī is now extinct, and the kākā did not colonise the forests of introduced *Pinus radiata* – deforestation, along with human hunters, ferrets and stoats, have caused overwhelming reduction of their numbers. As the availability of indigenous bird feathers and certain plant resources came under government and local body control in the twentieth and twenty-first centuries, practitioners found access to some of their traditional materials a time-consuming battle with bureaucracy. All these factors influence contemporary cloak makers today. The long-established weft twining techniques continue to survive and are still employed to create valuable and prestigious cloaks in Aotearoa. Classes that pass on the traditional skills are keenly attended. Some weavers prepare harakeke fibres in the time-honoured ways; others purchase industrially produced yarns and introduced varieties of feathers. Other innovative individuals are creating cloak-like garments by machine-stitching imported feathers onto commercially manufactured fabric backings. As fashions continue to evolve, the opening pepeha of this chapter becomes even more apt. Undoubtedly, things are not what they used to be.

3. Unpicked for the Voyage? Heirloom Dresses in Colonial New Zealand

Rosanne Livingstone and Valerie Carson

When the Greenwood family packed their luggage for the long arduous journey by ship from England to New Zealand in 1842, they made room for family heirlooms as well as clothing and furniture. In spite of the cramped conditions on board and the lack of space for both people and possessions, this family journeyed to Nelson with a family Bible, silverware, two eighteenth-century paintings, and an eighteenth-century silk dress among their precious belongings. The Burnett family also brought heirlooms with them from England. When they arrived in Whāngārei in 1852, in their luggage were a number of family treasures, including three eighteenth-century silk garments. According to family sources, these garments were 'unpicked for packing for the voyage'.[1] The Greenwoods also brought their silk dress in pieces. Immigrants were given lists of the items considered necessary for life in New Zealand, and most would not have been able to bring much more.[2] Only the reasonably affluent could afford to bring family heirlooms, and indeed they were probably the only people who possessed any. It is easy to see why Bibles, silverware and paintings were in the luggage of these families, but why did they also bring these garments to New Zealand?

These striking eighteenth-century pieces are now held by the Museum of New Zealand Te Papa Tongarewa (Te Papa). Although the museum has a number of eighteenth-century garments in its history collections, several of which were brought here by nineteenth-century immigrants, only the Greenwood dress and the three Burnett garments are known to have been unpicked before the voyage.[3] Believing this was a puzzle that needed solving, we decided to investigate further and thereby initiated what was to become an extensive and at times baffling research project. The textile experts and museum professionals we contacted thought it was probably common practice to unpick such dresses for packing: they were voluminous, and if packed intact, would take up considerable space in a trunk. Others knew of dresses that had been restyled and worn in the nineteenth century. But as some of this was based on anecdote or supposition, the

Greenwood and Burnett pieces provided a good case study with which to investigate further. As this chapter shows, the work required painstaking examination of the garments themselves, reading family papers and interviews and consultation with colleagues at museums and art galleries internationally. Reconstructing the steps we took reveals much about the pieces themselves, and about the cultural and social importance of such clothing as family heirlooms.

Handloom to heirloom

What makes an eighteenth-century dress so precious that it is handed down through generations as a family heirloom? The reason lies with the fibre and fabric from which it is made. As Philippa Scott points out, 'Silk is sumptuous, royal, heavenly; it is exotic, erotic, sensual. Most of all, it is simply sheer beauty.'[4] All four garments in this study are made from beautifully patterned silks; three are brocaded flowered silks and one is damask.[5] These silk fabrics were hand woven on a drawloom by a weaver and his assistant, or drawboy, who manipulated a series of harnesses and other mechanical devices attached to the loom to lift a set of warp threads forming a shed (space) through which supplementary coloured weft threads were inserted by the weaver. A sequence of manipulations was performed in a prescribed order to produce a complex figured pattern.[6] This method of weaving was extremely time-consuming. It has been estimated that it took at least three weeks for the weaver to prepare the loom, and another one to two weeks to weave a length of flowered silk fabric. Fabric woven on a drawloom was narrow, only about 19 inches (475 millimetres) in width, and at least 14 yards (12.5 metres) was needed for a typical eighteenth-century dress.[7]

Any fabric produced from silk was expensive. However, in England the price of weaving the fabric was in fact the least costly part of the process. Silk fibre had to be imported, and there were ongoing problems with sources of supply. The warp and weft threads came from different places: warp threads had to be strong and for this high-quality raw silk was obtained from Italy and China, while the silk for the weft thread came mostly from Persia, via Turkey or Sicily.[8] For comparatively little extra cost, highly skilled artisans, such as pattern designers, dyers and specialist weavers, were employed to make the fabrics even more sumptuous, and they were. Most of the silk fabric made in England was manufactured by the Flowered Branch of the London Weavers' Company, located in Spitalfields in London. To maintain their exclusivity, silk fabrics were manufactured in only small quantities and they were often made to order for garments worn by the rich. The well-to-do in the eighteenth century were highly attentive to their appearance and spent a substantial proportion of their income on clothing. A wealthy woman required a new wardrobe every year, for although the style of dress changed only gradually during the century, changes in fabric design occurred frequently.[9] The major design trends lasted several years but new colours and designs for silk

Gown and petticoat, Spitalfields, England, worn by Elizabeth Dandridge Aylett Henley, silk textile, c.1750, remodelled c.1770, silk brocaded with silk, bodice lined with linen, trimmings padded with cotton, reproduction stomacher. Family tradition states that Elizabeth willed it to her daughter-in-law to be cut up and used as furniture coverings, but the gown remained intact and was passed down through the family. ACCESSION # G1975-340, 1-2, IMAGE # TC1999-618, ABBY ALDRICH ROCKEFELLER FOLK ART MUSEUM, THE COLONIAL WILLIAMSBURG FOUNDATION, WILLIAMSBURG, VIRGINIA fabrics were produced seasonally. As a consequence, dresses very soon became unfashionable.

Over the course of the eighteenth century the designs of flowered silk fabrics underwent several transformations. According to costume and textile historian Natalie Rothstein, fashionable patterns of the 'bizarre' period in the early eighteenth century were characterised by elongated patterns and strange motifs, followed by the transitional 'luxuriant' period, leading to the 'lace' patterns of the 1720s.[10] In the following decades designers concentrated on 'representing well known flowers'.[11] People were hugely interested in gardening, and early to mid-eighteenth-century gardens contained a great diversity of flowers, shrubs and trees, both familiar, as well as unusual and exotic. The flowered silks of the period reflected this interest in nature.[12] The production of these naturalistic designs was assisted by advances in dye technology, aided by the fact that silk dyes readily. Naturalistic designs continued in popularity for a fairly long period; they lent themselves to the meandering rococo patterns that predominated in the middle of the century, although these patterns later became more stylised. After 1770 the neo-classical style became fashionable.

Eighteenth-century silk dresses were far too valuable to be thrown out. Instead, they might be sold to one of the many second-hand clothing dealers that existed at the time, passed on to servants, or bequeathed or given to less well-off relatives or friends. Sometimes they were put away to be altered and worn again years later, once the fabric was no longer noticeably out of date. It was simple to unpick eighteenth-century dresses, which were constructed using running stitches, and the voluminous skirts alone could provide enough fabric to make a crinoline dress in the nineteenth century.[13] Alternatively, they were altered to be worn as fancy dress, or the unpicked fabric made into church vestments and even patchwork quilts.[14] Nevertheless, some dresses were kept and handed down though the generations.

Why do some items become family treasures? We know from the histories of items in museum collections that there are many reasons: an item may have belonged to a famous ancestor or it might be related to an important event; it might be rare, an item of great beauty or have considerable monetary value. As the late Anne Burnett once told us, an item might be kept because some families, like her own, never threw things out.[15] The Greenwood dress and the three Burnett garments were carefully handed down, generation after generation, in their unpicked state. Were they originally intended to be kept as heirlooms, or were they kept so the fabric could be reused? And why were they brought to New Zealand?

The Greenwood family dress pieces

The Greenwood dress pieces are from an open robed dress dating from the mid-eighteenth century.[16] The fabric is brocaded flowered silk with an ivory ground,

This stomacher from the Greenwood dress is constructed from five pieces of ivory brocaded silk, with a hand-cut scalloped edge to prevent fraying. The stomacher is unboned and relatively short. Pin holes around the edges indicate that it was held in place by pins when worn. The bow was probably attached as a decoration on the sleeve above the flounce. GH007353, MUSEUM OF NEW ZEALAND TE PAPA TONGAREWA

the most popular colour of the period. Posies and smaller sprigs of anemone flowers, buds and berries are brocaded in eleven hues and tints of red, green and yellow over the subtle irregular warp striped ground.[17] This silk design is a typical rococo pattern of the mid-1750s (Plate 3). It is remarkable that the dress is almost complete. It consists of 26 pieces, which include the bodice, sleeves and flounces, rectangular skirt panels and two bows trimmed with silk Blonde lace. There is also a small stomacher (an inverted triangular panel filling in the front opening of the bodice), which is decorated with pearl buttons and Blonde lace arranged in a figure of eight imitating a laced-up stomacher. Missing are the matching petticoat robings (the trimmings down the centre front opening) and the falling lace cuffs. As so much of the dress is present, it would appear that it was purposely kept and treasured as a family heirloom.

Sarah and John Danforth Greenwood brought these silk dress pieces to New Zealand. Danforth Greenwood was born in England in 1803, the son of a London art dealer, John Greenwood, who was in turn the son of an American-born artist and art dealer, also named John Greenwood, who had settled in London in 1762.[18] Sarah also had a background in art. Baptised in London in 1809, the daughter of Mary and John Field, a wax chandler, she was well educated in art, languages and

music.[19] She was to become an accomplished artist and many of her later works, including pencil drawings and watercolour paintings, are held by New Zealand museums.[20] Sarah and Danforth had married in 1831, and were to have thirteen children. Danforth was a medical practitioner, but after his health failed in 1837 he moved his family to France, where he became a partner in what was to be an unsuccessful business venture. Sarah wrote to her grandmother in 1842, describing their plight and thanking her for a gift of money: 'The chief part of the money Danforth expended in books, giving us full information concerning the Colony of New Zealand, which I really think will be our ultimate home'.[21] Danforth raised the capital needed to purchase land in Wellington, Nelson and Motueka through the New Zealand Company, and the family, including seven children, boarded the *Phoebe* at Gravesend and set sail on 16 November 1842.[22] Because Danforth had been appointed the ship's surgeon superintendent, the family was entitled to a chief cabin and free passage, as well as a ton of freight free of charge. This meant that, unlike most other emigrants, the Greenwoods could include heirlooms as well as the more usual supplies in their luggage.[23]

Both Sarah and Danforth were prolific letter writers, sending detailed accounts of the voyage and their life in New Zealand to family and friends in

Sarah Greenwood (*née* Field), 1809–89, and Dr John Danforth Greenwood, 1803–90. 1103/1, DAVIS COLLECTION AND 114519/3 TYREE STUDIO COLLECTION, TASMAN BAYS HERITAGE TRUST/ THE NELSON PROVINCIAL MUSEUM

Mrs Humphrey Devereux, 1771, by John Singleton Copley (1738–1815), oil paint on canvas, 1005 x 805 mm. 1965-0013-1, MUSEUM OF NEW ZEALAND TE PAPA TONGAREWA

England. Many of the family's letters and documents still survive.[24] Although one of the eighteenth-century paintings brought out by the family, a portrait by the renowned American artist John Singleton Copley, is discussed in several of these documents, we found no mention of an ivory, flowered silk dress or dress pieces. The subject of the famed Copley painting, *Mrs Humphrey Devereux, 1771*, brought to New Zealand by the couple, is Danforth Greenwood's great-grandmother. Nine years after he moved to London, John Greenwood (senior) commissioned Copley to paint this portrait of his mother. His instructions to the artist were: 'I shall leave the picturesque disposition intirely [*sic*] to yourself and I shall only observe that gravity is the choice of dress'.[25] The dress Mrs Devereux is wearing in the portrait is made from dark brown silk satin, but she was 60 years old in 1771 so she could well have worn the ivory dress in the 1750s. English flowered silks were popular among the élite in the American colonies at that time.[26] The original owner of the dress remains unknown, but it could have initially belonged to any one of several female ancestors of either Danforth or Sarah.

More is known of the history of the dress pieces after they were brought to New Zealand. They came into the possession of Sarah and Danforth's daughter, Charlotte, their twelfth child, who was born at Motueka on 29 July 1849.[27] It is not known how or why she came by the dress pieces but perhaps she was given the dress pieces because of her interest in theatre. We know she wore 'A bright rose-bud chintz cut square with elbow sleeves and ruffles, looped up with pink bows over a green flounced . . . petticoat' for a play she took part in with her sister Katie in 1870.[28] By this time Charlotte was married to Dr William Kemp and living in Wellington. The dress pieces may have been her share of the family inheritance. Her elder brother John, writing not long after their father's death in 1890, said how hard it was to decide who should inherit the Copley painting. In the end it was given to the unmarried Greenwood daughters living in Wellington, because the sons had already been assisted with gifts of money.[29] John did not say what the married daughters received. Charlotte later moved to Sussex, England, where she lived with two of her daughters until her death.[30] The dress pieces remained in New Zealand, eventually passing to her granddaughter, Alison Hardwick-Smith (formerly Kemp). Not long before she died, Alison gave the dress pieces to her god-daughter, Jane Perry; Te Papa acquired them from Jane in 1998.

The Burnett family garment pieces

The articles from the Burnett family are from different decades. The earliest is a sack-back, open dress from about 1725.[31] It is a complex brocade weave of blue and ivory silk. The pattern is a stylised ornate Italianate design with palmettes, pomegranates, tulips, pinks, moss roses, artichokes, lilies, insects and delicately branching coral. There are eleven tints and tones of red and green scattered

LEFT Detail of the blue and ivory brocaded silk from the Burnett family's sack-back dress, c.1725. PC002090, MUSEUM OF NEW ZEALAND TE PAPA TONGAREWA

BELOW The edge of this sleeve flounce has been pinked and scalloped by hand. PC002090, MUSEUM OF NEW ZEALAND TE PAPA TONGAREWA

throughout the pattern (Plate 4).[32] The dress is partially unpicked and comprises sixteen pieces, which include bodice fronts, one sleeve and three flounces, skirt panels and the centre back bodice and skirt panel constructed from one fabric length, plus the sack-back length. Missing are the matching petticoat, stomacher, one sleeve, one sleeve flounce and the falling lace cuffs.

The second garment is an open robe constructed from yellow silk taffeta with narrow blue stripes brocaded with seven shades and tints of red and green, with tulips forming floral posies and sprigs in an all-over ivory meandering foliate pattern (Plate 5).[33] The design is possibly from the early 1740s.[34] The eight remaining pieces are entirely unpicked and include bodice fronts, skirt panels, one sleeve and flounce, and one robing. The sleeve flounce and robing are trimmed with ivory silk 'fly' gimp. Missing are further skirt panels, one sleeve and flounces, falling lace flounces, robings and petticoat. Whereas the blue and yellow garments are flowered brocaded silks, the third Burnett garment is brown silk satin weave damask.[35] It is a pelisse, a high-waisted, cross-over bodice overgarment or coat

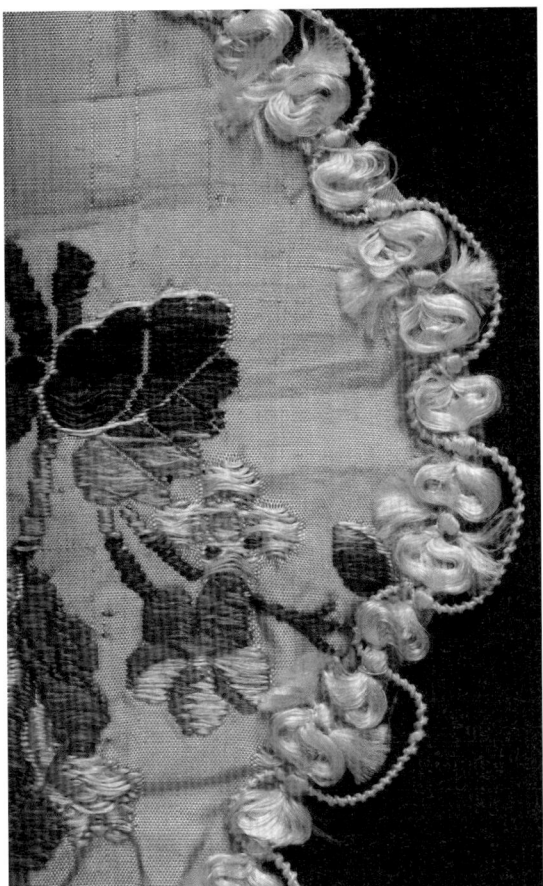 

LEFT Close-up detail of the sleeve flounce trimmed with ivory silk 'fly' gimp. RIGHT This proper left skirt panel from the open robe dress is constructed from two pieces of yellow brocaded silk taffeta (the smaller piece at the proper bottom left is upside down). The skirt opening is on the selvedge side, where unpicked running stitches remain from where robing was attached. Evidence of pleating can be seen along the top edge (the waist), and a pocket opening is on the hip. There is a soiled fold line on the hem. PC002091, MUSEUM OF NEW ZEALAND TE PAPA TONGAREWA

cut on the same lines as the thin muslin dresses of the period 1799–1803 (Plate 6). The flowers in the posies are stylised roses, pinks and buds.[36] The pelisse is still partially assembled, the bodice is almost intact and some of the skirt panels have been unpicked. Holes from the original seam and dart stitching and in some places unpicked threads are still visible.

Barbara Burnett (formerly Johnson) and her adult children brought these eighteenth-century garment pieces to New Zealand. The Burnett family was from Ovington, Northumberland, close to the Scottish border. According to family sources, Barbara was given the dresses by her Gregson relatives when she stayed with them sometime before her marriage to James Burnett in 1816. Mr Gregson was the factor (estate manager) of Prudhoe Castle, which was owned by the Duke of Northumberland. It is not known if the dresses originally belonged to a member of the Gregson family or to the Percys, the Duke of Northumberland's family, but a story handed down through the Burnett family was that one of the dresses, the blue and ivory flowered silk, had been worn at the court of Elizabeth I (1558–1603).[37] This story, like so many family myths, is probably based on facts that have become confused over time. Based on the fabric and styling, if the dress was worn at court, it would have been during the reign of George I (1714–27) or George II (1727–60). Whatever their origin, these garments represent three generations of a family's history: an exotic sack-back dress from the 1720s made from fabric typical of the 'lace' style patterns of the time, a rococo patterned dress from the mid-century and a damask pelisse from the very end of the century, when fashion changed dramatically.

Not long after James Burnett died in 1851, Barbara suffered a stroke. Despite this, she left England for New Zealand the following year with her daughters, Mary and Sarah, her sons, William and James, and James's wife Martha, aboard the *Joseph Fletcher*, a small clipper barque.[38] On their arrival in Auckland after 99 days at sea, Martha wrote to her mother that it was 'a most agreeable voyage' and Barbara had 'managed . . . wonderfully'.[39] Martha relayed that James had received advice on how best to invest the family's money, and mentioned the large quantity of luggage they were able to bring with them. Indeed, they required two cutters to take them and their luggage up to Whāngārei. The three eighteenth-century garments had been partially unpicked for packing by Mary and Sarah. Also among their heirlooms was an epaulet from the late James Burnett's yeomanry uniform. He had volunteered his services in Northumberland: according to a descendant, 'they often had to protect their cattle from the marauding Scots'.[40] Other personal items were among these treasures, including Mary's trousseau (she was to have married a clergyman in 1851, but the wedding was called off) and Barbara's paisley shawls, which were kept after her death and eventually became family heirlooms.

Barbara and her unmarried daughters settled permanently in Whāngārei, but James and Martha moved to Nelson in the late 1850s. James had found work with Julius Haast prospecting for coal on the West Coast. It seems likely that when Barbara died in 1861, either Mary or Sarah inherited the garment pieces. Later these were handed down through James and Martha's line, eventually coming into the custody of their great-granddaughter, Anne Burnett, who donated many items to Te Papa and the Colonial Cottage in Nairn Street, Wellington, in the 1980s. Did members of the Burnett family intend to reassemble the garments at a future date? The fact that the blue and brown garments were only partially unpicked supports this hypothesis. Or does the fact that pieces are missing mean that they were intended to be reused? We may never know. We are not even sure if all the pieces came to New Zealand, but we do know, from family sources, that decades later some of the yellow dress pieces were 'given away to the younger generation'.[41]

Collections of eighteenth-century dresses

A number of New Zealand museums have eighteenth-century dresses in their collections, as well as other garments and accessories. But were the garments brought to this country intact? In an attempt to answer this question, we contacted museums throughout New Zealand and Australia, ranging from large metropolitan museums to small cottage museums. We specifically asked if they had any eighteenth-century dresses in their collections that had been unpicked for packing for the voyage. Not one did. Only the Benalla Museum in Victoria, Australia had an eighteenth-century dress that had been brought to that country in pieces, but it was a 1770s sack-back dress believed to have been brought to the Antipodes by a descendant of the original owner in the 1960s.[42] This was a most unexpected finding. We were then faced with the question of whether the Greenwood and Burnett dresses were unique, or whether other dresses had also been unpicked for the voyage but their history was now unknown.

There is ample evidence of textiles brought to New Zealand that were either eighteenth-century dresses that had been altered, or were pieces of dress fabric that had been reused to make other items. An example of the latter is a patchwork quilt in the Te Papa collections.[43] The quilt was originally owned by the Reverend Vicesimus Lush of Ewelme Cottage, and his family, who arrived in Auckland in October 1850.[44] The quilt is constructed from a panel of silk patchwork in the 'tumbling block' design. This has been machine stitched on to eighteenth-century silk damask. The reverse is a combination of two different brocades and the damask, all of which are from unpicked dresses (Plates 7 and 8). The machine stitching is likely to have been carried out by Blanche, Lush's wife, after she acquired a sewing machine in 1866.[45]

Several other New Zealand museums have dresses that have been altered. Auckland War Memorial Museum has a dress from around 1820 that was remade from a 1780s cream silk brocade dress,[46] and Hawke's Bay Museum in Napier has an Edwardian dress in its collections that has been remade from an eighteenth-century dress.[47] Canterbury Museum has a mid-eighteenth-century embroidered gold silk dress that was extensively altered for wearing as fancy dress in the nineteenth century.[48] Some eighteenth-century silk dresses brought to New Zealand were altered and adapted to suit new situations, but others, like the Greenwood and Burnett dresses, remained family heirlooms until they were given to public museums.

Both the Greenwoods and Burnetts came from educated, middle-class English backgrounds. Both families possessed valuable heirlooms which they brought to New Zealand. They also recognised the importance of their family history, and kept the correspondence relating to their voyages and early years in New Zealand. In the late twentieth century, as the families became more dispersed and the awareness of their place in a national history grew, their heirlooms and correspondence were deposited for safekeeping in museums and libraries. This has ensured that the collections remain together and are preserved for the future. It is interesting and delightful to find that there was a personal connection between the two families. When Charlotte Greenwood married William Kemp in Nelson in 1870, Sarah and Danforth Greenwood invited 70 guests to the double wedding they held for her and her sister Frances. Among the guests were a Mr and Mrs Burnett.[49] It is very likely that they were James and Martha, the son and daughter-in-law of Barbara Burnett. In the early 1870s James Burnett was a justice of the peace in Nelson, along with Danforth Greenwood and two of his sons, John and Graham.[50]

Our original understanding that many eighteenth-century dresses were unpicked so they could be packed easily into a trunk for a voyage has not been supported by the evidence we have found to date. Such garments were highly valued and were preserved, either as potential sources of beautiful fabric or as family heirlooms. Some more affluent nineteenth-century immigrants found space for them in their trunks and brought them halfway around the world. As a consequence, even though New Zealand was not settled by Europeans until the nineteenth century, we have in this country many textile items from the previous century brought out by immigrants who wanted to maintain tangible links with both their ancestry and their places of origin.

4. Kilts as Costumes: Identity, Resistance and Tradition

Katie Pickles

In 1985, when I reported on an old girls' sherry party on the eve of Christchurch Girls' High School's move to new premises, I noted in the school magazine that some women had commented that 'something drastic had been done to the school uniform, and what clan did that kilt represent?'[1] My fascination with the kilt, a wrap-around skirt pleated at the rear and made of tartan fabric, was sparked. This chapter explores a variety of ways that the kilt has been worn, by men and women, warriors and schoolgirls, gay and straight, rich and poor, Pākehā and Māori, to reveal its contribution to New Zealand's history. In her work on colonial Australia, Margaret Maynard argues that dress practices signify 'the constant ever-changing human struggle for status and identity'.[2] Concerning the kilt in Highland Scottish society, Hugh Trevor-Roper has convincingly argued that its history was an 'invented tradition'.[3] Following their lead, I interpret the kilt's appearance, focusing on how, in the 'New World' of New Zealand, wearings of the kilt demonstrate the confluence of local, national and trans-national influences. This chapter investigates further what Tom Brooking and Jennie Coleman have described as the 'rich but often slippery area of discerning ethnic difference within a Pākehā culture', and James Belich's intuitive assertion of New Zealand as '*the* neo-Scotland'.[4] I seek to explain why people wore the kilt and discuss it as a garment imbued with meaning and serving a variety of interests. According to Robin Nicholson, tartan is 'so very interesting precisely because it can have such ambiguous and ambivalent meanings'.[5] In particular, kilts have been worn as costumes representing the politics of sexuality, identity, resistance and tradition.

Forming the kilt

By the time the Scottish settlers brought the kilt to New Zealand it had assumed its modern form. Contrary to popular legend the modern tartan kilt (in Gaelic the breacan philibeg) did not originate in ancient times as traditional Highland dress. Rather, the earliest form of Highland dress is thought to have been the saffron shirt (leine chroich), described as a 'voluminous garment of linen, much pleated, padded and quilted – maybe yellow'. In use until the end of the sixteenth century in Scotland, it is thought to have been brought from Ireland by the Scots who settled on the coast of Argyll in the seventh century AD. A major move towards the modern kilt was the belted plaid (breacan feile), consisting of a piece of fabric about 1½ by 6 yards (1.4 by 5.5 metres), made from two pieces of fabric sewn edge to edge. One piece was pleated and served as a kilt; the other was a cape that was adjusted to suit the weather.[6] At this stage of development the Scottish kilt had much in common with dress in other cultures. For example, in his work on traditional Māori clothing, Hirini Moko Mead considered the piupiu as a 'kilt'. Piupiu means to oscillate, or move to and fro, a feature of the Scottish kilt. It was made up of patterned tubular strands of flax attached to a waistband and, like the Scottish kilt, it could also be worn as a cape.[7]

The combination of the style of the Scottish kilt with the pattern of its fabric is important, as it became 'inseparable from the kilt and plaid of Highland dress'.[8] Plaid, more particularly tartan, is the result of the weaving technique that forms a geometrical pattern. Specifically, the fabric is made by using warp and weft made from spun sheep wool in a two over two under offset by one pattern. This gives a diagonal effect within straight bands of colour, particularly evident when bands of different colours intersect. Tartan is traditionally multi-coloured and patterns can be symmetrical, asymmetrical, repeating or non-repeating.[9] The technique was known in Scotland in the sixteenth century, perhaps coming from Flanders and reaching the Highlands via the Lowlands. Before industrialisation, the plaid fabric was made from natural dyes from native plants, rather than the stronger chemical dyes that came to replace them.[10] Vital to tartan fabric is the 'deep seated symbolism in the basic functionality of the tartan patterns'.[11] The mythology asserts that different clans had different tartans of ancient standing, and that different colours delineated rank and occupation. It is thought that tartans probably did arise for military identification and through the seventeenth century men fought in the belted plaid or also in trews (trousers). The inventor of the modern Scottish kilt was an English Quaker from Lancashire called Thomas Rawlinson. Seeking practical clothing for his workmen to wear when smelting iron ore at Invergarry, he developed the felie beg, hilibeg, or small kilt, an adaptation of what had gone before, in one piece, with pleats already sewn. Ironically, as Trevor-Roper has indicated, this modern garment was designed not to preserve a traditional Highland identity, but to assist its transformation – 'to bring them out of the heather and into the factory'.[12]

Traditions of resistance versus hegemony
The kilt arrived in New Zealand with a contentious political history. From being unknown in 1726, by 1746 it was named in a British parliamentary act that forbade

the Highland dress. Trevor-Roper argues that at the time of the 1745 Culloden rebellion the 'clan' tartans did not exist.[13] Afterwards, however, the British would never again tolerate a clan uprising in Scotland. One way of destroying their power was to outlaw the wearing of Highland dress, 'the tartan cloth, which had become synonymous with rebellion'.[14] Under a law that was in place for 35 years, wearing a kilt resulted in six months' imprisonment for a first offence and transportation for seven years for a second offence. Highland culture came into being through defining itself against what it was not – English. Before the 1707 Union with England, the central facets of Highland society were 'regarded by the large majority of Scotchmen as a sign of barbarism: the badge of roguish, idle, predatory, blackmailing Highlanders who were more of a nuisance than a threat to civilized, historic Scotland'.[15] After Culloden, Highland culture became central to the construction of a Scottishness that was grounded in rebellion and resistance. The kilt became part of Scottish national dress, 'a symbol of ancient glories, real and imaginary, [that] is worn with pride by exiles, and foreigners anxious to claim Scottish ancestry'.[16]

The kilt also became a symbol of hegemonic authority. Simultaneous with its outlawing, the British government appropriated Highland dress for Highland regiments that were loyal to the Crown. The first and most famous of these was the Highland Regiment, later the Black Watch. Formed in 1739, it was the only regiment allowed to wear kilts during the ban.[17] W. A. Thorburn attributes the survival of the tartan kilt to the Highland regiments of the British Army and considers the Black Watch tartan the 'oldest, and most genuine, tartan still in daily use'.[18] The regiment went on to gain an impressive reputation, performing well against Napoleon at Waterloo, and around the world Scots loyal to Britain formed regiments. According to Nicholson, 'the Highland soldier, the Highland officer and the Highland regiments had become a central feature in the glorious campaigns of the expanding British empire . . . . part of the uniform of British glory and British greatness'.[19]

The idea of the kilt as symbolic of rebellion and resistance has also flourished in New Zealand. The devastating Highland Clearances that lasted from the 1780s to the 1890s compounded such feelings. As part of this move to crush Highland society, families were evicted, dispossessed and deported.[20] This is a history that many Pākehā New Zealanders and New Zealanders of mixed Māori and Scottish ancestry hold as a part of their genealogical memory banks. As editor and writer Finlay Macdonald wrote in 2006: 'To cut the usual long story short, my father's side of the family came from the Western Isles of Scotland. Like many displaced and disinherited Highlanders, the men took to the sea and were eventually spread around the globe aboard Britain's huge merchant navy.'[21]

Adding another layer to its history, tartan became a visible fabric of colonisation as Māori traded land for blankets. Blankets served a similar purpose in Australia where, as Margaret Maynard has shown, they were given to Aboriginals expressly 'to reduce violence, gain control of and secure the frontier'.[22] Images of Māori wrapped in tartan blankets were similar to those of other colonised peoples around the world. From the time of the Industrial Revolution tartan was a cheap and durable fabric that was supplied in large amounts to clothe slaves in colonial outposts.[23] In 2005 Tūhoe Māori activist Tama Iti reasserted this association when he appeared wearing a crude kilt and firing a rifle during his tribe's Waitangi Tribunal hearing. He reminded spectators of this history of colonisation at the same time as he appropriated the fabric in an oppositional warrior tradition.

This tradition of Highland resistance to oppression was also simultaneously alive and well in the punk movement and among the Scottish new romantics of the 1970s and 1980s. And then during the 1990s the successful Hollywood films *Rob Roy* (starring Irish actor Liam Neeson) and *Braveheart* (about William Wallace and starring Australian-American Mel Gibson) led to a trans-national resurgence in Scottishness. Some 'stalwarts actually choose to wear the kilt as a sign of their Scottishness' and staff at Lewis Turrell's House of Scotland shop in Auckland note that more young people have bought kilts since the *Braveheart* movie.[24] Chris Laidlaw epitomised such a perspective in a piece titled 'Learning to Love the Kilt':

> I have come to like the grittiness of the Scottish tradition. I like the Celtic flavour, I like the fact that they stood up to the English and never really buckled. The movie 'Braveheart', for all its Hollywood license, certainly stirred something primal in me. The clearances of the 18th and 19th centuries are emblazoned on Scottish minds as an act of English infamy that provoked all Scots to distinguish themselves permanently from the English and that tradition has persisted ever since. All of us who are Scots by origin have inherited some of the residual anger at that chapter of inhumanity.[25]

The apolitical mythology of Highlander traditions in a Highland romantic wilderness also gained strength with regard to the kilt, epitomised in the writing of Sir Walter Scott (1771–1832). He was president of the Highland Society, founded in London in 1778 to encourage what were perceived as ancient Highland virtues and the preservation of ancient Highland tradition and clan identities. The kilt played a central part in these fabrications. Trevor-Roper argues that the major elements of this culture were 'largely modern', and Peter Womack's study of the myth of the Highlands shows that 'the whole concept of a distinct Highland culture and tradition is a retrospective invention' and that 'before the end of the seventeenth century the Highlanders of Scotland did not form a distinct people', but 'racially and culturally' were a 'colony of Ireland'.[26] The 'libels' that 'all Scots wear tartan, are devoted to bagpipe music, and are moved by the spirit of clanship . . . live on as items in the Scottish tourist package of the Twentieth century'.[27]

There was literal fabrication in the first half of the nineteenth century when tartans were codified. Colonel David Stewart's 1822 book claimed distinct patterns for different clans, tribes, families and districts. It was followed in 1842 by the *Vestiarium Scoticum* and then in 1844 the Sobieski Stuarts published *The Costume of the Clans*, in which they claimed that Highland dress 'was the fossil relic of the universal dress of the Middle Ages'. As well as being a 'badge of nationhood', tartan was 'a mark of genealogy and descent'.[28]

From being a wilderness costume worn for protection against the elements, the kilt was taken up by the upper classes as a marker of rank and genealogy. From the mid-nineteenth century tartan's popularity with British royalty cemented its traditional and hegemonic identity. It was the British establishment that was responsible for 'Scottish ceremonials'.[29] From her time at Balmoral Castle Queen Victoria led a vogue for tartan. Prince Albert designed a Balmoral tartan worn by the Royal Family, which opened the way for kilts to be worn at official events such as weddings, graduations, state functions and military parades, reinforcing the kilt as a military costume. There was a nineteenth-century vogue for box-pleats, which used less fabric than knife-pleats and were consequently popular with the War Office.[30]

The association between kilt wearing and authority and tradition was sustained in New Zealand from the time of colonisation. Successful Anglo-Celtic New Zealanders wore kilts and participated in martial activities. For example, politicians John McKenzie and Peter Fraser were both in the Seaforth Highlanders Volunteer Corps.[31] A number of prominent New Zealanders have worn kilts at official occasions. As a small boy, the Nobel Prize-winning scientist Ernest Rutherford wore a woollen Royal Stewart tartan dress. In 2003 the garment was considered to be of national significance, and textile specialist Tracey Wedge spent more than 40 hours conserving the outfit at a cost of more than $2000. Fabric was ordered from Scotland to patch holes in the moth-eaten 130-year-old garment.[32]

Invercargill National list MP Eric Roy wore a kilt when he gave his maiden speech in parliament in 1995. As he stated, 'it was noted that mine was not an address in reply, it was a reply in a dress'. In May 2000 he was injured in a hunting accident and, claiming to be unable to wear his trousers, he donned his kilt once more.[33] In an interesting cultural exchange, Minister of Māori Affairs Dover Samuels stated: 'I wish the Assistant Speaker well with his broken waewae (leg). I acknowledge the piupiu – the Scottish kilt – he has brought into the Chamber, which I think serves very well in terms of recognising the custom and tradition of our bicultural and multicultural nation.'[34]

Warrior traditions in New Zealand

The martial Scottish Highland identity developed in Scotland spread around the British Empire. John M. MacKenzie suggests that 'The Scottish soldier becomes

Prime Minister Peter Fraser, aged eighteen, in the uniform of the Seaforth Highlanders Volunteer Corps, c.1902. NASH320, 0520, ARCHIVES NEW ZEALAND TE RUA MAHARA O TE KĀWANATANGA, WELLINGTON

First sergeants of the Wanganui Highland Rifles, photographed in 1901. M/G/2A L, WHANGANUI REGIONAL MUSEUM

a major, some would say *the* major, icon of nineteenth-century Empire'.[35] The existence of a Scottish regiment in New Zealand has a chequered past, however. Stephen Ladanyi has found that, during the latter part of the nineteenth century, there were a number of Scottish companies among the volunteer units formed in reaction to the North Island Land Wars of the 1860s: there was fear that the unrest would spread south. Ladanyi estimates that, owing to the enthusiasm of Scottish settlers, at least thirteen Scottish units were formed between 1863 and 1906. Unsurprisingly these were concentrated where Scottish settlement had dominated: in the south of the South Island. Early examples were the No. 2 Company (Scottish) Dunedin Rifle Volunteers formed in 1863, the 1865 Dunedin Highland Rifle Volunteers, the 1873 Invercargill Highland Rifle Volunteers, the

The Wanganui Highland Rifles wearing the Gordon tartan, c.1900. M/G/6, WHANGANUI REGIONAL MUSEUM

1871 Wellington Highland Rifle Volunteers, the 1871 Auckland Scottish Rifle Volunteers and the Canterbury Scottish Volunteers.[36] These units required a momentum and energy that was not sustainable and they frequently disbanded a few years after their formation. It is likely, too, that in the second half of the nineteenth century the emphasis was on a united Anglo-Celtic settler front rather than on sectarian and diverse loyalties.

An environment more supportive of the cultivation of ethnic identities developed in the twentieth century. During the South African War, at the turn of the twentieth century, there was a revival in martial units, which appeared again in places of concentrated Scottish settlement, and also in large urban areas. Jock Phillips argues that the new urban male middle classes grasped for martial pursuits to stave off fears of effeminacy.[37] The Wanganui Highland Rifle Volunteers, established in 1900, wore the dress of the Gordon Highlanders, and their uniforms were made in Dunedin by Hallenstein Brothers. In the same year the Wellington Highland Rifle Volunteers and the Canterbury Highland Volunteer Rifles were formed, and in 1909 the Auckland Highland Rifle Volunteers.[38] The only mounted volunteer company was in the Scottish settlement of Waipu: the Scottish Horse Mounted Rifle Volunteers formed in 1906. Some of the early volunteer units lasted much longer than others but in 1911, following the 1909 Defence Act which abolished the Volunteer Force and established a compulsorily recruited Territorial Force, all remaining Highland units were absorbed into the Territorial Force and their distinctive dress and titles were lost. There were to be no New Zealand Highland soldiers in kilts during the Great War who could be dubbed by the Germans 'the ladies from hell'.[39]

It was not until 1937 that firm steps were taken to reintroduce troops wearing Highland uniform into the New Zealand Army. On 15 January 1939 approval was finally given for the formation of the New Zealand Scottish Regiment with companies of 125 men in Auckland, Wellington, Christchurch and Dunedin. A formal agreement to affiliate with the Black Watch was finalised in March 1939. Those intending to join were required to have Scottish ancestry. Scottish societies around New Zealand supported the formation of the regiment and raised funds towards the expensive uniforms. Yet in the Second World War New Zealand was the only dominion not to have a unit of Scots in its overseas forces, perhaps because the New Zealand Expeditionary Force was too small to sustain factions.[40] The Scottish Regiment had disbanded by 1943, although Scottish martial sentiments continued, from 1949, through compulsory military training: there were Scottish units in Christchurch and Dunedin.[41]

Inventing Kiwi culture

The military origins of Highland traditional dress as it emerged in the last quarter of the nineteenth century conjure up images of 'Civilian pipers as well as adult and child dancers from Ontario to Melbourne' wearing 'elaborate costumes in the belief that they are wearing a traditional Highland dress, when in fact they are dressed up as Edwardian soldiers'.[42] From the time Scots arrived in New Zealand kilts have made various appearances as a part of the invention and reinvention of Scottish identity and culture. Versions of a Highland warrior tradition found comfort in the wilderness of the 'New World', where Highland sports, dancing and pipe bands were naturalised.

The McAlpines Premier North Canterbury Pipe Band (Rangiora) at the Amuri Show, Rotherham, in North Canterbury, 2002.
PHOTOGRAPHER
JIM PICKLES

The Alexandra Pipe Band at the West Otago Show in Tapanui, 2003.
PHOTOGRAPHER JIM PICKLES

Highland dancers perform at the Ashburton Show in 2004.
PHOTOGRAPHER JIM PICKLES

Scottish societies kept traditions alive. By the turn of the twentieth century pipe bands and highland dancing were in full fling, often on display at Agricultural and Pastoral Association Shows. Here Scottish culture formed a part of local rural identity, a modern celebration of harvest festival and traditional ways. Replacing the dominance of men, women became involved in Scottish dancing from the early twentieth century. Tartan kilts and tam-o'-shanters were 'in true colonial fashion'.[43] New Zealand pipe bands appeared in kilts, doublets, sword belts, plaids, feather bonnets, spats and 'oversized horse-hair sporran[s]'.[44]

Maureen Molloy's case study of Scots at Waipu is one example of the formation of Scottishness. The first Caledonian Games were held at Waipu on 2 January 1871

The winners of the tent pitching and night alarm competitions at the Caledonian Sports at Turakina, photographed on 22 January 1907. MM/G/4L, WHANGANUI REGIONAL MUSEUM

and, with the exception of the war years, have been held annually on New Year's Day ever since. From the 1890s photographs of boys in Highland dress appeared in family albums and the presence of colourful tartan kilts is a mainstay of the event. Molloy argues that 'the kilt, tartan and bagpipes all immediately identify the event as having to do with "Scottishness"'.[45]

At the turn of the twentieth century developing technologies boosted the kilt's presence in New Zealand society and a kilt industry was established. Helean Kiltmakers in Dunedin was started in September 1901 by merchant tailor Patrick Joseph Helean, who had migrated to New Zealand as a child in 1873. He learned his military kiltmaking skills by employing staff who had previously served in the British Army. The business became well known for making the traditional pipe band kilts popular at the time.[46] Today, the trend is once again towards importing fabric. Companies such as Mitchell Kilt Hire in Hamilton and Highland Kilt Hire in Christchurch hire out kilts 'for weddings, graduation and other formal occasions'. Tartan developed into big business and high fashion. Clan and family tartans became an integral part of the whole concept of being Scottish: over 2000 setts (patterns) are officially listed. There is a Pride of New Zealand tartan, a

Patrick Hellier, New Zealand heavyweight champion, tosses the caber at the Waipu Highland Games on 2 January 2007.
PHOTOGRAPHER JOHN STONE, *NORTHERN ADVOCATE*

Dunedin district tartan and an Otago district tartan with designs copyrighted to The Suit Surgeons Ltd, Dunedin, New Zealand.[47]

Wearing kilts became part of a Celtic revival that was significant throughout the world at the end of the millennium. An interest in 'being Pakeha',[48] to use Michael King's phrase, meant searching for a 'traditional costume', and for some, the kilt sufficed. At weddings, funerals and official occasions men donned kilts, flagging their Scottish identity. For example, on the weddings page of the 6 March 2006 issue of the *New Zealand Woman's Weekly*, Antony Duncan 'has Scottish ancestry so he and Emma Snape added some "reel" Highland flavour to their Tauranga Wedding. The groom and his men wore kilts and Antony's dad played the bagpipes as Emma came down the aisle.'[49] Wearing kilts at weddings became an international phenomenon. Theresa M. Winge and Joanne B. Eicher suggested that from 1985 to 2002 many United States grooms wore kilts at their weddings as a largely unhistorical 'role dress play' through which they were able to assert choice and individuality rather than as an expression of their Scottish ancestry.[50]

At the beginning of the twenty-first century some New Zealand men attempted to perpetuate a mythological kilted past. In 2000 Matthew MacIntosh of Woodend Beach, north of Christchurch, claimed to be following in his grandfather's footsteps: 'I pretty much wear a kilt all the time when I am not working but I often wear a kilt while I am working as well.... My other one... is covered in cow manure.'[51] Champion New Zealand representative blade shearer 57-year-old Alex Macdonald, whose parents were Scottish, intended to wear a kilt to compete in the World Shearing Championships in Edinburgh in 2002.[52]

Tartan, and in particular the kilt, was associated with Highland warrior strength and sporting prowess and it is common for modern outdoor clothing to capitalise on this. For example, with a sense of Highland adventure New Zealand clothing label Scotch Kiwi, based in Bulls, connected tartan to the rugged outdoors. Its thermal underwear claimed to rise in temperature in the cold and wet and cool down in the heat. New Zealand ski team's Guy Davies endorsed the product saying, 'Scotch Kiwi Thermals keep me comfortable when I'm skiing on the edge or standing by the lift'.[53] Gary MacPherson, a Scot competing in the 2005 Coast to Coast, would have cycled, kayaked and run from the West to East Coast of the South Island in a kilt, except for the belief that it would cause too much chafing.[54] Rugby, that supreme exhibition of masculine prowess, reflects the association in the Otago team's name, the Highlanders: 'No big rugby match is complete without a kilted and bag-piped intermission.'[55]

Girls in kilts

'It can perhaps be said yet again,' wrote British historian James Scarlett in 1975, 'that the full male kilt is not for the ladies; there are many styles of skirt, plain and pleated, that are more suited to the female figure and all look infinitely better than does the full kilt.'[56] At the same time as Scarlett's book on kilts was published, New Zealand kilts for girls became a staple school uniform. Significantly, at a time when masculinity and femininity were considered polar opposites, the kilt was both the height of masculinity as a ceremonial military uniform, and the height of femininity as a school girls' uniform. The gender-bending involved in kilt wearing discomforts those who believe that the sexes should wear different clothing. When *Sunday Star-Times* columnist Rosemary McLeod assumed in 2006 that a kilt was a skirt, and hence women's clothing, and accused Prince Charles in a kilt of being in drag, correspondent F. L. Robson of Invercargill retorted that 'He is dressed in a kilt, and the kilt is a male garment. There is no such thing as a lady's kilt. Indeed, the kilt may be the only male garment left that has not been hijacked by feminists.' He continued that 'New Zealand schoolgirls do not have kilts as part of their uniform, they have plaid skirts which have never seen a kilt maker. New Zealand could not afford to dress school children in kilts

Anna Thomson from Ashburton, recipient of the Boarder's Bursary for 1997, tries on her new school uniform. The Rangi Ruru kilt was introduced in 1996, with a unique blue and gold tartan designed to match pre-existing school colours. Plaid summer dresses also encourage school identity.
RANGI RURU GIRLS' SCHOOL, CHRISTCHURCH

Avonside Girls' High School replaced its brown winter tunic with a kilt in 1975 it adopted the Hunting MacKinnon tartan because it matched the school colours of green and brown.[64]

Some schools in Christchurch did create their own tartans, for example Rangi Ruru Girls' School, St Michael's Church School, St Mark's School and Christchurch Girls' High School, which introduced an optional winter senior skirt in 1971. The main winter uniform was the navy-blue serge gym frock in use since 1926. In 1982 the fabric of the senior skirt was used in a winter kilt for all girls. Sarah Lees-Jeffries notes that 'Several schools changed to a kilt for girls' uniform at about this time'. These schools were part of a second wave of schools to adopt the kilt. Again, colour rather than an affiliation with particular clans appeared to be the key factor. Presbyterian Rangi Ruru created more than a tartan: the school houses are named after Scottish castles – Balmoral, Glamis, Doune, Stirling, Dunvegan and Braemar.[65]

Not all opinions of kilts as school uniforms have been positive. Kilts are expensive, with the average kilt requiring 5 to 9 metres of fabric at $100 per since there is seven yards of material in a civilian kilt.'[57] Both McLeod and Robson failed to grasp the reality of the kilt as a costume that clothes both women and men, and that challenges the limits of sex and gender.

Distinctive school uniforms in a variety of colours emerged in the early twentieth century. At the same time military training and military drill became popular and uniformity and conformity were an important part of inculcating citizenship.[58] In the mid-1920s gym slips were popular for girls because they were associated with greater movement during an interwar age of fitness. The numbers wearing them peaked after the Second World War. By the mid-1960s a cluster of schools had introduced a kilt in place of the now considered cumbersome gym slip. New Zealand schoolgirls paraded around in kilts exhibiting tartan patterns intended to be worn by Scottish warriors. In 1966 Papanui High School girls began wearing a kilt in the Black Watch authentic tartan.[59] Gym slips after all, had been associated with military-style exercise drill and conformity. And, as Charlotte Macdonald shows in her chapter in this volume, marching in uniforms influenced by Scottish military dress was a popular sport for New Zealand girls when kilts were introduced as school uniforms.[60] The various tartan clans were readily transferable to school 'clans' as instantly recognisable markers of identity and conformity.

Climate also played a role in the adoption of kilts. Although tartan fabric is used for school uniforms throughout the world, tartan kilts are less common. For example, girls' uniforms in Australia have polyviscose skirts for the lighter, warmer weather. Although some North Island schools did adopt a woollen kilt, climate helps to explain a North/South Island divide, whereby North Island uniforms are more likely to use tartan fabric. For example, in 1974 Napier Girls' High School introduced a winter skirt made from Napier tartan fabric. As one of the most recent schools to introduce a kilt for girls, featuring a hidden pocket, in 2000, Christchurch's Catholic Cathedral College cited warmth as the major reason.[61] The kilt at Dunedin's St Hilda's Collegiate School is in the school colours of grey, blue and white. The major advantages of the kilt were considered to be 'that they were adjustable both in width and length, they had a long life, were not easily soiled, and they would do away with the need for boarders to have a second garment. It was planned for the boarders, and ultimately destined for the whole school.'[62] The strong presence of Scottish culture and a kilt-making industry also aided the introduction of kilts as school uniforms.

How schools chose their tartans had little to do with the clans they represented. In many cases the school colours determined the choice. For example, Burnside High School in Christchurch selected the McKenzie tartan because it coordinated well with a green jersey and blazer. 'Green was deemed to be the preferred predominant colour as cabbage trees are a major part of our logo. There is a large stand of the trees on our site.'[63] Riccarton and Kaiapoi High Schools picked the authentic Napier tartan because it matched their blue and white colours. When

Palmerston North Girls' High School students in their kilts, 2004. *MANAWATU EVENING STANDARD*

metre.⁶⁶ Co-educational Mairehau High School, whose student catchment area covers a low socio-economic area of Christchurch, introduced the kilt for girls in 2002. According to the deputy principal, 'the students complained that the skirt was too cold and they saw other schools wearing a kilt and wanted the same'. Pauline Moore claims that the kilt has not been taken up in great numbers because it is so expensive.⁶⁷

The uniform kilts worn in the 1960s by the baby boom generation tended to mimic the fashion for mini skirts, but by the end of the century kilts had reached 'Edwardian lengths'.⁶⁸ In 2005 Christchurch fashion designer Barbara Lee, who designed uniforms for fifteen schools, including two in Christchurch, said that she preferred shorts; long kilts were 'seriously stupid and a waste of fabric'.⁶⁹ Kilts got stuck in bicycles, were heavy to wear and, if reaching the floor, caught dust and dirt that remained until dry cleaning in the school holidays. Another local way of wearing school kilts was evident at Waitaki Girls' High School in Oamaru, where the striking predominantly dark red McQueen tartan kilt is worn. In 2004 some students took to wearing pyjama bottoms under their kilts.⁷⁰

Girls in kilts had appropriated a military and ceremonial uniform for men, yet, as skirts, they became symbolic of society's assertion of compulsory gender difference. Why couldn't girls wear trousers to school? In May 2005 a public debate ensued over the actions of girls at Cashmere High School in Christchurch who refused to wear a kilted skirt after trousers for girls were banned. The school had been a pioneer in exploring unisex uniforms. In 1980 the old gym frock and summer tunic were replaced with unisex gold shirts, grey skirts or walk shorts, roman sandals without socks in summer, and yellow parkas for rainwear. In 2005 the trousers, with their high elastic waists and pleats, were badly out of fashion. Katia De Lu, the organiser of a petition that collected 300 signatures, including 21 from staff, said, 'I really want to wear trousers. Sometimes I have to bicycle to school, and a kilt on a bicycle isn't very good.' Public opinion was divided. Robert Mather, the owner of Lithgows, a school uniform shop, said he would not even put a pair of girl's trousers on display in his Riccarton shop. 'All the girls prefer to have the kilt; they love the kilt.' Meanwhile 'keep your pants on' was the opinion of younger people such as Olivia Pither and John Daniels, Year 6 pupils from Windsor Primary School. 'The girls who like to play sport are forever changing during the day because it is very unlady-like to play sport in a kilt.'[71] Would these pupils consider a man in a 'skirt' participating in Highland Games manly?

Queering the kilt

If different wearings of the kilt offer a challenge to constructions of ethnicity, masculinity and femininity, the most complex and interesting subversion comes in the challenge to heterosexuality at the end of the twentieth century.[72] Once kilts had become a costume to wear at a wedding, they were appropriated and playfully worn by gays and lesbians. Such attire was international in scope, part of what Shaun Cole considers to be the 'homogenisation of gay culture'. In July 1993 the *New York Times* reported that hundreds of men turned up to watch a Gay Pride Parade wearing short kilts, with heavy workboots, and that men had been spotted at discos dancing in kilts. The same year kilts were also noted as 'the latest gay fashion trend' in Canada: 'The kilt is a MASCULINE mode of dress that holds up on its own and allows a man to dress in other than jeans and polyester without looking feminine'.[73] More than playful gender-bending was at stake. In 2001 controversy broke out in Scotland over the registration of the rainbow tartan designed for gay men. Some believed the application by 'Queensferry' was an affront to what was perceived as 'a symbol of Scottish manhood, conjuring up an image of hearty Highlanders doing battle in the glens'.[74] Kilts were grounded in concepts of clan and genealogy, bloodlines and belonging; now subversive alternative masculine subjectivities were being fashioned.[75]

Kilts also became a costume of choice at New Zealand gay and lesbian alternative marriage ceremonies but, as with other instances, there was a continuing exchange between innovation and tradition. Gay and lesbian New Zealanders who wore kilts were expressing their ethnic identity. More generally, they were tapping into the enduring identity of the kilt as a costume of resistance – most strikingly against compulsory heterosexuality. In April 1995, Carmel Carroll, an opera singer, and Jess Denholm, a gardener, married in Auckland. 'The two women arrived at the ceremony together, and, in acknowledgement of Jess's Scottish heritage, were piped into the service . . . .' Carroll wore a concert gown but Denholm wore 'Scottish national dress with a black watch tartan kilt'.[76] Intriguingly, on this occasion, which was controversial for its potential mimicry and subversion of the family unit, Denholm wore a warrior costume – and not the tartan of the rebel clans, but that of the loyalists.

The fabric and form of an item of clothing so important in Scots identity has enjoyed a status far beyond its appeal to or impact on one ethnic grouping. Although the kilt's strong presence in New Zealand might suggest the existence and influence of 'Scottishness', most interesting is how legions of schoolgirls have taken over from parading Highland regiments, and how same-sex unions assert homosexual identities while dressing in a costume of heterosexual lineage. A traditionally male garment, renowned for its association with fighting and strength, the kilt has retained its shape but shifted to the opposite sex. A co-existence, and sometimes a tension, between tradition and hegemony and rebellion and resistance has enabled the kilt to be worn in many ways that reveal the complexities of the construction of sexuality, identity, resistance and tradition in New Zealand. Together the form of the kilt and the tartan pattern of the fabric have made provocative history.

5. Every Garment Tells a Story: Exploring Public Collections
David Butts

Each time I walk through the doors of the Hawke's Bay Art Gallery and Museum on Marine Parade in Napier, I know I am entering an institution with a collection of national importance.[1] In my mind's eye I can see the garments that lie in the basement storage areas beneath the public galleries. Special treasures come to mind. Some visitors may be drawn to the collection of taonga Māori or the collections of fine and applied arts, but I look to the small collection of eighteenth-century men's embroidered waistcoats. I do not fully understand why I am fascinated by these waistcoats. I am not a particularly fashion conscious individual, but I am intrigued by the notion that men of a certain station in European society once wore such garments as a measure of their status and sophistication. I trained as an archaeologist during the 1970s and entered the museum world to further my career. For a time I was able to do just that, but when I moved to the Hawke's Bay Art Gallery and Museum in 1982, the institution was beginning a major redevelopment project and I was required to work with other museum staff in developing new exhibitions and new storage facilities to house the museum's many and varied collections.[2] Although I had some experience working with taonga Māori and general historical collections from my time as curator at the Manawatu Museum in Palmerston North, the Napier collections had been developed over a longer period and were more varied, including wonderful collections of fine and applied arts. For the first time I had to turn my mind to creating exhibitions of ceramics, glass, silver, textiles and clothing.

A major part of the redevelopment entailed transforming the existing basement storerooms into modern museum storage facilities. During the 1980s the new science of preventive conservation of cultural materials had a significant impact on museum practice and on the care of clothing and textile collections in particular.[3] The collections had to be moved from the existing storerooms to another part of the museum while the work was done and it was during this relocation process that I first began to realise the richness of the clothing collections. Kākahu Māori (cloaks) emerged tightly folded from small acidic cardboard boxes in which they had been kept for decades, or were removed from the pipe racks over which they had been folded. Their fragility was only too apparent as we tried to move them with the minimum of damage. The black dust that results from the acidic action of the earth dyes, the feather fragments and the detached harakeke hukahuka (flax tags) indicated the care needed to handle these treasures. And yet these taonga tuku iho (treasures handed down) had stood the test of time and minimal storage conditions to remain as an invaluable reminder and resource for those who would trace their history and learn again the techniques of their creation.

The general clothing collection was also revealed in all its wonder and diversity. Although the storage conditions were basic, lacking the mobile shelving, acid-free tissue paper and boxes used today, museum staff and volunteers had cared for these treasures as best they could. As each box was opened a wealth of clothing history emerged, including an extraordinary range of dresses, military uniforms and children's clothing. There were the garments that mark the rituals of baptism, marriage and death – christening gowns, wedding dresses and mourning clothes, the finery of famous men and women, and the ceremonial and regional dress from many other parts of the world, including China and India.

I have enjoyed working with and observing other curators, collection managers and conservators for whom clothing is a passion. This chapter provides an opportunity to draw attention to the significant collection at the Hawke's Bay Art Gallery and Museum in order to emphasise its importance for historical research. My intention is not to provide a formal academic analysis of the collection, but rather to convey something of the pleasure that I have experienced in discovering it and enjoying its display in the many exhibitions created by the museum staff.[4] In doing so, I hope to elaborate the range of connections that can be made between garments in the collection and the social, cultural, political and economic lives of people in Hawke's Bay and beyond. I also want to provide some insight into the way in which collections evolve. The values attached to historical and contemporary clothing by originating communities, individual owners, collectors, curators and designers change greatly from one period to another and the acquisition of museum collections reflects these shifting values. Once garments enter a museum collection their social lives continue, although their significance also varies over time.

A selection of treasures

Although the Hawke's Bay Art Gallery and Museum was established in 1936 as the first public museum in Napier, its antecedents reach back to the Hawke's Bay Philosophical Institute's museum, which began in 1881. This was located in the Athenaeum, on the same site occupied by the gallery and museum today. It was curated from 1883 to 1890 by Augustus Hamilton, who was later appointed

Director of the Colonial Museum in Wellington. Hamilton encouraged Philosophical Institute members to deposit items in the museum and by 1890, when he departed to become Registrar of the University of Otago, the collection included a wide range of natural history specimens and taonga Māori, including a small number of kākahu Māori.[5] In the mid-1880s Hamilton realised that significant numbers of taonga Māori were being exported to Europe for both private and public collections and he encouraged local collectors to focus on acquiring them for the institute's collection.

From its establishment, the Hawke's Bay Art Gallery and Museum continued to collect taonga Māori, along with foreign ethnology, art and applied arts.[6] After the Second World War the ethnology collections grew most rapidly.[7] The museum's first director, Leo Bestall, was far more interested in the arts and the exotic than in documenting the daily lives of the European settlers in Hawke's Bay. It was not until the early 1960s, following the appointment of the second director, Jim Munro, that there was a growing recognition of the need to develop a collection of 'all manner of domestic and agricultural objects of the type used by our forebears in homes and farms'.[8] This broadening of the museum's collecting and exhibiting interests reflects both Munro's influence and a growing interest among academics and the wider community in New Zealand's social history. As the Pākehā communities in Hawke's Bay became increasingly conscious of their own history, the number of objects donated increased significantly: as many objects were acquired between 1977 and 1986 as had been in the previous 40 years.[9] Among these were many treasured items of clothing.

A collection of locally worn European styles of clothing was begun in 1936. Known as the general clothing collection, it initially grew only fitfully, although it did include interesting items, such as a uniform jacket of the 5th Royal Inniskilling Dragoon Guards (now known as the Royal Dragoon Guards). This slow beginning reflects the initial interest of the museum's supporters in the fine arts, taonga Māori and exotic items of all kinds. The collection of customary Māori clothing was purchased or gifted as part of the large collections of taonga Māori that had entered the museum by the 1960s. During the last quarter of the twentieth century very few kākahu Māori entered the collection, but the general clothing collection increased by more than 1500 items between 1980 and 2000. There were only ten dresses in the museum collection at the end of 1959; by 2000 there were 277. The museum's curators, who were particularly interested in developing the more contemporary sections of the collection, deliberately encouraged this emphasis. Towards the end of 2005 there were more than 2500 items in the general clothing collection, around 5 per cent of the museum's holdings. I have chosen to discuss five garments from the general clothing collection. While each has its own unique history, taken together they draw our attention to changing social practices, fashions and technologies, as well as a range of museological issues and opportunities.

Hew Steuart's embroidered waistcoat

Imagine my sense of discovery and revelation as I opened a box of men's embroidered waistcoats and discovered between each layer of acid-free tissue the most exquisitely decorated garments. The first was embroidered with delicate flowers in greens and mauves; the second, made of fine red wool, was embroidered with small fox heads; and the third, a waistcoat of cream silk satin, was embroidered with vertical bands of green, pink and yellow flowers. In a moment of aberrant enthusiasm, I had persuaded the museum director to purchase the third waistcoat at an auction in Auckland, even though it had no Hawke's Bay provenance. The museum currently houses four eighteenth- and nineteenth-century men's embroidered waistcoats, the three described above and one on loan, which has subtly beautiful whitework on white linen.

This last waistcoat was made for Hew Steuart, the second son of John Steuart, seventh Laird of Dalguise, Perthshire, Scotland, by his mother, Mary Steuart (*née* Finlay). Born in 1733, Steuart joined the British civil service and was posted to the Far East, eventually ending his career with an appointment as Governor of Fort Marlborough and President and Commander in Chief of Sumatra in 1780. He died at sea while returning home in 1782. When and where he wore the waistcoat is unknown. The front and pocket flaps of this high-necked, sleeveless waistcoat

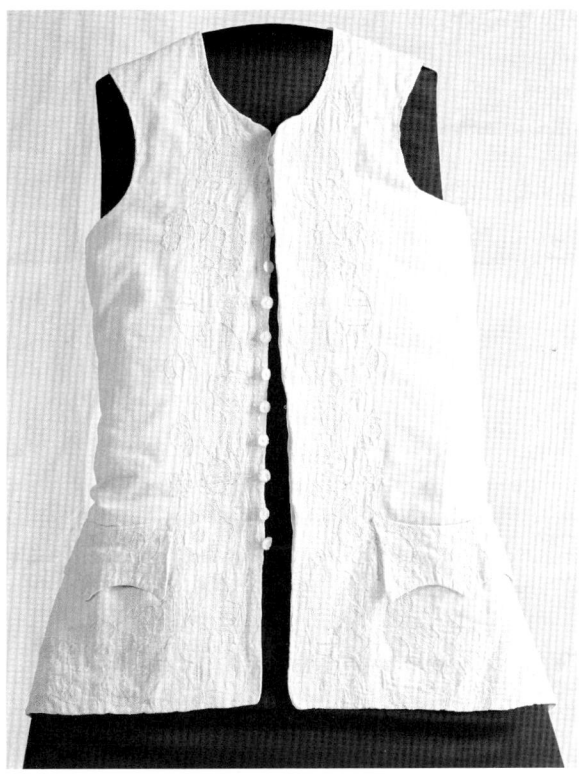

Hew Steuart's eighteenth-century waistcoat, and detail of buttons and embroidery (facing page).
93/113A, HAWKE'S BAY MUSEUM, PHOTOGRAPHER CLIVE RALPH

are made of white hand-spun, hand-woven linen, with whitework embroidery in a stylised pattern of flowers and leaf forms. The front fastening has twelve thread buttons of the Dorset cross-wheeled type on the right side and concealed buttonholes in a fly front strip on the left side. The back of the waistcoat is made of napped linen. It has two side vents and one back vent.

 I chose this linen waistcoat for its history, its construction and the fact that it is on loan. It was handed down through the Steuart family for many generations until it was bequeathed to a young man whose parents asked the museum to care for the waistcoat until he was old enough to assume the responsibility of ownership. After consultation with the museum the family had the waistcoat assessed and treated by Valerie Carson, a textile conservator at the Museum of New Zealand Te Papa Tongarewa (Te Papa). The trust shown by this family in placing the waistcoat in the museum is indicative of the institution's reputation in the region. When this young man was old enough he removed the waistcoat from the museum for a time, subsequently returning it, once again on loan. Museums are generally cautious about entering into loan agreements, but the Hawke's Bay Art Gallery and Museum has an established relationship with this family and recognises a responsibility to help them care for this significant treasure. While on loan, the waistcoat is accessible to those who have an interest in such garments and it can be used for exhibitions.

Such waistcoats prompt us to reflect on the changing nature of men's fashions and definitions of masculinity. They remind us of a time when élite male clothing was very different to that worn by most men today, and suggest that there was no disjunction between fine embroidery and such passions as horse riding, hunting and collecting fossils. A link could certainly be drawn between civilian garments, such as the embroidered waistcoats, and the elaborate military uniforms of this period. However, it should be noted that although this waistcoat was made before the full onset of 'the plain and uniform costume' of aristocratic men, characteristic of 'the gender ideology of masculine renunciation' of the late eighteenth and early nineteenth centuries, the whitework embroidery on white linen may reflect a certain constraint. This ideology is said to have emerged throughout the eighteenth century as the aristocracy sought to identify themselves with the 'values of industry and economy', which were increasingly important if they were to retain their claim to political authority in the face of middle class political activism.[10]

Dr William Spencer's 18th Royal Irish Regiment officer's tunic

An assistant surgeon in the 18th Royal Irish Regiment, Dr William Spencer saw active service during the New Zealand Wars from 1863 to 1866. He resigned in 1870, when the regiment returned to Australia, so that he could remain in Napier with his family. He was elected mayor from 1882 to 1885, and died there in 1897. Dr Spencer's tunic was donated to the museum in 1947 by his eldest daughter, Anna Elizabeth (known as Bessie), a former principal of Napier Girls' High School and founder of the first Women's Institute in New Zealand.[11] The tunic is made of a red serge cloth and lined with cream wool. It has a high navy blue collar, with raised decorations on each side in the form of a crown and a medallion, and navy blue cuffs elaborately decorated with silver bullion wire work. Each cuff has three buttons decorated with a silver harp under a crown. The back vent of the tunic is also decorated with silver bullion wire work. The tunic is showing some signs of wear and the right epaulet is missing.

It was Spencer's practice to continue wearing his military uniform on formal occasions. The *Hawke's Bay Herald* records his presence, with his wife, Anna, at a local ball on 9 August 1877:

> Dr Spencer: Full dress uniform of a Medical Officer of the 18th Royal Irish Regiment. Mrs Spencer: Parsee Lady – Oriental costume or sorree [sari] of white cashmere, with scarlet figured border; the scarf like end of the dress, falling from the head over the shoulder; scarlet short sleeved bodice with gold trimming; ornaments, necklace, earrings, bracelets from wrist to elbow, and crescent shaped jewel on the forehead.

EVERY GARMENT TELLS A STORY

Dr William Spencer's 18th Royal Irish Regiment officer's tunic and cuff detail. 47/113, HAWKE'S BAY MUSEUM, PHOTOGRAPHER CLIVE RALPH

They made a striking couple, the bright red, navy and silver of his military tunic contrasting with her white and scarlet costume. We may surmise that this particular wearing of his tunic was a measure not only of the pride Spencer felt as a military and medical man of Irish descent, but also part of the celebration of colonial splendour. Beyond such occasions, Spencer's military tunic can be associated with a number of wider historical themes, including military conflict, colonisation, medicine and politics, as well as drawing our attention to different cultural perspectives. For instance, the term 'red coats' may have quite different meanings for Māori than for Pākehā.

The museum holds a range of military uniforms, from those worn during the nineteenth-century conflicts in New Zealand and South Africa to those of the First and Second World Wars. They represent those who died here and overseas and those who returned to continue their lives in New Zealand. The history of families, communities and countries is often defined by these wars. In recent years there has been a revival of interest in the annual ANZAC remembrances and numerous war histories have been published. Major oral history projects, such as those undertaken with the families of D Company (Hawke's Bay) and C Company (Tairāwhiti) of the 28th Māori Battalion, have recorded the impact of these wars. The histories of which these uniforms speak continue to evolve as we gain a better understanding of the impact of these conflicts.

Bessie Thompson's christening gown

Christening gowns are common in museum clothing collections, as are wedding dresses. The Hawke's Bay Art Gallery and Museum collection includes about 20 christening gowns and about 30 wedding dresses, some with veils and associated items.[12] Both were worn for rites of passage and were typically white, a symbol of purity in the Christian faith, but their patterns of use were quite different. Christening gowns were often made by the mother or grandmother and frequently used for more than one child, sometimes in more than one generation. Wedding dresses were more likely to have been made by a dressmaker, worn by one bride and then stored until the material was used to make another garment, or the dress was discarded or donated to a museum. Christening gowns were more likely than wedding dresses to be passed down through family members, although veils were an exception. Christening gowns often made their way into museum collections because they had been valued by more than one generation.

A wedding and a christening come together in the story of one particular christening gown.[13] It was made in 1911 by Mildred Thompson for the christening of her first child, Mildred Bessie (Bessie) Thompson, from material cut from her own wedding gown. Born in Mauriceville, Mildred Jane Devonshire had married Australian Thomas Ernest Thompson in Levin on 30 November 1910.[14] The christening gown was used for Bessie's six siblings and then passed on to one of the children, who eventually donated it to the museum. Even though this garment was much treasured by the family, long use has left its mark, and it is this that makes this garment so interesting. The same family has donated a number of other children's items, including the tin baby's bath, purchased in 1911, that was used to bath the seven children who wore the christening gown. This example demonstrates the importance of relating the items in the clothing collections to other items from the same family or donor to give a composite picture of material life in earlier domestic settings.

The gown is made of Indian muslin, with white cotton embroidery down the centre of the bodice and around the base of the gown, typical of such garments. There is hand-made lace at the neck and sleeves and the hem is machine embroidered. There is a pull-through tie around the neck and around the base of the bodice is white eyelet braid with the ribbon missing. Three mother-of-pearl buttons fasten the gown at the back. This garment heralds the hopes and aspirations held in the early stages of life, as does the next one I have selected, which symbolises the step from adolescence to adulthood.

Hinemoa Collison's twenty-first birthday dress

Art deco has become synonymous with Napier. Since the 1980s the Art Deco Trust has encouraged the people of the city to recognise and maintain the distinctive townscape that was built after the 1931 earthquake, which killed 256 people. Much of the tourism marketing of the city is based on this identity. Each year the Art Deco Weekend attracts thousands of visitors to Napier to celebrate the architecture and enjoy the locally produced food and wine in the spirit of the optimism and renewal that characterised the region after the disaster, and still does today. As a result, the Hawke's Bay Art Gallery and Museum has developed a collection of art deco objects dating from the early 1920s until the mid-1930s. This initiative was begun by museum director Robert McGregor, who later took up the position of CEO of the Art Deco Trust. This collection now includes applied arts objects, such as angular glassware, figurines, scent bottles and ceramics, and textile items, such as carpets, clothes and accessories.

Hinemoa Collison is thought to have worn the beaded dress shown in Plate 9 (detail below) on her twenty-first birthday in 1922. A sleeveless shift-style dress made of green silk georgette, it has an elaborate geometric design beaded onto the bodice and skirt. Purchased in Paris by Hinemoa's mother, it was donated to the museum in 1984 with the original shoes. Hinemoa was the eldest daughter of Edward and Mary Collison, who farmed at Longlands near Hastings. Edward Collison had an interest in and admiration for Māori culture like many Pākehā at

Detail from Hinemoa Collison's twenty-first birthday dress, 1920s. 84/95, HAWKE'S BAY MUSEUM, PHOTOGRAPHER CLIVE RALPH

this time, and gave his three daughters Māori names. Hinemoa married Hedley G. Harvey in 1926 and had two daughters, one of whom donated the dress.[15]

This garment can be taken as evidence of the distance travelled from the constraints of Victorian fashion to the freedom of the 1920s. New Zealand, along with much of the rest of the world, had emerged from the sacrifice of war, when women had assumed new roles. Loose-fitting garments were popular, skirt lengths rose above the ankle, and the ideal female figure was as flat as an ironing board. The somewhat boyish women's fashions of the 1920s are widely believed to reflect women's new-found social and political status, but some historians have argued that this perception may be a matter of image rather than reality. In the words of New Zealand art historian Hamish Keith, in flapper fashion '[e]legance was a straight line', but many women found this hard to achieve.[16] Closer examination of fashions worn by Australasian women during this period suggests that a wide variety of clothing styles was worn, including more conservative designs. For many women, the 'freedom' of the 1920s still had (apron) strings attached.[17]

Barbara Penberthy's three-piece suit

The 1960s were also a time of new freedoms for some women and distinctive styles of clothing. Auckland designer Barbara Penberthy (*née* Lewis), operating under the trade name Babs Radon, received the Supreme Award at the 1963 National Gold Medal Wool Awards, held in Lower Hutt. Her beautifully tailored cream lambda ensemble, which included a sheath dress and three-quarter-length coat trimmed with marmot, was selected from 5000 competition entries. She received a kauri 'Oscar' from Queen Elizabeth II and the Duke of Edinburgh. Penberthy, by then known as Barbara Herrick, wore to the ceremony a three-piece suit she had designed herself, and she donated this to the museum in 1999. It consists of a short sleeveless top made of teal and black silk, a bias cut teal and black silk skirt, and a sleeveless, taffeta-lined, teal printed textured rayon jacket, gathered below the bust, with bows on either side. The museum collection also includes a number of dresses designed by Penberthy and sold in her Babs Radon store in Auckland. She collected numerous fashion awards and featured repeatedly on the pages of *Vogue* magazine. By the mid-1960s, Penberthy was widely respected as one of New Zealand's most successful fashion designers – this in a period, as Douglas Lloyd Jenkins has noted, 'in which the term "New Zealand fashion design" would not have sold a single dress'.[18]

> Looking back over the Babs Radon runway shows of the 1960s, we can see that Herrick was developing her take on what we now think of as a distinctively 60s look – somewhere between Doris Day in her Rock Hudson period and Jacqueline Kennedy before Ari. The look was crisp and smart. It focused on the good cutting and careful tailoring of quality materials – often wool.

Barbara Penberthy's three-piece suit and shoes, 1963. 99/21/1, HAWKE'S BAY MUSEUM, PHOTOGRAPHER CLIVE RALPH

Lloyd Jenkins goes on to say that, in

> a subtle, carefully tailored form of revenge against the limitations of 1960s society, Herrick dressed the very women who would change those attitudes. Because of this, she attracted to her label key figures like the feminist broadcaster Cherry Raymond, who were working to change other aspects of New Zealand women's lives.

The Penberthy suit highlights a major development in the clothing collection in the late 1990s when Claire Regnault was curator. Coming to the position with a well-developed interest in textile and clothing design, Regnault not only curated exhibitions about textile and clothing designers from Hawke's Bay and beyond, but also actively sought examples of their work for the collection. As her curatorial interests became known, the designers themselves and others began to direct such material to the museum. Within a relatively short period a significant collection of contemporary New Zealand textile and clothing design was accumulated and the museum's collection policy had been broadened.

When Regnault moved to a position at the Dowse Art Museum in Lower Hutt, the development of this collection declined and for some years it was uncertain whether it would be sustained at all. However, the appointment of Douglas Lloyd Jenkins as director of the museum in 2006 suggests that this focus may be revived, especially given his involvement in building up these collections and curating exhibitions about textile designers. Meanwhile, designers and other donors have continued to bring items of designer textiles and clothing to the museum. Although there have been significant costs associated with collecting in this area, including acid-free packing, storage space and staff time to document and care for the items, there have also been significant benefits. The representation in the museum collection of textile and clothing designers who have worked in the Hawke's Bay region has increased considerably, and more attention has been drawn to the existing textile and clothing collections, prompting a significant amount of retrospective work on their documentation and storage. Exhibitions drawing on the textile design and designer clothing collections have travelled throughout New Zealand and raised the profile of the museum as an institution holding a nationally significant collection of textiles and clothing.[19]

Māori clothing in transition

European waistcoats were not the only ones to catch my eye; I was also enthralled by a stunning waistcoat in the taonga Māori collection (Plate 10), with a purple silk back, with an attached buckle and strap for tightening, and woven front panels made from plain and purple dyed harakeke (flax). Pockets have been sewn onto the lower section of each front panel of the waistcoat and a small pocket is sewn to the upper section of the left-hand panel. The edges of each of the front panels and the pockets of the waistcoat are bound with a narrow purple tape that has been sewn to the body. The amount of wear on the waistcoat suggests that it was used regularly for a period before being set aside and preserved. Unfortunately, there is no known history recorded about it. I thought that it was perhaps a unique item but on a recent visit to Aratoi, the Wairarapa Museum of Art and History in Masterton, I was shown a second waistcoat made of harakeke by women from Te Ore Ore Marae, near Masterton. This garment was made for Augustus Cave, a local Pākehā farmer, in recognition of his relationship with the local Māori community. Strands of this waistcoat are thought to have been dyed with gentian violet to create the pattern in the same way as has been done with the Hawke's Bay Museum waistcoat. I began to wonder how many such garments there might be in public collections. Subsequent enquiries have located only one further example, held in the British Museum. These waistcoats are examples of European-style garments made using a blend of customary Māori and European materials and techniques. The dyed panels create dynamic designs that must have been as remarkable when they were created as they appear today. One can only imagine the impact a man would have made entering a room or standing to speak on the marae wearing one of these waistcoats.

They form a connection between the clothing of the early European settlement period and the customary kākahu Māori. The meeting of Polynesian and European clothing traditions is seen in many nineteenth-century photographs where people wear combinations of customary Māori clothing and European garments, with headdresses of feathers or European hats or the two traditions combined. This wonderfully creative response to new fashions is but one instance of Māori capacity to adapt in a rapidly changing political, social and economic environment.

The waistcoat is only one tiny part of the kākahu section of the taonga Māori collection at Hawke's Bay Art Gallery and Museum. Unfortunately this collection is not widely known to the local community or to visitors to the museum because it has rarely been on exhibition and there are no publications illustrating the breadth of the collection. Museum staff have, however, encouraged weavers and others to access the collection in storage for research purposes.

As at April 2005, the museum was caring for about 4340 taonga. Among them were 94 cloaks and rain capes, 37 piupiu and 7 rāpaki (loincloths).[20] This is the second largest collection of kākahu Māori in a regional museum collection in New Zealand.[21] It is no longer possible to date with any certainty the entry into the museum of a third of the kākahu, but it is known that most arrived into the museum before 1990.[22] Only two cloaks have been deposited in the museum since then. Since there is no substantial history of Māori families depositing kākahu in the museum, one can assume that non-Māori collectors and families in Hawke's Bay who hold kākahu are no longer depositing them in museums. Without further research it is not possible to determine whether there are still substantial numbers of kākahu held by non-Māori in private collections. It may be that most kākahu Māori in Hawke's Bay are now held by Māori families and the museum.

Of the 94 cloaks and rain capes in the collection, only 16 have a provenance beyond the name of the donor. Of these, nine are from one local Heretaunga Māori family and three others were presented by Māori to Pākehā individuals whose descendants have placed the cloaks in the museum. The largest single deposit is the 22 cloaks in the McLean Collection gifted to the museum by Lady Florence McLean in 1937 as part of the museum's foundation collection.[23] None of these has a recorded provenance and it cannot be assumed that they were all collected by runholder, politician and land agent Sir Donald McLean, since his son, Sir Douglas McLean, and daughter-in-law, Lady Florence McLean, both added to Sir Donald's collection.[24] When a collection is passed on to a museum after the primary collector has died, and there is no catalogue, it is highly unlikely that information will have been provided.[25] This situation was exacerbated in the period before the Second World War, when some museum staff either placed little value on recording the history of these taonga or the donors were no longer able to convey detailed provenance. Only 7 of the 37 piupiu in the collection have any provenance information recorded beyond the donor's name and in most cases this information is minimal.

Ecologist Lara Shepherd used an extensive reference database of mitochondrial DNA sequences to determine the provenance of brown kiwi feathers from kākahu Māori and kete (kits) from the Hawke's Bay Art Gallery and Museum collection.[26] Samples were taken from the base of feathers of fifteen cloaks. All the feathers sampled were from North Island brown kiwi (*Apteryx manelli*). The majority of haplotypes obtained were identical to those detected in modern and ancient brown kiwi populations from the Hawke's Bay and Bay of Plenty regions.[27] The absence of haplotypes from western and northern regions of the North Island in all but one sample makes it reasonably certain that these cloaks came from the East Coast. No cloaks had both eastern and western population haplotypes. Using this type of analysis, other museums will be able to determine the broad regions from which the feathers in cloaks have originated and thus determine the regional provenance of the taonga, although in most instances this will not enable the taonga to be assigned to a particular iwi.

The cloak types best represented in the collection are the feather cloaks (16 kahu huruhuru and 21 kahu kiwi) and korowai (27); a distant third are the kaitaka paepaeroa (8). The rarest types represented in the collection, with one of each, are the kahu kurī (dogskin cloak) and the kahu toi (cloak made of mountain cabbage tree). Although there is a need to allow for distinct regional patterns, the distribution of cloak types is very much what might be expected given the general history of cloak types outlined by Hirini Moko Mead.[28] He argues that kaitaka types were rarely made after about 1880 and that the korowai rose in prominence through the nineteenth century. The feather cloaks, he suggests, became more popular in the late nineteenth century; there was a transition to cloaks with both feathers and tāniko in the twentieth century. However, there appear to be only three such feather cloaks with tāniko borders in the collection, a smaller proportion than one might expect, given Mead's analysis. Kahu kurī were only rarely produced after 1850. There are only seven rain capes in the collection, which may reflect the more utilitarian nature of these garments and the fact that few seem to have been produced since the end of the nineteenth century.

Although there has been a revival of cloak and cape making since the 1970s, the Hawke's Bay Art Gallery and Museum has only acquired one garment from this period. This is a fibre sculpture, entitled 'Kapu 1/Cloud 1' in cape form by Rangi Kiu, acquired for the art collection in 1992. There is no evidence that the museum has sought to collect or document clothing developed for performances by kapa haka groups in Hawke's Bay in recent times. Piupiu, according to Mead, emerged in the nineteenth century and became more popular for performing groups in the twentieth century.[29] They were also produced commercially for the tourist trade. However, the small number acquired by the museum suggests that both collectors and the museum placed less value on items that were not considered traditional or authentic pre-European taonga.

The museum is the caretaker of the taonga Māori in the collection, and to ensure that they are treated appropriately and with respect and made accessible to tangata whenua (the people of the land, first settlers), the museum trustees and staff are guided in their policy and practice by Te Roopu Kaiawhi Taonga, the consultative committee that has representatives from each taiwhenua (district) of Ngāti Kahungunu. In 2002 consultant materials conservator and weaver Rangi Te Kanawa and museum staff completed a survey of the conservation requirements of half of the kākahu collection.[30] Digital images were taken for use in the museum's computerised collection database. These photographs also made it possible for staff and researchers to see the collection without having physical access.[31] During this conservation project local weavers and other interested people came into the museum to see the kākahu while they were more easily accessible. In 2003, in response to requests for further access to the collection, the museum developed a training project, Te Whakaruruhau: The Mantle of Care, in partnership with National Services Te Paerangi, to provide five workshops for weavers and others interested in learning more about kākahu Māori. Visitors to the conservation project had been impressed by the richness of the resource represented in the collection for weavers, artists and scholars. The workshops, tutored by Rangi Te Kanawa and museum staff, provided an introduction to the handling, storage and preventive conservation of kākahu, as well as an exploration of the weaving techniques and artistry evident in the collection.

During the conservation project, Rangi Te Kanawa identified one of the cloaks as one of the largest kaitaka paepaeroa she had seen in any collection in New Zealand or overseas (over, and Plate 11).[32] It is big enough to wrap twice around

Detail of the kaitaka paepaeroa (width: 2880 mm, length: 1650 mm). 38/39, HAWKE'S BAY MUSEUM, PHOTOGRAPHER CLIVE RALPH

the body of the wearer. The kaupapa (foundation) of the kaitaka paepaeroa has vertical wefts, characteristic of this type of cloak, and is made of muka (beaten and rubbed harakeke). Mead identifies the paepaeroa as a garment normally worn by persons of high standing.[33] The cloak has a tāniko border on both the kauko (side edges) and remu (bottom edge) composed of dyed and undyed muka and incorporating red, blue, green and yellow woollen thread. The ua (top edge) is finished with a red, blue and mauve twisted running thread. This cloak needed conservation treatment: the surface was cleaned, the folds and creases were relaxed with controlled humidity and some frayed elements were secured.[34] Although this kaitaka paepaeroa has no recorded history, Te Kanawa has dated it to the mid-nineteenth century, since it incorporates fibres introduced by Europeans to enhance the construction and decoration of garments. Connections may be drawn between the use of the polychrome cloak kaupapa, tāniko designs using introduced fibres, and painted wharenui (meeting houses) in the nineteenth century. It is unlikely that the use of such coloured fibres is entirely random. Some of the colours, such as red and blue, are known to have customary cultural significance.[35] Thus, although this paepaeroa has no known history, it remains an important taonga tuku iho. For Rangi Te Kanawa, such taonga are 'the very essence of our tūpuna':

> Throughout our lives we draw upon ngā taonga for a number of reasons: comfort, inspiration, guidance and representation. In return we must provide the best care possible so that the taonga will remain with us and future generations.[36]

The high-profile clothing collections of major metropolitan museums in Auckland, Wellington, Christchurch and Dunedin are well known to those interested in the history of clothing in New Zealand, but it is important to acknowledge the national and regional significance of the clothing collections in provincial museums such as the Hawke's Bay Art Gallery and Museum in Napier. Although the main centre institutions house large, nationally important collections of contemporary textiles and clothing, it is unlikely that Hawke's Bay Art Gallery and Museum would now deaccession items to areas in which they were originally created. A question remains as to whether the museum will continue to develop a national collection or take on a more regional character. There are also enough other gaps in the clothing collection to usefully engage any curator's desire to collect. The challenge, for example, will be to add to the collection items of men's work clothes and children's clothing from throughout the twentieth century. There are, as my selection has shown, excellent examples of the clothing of colonial élites, clothing associated with rites of passage, and contemporary designer clothing, but common everyday clothes have been largely overlooked by those who have had the museum collection in mind when disposing of items in their wardrobes, duchesses and tallboys. Perhaps this is because most people assume that museums will not be interested in the clothes that they wear to work or at the weekend, but wish only to collect items that are special either because of their design and materials or because of some notable association with a particular event or famous individual. However, museums are increasingly interested in collecting the full spectrum of contemporary clothing and accessories, particularly those produced in New Zealand. As local clothing manufacturers struggle to survive in the face of an increasingly international free trade environment, our museums should be concerned with collecting New Zealand-made clothing.

Clothing collections present their own challenges in storage and exhibition, but the increasing size of these collections and the growing number of clothing exhibitions in many New Zealand museums indicates that there is a demand to know more about the historical and contemporary nature of clothing and the role that it plays in our lives. As New Zealand museums increasingly recognise the need to make their clothing collections more accessible to the visiting public, specialist community groups, such as embroiderers, art and design students, and a wide range of scholars, there has been an improvement in the standard of documentation, storage and exhibition. Museum practitioners are increasingly aware of the need to maintain the tangible and intangible dimensions of our textile and clothing heritage. The challenge for museums is to maintain the physical integrity of collections and to record, research, interpret and make accessible the stories that help to bring collections alive. This involves maintaining relationships with individuals, families, even whole communities for whom these garments are taonga tuku iho, treasures that have been handed down from one generation to another, to carry cultural knowledge and inspiration into the future.

6. 'What are These, So Withered, and So Wild in their Attire?': Castaways' Clothing from the Auckland Islands

Jennifer Quérée

SATURDAY AFTERNOON, 30 NOVEMBER 1907 – THE TELEGRAPH LINES OUT OF Bluff ran hot as reporters scrambled to file sensational news of shipwreck and salvation.[1] By Monday morning newspapers across New Zealand carried bold headlines, inches high:

> WRECK AT THE AUCKLANDS
> LOSS OF THE FOUR-MASTED BARQUE DUNDONALD
> THIRTEEN LIVES LOST.
> SEVEN MONTHS ON DISAPPOINTMENT ISLAND.
> SURVIVORS LIVE ON SEALS AND SEA BIRDS.
> DARING VOYAGE IN CANVAS BOAT.
> CASTAWAYS RESCUED BY THE HINEMOA.[2]

The loss of the *Dundonald* was the latest in a series of such disasters in New Zealand's sub-Antarctic territories. Situated close to the major shipping route from Australia to Cape Horn, the poorly charted Auckland Islands had been the site of at least ten shipwrecks before 1907; 63 people had survived.[3] In 1868, public outcry about the hardships endured by castaways in this isolated and desolate region of the Southern Ocean had prompted the construction and provisioning of emergency depots on most of the islands. The *Otago Witness* reported on 4 April 1868:

> The *Amherst* reached Port Ross on the 1st February, and formed depot No. 1 on Enderby Island, containing clothing, blankets, compasses, matches, tools, &c. It was placed in a good position, and on it was written, 'The curse of the widow and the fatherless light upon the man who breaks open this box whilst he has a ship at his back'.

A second depot was erected in Carnley Harbour on Auckland Island, near the site of Musgrave's Hut, built by the crew of the *Grafton*, which went aground in

1864. Goats and pigs were landed as food supplies, and, the report noted, all the depots were made with 'care, and their positions distinctly defined'.[4] From 1887 to 1929 a New Zealand government steamship visited twice a year to check for shipwrecked sailors and to repair and replenish the depots.[5]

Clothing, and the desperate solutions to the lack of it, played a critical part in the survival of all the Auckland Islands castaways, not only for its protective role in an extremely harsh environment, but also in the struggle to maintain personal and social identity. In most accounts of shipwrecked or marooned mariners over the centuries there are frequent references to 'savages' or 'wild men'. These are always associated with dress – inadequate clothing, distressed or improvised garments (particularly when made from animal skins rather than woven cloth), and unshaven, dirty faces and bodies, together with long hair. It suggests that European minds have long associated such dress with barbarity, primitiveness or lack of civilisation. The pervasiveness of the 'wild man' concept has indeed been described as part of the fundamental make-up of Western European culture. By creating the 'Other', the individual establishes the nature of the norm. Constant comparison with the Other reinforces that norm. 'The wild man was created to answer the questions of civilized man,' comments one scholar. 'The European wild man reminds us that we might have been something else.'[6]

Individuals constantly negotiate their role or identity by resolving who to be, and how to conduct themselves, including how to present themselves through the medium of dress. In the castaway's situation, the circumstances severely reduce the means to create and maintain a 'normal' identity in this way. Photographs of rescued castaways can only hint at the shock, laced with apprehension, which their appearance initially aroused. Written descriptions, both by rescuers and the castaways themselves, reveal the fear that, with the loss of 'civilised' clothing, the wearers had sunk into a state of 'barbarity'. The rough, improvised garments and lack of personal hygiene were a source of intense psychological, as well as physical, discomfort and unease, for viewer and subject alike.

The earliest published account of shipwreck survivors in the Auckland Islands is *Castaway on the Auckland Isles*.[7] It was based on the private journal of Thomas Musgrave, master of the *Grafton*, which was driven aground in Carnley Harbour in January 1864. He and his crew of four – mate François Raynal, seamen A. McLean and George Harris and cook Henry Brown – were able to retrieve supplies and equipment from their beached craft, giving them an initial advantage that most Auckland Islands castaways lacked. In the hope of rescue, the *Grafton* men remained on the island for eighteen months, building a dwelling and improvising both tools and clothing. In late October 1864, according to Musgrave, they were 'not yet reduced to wearing seal-skin clothes entirely, but those which we do [wear] look most deplorable, although they are neither ragged nor dirty'.[8]

Raynal kept an official logbook, to which he added 'a brief narrative of our doings and adventures [and] sometimes . . . my individual impressions'.[9] This was published in 1892 as *Wrecked On A Reef*. He discussed the castaways' anxiety about the condition of their clothes, which even after a few weeks 'stood in great need of tailoring skill'.[10] The men's personal appearance and lack of cleanliness concerned them as much as the general filthiness and poor repair of their garments. 'A great question arose. We were threatened with the loss of self-respect, or of becoming to our own eyes an object of disgust.'[11] The *Grafton* men eventually rescued themselves by building a boat in which three of them sailed for help, landing on Stewart Island on 24 July 1865.[12] There 'after [a] bath, we were investing ourselves, to our great satisfaction, in dry, clean clothes, lent to us by our host, in place of our own miserable rags'.[13] The world of these castaways had begun to resume its proper forms as they rediscovered, through dress, their normal social and individual identities.

The American ship *General Grant* was wrecked on the Aucklands on 14 May 1866, with the loss of 68 passengers and crew. Of fifteen survivors, ten were finally discovered some eighteen months later, on 21 November 1867, by the brig *Amherst* of Invercargill, during a sealing voyage. Their number included Mrs Mary Ann Jewell, the only woman ever to survive a shipwreck on the islands. Captain Paddy Gilroy and his crew were initially suspicious and apprehensive of the group of unshaven, long-haired 'wild men' who greeted them, dressed bizarrely in animal skins. Were they savages or dangerous mutineers? Gilroy's impressions probably mirrored those of Captain Woodes Rogers of the ship *Duke*, which rescued Alexander Selkirk, the original 'Robinson Crusoe', in 1709, after four years and four months of isolation. Rogers observed, 'Immediately our Pinnace return'd from the shore, and brought abundance of Craw-fish, with a Man cloth'd in Goat-Skins, who looked wilder than the first Owners of them.'[14]

The *Amherst* left the Auckland Islands with the castaways on 6 January 1868, arriving at Bluff four days later. The 'picturesque' survivors, as they waited outside the courthouse at Bluff for the official inquiry into the disaster, were described as weather-beaten and clad in 'Robinson-Crusoe-looking costumes'.[15] In a letter to his father in Devon shortly afterwards, Joseph Jewell made particular reference to the castaways' clothing problems. He had stripped down to shirt and trousers in getting off the sinking ship, and his wife had some of her clothes torn off in the attempts to get her to safety in one of the *General Grant*'s boats. To add to their woes, within a short time

> the few clothes we had were wearing out fast and our boots were soon quite worn out; in fact some had none when they landed . . . The next thing we wanted was needles to try and keep our rags together, and those we made out of the bones of the albatross.[16]

Passenger James Teer, who kept a form of journal by writing with charcoal on split and dried sealskin, commented that the survivors spent nearly all their time (when not finding food) in mending their clothes. On 26 May 1866 he noted that:

> During this time, some of those bare footed tried to make shoes out of the seal's skin, but did not succeed very well. One day, I thought of the moccasin, and made a pair for P. McNevin. Soon after this, all hands were able to make them for themselves. These were good substitutes during our stay on the island.[17]

The skins of wild rabbits were turned into warm scarves during the icy sub-Antarctic winter months and the castaways eventually constructed complete outfits from the hide of the seals that formed a large part of their diet.[18] Initially, a major problem was their inability to properly cure the sealskins. They could only be dried, and as a result were stiff and 'as hard as bullock hide'.[19] As his account in the *Otago Witness* shows, Teer credited himself with the solution to this difficulty and described the process:

> [1 September 1866] We tried every means to manufacture seal's skin into clothes, as those we had left were all threadbare, and the skins we had to keep us warm at night were like boards. We scrubbed them with sand, and scraped them with glass, but to no purpose. At last I hit upon a successful plan. I was trying to get a patch for my trousers, and thought of paring the skins with a knife, but I cut a hole in every square inch; I saw the plan would answer by paring the dried skins close to the roots of the hair; the skin was then very soft, and by perseverance and practice I found that we would be able to make clothes much better than we imagined.
> [8 December 1866] We were at this time able to make coats, vests, and trousers out of sealskins. Those who had been at Musgrave's had nothing made of sealskin; but, they patched up their clothes with the remaining pieces of canvas.[20]
> [8 March 1867] Our original woollen clothes being all worn out, it took us all our time to mend and manufacture seal's skin coats, and make thread from the New Zealand flax.[21]

In its initial report of the rescue of the *General Grant* survivors, the *Otago Witness* also mentioned underclothing and caps in the castaways' clothing endeavours.[22]

Publicity photographs of the survivors, taken mostly in Melbourne, show a relatively sophisticated level of tailoring. This is probably due to the input of Mary Ann Jewell, and certainly the needlework and basic dressmaking skills that were part of nearly every woman's education in this period would have stood her in good stead. One recent biography of James Teer credits all the clothing production to him and Mary Ann Jewell, but this may be an exaggeration.[23] As Teer noted, 'all hands' were able to make their own moccasins. In addition to being able to 'hand, reef and steer', it was common for every ordinary seaman on

Joseph and Mary Ann Jewell photographed in their sealskin clothing after their return to Australia in 1868. Mrs Jewell reputedly earned good money from lecturing, in her sealskin costume, about her adventures and selling copies of photographs such as this. Joseph Jewell went to work for the railways in Victoria, eventually becoming a stationmaster. GH003129/5, C. HEWITT/MUSEUM OF NEW ZEALAND TE PAPA TONGAREWA board a merchant sailing ship to be his own tailor, mending worn and damaged clothing with scraps of discarded cloth and using a sewing kit or housewife (hussif) kept in his sea chest. However, Teer's experience of living for twenty years as a gold miner in isolated areas of Australia and New Zealand, and his time at sea, may have given him additional skills.

Apart from the moccasins, Mary Ann Jewell's sealskin clothing gives a good approximation of the fashion of the day. Her full skirt is sensibly shortened but otherwise follows the current silhouette. It is unclear whether the dress has a separate bodice, as this is concealed by a rather smart, fitted jacket with a small upright collar, and set-in sleeves that are cut in the typical, tapered 'banana' shape of the period. Her hair is covered by a low-crowned hat with upturned brim (or possibly, ear flaps). Joseph Jewell's sealskin suit comprises a high-fastening waistcoat or vest, short sack coat or jacket, trousers and a sou'wester-styled hat with a turned-up peak and flaps that probably turned down to cover the ears – an essential feature in the bitter climate of the Auckland Islands. His coat and waistcoat are fastened with round buttons, which may have survived from his original clothes, or which could have been fashioned from wood or bone. Another photograph of the couple shows that Joseph's coat had at least one deep patch pocket on the right hip.[24] The comfortable-looking, sturdy shoes worn by the Jewells appear to be based on the traditional hard-soled moccasin of indigenous North Americans, as suggested by Teer's remarks. An extended sole is sewn to an upper piece with an edge-to-edge seam, and (at least with Mary Ann Jewell's pair) a cord appears to secure the upper above the instep, near the ankle.

The clothing of passenger David Ashworth and seaman Aaron Hayman (over) shows similar features to Joseph Jewell's outfit.[25] Ashworth has a high-crowned hat with turned-up ear flaps, and a single-breasted jacket or short coat with either toggles or buttons and a deep patch pocket on the left side. His shirt (or perhaps some sort of vest) is tucked into trousers with a deep, buttoned fly opening, and his moccasins are of the same style as the Jewells'. Hayman, by contrast, wears a smock-like jerkin with a small collar and two patch pockets at hip level. His trousers are cut rather full and break well over his moccasins. He may be wearing a shirt or long vest beneath the jerkin and his cap is more of a pudding basin style, although it, too, has turned-up flaps. The sealskin appears to have been used with the hair on the outside for every piece of clothing worn by this group of castaways.

All this attire resembles conventional bourgeois and occupational styles of the period. Garments such as Joseph Jewell's waistcoat and Mary Ann Jewell's stylish jacket and skirt indicate the power of fashion, as an aspect of dress, in the attempt to maintain social identity in a tiny, isolated community. In Mary Ann's case, as the only woman in a group of nine men from varying socio-economic backgrounds, it probably also reinforced the Victorian concept of woman as an upholder of social mores and 'civilisation'.

David Ashworth, a 32-year-old passenger from the *General Grant*, photographed in Melbourne in 1868. He drowned in a failed attempt to salvage the ship's cargo of gold in May 1870. C. HEWITT/ COLLECTION OF GUNTER MUELLER, OAKHAM, MASSACHUSETTS

Fashionable or not, the castaways were glad to abandon their sealskin attire for proper garments, at least initially. Teer's journal entry for 22 November 1867, following their discovery by the brig *Amherst*, reads, 'When all of us were aboard, we had such clothes given us as could be well spared by both the officers and crew.'[26] Jewell wrote of the kindness 'received at the hands of the inhabitants of Bluff and Invercarjale [sic]', but their later reception in Australia perhaps explained the necessity of posing for the Victorian paparazzi.

> [The people of Bluff] soon had us out of our seal skin clothes and supplied us with everything of the best during the eight days we remained there. Mrs. Taylor, the wife of the superintendent of Southland, came down from Invercarjale in a special

Aaron Hayman, a member of the crew of the *General Grant*, photographed in Australia, 1868. It is believed that he went back to sea after the rescue. T. M. CLEAVES/COLLECTION OF GUNTER MUELLER, OAKHAM, MASSACHUSETTS

train and kindly took my wife to her own house to stay with her, and we were sent to a first-class hotel . . . When we arrived in Melbourne the Government could do nothing for us as we were under the American flag. The 'General Grant' having belonged to Boston, United States, and the American Consul said he could do nothing for us as we were all foreigners, and as none of us were fit for work they made a subscription, and we received £5 11s. 5d. each. It was not enough to pay for our board, much less clothing that we were in need of – only having the suit that we received in Southland.[27]

Mary Ann Jewell appears to have made good use of the photo opportunities afforded the castaways. For several years she sold copies of the portraits of herself and Joseph, as well as giving paid lectures in and around Melbourne, wearing her sealskin ensemble. She is reputed to have earned about A£600 by these efforts, and this undoubtedly helped to support the young couple, who had been left destitute by the disaster.[28] James Teer also found his castaway clothing useful when he returned to live on the West Coast of the South Island of New Zealand. For some years he made a career from speaking about his shipwreck experiences, touring the various gold mining communities and giving lectures dressed in his sealskin clothes.[29]

There were six more shipwrecks after the *General Grant*, and the last, the *Dundonald*, is probably the most comprehensively recorded – in Charles Eyre's dictated *Castaways of Disappointment Island*,[30] contemporary newspaper and scientific reports, letters and photographs and, many years later, a radio interview with Albert Roberts, the youngest and last survivor. As well as the physical struggle for survival, and the despair of not being found, the fear of identity loss and rejection as members of 'civilised society' is well documented in many of these accounts, and in every case it is strongly associated with dress.

A number of artefacts constructed by the castaways have survived, including several garments and dress-related items. The GSS *Hinemoa*, which discovered the men at Erebus Cove in Port Ross on Auckland Island, was carrying a large party of New Zealand scientists, among them Edgar Waite, Director of the Canterbury Museum in Christchurch.[31] Waite, anticipating the enormous public interest in this classic story of shipwreck and endurance, acquired a selection of 'relics' from the castaways. These included a collection of bird-bone needles and an awl, a sailcloth jerkin, and shoes and a cap made from 'sealskin'.[32] They continue to intrigue visitors to the Canterbury Museum today, not just as testimony to a remarkable story of hardship, courage and ingenuity, but also because of the general fascination with dress that is unfamiliar and outside the norm.

The Glasgow-owned steel barque *Dundonald* was a large bulk carrier, working the deep sea routes to China and Japan, South America and Australia. On Sunday 17 February 1907, the ship and her 28 crew left Sydney for Falmouth, intending to catch seasonal northerly and westerly winds to take the ship swiftly to Cape Horn. However, prolonged bad weather drove them far south. Shortly before 1.00 a.m. on 7 March, in a freezing semi-gale and dense fog, the *Dundonald* struck Disappointment Island in the Aucklands group, 40 miles (65 kilometres) south of her presumed position. During the night and the following morning, fifteen men managed to get ashore, scaling the masts, which were hard against the cliffs, and swinging hand over hand across a rope from the fore topgallant mast.

The plight of the *Dundonald*'s crew was unusual for the period because they had the misfortune to be wrecked on the only island within the Aucklands group that had no depot – it was thought impossible to get ashore from any shipwreck on its inhospitable coast. Of all the groups of castaways discussed, the *Dundonald* men had the least available resources. Some of the crew had been lightly clad in the first place, having just turned in at the end of their watch, and during the night many had thrown off their heavy weather gear – coats, caps and boots – in case they had to swim ashore. They had no food, only a couple of pocket knives, half a box of usable matches and a length of rope. Over the next few days, some more line, plus the gaff topsail and a sail from the topgallant mast were retrieved, but everything else on the wreck was submerged.

Jabez Peters, the oldest of the group, soon succumbed to shock and exposure, and nineteen days after they landed he died. 'Not having much clothes ourselves, we took off his coat, waistcoat and pants, and then laid him on the ground.'[33] Peters's clothes were then divided among his former shipmates by drawing lots, a common practice at sea when a death occurred. They were certainly in need of every extra piece of clothing or covering they could get. Some of the men had tried using birdskins for shoes but, being soft, these lasted only a few hours. Charles Eyre commented:

> Most of us were no better clothed than I was – and I had a thin pair of trousers, split all to pieces, a thin vest, fill of holes, a coat, but neither socks nor boots. A poor sort of protection against cold such as those in England rarely feel; and then, besides, everything we had on was soaking wet all the time, and it was utterly impossible to try to dry them.[34]

Eyre later said that by the beginning of May the castaways resembled 'Spring poets', a curious expression that seems to have been in vogue at the turn of the twentieth century. It appears to refer to the stereotypical 'Bohemians' depicted in literature and the musical halls and theatres of the day. These characters were based on the real Bohemians – poets and painters living originally in Paris in the mid-nineteenth century, who were characterised by their unkempt or downright shabby clothing, lack of hygiene and long hair and beards.[35] Daniel McLaughlin and Karl Knudsen commented that their hair and beards got very long, but of more concern was the increasing disrepair of their clothing. 'Every day we are looking more like savages . . . what clothes we do possess are getting very frail . . . we have to sleep in our clothes, so we have not much comfort. He is considered well-off who has a coat.'[36]

The castaways lived mainly on a diet of ground-nesting mollymawks or *Diomedea steadi*, the New Zealand white-capped albatross. This was later supplemented with muttonbird (the nocturnal sooty shearwater, *Puffinus griseus*), and, from early June, by 'seal' meat, after a sea lion rookery was discovered. This was considered 'wholesome and nutritious – far more so than the mollyhawk [sic] flesh we were eating; and in the next, sealskin makes good clothes, and we were now nearly naked'.[37]

As previous castaways had found, there was no means of properly curing the hides, so they were stretched over roughly lashed frames, scraped as clean as possible and kept near the fire to dry for two or three days. Eyre recorded that the men welcomed the prospects of renewing their clothing, 'even if the dresses which we should make would be something like that which Robinson Crusoe wore on his island. We had not fashions to study, and so long as we were warm we did not care.'[38]

One of the most pressing needs was footwear. Michael Pul, an Estonian seaman, provided the solution. McLaughlin and Knudsen gave a detailed account:

> The Russian said he would make slippers, the same as he had made at home, and are known as 'farm slippers' in Russia. These slippers are twelve inches long, and seven inches broad at the toes and about five and a half inches at the heel. You sew them up at both ends. Then you make holes [with awls] for the laces all round, about an inch apart. You put the laces in the hole, and when you have the shoes on, you haul tight the laces and knot them at the back, cross them on the foot and put them under, and haul tight and knot them on top of the foot. Having no socks, the mollyhawk [sic] skins came in very useful, as the wing part forms a sock; with the feathers turned inside they are very warm. The skin slippers fit well and are comfortable, so we think we are well off. Everybody wants skins for slippers. We consider this a very good patent.[39]

Apart from knives used for cutting the skin to shape, the tools for making these moccasins were furnished by the birds. Awls and needles were fashioned from

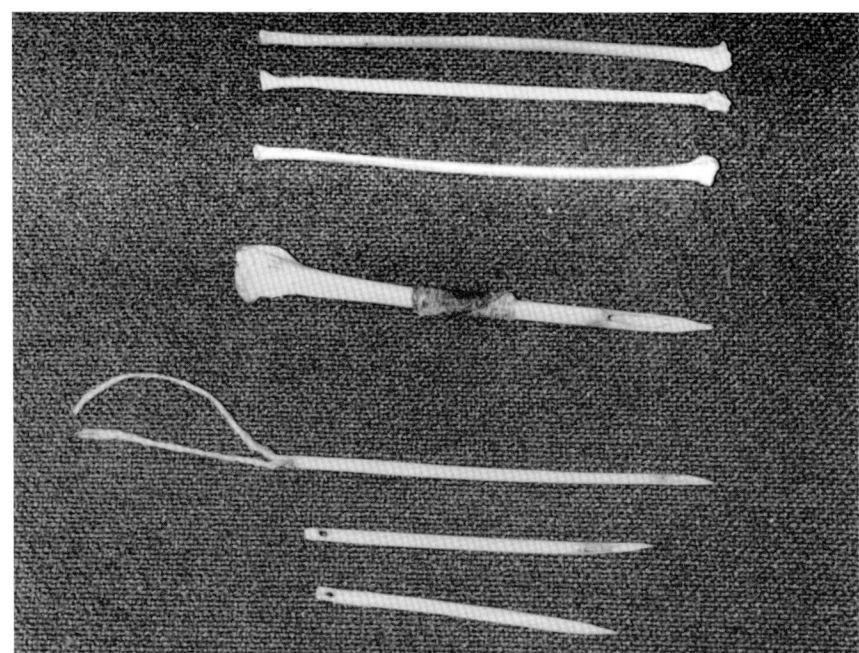

Muttonbird bones, awl and needles, 1907. The largest needle is still threaded with unravelled yarn from one of the sails from the *Dundonald*.
EC152.185-187,
J. QUÉRÉE/
CANTERBURY
MUSEUM
COLLECTION

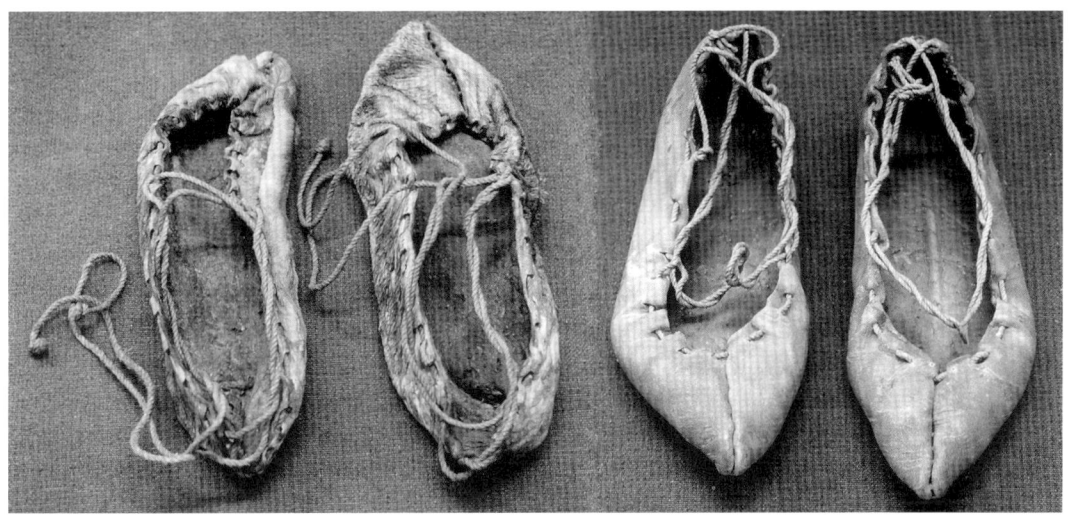

Seal or sea lion hide moccasins with linen cord ties, made by the *Dundonald* castaways in 1907. EC152.193-194, J. QUÉRÉE/CANTERBURY MUSEUM COLLECTION

muttonbird bones, as those of the mollymawk were too large. The bones were scraped clean and rubbed down to a point with a stone. Some pieces of wire had also been retrieved from the *Dundonald* and these were used to drill the eyes for the needles. Eyre thought the bone needles 'were almost as serviceable as the needles which are bought at shops. Of course, they were coarser and more clumsy, but that was an advantage . . . as our material was thick sealskin and ordinary needles would have been no good for the work.'[40] Pieces of sailcloth were unravelled for thread and finer cordage was used for the slipper lacing. This cord may have been from the life jackets the men had been instructed to put on when the ship first grounded.

The moccasins stiffened after a short time, but by then were moulded to the shape of the wearer's feet. Albert Roberts recalled that, when worn with the fur side outside, the shoes would last a fortnight, 'otherwise, wearing them with the fur in and the skin outside, they'd only last us a day'.[41]

The castaways now turned their hands to tailoring and produced coats, trousers and caps from sealskin and pieces of sailcloth. Eyre describes his wardrobe at this time as 'a pair of sealskin boots . . . and trousers which I had sewed together with one of the birdskin needles, and which were cut out of a bit of old sailcloth with a knife for a pair of scissors'.[42] The blood and sweat-stained jerkin in Canterbury Museum's collection is made from seven pieces of dark cream linen sailcloth, sewn together with two- and three-strand thread made from similar cloth unravelled. The same thread has been used to cobble together several tears in the fabric. It probably belonged to George Ivimey, as shown in the photograph (over) of some of the castaways outside the Port Ross depot hut in 1907.

Although a 1907 *Canterbury Times* photograph of the surviving sealskin cap (p. 89) shows it with fur attached, it is now completely hairless and very stiff.

Some of the *Dundonald* castaways wearing a mixture of depot clothing outside the Port Ross bunkhouse, November 1907. Albert Roberts (second from left) is barefooted, while George Ivimey (third from right) wears the canvas jerkin now in Canterbury Museum's collection. Two sea boots hang on nails at the end of the building. The castaways are, left to right: Santiago Marino, Albert Roberts, Harry Walters, Herman Querfeldt, Alf Finlow, George Ivimey, John Judge and Jan Putze.
PHILOSOPHICAL INSTITUTE OF CANTERBURY COLLECTION, REF: 17170, CANTERBURY MUSEUM

Formed from two pieces of semi-circular hide, it was stitched together with unravelled canvas yarn. Two ties, made from tapered pieces of skin sewn to the crown, secured the cap under the chin. All the stitching passed through diagonal or triangular holes punched with a bird bone awl. A small tear on the crown was repaired using a fibrous yarn made from grasses and other vegetation.

Sea lion skin was also used to make coats and blankets, which made life slightly more comfortable when winter set in. 'Our sealskin boots comforted our poor, torn feet, and were warm and nice; and our rough-and-ready clothing, though it was awful to look at from a tailor's point of view, was serviceable.'[43] A photograph taken in November 1907 (p. 90) shows deckhand George Ivimey in 'sealskin attire' – a large hat shaped rather like a tea cosy, and a pair of 'slippers'. Seated, he is holding another pair of moccasins and is covered from the waist down by a large sealskin blanket.

By the end of July, the men realised they were unlikely to be found on Disappointment Island, and the food was running out. Their only chance of survival was to reach the castaway depots on Auckland Island. Using the branches of the shrub *Hebe elliptica* they constructed three coracles (basket-shaped boats) covered with patchwork remnants of sailcloth. A crew of three – Michael Pul, Santiago Marino and Bob Ellis – paddled the first coracle to Auckland Island on 31 July, but returned on 10 August, having failed to find a depot. At the end of September, a fine day signalled the chance to attempt a crossing in the other two coracles. The first was launched successfully. The crew of the second coracle first stowed their bulky sealskin coats on board, along with Albert Roberts' sea boots – one of the few pairs to have survived.

Suddenly, just as everything was readied for departure, a huge wave 'sent [the boat] smash, crash, on the rocks'. The canvas covering was ripped to shreds and

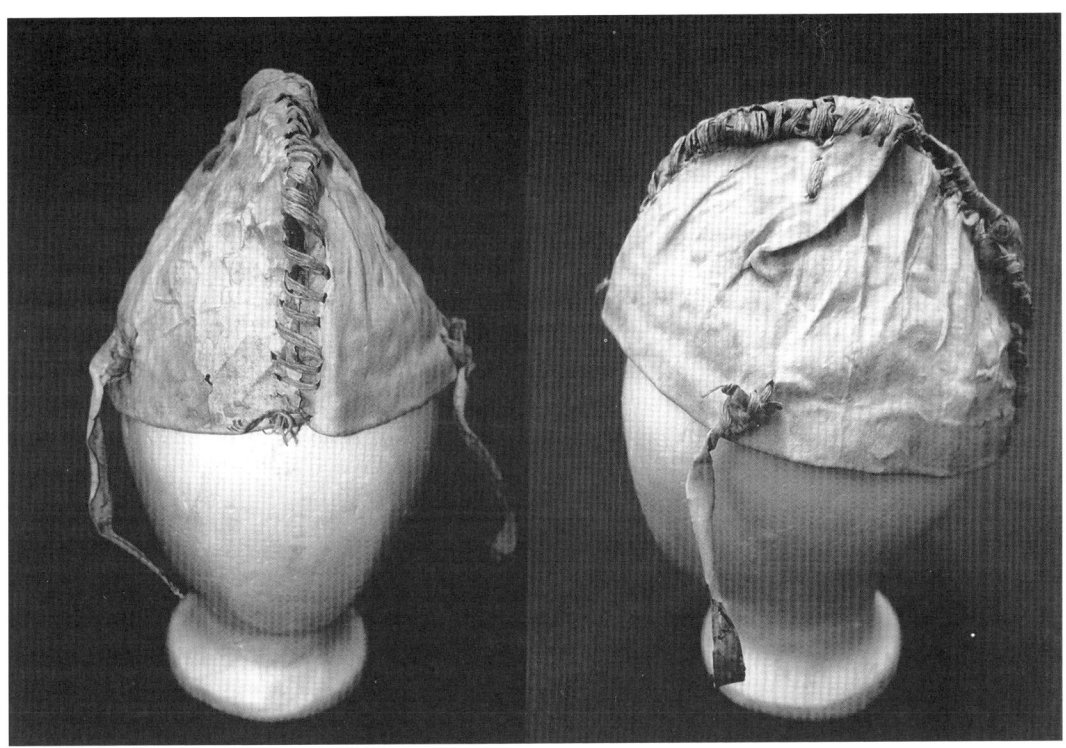

A seal or sea lion skin cap, made by one of the *Dundonald* castaways, 1907. EC152.188, J. QUÉRÉE/CANTERBURY MUSEUM COLLECTION

the framework shattered, Albert's prized boots were lost, and 'there were our precious coats floating out to sea!' Karl Knudsen and Charlie Eyre set off after them in the remaining coracle. 'But it was a hunt, for the waves had separated our coats, and one was drifting here and another there. Fortunately they floated, or we should have lost the lot; but as it was . . . we managed to capture the whole of them.'[44]

The castaways were now at the end of their tether. The birds had vanished completely and hardly a seal was to be found. The men were near starvation, living mostly on seaweed, the root of the endemic megaherb *Stilbocarpus polaris*, and grass. Those few clothes that had survived the shipwreck and nearly seven months of harsh conditions were falling to pieces. 'Our hair is very long and our faces very dirty; we look like savages,' reported McLaughlin and Knudsen.[45]

On 6 October, a final attempt was made to reach Auckland Island. Crewed by Eyre, John Grattan, Knudsen and Harry Walters, the last 'canvas-covered basket' reached the landing spot used by Pul, Ellis and Marino, only to be wrecked beyond repair on a hidden reef. The four men struggled ashore but now had no means of returning to their companions. After four days of fruitless searching for a depot in this area, they had little choice but to set out for the northern tip of the island, where they hoped a depot was located.

George Ivimey 'in sealskin attire' at Bluff, November 1907. E. PHILLIPS/ELMSLEY COLLECTION, POSTCARD #01512 DETAIL, REF: 17193, CANTERBURY MUSEUM

Dressing for the journey through Auckland Island's swamps and dense forests was by now a complicated process. Every piece of ragged garment had to be tied on, as by now all their buttons had been lost. The four headed northeast and by late afternoon reached what Eyre later identified as Meggs Hill, at the edge of a large valley filled with an almost impenetrable forest of tall rata trees (*Metrosideros umbellata*). 'By the time we came to the end of the valley our clothes were literally torn off our bodies.'[46]

Eventually the men reached the end of the forest and emerged into a little bay where they decided to camp for the night. Suddenly Grattan noticed something glimmering in the half-light. It proved to be a white-painted signpost, with the inscription 'Four Miles to the Provision Depot'. Within seconds they were off, and 'at last we raised a joyful shout, for there, rising above the dense bush of the forest, towering between thirty and forty feet in the air, we saw a ship's mast'.

> It was in the bush a little way from the beach . . . On we pushed, and just as we were turning into another little bay on the opposite shore we saw two white roofs, appearing over the forest timber . . . [We] came out into a little clearing, in which were two sturdy buildings.[47]

The *Dundonald* castaways photographed in front of the flagpole at the Port Ross depot on Auckland Island, November 1907. They are wearing clothing from the depot stores. BACK ROW, LEFT TO RIGHT: Michael Pul (Estonia), Bob Ellis (Adelaide, Australia), John ('Mickey') Grattan (Arklow, Ireland), John Judge (Cork, Ireland), Alf Finlow (Manchester, England), Harry Walters (Norway). MIDDLE ROW, LEFT TO RIGHT: Charles Eyre (Dulwich, England), John (Jack) Stewart (Cambridge, New Zealand), Daniel McLaughlin (Dunbartonshire, Scotland), Albert Roberts (Cardiff, Wales), Karl Knudsen (Ålesund, Norway). FRONT ROW, LEFT TO RIGHT: Jan Putze (Libo, Poland or Moravia), Santiago Marino (Chile), George Ivimey (Southampton, England), Herman Querfeldt (Germany).
PHILOSOPHICAL INSTITUTE OF CANTERBURY COLLECTION, REF: 4192, CANTERBURY MUSEUM

It was, at last, a relief depot, situated at Erebus Cove, Port Ross, near the original Hardwicke Settlement. This was founded in 1849, but because of the harsh environment, the lack of whales and the few visits by whaling vessels, it failed after three years. The buildings were dismantled and removed by departing settlers.

At daybreak Eyre and the others eagerly overhauled the contents of the storehouse. Everything was packaged in airtight zinc rolls, inside wooden boxes. As well as matches, tins of meat and biscuits, tools and hunting equipment, there were two large bars of soap, twelve thick woollen blankets and a dozen sturdy suits, together with twelve shirts, twelve pairs of boots and six sets of underpants.

> [W]e went down and washed ourselves solemnly; we cut each others hair and beards – decidedly not in the West End style, but more after the fashion prevalent in His Majesty's prisons; and then we donned our new clothes and boots, and I give you my word that when we had finished we did not know ourselves, much less each other.[48]

The New Zealand-manufactured clothing (seen in the photographs of the castaways taken by the *Hinemoa* scientists) consisted of single-breasted, high-buttoned jackets and waistcoats and narrow trousers, probably of coarse wool tweed in a brown and black hound's-tooth pattern. These three-piece suits were teamed with grey flannel shirts and mid-calf-length sea boots of heavy brown leather with hobnailed soles. Although none of the castaways gave a detailed description of their new outfits, we know what they looked like because in 1947, and during the 1960s, clothing was recovered from discontinued depots on the Antipodes and Snares Islands. A number of examples were gifted to various museums in New Zealand, including the Canterbury Museum and the Museum of New Zealand Te Papa Tongarewa.

Within a few days, the men rigged a sail for a boat found at the depot and returned to Disappointment Island to rescue their mates. Back at Erebus Cove, there were not enough suits, boots or underclothes for everyone and according to Eyre it was a case of 'first come, first served'. McLaughlin, however, wrote that he, as second mate, took charge of the stores and divided the clothing so that 'some got a jacket and others got pants and a waistcoat – everyone was satisfied'.[49] Later he recorded, 'We all indulge in a good wash, feeling much better with our new clothes. After getting our hair cut, and a wash, we look more like civilised men.'[50]

Nearby Enderby Island was the home of wild cattle, which the castaways were not slow to exploit. However, following their first hunting trip, 'We did not look very pleasant objects by the time we had done, what with the grease and the blood.'[51] As a result of this messy experience, the men decided to make some more clothing, to protect and preserve the decent clothes from the depot. Sails recovered from the Enderby boatshed were used to make hunting trousers. These were fastened with rope-yarn, wound like gaiters from ankle to knee 'to prevent them catching in the bush'.

> We used to wear sealskin shoes for hunting, as they were lighter than the leather boots we had found at the depot. We would leave our coats behind us, and clad in these shoes, canvas trousers and our shirts, we would proceed on our expedition.[52]

Having found a note from the crew of the GSS *Tutanekai*, the last government vessel to check on the depot, the castaways knew that rescue was certain, with a ship due before the year's end. About 5 a.m. on 16 November, Karl Knudsen woke everyone with the news that he had sighted a steamer heading into the cove.

> We started out of our bunks like mad – we did not even stop to put on our clothes; we rushed out through the door, and tore down to the beach just as we were . . . We could not believe our eyes at first . . . We shouted and cheered, we rushed back to the depot and got into our clothes and made ourselves look as respectable as possible, and then back again we rushed towards the beach . . . We cheered as

loud as we could yell . . . we tossed our caps in the air, we waved our hands – we behaved like so many madmen; and for every cheer we gave an answering cheer came back from the boat [the *Hinemoa*].[53]

Captain Bollons came ashore, but soon had to break the news that he could not immediately take them to New Zealand, because of the work of the *Hinemoa*'s scientific survey party. However, at midday on 29 November, the *Hinemoa* finally departed Port Ross, bound for Bluff. Mr Hamilton, the chief officer, observing the poor state of the depot clothing, somehow found extra garments for the men so they were all more adequately dressed.

The *Hinemoa* reached Bluff about 4 p.m. on Saturday afternoon, 30 November. Mr Hutton of the Sailors' Home booked the castaways into the best hotel in Bluff and on the Monday took them to a clothier's to be fitted out with new garments at the government's expense. Some appear to have received extra. Eyre wrote that 'one gentleman, named Macky, gave me a perfect new suit of clothes and boots, and everything else that I needed to make me look respectable'.[54] Albert Roberts remembered: 'We got £10 from the Government and all the clothes we wanted, but I got a special one from [Premier] Sir Joseph Ward, the best sea kit I ever had in my life'.[55]

Most of the castaways subsequently left New Zealand. Charles Eyre's closing paragraphs describe his arrival in London, having worked his way home on a cargo ship.

> I was in my working gear, with my sea-boots on, and . . . I was pretty well soaked through . . . [T]he officer told me that my father had come on board, and was waiting to see me . . . Well, I went aft double quick [and] after the greetings were over, I dashed down to wash and dress myself, and to smarten up generally. It would not have done to go home in that condition.[56]

Dress signifies more than mere protection from the elements. As a study of castaways' clothing demonstrates, it also expresses and transmits identity, both as self and as a member of a group. 'Fashion', as an element of dress, can influence the construction of that identity, even in the most extreme situations. As Joanne Entwhistle has noted, 'bodies that do not conform, bodies that flout the conventions of their culture and go without the appropriate clothes are subversive of the most basic social codes, and risk exclusion, scorn or ridicule . . . Dress is fundamental to microsocial order.'[57] Far away from the tailors of the West End, with only their fellow unfortunates for company, the castaways of the Auckland Islands fought to maintain their social and personal identities by constructing garments that not only shielded them from the harsh environment but also attempted to follow the forms of dress appropriate to members of 'civilised' Western society.

7. Weaving a Journey: The Story of a Unique Cloak

Awhina Tamarapa

This chapter tells the story of a unique kahu waero, a rare type of dog-hair cloak, held in the collection of the Museum of New Zealand Te Papa Tongarewa. It reconstructs the remarkable and poignant journey from maker to museum of this kahu waero, woven by Te Wharetoroa Tiniraupeka, also known as Margaret Graham, of Ngāti Tunohopu, Ngāti Whakaue, Te Arawa. This journey reflects the fate of many taonga Māori that enter museum collections, which gather connections with many people over time. By weaving a history for the cloak, past relationships have been revitalised and connections with descendants made. As the cloak has moved between one context and another – from a weaver's expert hands, to a museum collection, to the collector's market and back to a museum again – it has become a metaphor for the future: a symbol of continuity, endurance and inspiration.

As the cloak's history is revealed, so are the exceptional qualities of its maker. It is fascinating to uncover the complex female voices of the Māori past. Many unsung women of all cultures deserve acknowledgement in the fabric of our shared histories. The accounts of Māori women from this period and the memories of their descendants are treasures in themselves. They should never be forgotten. Like their taonga, the treasures they leave behind, their lives are legacies, to inspire and enrich future generations.

Working with taonga Māori at Te Papa

Finding the connections between whānau (family), hapū (sub-tribes) and iwi (tribes) with particular taonga in the museum is one of the most rewarding aspects of curatorial work. In the care and management of the taonga Māori held by Te Papa, an important aim is to strengthen the knowledge base of the taonga in its care and to nurture relationships with descendants, organisations and community groups. The guiding principle of our work is mana taonga, in which Te Papa 'recognises the role of communities in enhancing the care and understanding of collections and taonga'.[1]

Acknowledging the whakapapa (genealogical ties) and spiritual connections of taonga to whānau, hapū and iwi underpins the museum's endorsement of the principle of mana taonga. This extends across all the collections and their descendant or source communities. It is especially moving when one's research reveals personal links or whakapapa to the taonga and its descendants, as happened in this instance. Experiencing such connections is a constant reminder that one is implicitly bound within the fabric, the ever-evolving network, of relationships past and present. Recognising these complexities and inherent obligations is a part of my growing understanding of the dynamic nature of mātauranga Māori (Māori customary knowledge) and the values of our ancestors that we, in turn, pass on to future generations.[2] As museum kaitiaki (guardians) we can constantly move between the physical presence of the taonga in our museum and the people who recall the histories, significance and relevance of the taonga to their lives.

The majority of taonga that make up Te Papa's Māori collection were steadily deposited, gifted, purchased and exchanged by individual collectors – both professional and amateur – scholars, scientists and ethnologists.[3] Dr James Hector, who was appointed the first Director of the New Zealand Geological Survey and Colonial Museum in 1865, also actively exchanged collections both nationally and internationally.[4] Records about those taonga as they entered the museum therefore vary greatly in the amount and accuracy of information they contain. Hundreds of items came from private collections and some collectors were more fastidious in their recording of provenance than others.[5] Large amounts of material were catalogued by brief description only. Frequently there are perplexing designations written in the early museum registers, such as 'carved slab' for ancestral carvings and 'mats' for cloaks. From a total of approximately 40,000 taonga Māori cared for by Te Papa, an estimated 60 per cent have no information regarding origin. It has been estimated that just 4 per cent of taonga can be attributed to one or more iwi.[6]

To complicate matters of identification and interpretation, recorded information was frequently misleading. The identification of tribal areas was often broad and non-specific, such as 'East Coast' or 'Taranaki'. Today, tribal details are considered vital, not only for correct identification but also to interpret accurately the symbolism and meaning surrounding the taonga in question. To add more confusion, although a taonga may have distinctive tribal characteristics based on artistic style and convention, this does not tell us its entire history. Intertribal relationships, gift giving, commissions and so forth cannot be determined without knowing the full story of a taonga.

It is easy to appreciate how tangled the threads of history may become for taonga in museums. Like the cloak at the heart of this chapter, they travel time and again from creator to collector to museum. Public auction houses also feature as part of their histories. Despite these factors, and not forgetting some of the more dubious collectors and their motives, we need to acknowledge the value of preserving New Zealand's unique cultural heritage.

Uncovering the cloak's history

This story begins in August 1991, when the kahu waero first appeared – or rather, reappeared – at the National Museum, the successor to the Colonial Museum, now Te Papa. The cloak came into the museum to be examined and registered before its sale at a public auction house in Wellington. This procedure is part of specific requirements under the Protected Objects Act, formerly known as the Antiquities Act, which is administered by the Ministry for Culture and Heritage. The act monitors and regulates the private ownership, trade and movement of objects of cultural and historical value to New Zealand.

I remember quite clearly the moment we unwrapped the cloak from its covering of stiff brown paper. We could not believe what we saw. As a young intern, I had never encountered anything like it. In our profession, we are always struck by the sheer beauty and skill of manufacture of many taonga, but a few, like this, are outstanding.

The most remarkable aspect of the cloak was its rarity. It was finely woven, decorated with tassels of white dog hair. The only clue to its past was a small swing label attached to the back of the cloak, which had written on it 'Deposited G. M. Graham. Rotorua'. On the other side of the label were the numbers 4827 and 158/30, which we suspected were museum registration numbers.

The National Museum purchased the cloak at the auction on 19 September 1991 for $5000. At the time, this was a very low price. The buying and selling of taonga Māori through public auction in New Zealand and overseas is a difficult and contentious issue for some Māori. Many ancestral taonga are regarded as priceless and selling taonga for commercial interests is of particular concern; spiralling prices make it harder for descendant families to buy anything. The primary interest of the National Museum was to retain the cloak as an item of significant cultural and historical value. It was rare and of considerable age. There was nothing like it in the weaving collection. Future research might one day uncover its provenance and weavers would certainly be able to study its construction and methods of manufacture.

Kahu waero – the most highly regarded cloak

The Polynesian dog, or kurī, was the only surviving domesticated animal that came to New Zealand with the ancestors of the Māori. Kurī pelts were used to make the highly esteemed dog-hair cloaks.[7] Usually the pelts were cut into narrow strips and attached vertically to the closely woven base of the cloak. The result was a very strong, heavy garment, perfect for protection and warmth.

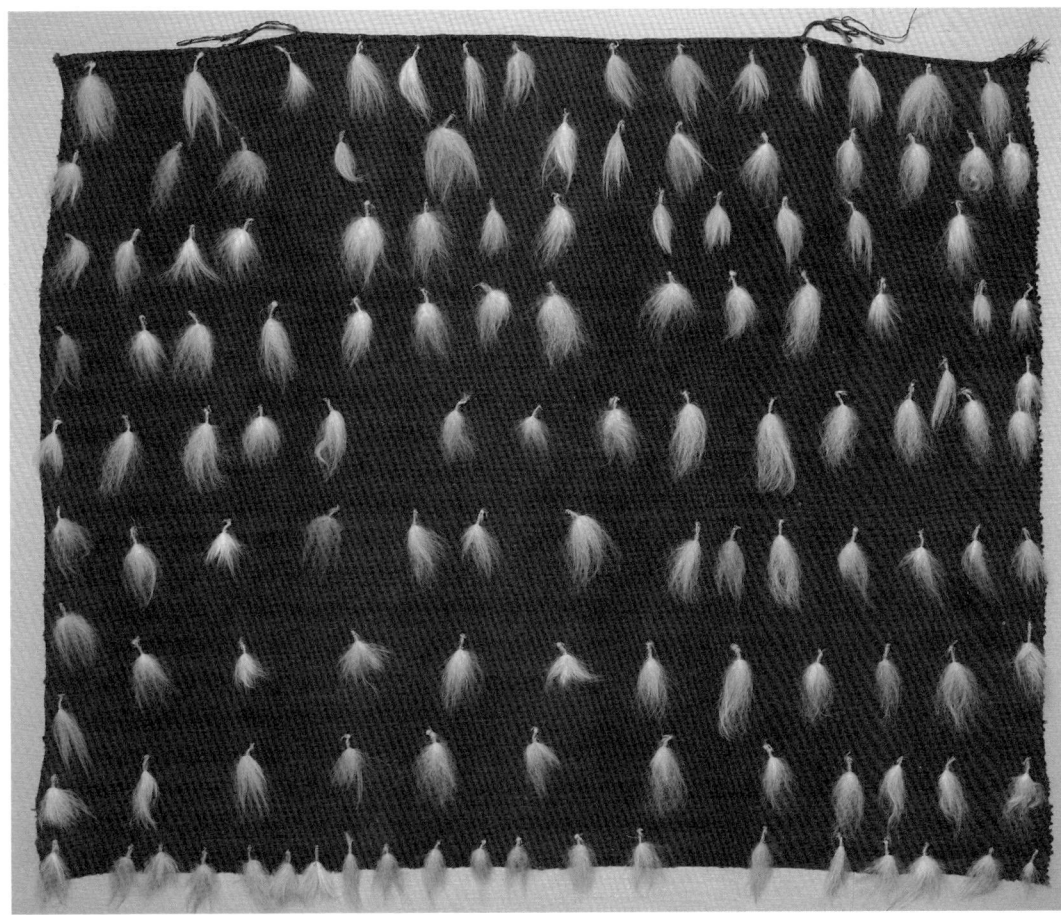

Arrangements of white, brown and black dog hair were used in various blocks or stripes of colours to create a striking effect. A rarer type of dogskin cloak also existed, made of whole dogskins sewn together.[8] Early European observers noted that kahu kurī were worn only by chiefs and were considered 'war cloaks', which were greatly valued.[9] Joseph Banks observed that 'the great pride of their dress seems to consist in dogs fur, which they use so sparingly that to avoid waste they cut into long strips and sew them at a distance from each other upon their Cloth, varying often the colours prettily enough'.[10]

The kahu waero was the most highly regarded of all dogskin cloaks, given the value attached to the tails of white-haired dogs:

> The white haired dogs were greatly prized especially if they had long-haired tails. Such were indeed objects of envy and were fitting presents for a king. These dogs were taken the best possible care of; they slept in a house on clean mats, so that

Kahu waero cloak, woven by Te Wharetoroa Tiniraupeka. ME 15529, MUSEUM OF NEW ZEALAND TE PAPA TONGAREWA their precious tails should be kept as white as possible. Their tails were curiously and regularly shaved, and the hair preserved for ornamental use. This operation of shaving its tail was quite unique (and would take some time to describe), and was never performed by a common person.[11]

As Chapter 2 of this volume notes, an eighteenth-century example of a kahu waero resides in the Pitt Rivers Museum at the University of Oxford. It was one of several taonga for which new information came to light in 2002. Through careful research, Jeremy Coote, Joint Head of Collections at the Pitt Rivers Museum, was able to link the kahu waero and other taonga to Captain James Cook's first voyage to New Zealand and the Pacific. Coote determined that the cloak was part of a collection from botanist and science patron Joseph Banks, who accompanied Cook on this voyage. By 1773 Banks had sent a collection of seventeen Tahitian and thirteen Māori items to Christ Church College, Oxford. In the 1880s the collection came into the Pitt Rivers Museum in two parts. Unfortunately, the second part of the collection entered the museum without any association to Banks, that is, until Coote uncovered crucial information and was able to deduce its origin.[12]

The making of the cloak
The materials employed in Te Wharetoroa's cloak are also customary. It is made from muka, the fine, long inner fibre of harakeke or flax. Muka is the preferred fibre for cloak making as it has soft, silk-like qualities and is extremely strong. Weavers know which varieties of harakeke are suitable for different purposes, for instance, for baskets, floor mats, waist garments or cordage. The finest quality muka is used for cloak making. To prepare muka, a weaver selects and cuts the desired amount of leaves of the harakeke in the manner taught. The hard midriff, edges and take (base) of the flax leaves are removed. Each leaf is halved and then split again into narrower strips. The muka is skilfully separated from the outer epidermal matter of the harakeke leaf by making a shallow cut across the centre of the dull side of the leaf. Starting from the centre, the leaf is pulled tautly across the straight edge of a mussel shell and this action separates the green matter of the leaf from the muka. The process is repeated on the other side of the leaf.

Valerie Carson, Te Papa's textile conservator, examined and treated the cloak once it came into the museum collection. She recalls making an instant connection to the cloak because it was so beautiful. Initially she thought that it was very old, based on the appearance of the weave. On closer examination, she made some interesting discoveries. The foundation of the cloak was a rich, dark brown colour and the weaving was particularly fine. The weft threads (aho) were formed using a technique called double paired twining. She determined that the cloak was dyed after the entire weaving process, which was not common. The

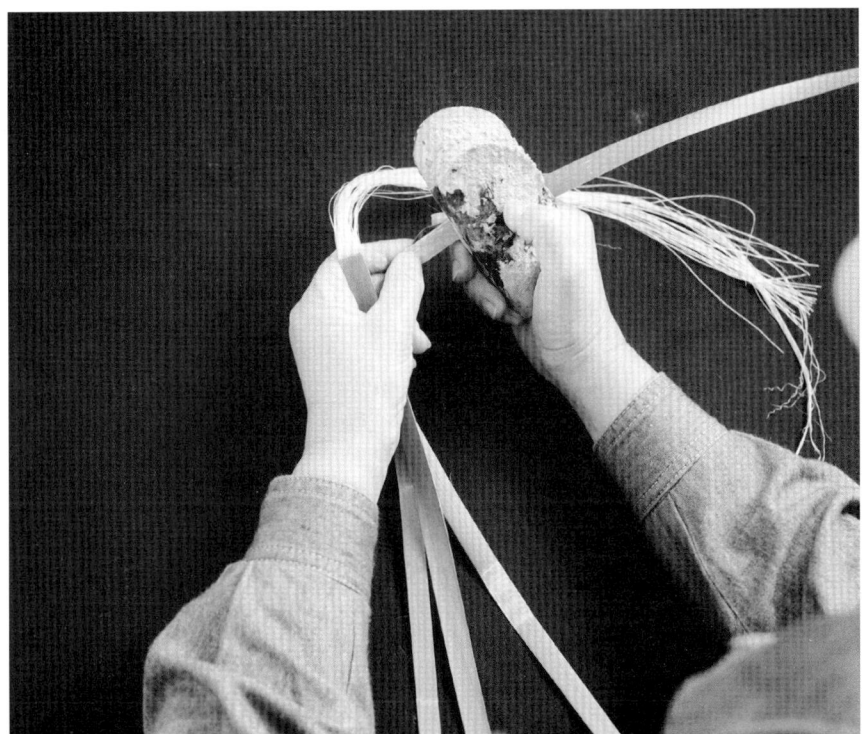

Master weaver Erenora Puketapu-Hetet (1941–2006) demonstrates the hāro (to scrape clean) process involved in extracting muka, the fine, silky inner fibre, from a strand of harakeke.
MA_F.000582/01, MUSEUM OF NEW ZEALAND TE PAPA TONGAREWA

cloak was decorated with tassels of dog hair intricately bound with undyed muka strands in a series of buttonhole stitches attached to the foundation of the cloak in evenly spaced rows. Carson noted that at both upper corners there were two holes consistent with the use of cloak pins, which fastened the top edge of the garment together. They were usually slender and crescent shaped, and fashioned from bone, shell or stone. Someone had repaired the hole at the right proper corner with brown dyed muka thread.

There were other areas of the cloak where the same brown muka thread appears as overstitching. [13] This was at the left proper outer edge, and approximately 38 centimetres along the right proper lower edge. The overstitching appears to be repair work by someone skilled in using muka thread – perhaps Te Wharetoroa repaired this cloak at some point in its life, before she dyed it? Another very interesting feature is that the lower edge of the cloak has been cut right across. Could a woven tāniko border once have graced the bottom of the cloak?[14]

Since the cloak's acquisition in 1991, it has featured in museum publications and been exhibited twice. In 1993 it was included in the exhibition *Nga Puna Roimata o Te Arawa*, which celebrated the arts and talents of Te Arawa women elders through early photographs and taonga. At the time we had no idea of the full story behind this cloak, but because of the information on the swing label,

Detail of the kaupapa (or foundation) of the kahu waero woven by Te Wharetoroa. The double paired muka aho (weft threads) are termed whatu aho rua. The dog-hair tassels and fine muka binding are evident. MUSEUM OF NEW ZEALAND TE PAPA TONGAREWA, PHOTOGRAPHER NORMAN HEKE

we knew that it must have had some connection to Rotorua and its people at one point in its history.[15] The exhibition was also shown at the Rotorua Museum of Art and History Te Whare Taonga o Te Arawa later that year. In 2002 the cloak was displayed in a contemporary Māori art exhibition, *Taiāwhio: Continuity and Change*. A few taonga from the museum's collection were included in each segment of this exhibition to act as anchor-points or references to ancestral origins and values. The kahu waero acted as one of these links.[16]

At this stage, we still knew no more about the cloak's origins and history. One day in 2003, however, fellow curator Matiu Baker was reading through Te Papa's archives. He came across documents compiled by collection manager, Ross O'Rourke, about the Danish collector Sygvard Dannefaerd, who came to New Zealand in 1874 at the age of 20. Dannefaerd began his career as a 'curio merchant' in 1877 and was also known as a jeweller, naturalist and lapidary specialist. He operated his own business initially in Queen Street, Auckland,

A Te Arawa elder, said to be Kiharoa Akuhata, wearing the kahu waero at a reception for the officers of the American Atlantic Fleet in Rotorua, 13 August 1908. He is standing next to Dr Peter Buck (Te Rangi Hiroa). However, the elder may be Kiharoa's older brother, Eruera Te Uremutu, as there is another photograph, in the Alexander Turnbull Library (½-00 1921-G), of the two men outside a carved house named Tauwhitu at Ōhinemutu in January 1908. B.019347, MUSEUM OF NEW ZEALAND TE PAPA TONGAREWA

and then at another shop in Hinemoa Street, Rotorua, from 1906 to 1920. The documents included information on the kahu waero.[17] The story of the cloak was beginning to unfold.

According to the records, Dannefaerd wrote to Augustus Hamilton, Director of the Dominion Museum (Te Papa's forerunner), on 26 October 1909 offering a 'black mat with white tufts' for sale for £12. The 'mat', said Dannefaerd, had been worn by chief Kiharoa at a reception for the officers of the American Fleet in Rotorua.[18] From 16 December 1907 to 22 February 1909, four squadrons of sixteen United States Navy battleships and their escorts, later known as the Great White Fleet, circumnavigated the world to display the new naval power of America under President Theodore Roosevelt at a time of growing tension with Japan. The fleet made a seven-day visit to New Zealand, berthing at the port of Auckland from 9 to 15 August 1908.

The opening of the therapeutic spa known as the Bath House, today's Rotorua Museum, coincided with the fleet's visit. On 13 August 1908, Rear-Admiral Charles S. Sperry and some 200 members of the fleet were given a reception by the Te Arawa people at the opening.[19] Premier Sir Joseph Ward and Te Rangi Hiroa (Dr Peter Buck), then the District Health Officer, were also present. James McDonald, employed as a photographer for the Department of Tourist and Health Resorts, filmed and photographed the event.[20]

The following year, Hamilton bought the cloak worn by Kiharoa. He had acquired a number of taonga from Dannefaerd over the years, some of which

Interior view of the main hall of the Dominion Museum, Museum Street, Wellington, photographed by director Augustus Hamilton, about 1910. MA_C.001050, MUSEUM OF NEW ZEALAND TE PAPA TONGAREWA

were very old and tapu (sacred). In due course, the cloak was displayed at the museum in a case specifically designated for Māori clothing. Hamilton did not know that this kahu waero had been taken from Te Wharetoroa Tiniraupeka's home before Dannefaerd acquired it. Twelve years later, in 1921, Te Wharetoroa and George Samuel Graham visited the museum and were surprised to see the lost cloak. On their return to Auckland Te Wharetoroa wrote to James McDonald, the museum's acting director:

> On my visit to Wellington I identified a Maori garment (a waero with dog hair tufts) in your Museum as being the identical one made by me and stolen from my home at Ohinemutu some twelve years or so ago. I was away from home at the time and it disappeared with other things . . . I have no idea whatever who took it or sold it to the museum – if it was bought. All I know is I was much distressed at the time of its disappearance.[21]

Graham also requested the return of the cloak:

When we were in Wellington Te Wharetoroa identified a certain Maori mat as her property – and she has asked me to write you. Personally I remember it well in their home at 'Tiki' Ohinemutu quite 15 years ago – and recognised it at once when we saw it in the case. During her absence from home this and many other valuables were taken – and no enquiries whatever resulted in their recovery.

I would suggest that as the article is not an antique merely a passable specimen of a Maori 'waero' – that it should be returned to the owner. I am sure you will persuade the Museum authorities to do what is just. Mr Best will point out the particular garment in question.[22]

The Mr Best referred to in the letter was ethnologist Elsdon Best, who was employed by the museum and published many books and articles on Māori material culture and history.[23]

McDonald wrote back to Graham, noting that:

With reference to the garment claimed by Te Wharetoroa, Mr. Best has pointed out to me and on referring to our Register I find that it was bought from Mr. Dannefaerd, Rotorua, and is marked as having belonged to Kiharoa. I cannot think that he would have offered it for sale had he known it to be a stolen garment but the name of the alleged owner may help you and Wharetoroa to find out how it passed into the hands of Mr. Dannefaerd . . .[24]

The next day Graham replied.

Te Wharetoroa says that Kiharoa was an elderly man of Ohinemutu – he is dead some years now, also unfortunately Mr Dannefaerd – who would have been able to give us all the[?] details. Te Kiharoa had no right to possession of the garment and Te Wharetoroa has no means of ascertaining how he came by it. He now being dead, she does not care to impute more than that.

Wharetoroa herself dyed the garment in the mud-pool at Waikuta, and affixed the dog-hair tufts. It is, though well made, therefore not an ancient object – and probably the Museum authorities will return it to her, as the family value it for sentimental reasons – having for some considerable time before its 'overhaul' and since then been used on the dead persons of the family prior to burial.

I am sure you will be satisfied that I would not countenance anything other than a genuine claim against your Museum – being myself an enthusiast in respect of such matters – and I consider that all articles of Maori Art should be in our Museums.[25]

After further correspondence between Graham and McDonald, with apologies for delays, McDonald wrote a memorandum to the Under Secretary for Internal Affairs, dated 27 April 1922. In it he told the story to date and explained that Hamilton had entered the purchase in the museum register in December

1909: 'No.1911 Black mat covered with tufts of white hair (Kiharoa's mat) purchased from Danneford'; the garment was marked 'Formerly belonged to Kiharoa'. McDonald reported that the only existing correspondence was that between Dannefaerd and Hamilton, and 'a search in the Treasury records from December, 1909 to April, 1910 does not disclose any payment having being made'. McDonald could only assume that:

> Mr. Hamilton either purchased it privately, and placed it with his own collection at that time on exhibit here or received it on deposit. With the purchase of the Hamilton collection in 1914, the garment became the property of the Museum.
>   Mr. Best states that the cloak is of recent manufacture and is an imitation of the ancient garment known as Kahu Waero. It has, therefore, but slight intrinsic value but is useful as an exhibit to show a former style of garment. Mr. Graham has asked on behalf of the Maori lady Wharetoroa who I understand is his wife [the pair were not in fact married] that the cloak be returned to him for delivery to her. Mr. Graham is well known to Mr. Best. He is a prominent member of the Auckland Institute, and a frequent contributor of papers on Maori subjects to the Journal of Polynesian Society . . . The claim made by him on behalf of Wharetoroa appears to be perfectly genuine and I recommend, therefore, that the garment be returned.[26]

Eventually the cloak was returned. Graham wrote to McDonald to confirm that the cloak had arrived at his Wyndham Chambers address in Auckland on 3 May 1922.[27] It is not known whether Te Wharetoroa took ownership of the cloak at this point. We do know, however, that the cloak was accessioned on 1 May 1930 into the large Hori Montrose Graham Māori and Pacific Collection that began to be deposited in the Auckland Museum from 1910. (It was named for George (Hori) Montrose Graham, G. S. Graham's son.) Its registration number was 4827 and accession number was 158/30 (the numbers attached to the cloak when it came into the National Museum for inspection in 1991).

From 22 July 1941 until 17 September 1946, taonga deposited in the name of G. M. Graham were returned to him by the Auckland Museum, on his written authority. They were uplifted by his daughter Beatrice Mika and granddaughter Josephine Mika. The cloak was returned with several other taonga on 17 September 1946. At this point the cloak drops out of sight until 1991. It is known, however, that a number of items in Graham's collection were at some point purchased by a Wellington-based jeweller and artefacts collector known as Andrew Miet.

Beginning the reconnection

Beyond the recounting of the cloak's entry into the National and Auckland Museums, there was little other information about its maker and the larger connections between Te Wharetoroa, George S. Graham and their families. I began to assemble the life histories of these two individuals and interviewed their descendants in order to flesh out this rather sparse, yet intriguing, account.

The weaver of the cloak, Te Wharetoroa Tiniraupeka, or Margaret Graham, was born in August 1863 at Tarawera, in the volcanic region of the Rotorua Lakes. Growing up, she would have seen increasing numbers of tourists visiting the area, drawn especially by the famous Pink and White Terraces. Known as the eighth wonder of the world, these beautiful silica terraces and the natural beauty of the geothermal area were a major international attraction. On 10 June 1886, when Te Wharetoroa was 23, they were destroyed in the great eruption of Mount Tarawera.[28] The daughter of Tiniraupeka and Kirihuruhuru, Te Wharetoroa became a woman of standing in her community; she was remembered as a formidable kuia (respected elder woman) of her people. She died in 1964, aged 101, and is buried at Te Wainui, Whakatāne.

As part of the process of reconnecting the cloak to its original family, I interviewed the woman who grew up with Te Wharetoroa: the late Whakatoro Iritana Hilda Inia, known as Hilda. She was accompanied by her daughter, Audrey McCaull. The interview took place at the family home at Waikuta on 9 October 2005. A respected kuia of Ngāti Whakaue, Ngāti Pikiao and Tainui, Hilda was Te Wharetoroa's grandniece. Born in 1927, she was also the daughter of George Montrose Graham, and the granddaughter of George Samuel Graham.

Māori children were often raised by their grandparents or elders. This led to many cross-family and cross-generational ties. Hilda and her older sister Kirihuruhuru were raised by Te Wharetoroa as her mokopuna (grandchildren). Te Wharetoroa was also a sister of Te Kira, their grandfather, and raised his children as her own. One of them was Hilda's mother, Rangihuia, who later married George Montrose Graham and had two girls and a boy, named George, who died when he was nine years old. George Montrose was the son of Mary Magdalene Hapi and George Samuel Graham, who had formed a close relationship with Te Wharetoroa.

At one point Te Wharetoroa was living in Devonport, Auckland, caring for her family's children and mining gum for a living. Later she moved back to Ōhinemutu in Rotorua. Hilda described her in this way:

> She was to herself. You couldn't even compare her with anybody. She was a very clever lady, very Pākehā and Māori. She could write beautiful Pākeha, she could write letters, and she even went to Parliament, something to do with the wharenui at Wainui . . . My kuia was a business lady. She could switch to business.[29]

Hilda says she was about three months old when her kuia took her. They lived at Ōhinemutu and at Waikuta, on the present-day outskirts of Rotorua, near Ngongotaha. They also lived at Te Wainui, Whakatāne, for a time.

Te Wharetoroa Tiniraupeka, aged about 23. She wears a huia feather in her hair, symbolic of rangatira (chiefly) status, and a pounamu (jade) hei tiki around her neck. Her garments are a kahu huruhuru (feather cloak) over a korowai (a fine cloak decorated with muka cords or tassels) with a deep tāniko (geometric patterned weaving) border. She is holding an elaborately carved wahaika (short hand-held weapon). AUDREY MCCAULL

George Montrose Graham,
c.1950. AUDREY MCCAULL

It was lovely . . . I was sort of a real kuia's girl . . . Kiri was two to three years older than me. I loved it, anything my kuia did, or wherever she went, I was right behind her all the time. We stayed more or less between these places, but we didn't go to Wainui until I was about eight or nine years old. Before that we used to stay at Ohinemutu and we used to walk. We never had a car. We'd come out here to Waikuta, and she would do her gardens. Next morning we'd get up and we'd walk, we'd go again.[30]

The distance between Ohinemutu and Waikuta is about 7 kilometres.

At Waikuta Te Wharetoroa had a little whare (home) named Te Kurī. It had a dirt floor, which was as hard and strong as concrete and cleaned every day. Hilda says the old people worked hard. She remembers many of the kuia especially. 'They were lovely old kuia here, and at Whakatane, always hard working people . . . you were always welcome in their home, you'd call in their home anytime . . . you don't mind staying with them because they were so nice, it's a life that you'll never see again.'[31]

When Te Wharetoroa came back to Rotorua she started up what Hilda described as a 'curio place', or a shop for tourists, at Ohinemutu, in a whare rebuilt as a church in 1913. As well as weaving, Te Wharetoroa was also known to have carved small items, including a small tekoteko (carved figure), which the family

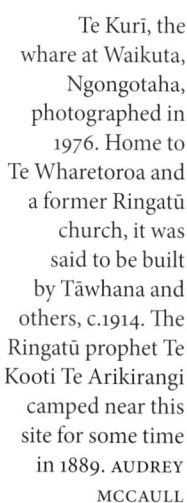

Te Kurī, the whare at Waikuta, Ngongotaha, photographed in 1976. Home to Te Wharetoroa and a former Ringatū church, it was said to be built by Tāwhana and others, c.1914. The Ringatū prophet Te Kooti Te Arikirangi camped near this site for some time in 1889. AUDREY MCCAULL

still has.³² Besides having business acumen, Te Wharetoroa was a devoted follower of religious prophet and leader Te Kooti Arikirangi Te Tūruki and adhered to the Ringatū faith. The rebuilt whare was named Tiki, after the original house, which had originally stood a little further down the slope. It was carved by Tene Waitere of Ngāti Tarāwhai.³³

> Her one reason [for rebuilding the house] was her faith. We used to have tekau mā ruas [the twelfth of every month, a significant day in the Ringatū church calendar] and they used to come from Ruātoki, from Whakatāne, and we had it all at Tiki, everything was at Tiki, she lived for those things. And that was what Tiki was really done for, for that. My koro [grandfather], he had a thing for a lot of greenstone and things like that, he was given a lot [through] his job, cause people have money, but they used to give him greenstone and kuia Wharetoroa used to make kits and carvings. Pākehā used to come around and come inside and have a look, buy things from her.³⁴

Hilda recalled her kuia's business sense:

> When we moved to Wainui she bought a couple of trucks and a car and started up her business out there. She and my uncle George and Mum's second husband, Charlie Marsh, and my uncle Bill, used to go up into the bush and it had a lot of

The whare whakairo (carved house) named Tiki, photographed by James McDonald in 1920, was carved by Tene Waitere of Ngāti Tarāwhai in 1913. Te Wharetoroa held Ringatū services there and it was originally home to the cloak.
MA_B.000099,
MUSEUM OF NEW ZEALAND TE PAPA TONGAREWA

white mānuka there. White mānuka was hard to get here [Rotorua] and she knew a fisherman over here, so she said to him, 'Would you like me to cut you some mānuka to smoke your fish?' and course he liked white mānuka to smoke his fish but he couldn't get any and she said to him, 'Would you like me to get it?' and he said, 'Yes. I'd like that, Margaret.' That was her Pākehā name, Margaret. 'Okay, you guarantee that you'll take my order, and I'll have your mānuka here all the time.' He had a fish shop right in town where she delivered it, and she would pick some paopao [*Scirpus lacustris*] and take it back to Whakatāne for that crowd to make some whāriki [woven floor mats].'

Hilda remembered Te Wharetoroa's skills. 'She weaved, she carved, she did all those kinds of things. She'd sit there doing that. She did carving, she'd do patu [hand-held weapons], she'd do it all herself, polish it up . . . little kete with muka and feathers. She used to make kākahu [cloaks], she was a great one for that.' Hilda recalled a dog that her koro George had brought down from Auckland. It had long, coarse hair, 'like string – hard – you don't pet it and enjoy it'. The dog was fed 'like a baby', but came to a tragic end when it fell into a hot pool. Hilda said that her kuia then had the dog 'scint' (shorn) of its hair, which she thought was used for a cloak.

George Samuel Graham was born in Auckland in 1874. His parents were James Bannatyne Graham, a lawyer and insurance manager, and Elizabeth

George Samuel Graham (1874–1952) in the late 1920s. AUDREY MCCAULL

Sheehan. George was an accountant and then practised law, later working with his father from 1919 to 1929. He also worked independently as an accountant and native agent. George S. Graham had a lifelong interest in Māori culture. He collected and translated many manuscripts of Māori history, several of which were published. They include histories of the Auckland region and of Te Arawa, Ngāti Toa and Te Ātiawa.[35]

Graham founded the Te Ākarana Māori Association and was a member of the Polynesian Society from 1902. He was a life member of the Auckland Institute and Museum, the precursor to the Auckland Museum, and in 1922 founded its Anthropology and Maori Race Section, which was dedicated to recording the history of and advancing knowledge about Māori. As we have seen, his collection of taonga was deposited in the Auckland Museum, and named after his son. Te Wharetoroa's cloak was to become part of this collection.

George Graham married Mary Magdalene Hapi of Waikato and Ngāti Whanaunga iwi in 1899. They had seven children but separated in 1912. George subsequently had relationships with Te Wharetoroa and with Mare Pōtatau of Ngāti Mahuta. He died in 1952, in Rotorua, survived by three sons and two daughters. Hilda remembered him fondly.[36] She also commented on what may have happened between Te Wharetoroa and Graham, giving a fascinating personal insight into the journey of this cloak.

> My kuia and koro had a big row, before my koro died, they had a big fight, because she said to my koro, 'All your wealth, everything you got, come from me, your knowledge on Māoritanga and everything . . .', because every time he came down it was 'Whare – pehea mea te mea' [how about this and that], and she used to tell him . . . She said to him, 'Ngā mea i roto i a Tiki kei a koe katoa, [the things inside Tiki the wharenui are all with you] you took them all, all the carving, all the greenstone, you never left anything.' So he said, 'I thought, instead of fighting over it, Whare, I'd thought I'd put them in the museum.'[37]

Some in the family wanted to consider bringing the cloak back home but Hilda disagreed:

> But they are safe in the museum . . . as far as I'm concerned, it will always be there . . . if they want to see it they only have to look at the books, they'll see where it is . . . by bringing it home, ka aha? [and what?] it's going to last longer, generations change, they're changing now.[38]

After the interview, Hilda and Audrey took me and my son Eruera into Te Kurī, their present-day wharenui, built on the site of the original Te Kurī. The wharenui is a large open room where extended family and visitors stay. Framed photographs of George Montrose and George Samuel Graham grace the walls, alongside other tīpuna (ancestors). It is a comfortable, welcoming place. It was here that Hilda mentioned the family vision of one day resurrecting the wharenui Tiki at Ōhinemutu, as a whare taonga (museum), just as Te Wharetoroa had over a century ago. Perhaps the cloak may travel again to the homes of Te Wharetoroa and be an inspiration for her mokopuna. The journey that this unique cloak has made through time is fascinating and complex. This chapter has related only some of the history of the cloak and its connection to Te Wharetoroa. Clearly, there is more to be uncovered and further connections to be made between this taonga and its people.

On Thursday, 7 September 2006, Hilda Inia passed away peacefully at her home. This chapter is dedicated to her. May her final wishes be remembered and come to pass.

8. Hand-Me-Downs and Respectability: Clothing and the Needy

Bronwyn Labrum

Every November, a colourful sight greets visitors and locals as the South Island town of Oamaru steps back into the nineteenth century.

> Ladies and gentleman in all their finery stroll along Thames Street, sip tea from china cups at the elegant Garden party, and swirl to an olde-worlde waltz tune at the glamorous Heritage Ball. Musicians and entertainers, swaggers and servants, rascals and ruffians, tradesfolk and mountebanks – all lend character and colour to the boisterous street scene of the Victorian Fete Day.[1]

When I visited in 2005, however, respectability and elegance, rather than the rough and the ne'er-do-well, were on display. I could count on one hand the number of men (and it was always men) who dressed down to play their part; most were trying to outdo each other in the costume stakes. Yet the late nineteenth century in North Otago 'was not an age of elegance' and especially during depressed times, destitution, unemployment and homelessness were all familiar to local townspeople.[2]

As with the competitive dressing displayed in the 'whirlwind of parades and dances, tea parties and train rides' at Oamaru's Victorian Heritage Festival,[3] most histories focus on clothing that is meant to be seen and that elicits approval, admiration and even envy. Many accounts slide effortlessly from clothing to style and fashion. Yet what was worn by those in straitened circumstances is a no less important story. Influential images from the 'Sugar Bag Years' of the 1930s Depression – women taking in mending and washing to make ends meet, the embarrassment of wearing dirty clothes to school or going without shoes – are also part of our history. Repeated mending and 'making do', forgoing the expected hats and stockings, wearing old clothes to work, even donning cut-down flour bags – these are the staple repertoire of memories, images and documents from the 1930s and 1940s. As one woman seeking help from the Wellington Hospital

A miner's wife tries to keep an eye on her child while sewing outside among the poultry and the washing in Buller, c.1945. Her hand-operated sewing machine was easily portable and required no electricity, making it ideal for such rudimentary surroundings. Its style dated from the late nineteenth century although electric models had been introduced in the early years of the twentieth century.
F-1158951/2, ALEXANDER TURNBULL LIBRARY, WELLINGTON, NEW ZEALAND

Board in 1932 told the prime minister: 'I reckon before long we will be back to Adam and Eve, just wear a fig leaf, or a cabbage leaf, as there are no figs in New Zealand that I know of'.[4]

Turning away from the familiar imagery, it is important to consider how the clothes of the poor and the needy were often passed down through successive family members, distributed by charities, churches and members of the community or sold at second-hand clothes shops. Through these processes clothing becomes an indicator of status or lack of it, and of conformity with or forced departure from social and community norms. In these circumstances cherished notions of egalitarianism and social difference were rearticulated. As those investigating the experiences of residents in the South Dunedin suburb of Caversham over the first half of the twentieth century discovered, 'where families found themselves in a more perilous financial position, clothing and fabric circulated in a complex informal economy', through home sewing, adaptive reuse and passing on clothes in and between families. These necessary practices were not shameful. Indeed, despite their insecurity, the poor and needy also wanted to fit in and to look good, if not 'flash'.[5] As Mavis Liverpool recounted:

People used to swap things or loan things so that the kids would be nice. The kids had nothing so that if there was a school concert coming up, if you had a good dress somebody else would loan you a cardigan to go with it so you'd look nice. I always remember I had a striped blazer, where that ever came from I don't know.⁶

If the surviving archival evidence of clothing and the needy is thin, the material evidence of clothing's relationship to poverty and need is sparse indeed. Working clothes were intended to be worn out and frequently ended up as cleaning rags and dusters, unlike much of the 'best' clothing, which has survived in families or museum collections. Occasionally, the less privileged aspects of life are represented in institutions. For example, the South Canterbury Museum has a piece of drafting paper attached to material. After it was washed it was used as fabric during rationing in the Second World War. Similarly, Te Papa has two intriguing pairs of 'austerity shoes' from around 1940, in most respects similar to every other pair of black men's leather shoes, except that they have thick wooden soles. They were sold in Auckland by George Underwood, who was a bootmaker and importer in the 1920s. It is surmised that he returned to his original trade during the Depression and early war years to 'produce footwear suitable for the times'.⁷

Men's 'austerity' shoes, with wooden soles and leather uppers, c.1940. PC003902/3903, MUSEUM OF NEW ZEALAND TE PAPA TONGAREWA

Yet despite the erratic nature of evidence it is clear that there were both strong continuities and important changes in the relationship between clothing and the needy over the late nineteenth and twentieth centuries. The provision of adequate clothing, as well as food and shelter, was a recurring topic for those in need and those attempting to provide assistance. A range of activities and incidences are apparent, from local and state provision of clothing as part of welfare services, to the importance of fitting into others' expectations, and the role of second-hand clothing in this. In focusing on the deprived, my work joins a small group of English studies which have explored clothing the poor in earlier periods. These scholars have shown how 'the dress of the poor takes on the role of a bodily marker, which alongside other bodily markers constructs the social, cultural and racial identity of those wearing it as self/other . . . . dress actively produced distinctions of gender, class and race, or more particularly fitness for purpose'. In the Victorian period, for example, 'Frayed seams/the disarray/the absence of dress suggested transgression and a failure of the boundary of culture/nature, a boundary that was meant to exist between human and animal, civilised and savage'.[8]

Making do in the nineteenth century

Immigrants to New Zealand expected to escape the poverty and degradation of their homelands, but found that the old world ills followed them into the new world. Within a few years of settlement the governor and other officials were employing the destitute themselves, setting up relief work schemes and handing out rations and clothing to both Māori and Pākehā.[9] As settlements grew and local governments developed more formal, but still miserly, systems of charitable aid, boots, clothing, and blankets became standard items of 'outdoor relief'. Case notes from the Otago Charitable Aid Board in the 1890s, for example, 'show homes entirely without furniture, only a few filthy mattresses and bundles of cast-off clothing as bedding'. Relieving officers who dispensed the aid saw 'naked and half-starved' children who lacked shoes and boots.[10] The provision of boots so men could work was a recurrent issue. Welfare workers were quick to make judgements about those who were exploiting the system, especially in the small communities of late nineteenth-century New Zealand. The Wellington Benevolent Trustees heard at a meeting in 1897 about a recipient who 'put on her oldest rags when applying for relief "yet who was very well dressed on other occasions"'.[11]

Because of their reliance on imported goods and the lack of local industry and labour, new arrivals often had difficulty in obtaining clothing. The Taranaki surveyor Edwin Harris and his family escaped with only their lives when fire destroyed his raupō whare in the early winter of 1841. Since other settlers had few things to contribute, his wife gathered up the burnt articles, made cloth shoes for the children and 'many little things sewed together came in useful until we could receive an outfit from England which arrived twelve months after'.[12] Later in the century, as Chapter 3 of this volume shows, old garments were remade. Two of Edwin Harris's daughters, by then living in Nelson, renovated an old white silk dress with 'a ninepenny packet of dye and hours of patient sewing' and converted a blue ball gown with black velveteen trimmings and restyling.[13]

The importance of clothing for men's work and survival is illustrated in the life and career of James Cox, a casual labourer who moved around the lower North Island in the late nineteenth century, endlessly searching for work. Cox emigrated to New Zealand in 1880 and, according to Miles Fairburn, soon adopted 'colonial clothes' and had learnt how to pack a 'swag'.[14] His copious diary entries mention the wear and tear on his clothes, even when he had employment at a flax mill near Foxton for several years. Initially the work was erratic, the wages low and accommodation and food poor. At Christmas 1888 he wrote: 'My shoes are got very bad and I have only one shirt I can wear and that's nearly worn out so I am in

A swagger resting outside a hut with his swag and billy on his back, possibly at Waipiro Bay on the East Coast, c.1900. Note his hobnailed boots, bowyangs (straps around the knees which held up trousers), scarf, heavy jacket and pipe. For nearly 100 years swaggers were a common sight on rural roads, forming a mobile workforce, walking huge distances from station to station, hoping to pick up seasonal work but enjoying a life of freedom. Better communications, including rural mail and telephones, railways, and welfare benefits all reduced the number of men on the roads so that the swagger huts and plates of stew and bread were mostly a thing of the past by the 1920s. G204181/2, ALEXANDER TURNBULL LIBRARY, WELLINGTON, NEW ZEALAND rather evil case and cannot get either money or goods from the firm'.[15] Conditions picked up and Cox's permanent station at the mill was at the 'wash', meaning that he swirled hanks of flax fibre in a water trough and then pegged them out to dry. He got completely soaked daily from waist to feet, having to experiment repeatedly with improvised protective clothing in an effort to keep dry. The boss supplied him with ordinary leggings and then overalls, but to no avail. He finally paid for his own waterproof apron and a pair of second-hand sea boots.[16] A 'respectable man', Cox bemoaned the lack of a 'decent suit of clothes' three years later when the flax milling business dried up.[17] A year of vagrancy followed, with shoes now the constant problem. For almost the next ten years he worked for the same contractors but suffered sharp and unpredictable drops in income. Then for the last period of his working life, of about 16 years, until the age of 72, he did a series of odd jobs interspersed with bouts of steady employment.

Cox washed, repaired and altered his own clothes: Fairburn argues that he probably knew as many handy hints as most colonial wives. He rubbed dubbin on his boots and resoled them. He 'did not buy clothes until he needed them badly' and waited for a 'good earning year' to purchase what were usually work clothes. Between 1888 and 1918 he bought only three suits, the first second-hand and the other two new. Only once, in 1913, does he record in his diary that he was 'well-supplied with clothing', after he replaced his worn-out work clothes with 'a working coat and vest, 3 undershirts, 2 prs Drawers . . . a pair of Denim Trousers' and 'a pair of leather leggings'. This was a shopping spree indeed.[18]

Lest Cox be thought of as a singular case, Ned Slattery (the swagger also known as 'The Shiner') took great care with, and worried about, his appearance. Although he was to be remembered as the archetypal 'work-shy' confidence trickster, he was

> fastidious with his attire and affected a down-at-heel gentlemanly appearance. He wore a battered and holed straw boater tied to his lapel with a bootlace, a starched or celluloid collar around his neck, a dark tie faded green by the sun, a waistcoat, shrunken dark trousers, carefully fitted boots, and he carried a cane or an umbrella (or at least the handle thereof) under his arm. In his later years only vestiges of decayed gentility seemed to remain, and he began wearing a handkerchief under a cap and another around his neck to protect himself against the sun.[19]

Institutional clothing

Elderly and run-down men like Cox and Shiner often ended up in homes for the aged, where they far outnumbered the female residents. Those men aged 65 and over became the primary residents of the country's benevolent institutions and by the 1880s were identified as a national social problem.[20] The total numbers of elderly increased by 50 per cent between 1896 and 1901 as the settler population

'Pensioner at home', Onehunga, part of a series, 'Old Age Pensioners: the Old Age Pension Act, 1898, in operation' by photographer Enos Silvanus Pegler. This respectable and able-bodied gent is also helping himself by hoeing the vegetables in his home garden. F22951/2, ALEXANDER TURNBULL LIBRARY, WELLINGTON, NEW ZEALAND/ ARCHIVES NEW ZEALAND TE RUA MAHARA O TE KĀWANATANGA, HEAD OFFICE

aged, and the majority who were institutionalised were those men without wives or children or other close family to assist them. They were also ineligible for the old age pension that was available from 1898 because of the moral and residency clauses, and increasingly rigid means-testing. Institutional responses to this mounting problem proliferated. In 1885, for example, there were Old Men's and Old Women's Refuges in Auckland, the Otago Benevolent Institution at Caversham, the Napier Refuge, the Ashburton Old Men's Home and one in Nelson. By 1920 there were 20 institutions under the jurisdiction of hospital and charitable aid boards. Although residing in an institution was often a far better solution than facing life alone, some homes were anything but 'homely'. Auckland's Costley Home of the Aged Poor, with its pretentious façade, ornamental balustrades and Corinthian columns, was in reality dirty and comfortless. Lice and bed bugs were rife and bed linen and clothing were left unwashed in bad weather because laundry work from outside the home took priority. Officials from a 1903 Royal Commission on the Costley Home noted that even fresh linen appeared half washed and that inmates' clothing was thin and dirty.

Here the informal economy of clothing might take on unanticipated aspects. Although obtaining clothing was not the problem, as all residents were issued with garments, however meagre, what that clothing meant and how it was used (and misused) was something else again. As Margaret Tennant has shown, these old men were not easily institutionalised. Their resistance, through non-cooperation and other inventive tactics, and the perverse pleasure they took in battling the authorities extended to clothing. In the 1890s the two charges of buying illicit alcohol and pawning clothes to pay for it often ran together.[21]

Homes for the elderly indigent were just one kind of institutional response to social problems in the nineteenth century and were part of a wide-ranging and growing system of reformatories, industrial schools for wayward children, rescue homes for unmarried mothers, prisons and lunatic asylums.[22] The first lunatics' building was established at Karori in Wellington in 1854 and over the next three decades institutions were established in the main cities and in major towns such as Nelson. The earliest asylums were attached to hospitals and gaols and were financed by public subscriptions, as hospitals were. But the marked lack of public interest and enthusiasm, the stigmatisation of the insane, as they were termed, and the fact that New Zealand's population was not big enough to sustain a dual public and private system, forced provincial governments to administer and fund the new asylums. The Department of Lunatic Asylums was the first state social service established after the abolition of the provinces in 1876.[23]

Clothing issues loomed large in these increasingly isolated and overcrowded institutions. At the Auckland Lunatic Asylum, for example, staff found that strong dresses (made of canvas, like straitjackets) prevented 'unnecessary waste of clothing'.[24] Indeed concern with respectability and self-presentation started with committal to the asylum, a formal medico-legal process that involved 'rituals of humiliation' and elements of self-mortification.[25] Charles J., admitted in 1890, appeared to speak for many when he declared that he was an 'inmate', not a 'patient'.[26] On arrival, all personal property, clothes and money were taken and passed to the Public Trustee, who also administered individual estates. Patients were then bathed and dressed and the men had their hair cut. Patient clothing was, at best, 'serviceable and provided adequate warmth'.[27] Although there was no conscious decision to create a uniform, a standard dress became the norm. Superintendents and inspectors made numerous comments on the shabby and dowdy nature of the patients' appearance and the prison-like style of the dress.

> There are few patients so far lost as not to be able to appreciate the distinction between the ordinary dress of civilians and that which is furnished to them on their admission. A consciousness of degradation owing to the change may exercise a prejudicial influence on many patients, and may obviate or retard their progress towards recovery.[28]

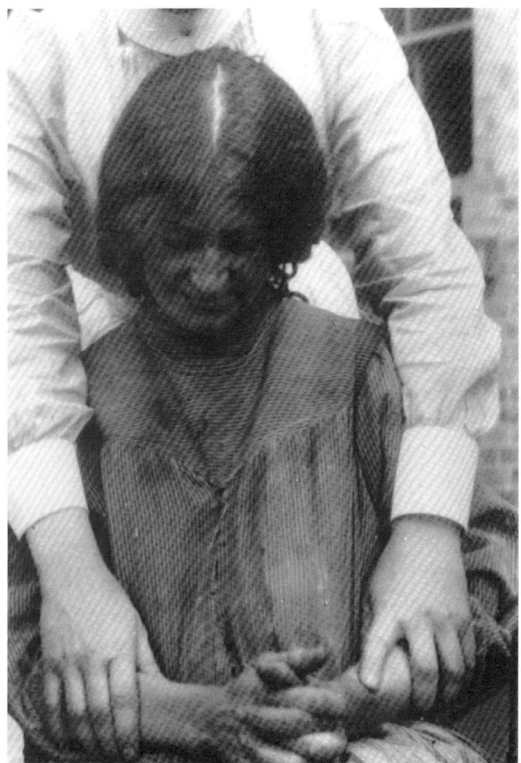 

LEFT: This 26-year-old married woman was admitted to the Auckland Mental Hospital in August 1910 and was discharged in November that year. According to her case notes she was in poor health and condition. Her reported cause of insanity was 'puerperal' or sepsis and fever following childbirth. She had been suffering from that for three weeks before committal. YCAA 1048/11, P.357, ARCHIVES NEW ZEALAND TE RUA MAHARA O TE KĀWANATANGA, AUCKLAND REGIONAL OFFICE. RIGHT: The starched white apron and clean and crisp demeanour of this female assistant at the Auckland Mental Hospital, c.1890s, contrasts strongly with the clothing of the patients. The assistant's weary look may counteract the air of authority and control, but the jangling keys at her side tell another story. B3493, AUCKLAND MUSEUM, PHOTOGRAPHER MARGARET MATILDA WHITE

Men wore moleskin trousers and coats, and blue striped or pink checked shirts. Women had calico combinations, cotton petticoats and galatea cloth frocks that were 'shapeless, heavy, dark, unattractive', with 'dozens cut from the one pattern'.[29] Flannels and jerseys were distributed in colder weather, although many patients suffered from leaky boots and were too lightly clad. Only in the mid-1880s did all patients receive a second set of clothing. As M. A. Crowther has noted of the English workhouse, 'the indignity of being bathed by an attendant', standard 'convenience haircuts' and even a partial uniform diminished the inmates' control over their appearance; they 'were always distinguishable from outsiders'.[30] Not all succumbed to passive institutionalisation. The asylum regime provoked forms of protest and subversion, which were 'not an unfortunate

PLATE 1 'Still life: Self portrait' [also known as 'The Red Beret'], c. 1935, Frances Hodgkins (1869-1947), New Zealand/England, 610 x 710mm, oil on plywood. 1999-0017-1, MUSEUM OF NEW ZEALAND TE PAPA TONGAREWA

PLATE 2 Kākahu kura (width: 1310 mm, length: 1120 mm). One of the few prestigious kākahu kura known to still exist in New Zealand, and made entirely of kākā feathers and *Phormium tenax*, this cloak is an important example of the traditional Māori practice of gift exchange. Estimated to have been made about 1850, it belonged to a Taupō-Tūwharetoa chief identified only as 'Chief Baker', who presented it to US naval officer John Hall on his departure from New Zealand during the Second World War. Hall had frequent contact with the Baker family in Taupō and became a good friend who generously provided them with supplies. ME15838, MUSEUM OF NEW ZEALAND TE PAPA TONGAREWA

PLATE 3 (ABOVE) Detail of the ivory silk brocade from the Greenwood family dress pieces showing a posy of anemone flowers, buds and berries, mid-1750s. The reverse of the posy shows the floating supplementary silk wefts inserted into the weave. GH007353, MUSEUM OF NEW ZEALAND
TE PAPA TONGAREWA

PLATE 4 (RIGHT) Details of a brocaded silk flower on the Burnett blue and ivory silk dress showing its reverse with the floating supplementary silk wefts inserted into the weave. The intense greens of the flower provide flashes of colour in a subtle background 'sea' of fine coral. PC002090, MUSEUM OF NEW ZEALAND TE PAPA TONGAREWA

PLATE 5 (ABOVE LEFT) Detail of the yellow silk brocaded taffeta from the Burnett family's open robe dress pieces showing a posy of flowers, including a tulip, c.1740s. PC002091, MUSEUM OF NEW ZEALAND TE PAPA TONGAREWA

PLATE 6 (ABOVE RIGHT) Detail of the brown silk satin damask from the late-eighteenth-century Burnett pelisse. Light catches the raised pattern of the flowers in this monochromatic textile. PC002089, MUSEUM OF NEW ZEALAND TE PAPA TONGAREWA

PLATE 7 (LEFT) Detail of a brocaded reddish violet silk taffeta from the reverse of the quilt owned by the Lush family. A serpentine pattern is overlaid with sprays of leaves. Posies of roses and daisies, and sprigs of buttercups complete the pattern.

PLATE 8 (ABOVE) Detail of brocaded ivory silk taffeta from the reverse of the quilt, with colourful sprigs of flowers. Two pieces of the taffeta have been joined in the centre. A tie with buttonhole edging sits across the join. It is not quilted in a traditional manner; rather the layers are held together by these decorative ties. PC003958, MUSEUM OF NEW ZEALAND TE PAPA TONGAREWA

PLATE 9 Hinemoa Collison's twenty-first birthday dress and shoes, 1920s. 84/95, HAWKE'S BAY MUSEUM, PHOTOGRAPHER CLIVE RALPH

PLATE 10 One of three known European-style waistcoats which combine Māori and European techniques and materials. Date and maker unknown.
45/209, HAWKE'S BAY MUSEUM, PHOTOGRAPHER CLIVE RALPH

PLATE 11 Detail of the kaitaka paepaeroa tāniko border (width: 2880 mm, length: 1650 mm). It has coloured woollen thread in this border and along the ua (top edge) and is thought to date from the mid-nineteenth century. The maker is unknown. 38/39, HAWKE'S BAY MUSEUM, PHOTOGRAPHER CLIVE RALPH

PLATE 12 Ruhia Pōrutu's glossy white kaitaka with tāniko borders at the front edges and hemline is a superb example of the type of cloak worn by Te Rarawa chief Hakitara at the signing of the Treaty of Waitangi in 1840. Woven entirely from muka, using the weft twining process called 'whatu', the garment relies on the preparation of the fibre and the skill of the weaver for its particular beauty. DE000107, MUSEUM OF NEW ZEALAND TE PAPA TONGAREWA

PLATE 13 Australian Gown of the Year, 1970, created by Pauline Kingston.
JANE MALTHUS

PLATE 14 Rosalie Gwilliam's 1975 padded cape-sleeved coat.
JANE MALTHUS

PLATE 15 Beverley Horne's hand-spun, hand-dyed, hand-woven dress in Corriedale wool and lynx yarn, c.1972. JANE MALTHUS

anomaly, but an inevitable feature of institutional life'.[31] Destroying clothing was a recurring means of modifying institutional life and its impact. Many deliberately refused to eat, mutilated themselves and attempted, sometimes successfully, to escape. A more profound if less spectacular form of resistance took the form of complaining, especially to official visitors on their periodic visits.

This spirit of individualism persisted in other institutions where the avowed context was control and punishment, rather than care. For example, in a bid to ensure they did not abscond, the inmates of the Dunedin Female Refuge, a home for unmarried mothers, had their clothing taken from them upon entry and were charged with larceny if found outside the home in institutional clothing.[32] Those sent to the Te Oranga Reformatory for delinquent young women, near Christchurch, in the early twentieth century were subject to a number of punishments to do with clothing and appearance. These were symbolic, as Bronwyn Dalley has argued, and relied on humiliation more than physical discomfort, but it is significant that they took this form. Offenders were made to wear a runaway or punishment dress and their hair was cropped short as a distinctly feminine form of chastisement. The dress was garish and its colour and 'attached appendages' were meant to be 'an affront to a young woman's sense of tidy outward appearance'. Dalley notes that, in practice, this goal was thwarted. Other inmates took little notice and the wearer 'may even have felt a sense of individuality or drama in an environment where everyone else wore drab clothing'.[33] Hair-cutting was more humiliating and its effects lasted longer, although it was publicly condemned in the local press after its use was reported. At a time when women wore their hair long as a sign of their adult femininity, it was clearly meant to single out such offenders and make them appear masculine. Attempts by institutional managers to punish and shame were regularly used in other establishments in the early twentieth century. According to a 1905 official inquiry, 'Crude psychological victimisation' was visited on children at the Lyttelton Orphanage in a number of ways, and once again clothing was an integral part of this practice. As well as being forbidden to talk for a month, and taunted about their backgrounds, children were dressed in 'grotesque costumes' for outings.[34]

'Decency' and the welfare state

A different 'worn world' of clothing is revealed in welfare records from the 1950s and 1960s.[35] By this time a welfare state, introduced by the 1935 Labour government, had superseded charitable aid, the miserly old age pension, the widow's pension (1911) and family allowances (1926). The 1938 Social Security Act took government support for families to a new and unprecedented level. It established a separate Department of Social Security to administer the package, which provided a much wider range of benefits at slightly more generous rates.

Girls from St Joseph's Orphanage in Upper Hutt, wearing new dresses provided by an anonymous donor, 14 December 1968. The donor of the dresses also arranged for the girls to be bused to Wellington to see the pantomime *The Princess and the Swineherd*. EP/1968/5444/18A, DOMINION POST COLLECTION, ALEXANDER TURNBULL LIBRARY, WELLINGTON, NEW ZEALAND

These included a full range of means-tested benefits for the aged, unemployed, invalid, the sick, widows without children, deserted wives and orphans, as well as family benefits. Superannuation for those aged 65 and older and the new subsidised medical scheme became universal entitlements. There was also a new emergency benefit, whose recipients included all those who were ineligible by a legal technicality to receive other benefits, and would therefore suffer 'hardship'. Free primary and secondary education, a community-based preventive health scheme, a free public hospital system, including free antenatal and maternity care, and a state housing programme with mortgage relief bolstered the extremely broad nature of the provision by contemporary standards. Social Security provided 'cradle to the grave' support; the policies were designed to provide a family with 'an income sufficient . . . with everything to make a "home" and "home life" in the best sense of the meaning of those terms'.[36]

Alongside the office-based provision of statutory benefits, a growing number of social workers in the Departments of Child Welfare and Social Security facilitated other less publicised forms of material assistance, and gave advice and information. Their work shows how important attire was to the attainment of a 'decent family life' and increasingly, how influential the requirements of school uniforms were for both parents and children. Social workers dealt with the challenges of supplying clothing, including footwear and blankets, on an almost daily basis. Clothing constituted part of the definition of 'need' in specific ways. Notions of need in these terms shifted perceptibly in the post-war period as compulsory education became ingrained, and secondary schooling grew more widespread. The emphasis on schooling and the wearing of uniforms had major implications for family budgets. The public presentation of the self was under greater scrutiny, particularly as the emphasis changed from providing families with the 'main essentials of life' to enabling them to live 'a decent life'. Moreover, as the state social work apparatus expanded, supervision of spending on clothing and its appropriate use also increased.[37]

Special assistance, a discretionary form of supplementary payment or 'top-up' to the fixed statutory benefits, later renamed supplementary assistance, helped parents to buy school uniforms, blankets and clothing, and to pay the rent. Fronting up to Social Security officers and the volunteers also employed in this programme could be daunting, especially if requests for a clothing allowance required such things as a list of the number of pairs of underpants owned and required.[38]

The way supplementary assistance helped families to buy clothing illustrates contemporary, and to our eyes, very accommodating, notions of 'decency'. In February 1952, for example, the Social Security Commissioner decreed that his committee would re-examine cases for assistance with the purchase of clothing that had been declined. These included widows with children:

> where the applicant had been forced over a lengthy period to pay high rent, live almost entirely on the benefit [to] maintain a family, or has incurred extraordinary expenditure. In such cases where they have been unable to maintain a wardrobe at a reasonable standard or find difficulty in buying clothes for dependent children.[39]

Mrs Carson described the 'tremendous moral uplift' she felt when she received financial assistance for rent and clothing in 1955. 'For the first time the children have lived in a decent home and had clothes no different from other people.'[40]

The provision of clothing and its production was a feminine domain. According to the rural women interviewed by Sally Parker about this period, 'Keeping her family clothed in home-made garments was the goal of every self-respecting farm woman'. Clothes bought from the shops were seen as 'a luxury, reserved for the idle rich'.[41] Yet others appeared to live to a different standard. In a 1957 case, Mrs Williams admitted that she could not stop herself from buying items for her family of 7 children aged between 1 and 21. She made continual purchases for the house and the children, getting the family deeper and deeper into debt. If Mrs Williams saw her children in need of clothing, she would acquire it; she was not one to make do. Rather than simply 'managing' or aspiring to the self-respecting feminine ideals of home-made goods, Mrs Williams succumbed to the consumer temptations that the post-war economy had made newly available.

The material enticements of the booming economy were hard to resist. Families and individuals got into trouble by buying cars or other goods on time payment, accumulating building society debts, and running up popular sources of credit such as those offered by the Farmers' Trading Company. The young had greater access than their parents to money, clothes, entertainment and new lifestyles, as they lapped up popular culture from North America through Hollywood movies, books, comics, speech and music.[42] And if they could not pay immediately, they put away the latest matador pants, pencil slim skirts or go-go boots on the system of revolving credit where a small deposit was followed by weekly payments, often doing so at several stores simultaneously. They sometimes did this without the knowledge of their parents, who discovered the transactions only when it came time to pay the bills.[43]

Family budgets also had to stretch because of rising educational expectations in the post-war decades. Changes in schooling, especially in the length of children's participation, contributed to financial woes. The school leaving age was increased to fifteen in 1944. This alteration reflected the growing provision of free secondary education: in 1936, the government had abolished the proficiency examination, which allocated free places in secondary schools, so that everyone could now attend. After the Second World War, numbers attending school grew sharply. Between 1945 and 1970, the primary school population doubled and the secondary school population expanded three and half times, owing to the 'marriage boom' and the number of pupils entering secondary school younger and staying longer.[44]

School uniforms for the mushrooming technical colleges, intermediate schools and colleges, as well as books and stationary, were new items that many families could not easily afford. At the end of 1954, for example, Mrs Bass requested help in buying clothing and schoolbooks for her son who wanted to attend Wellington College the following year. As she explained, she had been 'recently informed of the assistance offered by the State to those of us who are in need of financial help in preparing our children for Secondary School education'. Since divorcing her husband ten years earlier, Mrs Bass had lived alone with her only child. She currently received the invalid and emergency benefits. The District Child Welfare Officer authorised a grant of £20 for clothes and £5 for books.[45] Officers continued to arrange clothing assistance in conjunction with voluntary societies, churches, the Red Cross Society or the Mayor's Relief Fund.

As well as drawing attention to the presentation of the self, the ability to purchase clothes 'could make the difference between regular and sporadic school attendance'.⁴⁶ Writer Janet Frame's memories of the vexed question of obtaining and looking after appropriate clothes for successive schools make explicit what is often implicit in welfare case files. Recalling her primary school days, she wrote:

> Anyone observing me during those days would have seen an anxious child full of twitches and tics, standing alone in a playground at school, wearing day after day the same hand-me-down tartan skirt that was almost stiff with constant wear, for it was all I had to wear: a freckle-faced, frizzy-haired little girl who was somehow 'dirty' because the lady doctor chose her with the other known 'dirty and poor' children for a special examination.⁴⁷

Going on to junior high school meant a special and compulsory uniform for two seasons: tunic, hats, blouses, stockings, pants and shoes. 'Fortunately, the Dux medal . . . had also reminded relations who might have forgotten that the Frame girls might need clothing . . . . so there arrived a parcel of . . . "aunt-smelling" clothes in "aunts' colours" . . . which we divided amongst ourselves but which did not help towards a school uniform'. Her mother made a 'disastrously sewn' tunic with grey flannel bought 'on tick'.⁴⁸ In the summer before senior high school she 'dreaded returning' because she needed yet another uniform. She noted that 'schools were so particular about our having the correct uniform, and anything that made one's appearance different from the others was a cause for alarm and worry'. Frame's last year at school was dominated by her too-tight uniform that was 'torn and patched and patched again' because it was no use getting a new one before she left.⁴⁹

For Māori, who were shifting from rural areas to the cities in ever-increasing numbers from the 1940s, the problems of transferring to an urban, cash-based society, and the attempt to mirror Pākehā lifestyles, led to specific forms of need. Welfare officers made ubiquitous judgements about Māori worthiness to receive benefits, handle money and adapt to 'modern life'.⁵⁰ The officers frequently responded to headmasters' written enquiries about the alleged neglect and poor feeding of schoolchildren, their poor appearance, and clothing and related issues. In one case, a headmaster was advised to contact a Māori welfare officer about the spending of Social Security money on clothing for some of his pupils.⁵¹ The complaints and negative observations of welfare staff, teachers and members of the community were comments on 'Māoriness' as much as on poverty and were imbued with moral value judgements, which the Māori parents involved did not necessarily share.

'Lady' welfare officers from Māori Affairs, district nurses and local members of the Māori Women's Welfare League were often brought into such cases, dealing extensively with charity organisations and the circulation of clothing in the community. Some male officers were impatient to be seen as moving beyond charity and such basic welfare work. One reported that he felt whakamā

Children arriving at Te Kaha Native School, Opōtiki, c.1944. Māori pupils were often criticised for their state of dress by school staff and members of the community. These children attempt to look presentable, despite a lack of shoes and the apparent varying quality of uniform pieces they wore. F-1105-1/4, JOHN PASCOE COLLECTION, ALEXANDER TURNBULL LIBRARY, WELLINGTON, NEW ZEALAND

(ashamed) when he received an offer of a parcel of used clothing for the needy; he handed it over to the Māori Women's Welfare League to distribute instead. The extraordinarily wide range of work undertaken by Katie Graham, who worked as an honorary Māori welfare officer in Palmerston North in 1966, included distributing parcels of clothing to the needy.[52]

Second-hand clothing and community

Some twentieth-century social workers may have baulked at participating in the informal economy of clothing, but the circulation of used clothing has a long history, which New Zealand settlers drew upon. The adaptation of clothing handed down in families acknowledges the eighteenth-century tradition of the second-hand garment trade, which was far more organised and extensive than has been previously acknowledged.[53] Also important in the nineteenth century was parish clothing provision and its key role in maintaining a sense of local social justice is evident.[54] New Zealand churches of all denominations have long had a history of running second-hand clothing shops, referred to as 'goodwill', 'charity', 'opportunity' or 'thrift' shops. The Methodist church provides an instructive case study of this phenomenon, beginning with city missions, such as the Helping Hand Mission in Auckland's Freemans Bay, established in 1885, and the Dunedin Methodist Central Mission in 1890. The 'Social Creed' of the church became influential from the 1920s and the regional institutions responded to the 1930s Depression by 'marshalling community resources to clothe and feed those most affected by high unemployment'.[55] As the central and local governments failed to respond adequately to the crisis, city missioners became vocal advocates for both relief and structural change.

Charities, churches and friends helped those who struggled to assemble even basic items of clothing all through this period. Collections of donated clothing were distributed to people who could not afford shop prices. Initially, this was done on a charitable basis, with no money changing hands. Then in 1927 the Auckland City Mission decided to charge a nominal sum for the clothing to 'remove the stigma of charity' and 'preserve recipients' pride'.[56] Yet help given in this way was a double-edged sword, as Rita Snowden, a Methodist deaconess, recalled of the 1930s:

> Weekly jumble sales . . . were reckoned one way of dealing with this need for independence; there people could pay a little for the garments they took away.

Boys at a Wellington City Mission camp, 1920s. F-101985-1/2, ALEXANDER TURNBULL LIBRARY, WELLINGTON, NEW ZEALAND

And crowds came – with unmannerly pushing and shoving all too often so that I still think of the jumble sales as 'the lowest form of human activity'. We had to contrive to keep dealers out; and to give our own people a fair chance we issued tickets at our weekday meetings. At one stage, a courageous male member of our staff stationed himself at the foot of our steep hill, to turn back under guard, outside buyers who came down pulling stolen goods out of their bloomer-legs. It was a humiliating business.[57]

Second-hand clothing shops altered again in the post-war period, as the welfare environment changed: Methodists placed greater stress on social service and community development than on evangelism. The Manawatu Methodist Social Service Centre, for example, opened its long-running opportunity shop, Highbury House, in 1969. Such ventures were both financially successful for the parish – Highbury House funded the service centre's programmes and initiatives throughout the 1970s and beyond – and also a meaningful outlet for community activity and service by its volunteers. The work was often onerous. As well as providing clothing for individuals, the shop ran an extensive textile-recycling programme, which supplemented the money made from sales. Volunteers sorted

'Warm clothes for everyone', *New Zealand Free Lance*, 1 July, 1931. Volunteers in the basement of the Hope Gibbons building sorting out some of the 11,000 bundles of clothes collected during this drive in Wellington. C16208, ALEXANDER TURNBULL LIBRARY, WELLINGTON, NEW ZEALAND

Mrs Nancy Rodda models a frock for a prospective buyer in the Wellington City Mission shop in Lower Hutt, 1967. Mrs Beth McWha adjusts the hemline while Mrs Helen Bryant, standing by the buyer, looks on.
EP/1967/2113, DOMINION POST COLLECTION, ALEXANDER TURNBULL LIBRARY, WELLINGTON, NEW ZEALAND

donations and processed items unsuitable for resale into rags. Up to 100 rostered volunteers would collect garments, prepare and sort them, cut them into rags and serve in the shop.

Many volunteers recounted 'the mutual satisfaction of customers and staff when the "right" garments were matched to new owners'.[58] When the shop had been open seven weeks, a tally of business conducted noted that 'Anything at all will sell in the shop'.[59] It then went on to list items such as underwear, 'especially woollen for men and children from toddlers to about 10yrs. This includes pyjamas especially large men's. These last two items are practically non-existent and sell as soon as they come into the shop.'[60] The inventory included jerseys and cardigans, working boots, shoes and warm working shirts, large size 'frocks and cardies' for women, 'naps', warm coats for children and 'all types of bedding, blankets, rugs, sheets, towels, pillowslips and teatowels'. The compiler noted that: 'This area seems starved of anything and everything that helps to make for comfortable living and helps the housewife get a lift out of her home'.[61]

It is difficult to reconstruct the experience of shopping for second-hand clothes, but the recollections of workers at Highbury House give a good indication of the needs that were being met. Pensioners were very good customers, often stopping for a cup of tea and a chat and providing advice about gardening. One recalled: 'I now have rows of onions about as long as Cook St coming along nicely with carrots and parsnips and all the rest [in my mind]. He is a dear and is still waiting for a woollen singlet.'[62] Young mothers, including the unmarried, were desperate for nappies and baby clothes.

> These people especially the Maori are very grateful for the fact that the shop is now there for them to help keep the children warm. I notice that they do no buying for themselves till they have got their kiddies warm clothing. They are all wonderful people coming in with their tales of tragedy and happiness and one learns to listen and cry with them.[63]

Not only the poor and needy were avid customers, however. The catalogue compiled in the early weeks of Highbury House's operations also mentioned a different type of customer: 'The High School aged boy asks for waistcoats and old pin stripe suits and will buy them if in stock'.[64] Tertiary students had long been rifling through the racks for orientation garb and 'grunge' clothing. From the late 1960s second-hand clothing shops proliferated. As Elizabeth Smither's evocative poem, 'In the second-hand clothes shop', acknowledges:

> Lounge lizards and ladies of the night
> Have been here and gone off in disguise
> All it takes for a safari is a cork hat
> It takes an eagle eye to gut the racks . . . .
>
> Furtively tumbling labels, trying on
> Another's skin that fits us like a lamp.[65]

The late twentieth century witnessed a new phenomenon: the currency of designer labels, which gave rise to the terms 'pre-loved' and 'vintage' in an effort to demarcate them. People looking for these types of garments were motivated more by fashion and the notion of 'retro-chic' than by need.[66] The varied uses and meanings of second-hand clothes in the later twentieth century reflected a greater diversity in society at large, where generation gaps, a new urban culture, the impact of tertiary education, new media and other contemporary issues made for 'loud voices and conflicting principles'.[67] Changing community norms and standards were as apparent in the second-hand clothing bin as they were in the wider society.

Looking to those who were marginalised and impoverished provides a useful corrective to the typical histories of clothing. Vignettes of wearing hand-me-downs, recycling or buying second-hand clothes, submitting to social worker assessments or going without, show clearly how integral clothing is to a range of key historical experiences. The tales in this chapter highlight a number of themes: issues of respectability, feelings of embarrassment and shame at being differently or less well clothed (or being considered so by others) and later notions that 'decent' clothing was part of participating in modern society. They also reveal that second-hand clothing meant different things according to time, place and need. It is important to put these experiences alongside others in our accounts of the past, lest we construct a clothing heritage that is more about an ideal rather than any reality, and does not tell us what life was really like.

9. 'Just the Thing': Shopping for Clothes in Palmerston North

Fiona McKergow

It is 3 January 1877 and you are browsing the front page of the newly established *Manawatu Times*.[1] Your eye catches the headline 'IMPORTANT NOTICE', placed by Thomas Nelson, a general storekeeper, who was one of a handful of sole traders in drapery, clothing and footwear, among other domestic goods, in the soon to be created borough of Palmerston North.[2] To maintain his 'liberal patronage', Nelson offered a spacious shopfront with a large and varied stock of 'first-class articles' and a fair balance of price and profit. His shop provided the services of a 'workmanlike' watchmaker and jeweller and a department for women and children, where sale items may have proved tempting. Nelson's enterprise is one element in the complex and fascinating story of how New Zealanders have acquired their clothing in the past.[3] Today most of us have little or no involvement in the production of our clothing and are almost totally dependent on a relatively cheap global marketplace. This has not always been the case, although readymade clothing – 'apparel and slops', boots and shoes, hats and caps, and millinery – was available from the time of initial European settlement and in large quantities, especially for men, from at least the late 1860s.[4] Since then New Zealanders, both Māori and Pākehā, have acquired clothing in a wide variety of ways. These include making clothing from locally gathered and prepared plant and animal fibres; purchasing fabric to make garments at home by hand or machine; commissioning tailors, dressmakers and a range of other specialists; and buying ready-to-wear items directly from shops, both new and second-hand, or indirectly from mail order catalogues. Individuals also dealt with hawkers; received clothing as gifts or loans from relatives, friends and employers; were allocated clothing and footwear in the form of charitable aid; and begged for or stole garments.

In this chapter I explore the buying and selling of clothing and home sewing supplies in Palmerston North between the 1870s and 1920s. Related historical studies in New Zealand have investigated key sites, such as department stores, specific sewing trades, such as dressmaking, and important urban centres, such as Dunedin.⁵ I offer a complementary approach by exploring the range of clothing retail trades that operated in a provincial town over time. As well as 'big stores' – as department stores were initially known – with their advantageous economies of scale and limited liability status, I include Palmerston North's draperies, which sold both home sewing supplies and ready-to-wear clothing, and its sewing trades, such as tailoring and dressmaking, in an attempt to balance commerce and craft. What the people of Palmerston North chose to wear is also an important part of this story. Their relative preferences for home, custom and readymade clothing were an essential ingredient in the evolving nature of clothes and clothes shopping.

Unpacking colonial shopping

Shops were the cogs of British colonial expansion. They may initially appear to be a small part of the colonising process in New Zealand but they were an enormously successful means of introducing and dispersing British culture, commodities and systems of exchange. During the nineteenth century, Britain derived immense self-confidence and power from its ability to translate handcraft skills into industrial manufacturing processes. Scientific discoveries and inventions were increasingly underpinning British economic life, enhanced by the more rapid extraction and transportation of raw materials at home and from the distant shores of empire.⁶ Britain produced an astonishing range of goods, which swamped its domestic and colonial markets, and made its imperial

Thomas Nelson ran this advertisement in the *Manawatu Times* during December 1876 and January 1877. Other general stores on The Square were owned by John W. Liddell, a general storekeeper at Foxton whose branch store in Palmerston North was under the management of John Hanson, and Samuel Abrahams, a boot and shoemaker by trade and later one of the town's mayors. These stores sold a wide range of goods for domestic use. There were a similar number of hotels located on The Square at this time, offering a variety of services for both boarders and travellers. NATIONAL LIBRARY OF NEW ZEALAND TE PUNA MĀTAURANGA O AOTEAROA

IMPORTANT NOTICE.

THOMAS NELSON,
GENERAL STOREKEEPER,
PALMERSTON NORTH,

Whilst thanking the inhabitants of this and surrounding districts for the very liberal patronage accorded him during the last two years, has much pleasure in intimating that he has just opened his

NEW AND COMMODIOUS STORE
IN THE SQUARE,

Which will be found replete with a large and varied stock of Goods, consisting of—

    Drapery, Clothing, Boots and Shoes, Groceries, Ironmongery, Tinware, Glass, China, and Earthenware, Stationery, Fancy Goods, &c., &c., &c.,

And trusts that by continuing as hitherto to supply none but first-class articles at the lowest price consistent with a fair living profit, to merit a continuance of past favors.

TO THE LADIES.

Now showing in the Drapery Department some specialities in Ladies' and Children's Costumes.

ALSO,

A splendid assortment of Vulcanite Goods, consisting of—

    Earrings, Brooches, Bracelets, Hair Ornaments, &c., &c.,

In every variety of style and design, which will be sold CHEAP to effect a clearance.

T. N. further intimates that he has secured the services of a first-class WATCHMAKER AND JEWELLER, And assures the public that all work with which he may be entrusted will be performed promptly and in a thoroughly workmanlike manner.

N.B.—A splendid assortment of Toys suitable for Christmas presents, comprising some of the most amusing novelties of the day.

Wines and Spirits sold wholesale.

Look out for T. Nelson's PRICE LIST, which will shortly be issued.

NOTE THE ADDRESS—
T. NELSON,
THE SQUARE,
PALMERSTON NORTH.

The LITTLE WONDER
That keeps the prices under.

'Tis not in mortals to command success ; But I'll do more— deserve it.

aims and its domestic pleasures more difficult to separate. Abundance, rather than sufficiency, had become one of Britain's most vital ambitions. Quite simply, its people were increasingly able to exercise their enchantment with things – new things – and the comfort and status they appeared to offer.[7] For many the spiritual and communal dimensions of life were providing less security and they turned to materialist goals. The circumstances that stimulated and accelerated British consumerism are the subject of numerous historical studies.[8] An upsurge in new shops, new products and new marketing methods (many of which originated in North America), not only changed the face of British cities and towns, but also the everyday needs and expectations of their inhabitants.[9]

Most British colonists shared a fundamental belief in the civilising influence of their commodities.[10] Human progress went hand in hand with advances in material well-being, or so they believed. These were just some of the precepts that influenced the nature of Britain's colonial relationship with Māori. Of more importance to this story is the fact that merchants and shopkeepers imported large quantities of British goods, whose increasing availability held a contradictory potential for Māori communities.[11] However circumstances unfolded for particular iwi, hapū and whānau, there is no doubt that these commodities offered alternative ways of living that they needed to confront. Even a range of apparently unexceptional items like parasols, ploughs and prams offered different ways of dressing (being sun-shy), cultivating (using techniques of heavy tillage) and communicating (carrying babies without body contact). Māori adopted some and not others; they modified many.[12] They acquired great numbers of woollen blankets, which they wrapped around the shoulders like kākahu (cloaks), along with items of European clothing that they wore in combination with or as a complete alternative to customary clothing.[13] Unlike prepared flax, with which Māori did considerable trade, there is little evidence that they traded items made from it as commodities with British settlers.[14] This was not the case for kete (kits) and other items that were easily and quickly produced from strips of flax leaf and other plant materials.[15] It was an unequal contest, however, as clothing and textiles were at the forefront of modern forms of British consumerism.

Importers, merchants and shopkeepers ensured that British drapery, clothing and footwear reached customers throughout New Zealand, and with time, they benefited from the widening scope of telegraph, steamship, rail and road systems within the colony. Shops, and the distribution networks that supplied them, offered work, as well as goods, and were integral to the establishment of new towns. They kept settlers in material contentment a long way from 'Home', and increasingly gave them a sense of 'home'. As townships grew, general stores lost their initial advantage to a wide range of specialists: tailors, dressmakers, milliners, mantlemakers, corsetmakers, drapers, haberdashers, clothiers, outfitters, mercers, furriers, boot and shoemakers, even military lace men. And as colonial New Zealand matured sufficiently to boast a clothing industry of its own, centred on Dunedin, shops began to sell colonial-made goods in greater quantities, especially for men and boys.[16] For instance, in 1873 Bendix Hallenstein opened a Dunedin factory producing men's and boys' clothing, which was replicated around the country as the New Zealand Clothing Factory.[17] Such businesses provided substantial work opportunities, particularly for young women, but were not exempt from charges of sweated labour, which the government legislated against in the same year. The issue of labour conditions came to a head with the appointment of the parliamentary Sweating Commission in 1890.[18]

Shops were clustered in the middle of towns. In New Zealand, the practice of 'going shopping' was a product of the nineteenth-century growth of towns. Because women were regarded as the principal shoppers in most households, they routinely occupied the public space created in these new town centres, alongside men. For most women, shopping for clothing actually meant shopping for dress materials to make up at home for themselves and their children (men wore factory or tailor-made clothing). Drapery stores were an essential part of their shopping round, whether they wanted to replace a missing button or to embark on more ambitious sewing tasks. Large drapery stores provided dressmaking (and tailoring) services for those who could afford them. With time, the profit incentive for many drapers rested on turning over stocks of readymade clothing for women, in addition to the sale of fabrics and sundries, and making up and alteration services. During the early twentieth century, the dispersal of better quality and more varied factory-produced clothing was to entrench the exclusivity offered by tailors and dressmakers, but this impact was somewhat offset by rising standards of living.[19] Some drapers were able to expand their businesses into big stores, which later consolidated as department stores and had their heyday from the 1920s to the 1960s. By then, they devised new forms of clothes shopping, as a sensual fashion experience and an extension of leisure.

From Papaioea to Palmerston North

In 1866, the town of Palmerston North was little more than an idea mapped out with a theodolite and coloured ink by government surveyor, J. T. Stewart. A large town square was proposed for a clearing, known as Papaioea, situated on stony river terraces dotted with ox-bow lakes. It was based on Rangitāne's 1864 sale to the government of a 250,000-acre (100,000-hectare) block of land, known as Te Ahu-a-Tūranga. Stewart was well acquainted with Manawatū as he had also surveyed the river and its tributaries in the late 1850s. He later recalled: 'Boots and shoes gave way in this water & gravel travelling and the party, except the Maories [sic] whose feet were stone proof, were reduced to wearing sandals made of the dry leaves of the Ti or cabbage tree, or to covering their feet with pig skins with the hairy side out laced over the remains of their shoes'.[20] As road lines were cut and surveying began in earnest, trade from Te Awahou (now Foxton) and

Torkil and Kari Gundersen with their children outside their Main Street home, in the early 1880s. The sign above the door reads 'Tailor & Habit Maker', indicating that Gundersen made everyday tailored outfits for men as well as more specialised garments of rank and profession.
C. A. ANDERSON PAPERS, BC404, PALMERSTON NORTH CITY LIBRARY

other riverside settlements gave inland Rangitāne and the first European settlers increased access to garments such as thick cotton and woollen shirts, heavy trousers, blouses and skirts, leather boots and shoes, caps and hats, and other textile items, such as blankets and bedding.[21] Settlers purchased town sections and The Square slowly materialised in join-the-dots fashion, with unoccupied or grazed stretches of land punctuated by modest buildings of corrugated iron, timber and brick. One housed the first general store, run from 1871 by Louisa and George Snelson, who was also an auctioneer, land agent and the town's first mayor.[22] Papaioea became Palmerston North, with timber milling, rail and pastoral farming at the heart of its expansion.

The first permanent buildings on the margins of The Square had the stylistic unity typical of new or emerging towns. Shop frontages were simple, with wide, angled or gently curved corrugated iron verandas and minimal signage giving the proprietor's name and trade in paint on fascia and gilt on windows. With their large square panes or semi-circular arches placed each side of double or partially glazed doors, feature windows drew attention to the shop entrance, in contrast to the sash windows and solid single doors of private quarters.[23] Larger goods might be put on view outside, or stacked for delivery at the entrance. From the daytime brightness of the street, customers took a single step through the doorway into dimly lit and plainly stocked interiors. By the early 1890s, buildings on The Square had connected up, like the winnings on a Monopoly board, forming a defined civic area and shopping precinct. Shopkeepers jostled for command of the street frontage. Those in heavy trades took up premises elsewhere, leaving The Square to drapers, bootmakers, paperhangers, butchers, hotelkeepers, bankers and the like.[24] If the new township of Palmerston North was being populated swiftly – from 193 in 1874 to 4303 15 years later – so too was the surrounding countryside.[25] Manawatū experienced one of the most dramatic, and irreversible, landscape changes in the entire country, caused by timber fellers, railworkers, farmers and farm labourers who came, with and without families, from European countries as disparate as England, Ireland, Scotland, Denmark, Norway, Sweden, Germany and Poland. Mostly these newcomers needed affordable, hard-wearing and practical forms of clothing and footwear.

The first tailor to set up business in Palmerston North was probably Torkil Gundersen, a Norwegian who arrived in 1871 with his wife, Kari, as part of a public works scheme run by the New Zealand government. The authorities feared that his trade, and those of a miller and a machinist, 'may have unfitted them for the rougher work of bush clearing and splitting'.[26] The following year he returned to his original trade, in addition to public works and land clearance. Torkil and Kari Gundersen were one of eighteen young married couples (with seventeen small children between them) to arrive on the *Celaeno*, the first immigrant ship from Norway.[27] We can assume that some of Torkil Gundersen's clients were Norwegian, although it is clear that Norwegian women brought a strong tradition of homespun clothing to their new land. After welcoming them, Arthur Follett Halcombe, the Wellington Provincial Secretary, wrote: 'During the long winter months, the women employed themselves in spinning and weaving; and I was assured by them with no little pride, that every article of clothing worn by the men, from the knitted woollen shirt to the warm blue frieze coats, was entirely of home manufacture'.[28] By 1879 Torkil Gundersen worked from the family's Main Street home, making items such as uniforms for the Militia Volunteers, for which he had some difficulty getting paid.[29] Struggling to pay their bills, the Gundersens left Palmerston North for North America in 1884, with their four children.[30]

Palmerston North's first dressmaker is elusive. She may have been Mrs E. Marsh, who in the *Manawatu Times* of February 1877: 'Begs to announce to the inhabitants of Palmerston and surrounding districts, that she has re-opened her business as DRESSMAKER, And added to it that of MILLINERY, Having secured the services of a COMPETENT MILLINER Just arrived from England'.[31] She was therefore in the position to offer a more complete outfitting service, after the possible interruption to her business by the birth of a child or ill-health. As was customary, she 'thanks her numerous patrons for their past favours', and specified 'LADIES' OWN MATERIALS MADE UP'. Since it required very little stock, a dressmaking business could be easily set up or closed down.[32] There was no apparent obligation to buy from her husband, a general storekeeper at Terrace End, who a year later notified the public that he: 'Has now completed his extensive alterations, and made large additions to his Drapery, Grocery and Ironmongery Stocks. He is now in the position to compete with any Store in the district.'[33] In March 1877, a Miss M. Alderson advertised her services as a dressmaker and milliner at 'The House lately in occupation of Mr P. Stewart, Main Street,

Few nineteenth-century garments made by dressmakers have labels. The skilful cut and construction of this lilac (once brilliant blue) grosgrain silk wedding gown may be the work of a dressmaker. There is crude hand stitching on the recent embellishments of black nylon and cream lace, possibly from later use in repertory theatre. Mary Susan Hocking, a long-time resident of Manawatū, wore this two-piece gown in 1882 when she married contractor James Henry Hosking. The fitted bodice consists of fifteen carefully shaped pieces, and has deep inverted pleats at the back (see detail) that are weighted with lead discs to fan over a bustle. The skirt has eight major pieces, including a deeply pleated overskirt to accommodate a bustle, a heavy lining and a hemline protector. The gown is decorated with neatly ruched and pleated bands of matching fabric. PHOTOGRAPHS BY GRAEME BROWN WITH ASSISTANCE FROM CINDY LILBURN, 85/88/29, FIELDING BOROUGH COUNCIL COLLECTION, TE MANAWA

Palmerston North'.[34] Initially, she had requested 'A Situation as Housekeeper or Housemaid in a gentleman's family', so it is possible that she was doing both types of work.[35] Both dressmakers' situations reveal the often fragmented nature of this occupation. Given the centrality of sewing to women's domestic work, it is likely that many took up informal sewing jobs, for cash or in kind, as a way of assisting with household finances.[36]

Staff outside 'THE BON MARCHÉ', C. M. Ross & Co., The Square, in the mid-1890s. Charles Ross, seventh from the left with his thumbs in his pockets, declared he employed 'only first class talent'. He purchased the Bon Marché from J. C. Fowler in June 1883, having entered the local drapery trade the previous year. Named after the vast iron and glass store built in Paris by Aristide Boucicault between 1871 and 1887, it was designed by Palmerston North architect Ludolph West. The building has an entrance on the left that leads to 'gentlemen's outfitting and clothing, and tailoring departments' and another on the right for 'family drapery, hosiery, haberdashery, mantle, dress, and millinery departments'. PHOTOGRAPH BY A. E. HOBBS, BC48, PALMERSTON NORTH CITY LIBRARY

By the early 1890s, residents of Palmerston North and its surrounding districts were served by bigger and better shops, which sold a more varied range of drapery, clothing and footwear. For instance, some drapers had established their own workrooms, where they could employ tailors, tailoresses, dressmakers and milliners to make custom and readymade items.[37] For home sewers, there was now a ready supply of sewing machines. Ten years before draper J. C. Fowler had observed: 'The sales [of sewing machines] are quite unprecedented – so much so, that we are compelled to sell them in rotation as customers' names are put down in the list'.[38] These changes enriched the available range of clothing across a broad production base – home, custom and readymade. The needs of an expanded population were more diverse and growth automatically added new layers of complexity to individual lives and social relationships. Family occasions, such as christenings, weddings and funerals, and community events, such the annual show run by the Manawatu & West Coast Agricultural & Pastoral Association, horse races and sports matches, demanded a level of finery or garment specialisation that could now be more easily satisfied locally.

The clothing retail trades offered significant business and employment opportunities for both men and women throughout New Zealand. Among the working-age men resident in Palmerston North in 1893 there were 28 boot and shoemakers and dealers, 21 tailors, 21 drapers, 15 general storekeepers, a clothier, a hatter, a hosiery manufacturer and a military lace man. In the same year women in paid employment included 36 dressmakers, 7 milliners, 5 tailoresses, 4 storekeepers, 2 machinists (one of them a tailor's machinist), a draper, a corsetmaker and a seamstress.[39] The number of shops this level of employment represents is not easy to define, but we know that one of the most successful drapers of this time, and a key employer, was Charles McIntosh Ross (see previous page).[40] Unlike the southern city of Dunedin, the majority of drapers in Palmerston North were men.[41] The exceptions were Elizabeth George, who ran a drapery business with her husband and son from 1883, and Mrs C. J. Hansen, who set up premises on The Square as a corset and surgical belt manufacturer and general draper in 1889.[42]

View of The Square between Main Street West and Church Street West (out of photograph on left), c.1890. Warnock, Kelly & Adkin, 'CASH DRAPERS AND CLOTHIERS', was a branch of a Wellington-based firm, established as a rival to Kirkcaldie & Stains Ltd when three of its senior staff, T. Warnock, William Adkin and Mrs Kelly, walked out in 1885. The other commercial premises in this view include a land office, chemist, bookshop, restaurant, newspaper office and hotel. Wertheim sewing machines are sold by Grace, Clark & Co., a music shop.
PHOTOGRAPH BY GEORGE SHAILER, SQ12, PALMERSTON NORTH CITY LIBRARY

By now the extent of women's involvement in the sewing trades comes into view more clearly. Numerous dressmakers and milliners, such as Mrs Amelia Green, 'a native of England . . . who learned her trade at New Plymouth', and the Misses Fife, 'Anglo and Parisian Dressmakers', ran businesses on their own account, and may have trained other women.[43] Their presence refutes the widespread assumption that business was a masculine concern in the nineteenth century.[44] Contrary to usual expectations, it also tells us that both married and single women participated in business. However, in the early twentieth century the growing diversity of readymade clothing and the emergence of big stores narrowed the scope of independent commercial opportunities for women in clothing retailing. With the availability of simple, factory-produced hat shapes, in straw or felt for instance, and flowers, feathers and trims from haberdashery counters, milliners suffered encroachments into their trade. In 1905, Palmerston North had eight milliners, an increase of only one in twelve years, despite vigorous population growth (up to 10,239 in 1906). Similarly, there were only five additional dressmakers. The number of tailoresses, however, jumped to seventeen, another reflection of a shifting preference away from custom-made

Male and female workers at F. Johansen & Co. bootmakers, c.1905. The division of labour is apparent in this workshop: women stitch and men cut. Earlier generations of bootmakers did their work 'on the knee', but here we see the use of stitching, finishing, trimming and riveting machines, which simplified and hastened some tasks, but required skill to operate them. A bootmaker still needed an aptitude for choosing and preparing leather.
PETERSEN COLLECTION, BC390, PALMERSTON NORTH CITY LIBRARY

clothing. The move away from craft skill does not appear to have affected men in the clothing retail trades to quite the same degree, given a rough doubling of their numbers. In 1905 there were 51 boot and shoemakers, dealers and importers, 48 drapers and draper's assistants, and 42 tailors and tailor's assistants, among other male specialists.[45]

The trajectory for home sewing is more difficult to trace because such activities were not well documented.[46] On the one hand, women might be less tied to routine household sewing, because of the increased availability of readymade clothing, but on the other hand, the combined advantages of domestic sewing machines and commercial paper patterns boosted creative home dressmaking and widened women's access to fashion.[47] Certainly there were enterprising individuals thinking along these lines, such as English inventor Miss L. Roberts, who toured New Zealand in 1904 promoting her 'Imperial System of Dresscutting', available in Palmerston North in a two-hour lesson at a 'School of Dress' above the premises of tailor Emil Olaus Olsen.[48] Other schemes 'to reduce the art of cutting out and fitting to its simplest terms' emerged over time, such as the 'Ideal Home Chart' for dressmaking demonstrated by Miss Bagley at Collinson & Cunninghame Ltd.[49] In addition to the economic advantages of home sewing, the growing simplicity of women's clothing styles also helped to maintain its underlying viability. It also allowed originality and control of the final appearance. In the early twentieth century, the choices between home, custom and readymade clothing appear to have co-existed in an uneasy balance between economy, originality and convenience.

If you took a walk around The Square in 1920, you would see a modest agricultural service town with its 'famous square and its splendid blaze of floral colour, giving an impression of a garden city laid out on town-planning lines'.[50] Around and adjacent to The Square were 'twenty-four establishments engaged in the buying and selling of wearing apparel and general drapery and mercery goods'. Foremost among these were Palmerston North's big stores: Collinson & Cunninghame Ltd (1904–83), C. M. Ross Co. Ltd (1883–1959) and the Premier Drapery Company Co. Ltd (1915–56), each with generous street frontages for window displays.[51] For a select female clientele there were dressmaking establishments, such as 'Maison Louise au beau monde', which dealt 'exclusively in ladies' blouses, dinner gowns and fine underwear'. For the equivalent male custom, there were menswear specialists, such as A. J. McMahon, a mercer and clothier: 'No price tickets appear on the goods ... the inherent quality of the merchandise being their own statement of value.'[52] Men could purchase clothing from W. H. Skinner, 'The Working Men's Outfitter', just off The Square, whose comforting slogan was 'we know small profits and a large turnover go together'.[53] Second-hand clothes and boots were available at Penketh's in George Street, a block away.[54] This range of clothing outlets reveals the level of conscious social differentiation in terms of both class (price tickets versus no tickets) and gender (big stores with separate male and female entrances). By now there were few shops that relied solely on making clothing for sale, and some were growing on a scale that would have been unimaginable 50 years earlier.

Shifting sales techniques

There were remarkable changes during the late nineteenth and early twentieth centuries in the nature of shopping, particularly in terms of how shops promoted and displayed goods and the way purchases were transacted. Some accepted retail techniques took on a new importance. The growing number of drapery businesses in Palmerston North from the 1890s meant that many shopkeepers faced stiff competition. J. B. Hamilton was one of the first to offer discount sales during the winter and summer months.[55] In mid-1882 discounted items included ulsters, costumes and jackets in 'every style' for girls, while for boys there were strong tweed trousers, strong tweed suits, tweed pole caps, ulsters and overcoats. There were satin cloths in 'new colors', new dress serges, ulsters with hoods and fur-trimmed jackets for women, while for men there were 'extra heavy' mole trousers, tweed galatea coats, dark winter suits, merino undershirts, merino drawers and strong elastic braces.[56] As the sale progressed additional items were offered such as women's merino stockings, ladies' beaver hats, boys' velveteen blouses and infants' merino pelisses.[57] By the 1920s huge biannual sales of drapery, clothing and footwear were an integral part of the retail landscape. For their seasonal clearance sales, C. M. Ross placed regular full-page newspaper advertisements, which gave a price reduction and a description for every item on sale. In January 1922 there was a 'DRASTIC SHOWROOM CLEARANCE', as well as sale prices for children's outfits, such as 'wash suits', 'High Grade' men's and women's footwear, women's underclothing (nightdresses, camisoles, undervests, combinations, and 'sports corsets'), veils and veilings, neckwear (collars, jabots, scarves), handkerchiefs and dress fabrics (taffeta, eolienne, bengaline, gabardine, suitings and serges).[58] Seasonal sales cleared old stock and won customer loyalty, and helped those on tight budgets.

Mail-order services were an important means of reaching outlying customers in the late nineteenth and early twentieth centuries. Initially they were available from major retailers in Wellington, the largest city in the region. For instance, fashionable goods for provincial women, including fabrics ('Black Norwich Grenadine' and 'fancy printed muslins'), readymade costumes (cambric, pique, mohair and Japanese silk), and millinery ('the latest in Ladies French Millinery Bonnets'), were supplied by mail order from James Smith Ltd, Cuba Street, Wellington.[59] Kirkcaldie & Stains Ltd also offered extensive mail-order services.[60] Newspapers initially carried such information, but later shoppers had the use of catalogues for such purchases. Those produced by Collinson & Cunninghame during the 1910s and 1920s listed an enormous range of goods: manchester,

Collars, collar studs, men's soft and hard felt hats, panama hats and straw boaters are among the items available from Collinson & Cunninghame Ltd's spring and summer 1913–14 mail order catalogue. In the early twentieth century, men were also enthusiastic consumers of stylish apparel and targets of retailers' marketing strategies. Detachable white collars were made from a wide range of materials, including linen and celluloid, as shown here, and also highly starched cotton, paper and rubber. Styles varied in the shape of the points, height, stiffness and finish. Worn in tandem with the bowler hat, they symbolised middle-class respectability. COLLINSON & CUNNINGHAME COLLECTION, TE MANAWA

linoleum and carpet, bedding, upholstered furniture, dress, ladies' underclothing, children's, fancy and foreign fancy, haberdashery, art needlework, hosiery, and clothing (in other words, menswear).[61] For each article of clothing, details of styles, fabrics, colours, fastenings, special features, available sizes and prices were given. Stylised fashion drawings were interspersed with sales advice and the occasional homily. In the store's spring and summer catalogue of 1929–30, slender female figures in girdles, brassieres and corselettes illustrate a popular notion: 'Perfect fitting corsetry is a necessity for perfect health'.[62] Clothing retailers were beginning to reach beyond the selling of products and fashions to the selling of ideas.

Window displays and shop interiors changed significantly during the early twentieth century as window dressing and interior design were professionalised. For instance, Collinson & Cunninghame crammed a gaslit window with Petone and Kaiapoi woollen wear for New Zealand Industries Week in June 1909. The window mirrored the nature of the store's interior displays. No matter which one of the many departments customers entered – from haberdashery to gents' outfitting, the ladies showroom to infantswear – they were surrounded by goods.

Petone and Roslyn Woollen Mills are represented in this New Zealand Industries Week display at Collinson & Cunninghame Ltd, June 1909. For decades retailers of men's clothing had promoted items of New Zealand manufacture, in particular boots and 'colonial' suits. As one local retailer stated in July 1888: 'Those who desire to encourage COLONIAL INDUSTRY, SAVE MONEY, And at the same time be Respectably Attired, cannot do better than invest in the first-rate TAILOR-MADE COLONIAL TWEED SUITS.' COLLINSON & CUNNINGHAME COLLECTION, 86/133/39, TE MANAWA

Stock was displayed from the ceiling cavity suspended on rails, in shelves that scaled the walls, crowding heavy, dark wooden counters, even stacked up from the floor. This was true emporium-style shopping. New retail practices brought a deliberate shift to more restrained and controlled display methods. By 1920 the store's interiors were more spaciously arranged, allowing the customer freedom of movement. There was deliberate use of display furniture, such as tables with stands for hats and glass-sided showcases housing exquisitely turned out mannequins. This tendency was boosted at the end of the decade, when pale cabinets with sleek, rounded lines and chrome fittings and plain floor coverings replaced the heavy, dark cabinets and elaborate, flowery carpets. The days of modern shopping in Palmerston North were beginning.

It is clear from photographic evidence that shopping for drapery, clothing and footwear became a more choreographed activity as retailers grew more attuned to the personal pleasures of browsing and the monetary rewards of providing an elegant environment for this to take place. With the advent of well-presented interiors, generous internal signage, good sightlines, beautiful display tables and

'Gents' Outfitting Dept.' at Collinson & Cunninghame Ltd, 1910. This department sold an array of readymade men's items, such as hats, collars, ties, shirts, jerseys, handkerchiefs, gloves, braces, belts, underwear, socks, blankets, bags, studs and links. It is comfortably – but not luxuriously or artistically – fitted out with bentwood chairs and serving counters. With the arrival of professional 'display men', such as Collinson & Cunninghame Ltd's award-winning Claude Dixon, there was a heightened sensitivity to style in shop interiors following the First World War.
COLLINSON & CUNNINGHAME COLLECTION, 86/133/66, TE MANAWA

showcases, shopping could involve less personal interaction with staff. Previously customers could not easily locate what they were after without the help of a sales assistant. Although there was now greater scope for customers to deliberate over displayed items, a staff member was never far away. These interactions were guided by commonly understood formalities, such as appropriate terms of address and the etiquette of touch and gesture involved in fittings or assessing the desirability of a garment for a customer.[63] Now clinching a sale was the underlying goal, and here the new display methods were of critical value. So, too, were sales campaigns.

These often used a combination of newspaper advertising and shop window displays. For instance, during 1915 staff at Collinson & Cunninghame were concerned that the sale of dressmaking materials was decreasing as a greater variety of readymade garments became available, so special efforts were made to regain this custom. A sales campaign – 'Any Skirt Cut Free During Sewing Week' – was organised.[64] 'Dressmaking in the home is somewhat of a decadent art,' explained Harold Vivian, the head of advertising. 'People go out more than they did, the "pictures" give folk fewer evenings at home. The increased popularity of ready-to-wears has cut into the dress goods trade very considerably.'[65] A series of advertisements in the local newspapers and a prominently dressed window were the key forms of publicity. The shop's biggest window (nearly 20 feet, or 6 metres, in length) was dressed with suitable skirt fabrics. These were ticketed with the

A display of women's daywear at C. M. Ross Co. Ltd soon after the opening of the new four-storey building on The Square in 1927. Its modern commercial aesthetic, celebrating colour, light and form, made a stunning visual impact in Palmerston North. The displays normalised the world of commodities, as well as stimulating desire. BC298, PALMERSTON NORTH CITY LIBRARY

complete cost of fabric, trimming, buttons, pattern and lining, so that 'nothing was left to the imagination of the prospective purchaser'. Two draped dummies and a female figure seated at a treadle sewing machine, 'to suggest sewing in the home', acted as eye-catchers, along with a big sign announcing 'Sewing Week'.[66] It was 'a popular-priced sales campaign', based on the assumption that 'the very best class of people would not be influenced by the idea of making up their own materials'.[67] Collinson & Cunninghame continued this particular promotion into the 1920s, when dress goods staff were pleased to observe 'the revival that is evident in home-dressmaking, for it pays to make one's own dresses'.[68]

Mannequin parades, which became more frequent in Palmerston North during the 1920s, were a measure of the acceptance of manufactured clothing by women of all social classes. By presenting such events, retailers aimed to capitalise on the combined pleasures of fashion and female sociability. For instance, Collinson & Cunninghame organised a series of mid-afternoon parades in May 1928. With live music, models displayed sixteen of the 'newest gowns for day and evening wear'. 'Daytime modes perforce go sombrely', read the programme, while 'fashion whispers secrets of the vogue for evening'. The cheapest item of day wear was 59s 6d ($235 in today's prices): 'A chic little jumper frock in leaf green kasha, with an unusual design in diamond effect in a darker shade.' The most expensive evening gown was 11 guineas ($909): 'Model evening gown in gold georgette, featuring new bouffant hip effect and uneven hemline in gold lace. This smart frock is a Parisian creation.'[69] These prices were affordable only to women in Palmerston North's middle and upper income brackets. The shows revolved around the lure of products from five European fashion centres: Paris, Vienna, London, Nice and Milan. New Zealanders regarded Europe as the centre of culture and sophistication.

Events like this reveal the extent to which fashion could be a sensual and social pleasure. The eye might be charmed by combinations of colours ('so wondrous an alliance as apricot and lettuce green'), fabrics ('larkspur shot taffeta with appliqued insets of gold lace') and styles ('Vandyked hem', 'beaded panels'), just as the ear might be beguiled by the music.[70] The advertising staff addressed the women who attended these parades as 'devotees', not 'customers'. While this term encompassed shared interests, lifestyles and incomes, it also allowed a tasteful distance from the commercial imperatives of the store. Shopping for clothes was a form of recreation to be enthusiastically followed. Whether the participants bought any items of clothing or not, such events were a social outlet where they could share anecdotes and intimacies, or laugh and grumble as they chose. Retailers anticipated that the combination of female sociability and slick presentation would encourage these women to buy fashionable ready-made garments. Celanese (synthetic) silk hose were offered as sale items, and may have provided for women who did not have the means to pay for more expensive items. Those with the necessary time and skills to make cheaper, home-made versions of these high fashion garments, may have been inspired by such shows to select suitable materials. As Wendy Gamber has explained, 'The victory of mass production and large-scale retailing . . . was neither instantaneous nor absolute.'[71]

Emily Mildon goes shopping

Emily Mildon's clothing accounts provide extraordinary insight into one woman's clothes shopping habits over many years. Born Emily Whitley, the only daughter of an Auckland kauri gum broker, general merchant and importer, she came to live at a Kairanga farm, west of Palmerston North, on her marriage to Percy Mildon in 1905. A petite and pretty woman, Mildon had been accustomed to a considerable luxury in her clothing. Her accounts, which date from 1913, show a precise pattern in her clothes shopping. Of the three big stores operating in Palmerston North, it was C. M. Ross that gained her faithful custom for everyday purchases. She bought a wide range of clothing, footwear, fabric and furnishings from this general drapery, furnishing and boot emporium. These purchases ranged from buttons at 2d ($1.32) each in 1913 to an ermine necklet at £7 17s 6d ($640) in 1923. On most occasions she purchased more than one item. Many shopping trips involved buying both clothing and furnishings, especially in 1924, a boom year in farm production, when the Mildon home was extensively

Emily Mildon was photographed wearing this salmon pink dress before her marriage in 1905. It is in the collection of Te Manawa. The bodice has a sweetheart neckline decorated with cream guipure lace edged with an embroidered leaf motif and pink, yellow and green glass gems. Artificial flowers add to the effect. The lightly boned bodice laces at the back. The waistband of the skirt measures only 20 inches (51 cm) around. Pintucked like the bodice, the skirt has a deep flounce, trimmed with bands of needlelace, and a small train. Its stiff white cotton lining has dust ruffles to protect the outer fabric. RICHARD AND GERALDINE MILDON

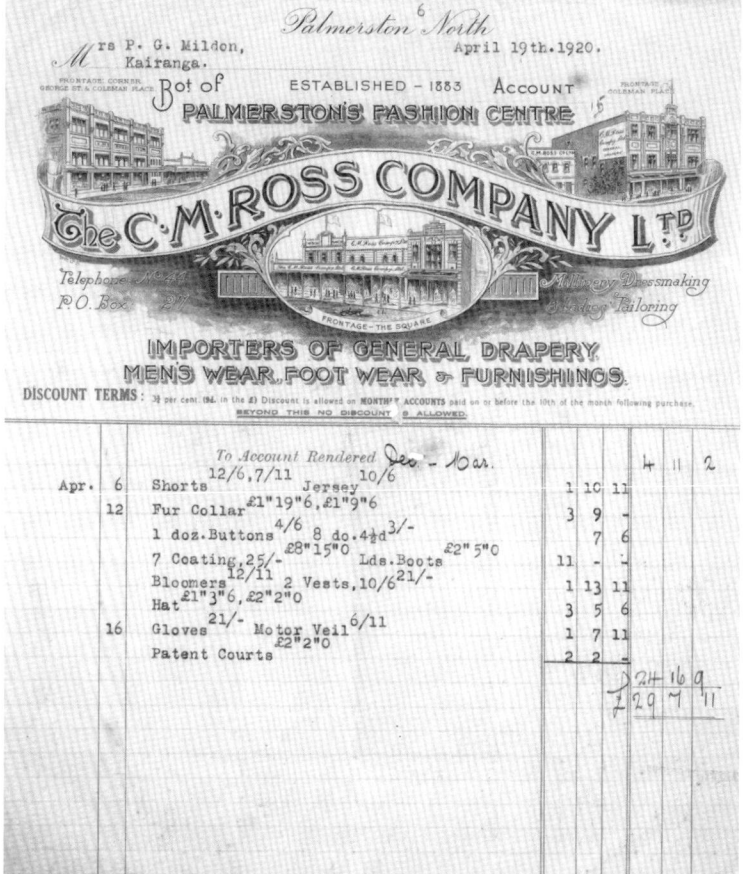

Emily Mildon's invoice from C. M. Ross Co. Ltd for April 1920 shows purchases of dressmaking items, including a fur collar, coating and buttons, as well as underwear and accessories. It is likely that the shorts and jersey were for her two sons. The family had recently purchased a two-seater Swift that she never learned to drive, hence the purchase of a 'motor veil'. RICHARD AND GERALDINE MILDON

remodelled and enlarged. Mildon regarded C. M. Ross as the best local source of everyday clothing and household items. Although she paid for dressmaking materials, Emily Mildon is not known to have sewn her own clothes or to have owned a sewing machine.

During the 1920s Mildon was a regular customer of dressmaker Madame de Luen. It was from her rooms in Coleman Place, directly opposite C. M. Ross, that she bought many of her more luxurious items of clothing. Elizabeth de Luen (formerly McDonald) had married into an established tailoring family, but ran her own business in premises handy to those of her husband, Arthur de Luen, on The Square.[72] Most of Mildon's purchases appear to have been custom made, such as a dinner frock costing £16 16s ($1250) in 1920, but others were not, confirming the need for dressmakers to supplement their incomes by stocking off-the-rack items, owing to the competitive pricing and convenience of the big stores. This, along with the deliberate provision of a place to rest, is revealed in an

Elizabeth Macaulay and Charles Thompson on their wedding day, 21 August 1929. Madame De Luen made the bride's loose-fitting cream silk dress. It has a scooped neckline, three-quarter-length sleeves, a slightly dropped waist and a draped skirt. Now in Te Manawa's collection, the dress is made from a delicate ivory silk georgette, and with great precision. Silver lamé lines the bias-cut frills on the sleeves and forms the large bow at the left hip. The skirt was cut in one piece, a large oval, which falls into an uneven hemline dipping at each side. This garment demonstrates the dramatic move towards comfort and simplicity in women's clothing by the 1920s. Charles Thompson wore an evening suit, providing the usual dark contrast to the lightness and brightness of the bride. BEV THOMPSON

advertisement: 'LADIES! You will certainly be charmed if you visit MADAME DE LUEN'S upstairs salon, where Adorable Gowns, Lingerie, Etc., are on view. You may come up and rest, it is so secluded, and you will not be pressed to buy.'[73] Occasionally Mildon was completely outfitted by Madame de Luen, for instance on three visits in one week during February 1922 she was supplied with a georgette frock, a cream coat frock, two singlets, an underskirt, two pairs of knickers, a corset and a dressing gown. The bill for that month amounted to £43 12s 6d ($3375). On other occasions the bill was much more modest, for instance an alteration to a frock for £1 5s ($98) in October 1924.

Madame de Luen and her staff were particularly busy in good years on the Mildon farm, though this extra income may have made Mildon, or possibly her husband, careless with payments. Madame de Luen wrote on an overdue account in March 1922: 'Very many thanks for your kind response, regret having to ask, but my Bank Manager is very exacting'. This apparently straightforward comment speaks volumes about the relationship between dressmakers and their clients. Cutting and fitting anything from a frock to a pair of knickers automatically narrowed any personal distance between a dressmaker, her staff and a client, particularly a regular one like Mildon. The dressmaker often had to maintain a delicate balancing act between managing the financial requirements of her business and continuing cordial relations, even a level of friendship, with her clients.[74] A bank manager could be usefully deployed both as an alter ego and as an ally. Dressmakers were dependent on these clients for their livelihood, and this was especially the case for Madame de Luen after her husband retired from business in the early 1920s.[75] Although Mildon had other options for her choice of dressmaker in Palmerston North, she did business only with Madame de Luen.

Mildon did not restrict herself to shopping for clothes in Palmerston North. Trips to Wellington, usually made in April or May, involved visits to some of that city's more exclusive retailers, such as F. N. Spackman, Hayward Ltd and Miss Mainwaring, as did trips to visit her family in Auckland. Many of the items were expensive, such as an evening frock bought from Epsom dress specialist Elsie Ginn, in February 1926. It cost £18 10s ($1414). Luxury clothing may have given some solace to a woman who was by now unhappily married, but there is also ample evidence of Mildon having clothing altered and remodelled.[76] For example, in September 1926, she went to Henry Blandford, a manufacturing furrier and owner of what was expected to be 'one of Palmerston's leading industries in the near future', for alterations to a black fur coat.[77] Her clothing accounts give a sense of carefully chosen, much enjoyed garments that were worn well. But her expensive purchases kept her at some distance from a rural community that she found 'scarcely to her taste'.[78] Her husband's farming life was unsatisfying to this city-born woman, whose elegance is seen in family photographs. A reversed purchase made for Mildon by her husband Percy from Whitley & Sons, her father's firm, gives the sense of a mismatched pair. In August 1925 he ordered a 7s 9d ($30) bed jacket that was immediately exchanged for a kimono costing £9 ($704) or 23 times as much.

Although we know when and where Mildon shopped, what she purchased and how much she spent, with the exception of possible cash purchases, her personal motivations can only be guessed at. Her shopping patterns show a remarkable degree of loyalty to particular clothing retailers. She dressed in both custom and readymade clothing, and in this way bridged not only old and new forms of clothes shopping, but also exclusive and popular types of clothing. Her frequent purchases over many years leave us with the impression of a woman who bought clothes as an enjoyable leisure activity and a means of upholding her social identify and status. The sustained pleasure of selecting fabrics, attending fittings and waiting for a unique garment to materialise in a dressmaker's salon was a perfect foil to the immediate gratification of an off-the-rack purchase. Although Mildon lived most of her life in the small farming settlement of Kairanga, she did not consider herself socially or psychologically part of that community. Clothing was an effective means of defining herself as more affluent and metropolitan than her neighbours.

The consumption of clothing is an expression of specific needs and desires and has an important effect on individual lives and social relationships.[79] As the rawness of early settlement diminished, and the needs and expectations of the predominantly Pākehā residents of Palmerston North and its surrounding districts became more varied and complex, so did the operations of retailers. Beyond the virtues of the articles themselves, which at first rested on sheer availability, quality and value for money, there were new layers of expectation that had as much to do with modernity and leisure as class and gender. Whether men bought a 'Colonial-made' flannel undershirt in the 1870s, or a 'motoring hat' half a century later, they were in fact buying more than the article in hand; they were buying ideas. Likewise, when women bought a 'trimmed bonnet' or 'filmy stockings', they too were acquiring notions about who they were, or wanted to be, concepts that went to the very heart of their sense of being. Whether or not these items were 'just the thing', at point of purchase and in wear they were a vital part of the economic and social fabric of the province, and as such, always more than 'just a thing'.

10. On the Beach: Or the 'Unbearable Scandal' of Shrinking Swimwear

Caroline Daley

Once upon a time there was a Bathing Suit which differed from all its associates, for it was modest. It was much distressed at being so much talked about and caricatured in the papers . . . No one would believe that a retiring disposition could belong to a bathing suit, and it was merely laughed at for its attempted vindication of its character.

But after thinking for a very long time on a possible course of action, it remembered that everyone called the violet modest, and determined to go and ask the little flower what it did to get up such an international reputation. So the Bathing Suit came to the Violet and asked it the momentous question, 'What do you do to make people all call you modest?'

The Violet dropped her pretty head, and softly answered, 'I shrink!'

So the Bathing Suit went away and began to shrink, and the more it shrank the more it got itself talked about, until at last there was an unbearable scandal.[1]

THE UNBEARABLE SCANDAL OF SHRINKING SWIMWEAR WAS AN ENDURING story in twentieth-century New Zealand. It was a tale that could be told about bathing suits for any summer up to the 1960s. By then local women were baring all in bikinis small enough to be threaded through a wedding ring and men were sauntering down the beach in Speedos that left little to the imagination.[2] Bathing suits had shrunk to almost nothing. But the story of the Bathing Suit and the shrinking Violet was not written in the 1960s. It appeared in the *Graphic* in 1904, when outfits such as the pink serge bathing costume with a coarse guipure insertion opposite (left), or white serge with scarlet silk stitching and matching sash (centre) or navy with contrasting white braid, were worn by society ladies. Given that only a few years before women apparently wore corsets under their bathing costumes and each bathing suit required a dozen yards of fabric, was full-skirted and incorporated long bloomers, 1904's jaunty little outfits were indeed a scandalous, shrunken version of their Victorian counterparts.[3]

Exploring how and why swimwear shrank so far and so fast is in part a tale of technological innovation: new fabrics allowed for lighter, tighter outfits that

Three costumes for fashionable Edwardian ladies. Still better suited for promenading than bathing or swimming, such outfits would soon be replaced by one-piece swimsuits that bared more than arms and lower legs. NEW ZEALAND GRAPHIC, 30 JANUARY 1904, P. 67

would make any shrinking violet wish that the beach would swallow her up. It is also a tale of changing social and cultural values and habits – of consumption, modernity, and understandings of gender that challenged conventions. Most of these stories are not peculiar to New Zealand. The outfits worn on local beaches were imported from the major manufacturers of Australia and the United States, or made locally to international designs. The debates that raged about indecent costumes worn at beaches in New Brighton, Lyall Bay and Ponsonby were echoes of arguments heard in Bondi, Blackpool and Ocean Grove, New Jersey.[4] These arguments were never about all beach-goers. Many of those who took to the sand and waves paid little attention to what they wore. But for those who tried to be in the vanguard of fashion swimwear took on increased importance as the century progressed. It is through their stories that we can see how New Zealand was part of a wider world of fashion and 'scandal' and how New Zealanders both endured and enjoyed their rapidly shrinking swimwear.

The first of these local stories takes place in the early years of the twentieth century, when a new emphasis on health and physical culture swept the country. Going to the beach to swim, rather than for a picnic and a paddle, suited this changing climate. All summer, at beaches around New Zealand, surf bathers took to the waves, safe in the knowledge that, should their aquatic prowess let them down, newly formed surf lifesaving clubs had the rescue reel at the ready.[5]

Despite the dangers of the surf, bathing at the beach was touted as being far more beneficial than wallowing in the foetid water of a swimming pool. As the waves crashed around them and the sun bronzed their pale flesh, beach-goers could breathe in the fresh sea air and treat their bodies to an invigorating, healthful experience that was not possible in the stifling city. Of course, most New Zealanders did not live in cities at the time, and these hardly seem to have bustled, but this did not prevent contemporaries from worrying about the harmful effects of urban life. Standing on the sand and stripping off the claustrophobic clothes of the city, they could make themselves anew.[6]

This new self, in its bathing suit and little else, worried local authorities. Some, fearing the effect of bodies cavorting in the surf, went so far as to prohibit sea swimming during daylight hours.[7] Others tried to prevent mixed sea bathing: in council-run swimming pools no such behaviour was allowed.[8] Most passed by-laws imposing strict swimwear regulations on beach goers. Dark, neck-to-knee bathing suits had to be worn in the sea. These might be one-piece bathing suits, similar to the combination underwear recently adopted by men. Unlike men's underwear, though, these neck-to-knee outfits were navy or black, often with a stripe or two. Some had sleeves, but many swimmers preferred a sleeveless version.[9] A number of councils required men to wear trunks under or over the one piece for added protection. Other swimmers, including many women, wore 'Canadian costumes', woollen knickers that came well down the thighs with a guernsey top. (These were sometimes called 'Colonial bathing costumes'.)[10] When swimmers were not in the water their bodies had to be covered. Councils seemed to think that raincoats offered an appropriate form of covering as swimmers made their way down to the waves.[11] Sunbathing before or after a swim was regarded as 'loitering' so was not allowed, and despite the fact that few beaches had adequate changing sheds, swimmers were forbidden from disrobing on the beach.

Such regulations are a perfect fit with the idea that early twentieth-century New Zealand was a puritanical, repressed, 'tight' society, where healthful leisure might be allowed but pleasure was strictly off-limits.[12] But this fit is about as snug as a woollen bathing suit after a few dips in the briny. Neck-to-knee swimwear soon lost its shape. With a little interrogation the idea that New Zealand was a tight society also begins to sag.

The costume by-laws that may strike us as ridiculous were not unique to New Zealand. In Australia, the United States, Britain and in various other parts of the world, beach-goers were being told to wear raincoats on the beach and warned that if the leg of their bathing suit was more than 3 inches above their knee they would be removed from the beach and fined for the offence.[13] If New Zealand was repressed then so was much of the Western world. But should the presence of such regulations be understood as actual repression? In New Zealand, as elsewhere, these rules seem to have been as annoying to beach-goers as the itchy woollen bathing suits they were meant to wear. Everywhere swimmers challenged such regulations, and in most places they succeeded in changing beach-going, and eventually the by-laws associated with it.

A few hardy souls decided that any form of swimwear was unnatural and undesirable. They literally stripped off at the beach, much to the astonishment of those around them. Passengers on a boat leaving Onehunga were said to have been surprised by the sight of men bathing off the wharf in 'scanty attire' and shocked by those who had not even bothered to put on trunks, let alone a bathing suit. But while the *New Zealand Herald* was indignant about such behaviour, *Truth* thought it was time for New Zealand to get used to Trilby's 'altogether'.[14] As *Truth* noted, 'society "wimmin" in the dress circles of theatres' wore fewer clothes than was allowed on our beaches.[15]

It was some years before any beach in New Zealand was designated 'free', or clothing optional, but even before the Great War beach-goers were seeing how much give there was in bathing by-laws. Their first tug at the regulations came courtesy of swimwear manufacturers. By 1909 it was impossible to buy council-approved neck-to-knee bathing suits. Legs of swimwear had already crept higher and necks scooped lower than local body regulations stipulated.[16] Swimmers wore outfits described as having 'a distinctly Continental cut and texture', that is, swimwear that was tighter and briefer than some thought proper. Although they were 'elegant', some onlookers regarded them as 'scarcely sufficient or decent'.[17] When swimmers emerged from the waves wearing garments that 'would put to shame an uncivilized South Sea Islander', letters to the editor inevitably followed.[18]

But the howls of complaint were barely heard above the crashing waves on the beach. Swimmers seem to have decided that the by-laws were there to be breached. Not only did they buy the new continental costumes, but they pushed back the wool and cotton covering their bodies. At Takapuna it was common to see men roll up the legs of their costumes and fold down the top so that they could lie in the sand 'in as near a state of nature as they very well can'.[19] In Napier men went further, lying on the shingle of Marine Parade with nothing more than a towel over their hips.[20] The 'modern woman', too, was no longer satisfied with the 'voluminous ill-fitting garment, [and] its attendant "sponge-bag" cap' of previous years. She wanted to copy her 'Continental cousins' and wear a sleek, tight-fitting outfit.[21] Such breaches of the by-laws shocked some. They were appalled by the 'young men who swagger up and down the beach in inadequate costumes, talking loudly and using indecent language'.[22] They worried about the 'blackguard' surf bathers who lolled 'semi-nude' on the beach, 'basking their naked bodies in the sun like human alligators watching for their prey'.[23] But for every defender of neck-to-knee bathing suits there was an advocate for continental swimwear. 'Baldhead', for example, was annoyed with puritans who wanted swimmers to wear 'a coat and pants of corrugated iron'. He could think of nothing better than for 'healthy, jolly girls, full of life, to be gambolling on a beach, or strong, well-made athletes

At fashionable Milford and Takapuna, councillors conceded that they had lost the battle of the bathing costume, allowing Miss 1927 to wear her sleek, one-piece suits. Not all local bodies were so accommodating. They continued to insist that Canadian costumes were worn despite beach-goers choosing American, 'Coney Island' suits instead. AUCKLAND STAR, 22 OCTOBER 1927, P. 12

"The beach inspector has recommended the wearing of the 'Coney Island' bathing suit at Takapuna and Milford beaches." This was adopted at a meeting of the Takapuna Borough Council this week, and Misses Takapuna and Milford both say that the inspector is a perfect dear.

to run about with bathing trunks only'.[24] 'The Altogether or Not at All' agreed that the sight of 'glistening skin' was 'far more attractive' than saggy woollen bathing suits. Lamenting that not all of the women had the shape of Venus, he nonetheless enjoyed watching women in fitted swimwear that 'display[s] every lovely curve and crease as the sportive mermaids rear themselves to the embrace of Father Neptune, or as they race along the sands like Dryads of our dreams, or sprawl out alongside an Adonis for a flirtation and a sunbath'.[25]

Many beach-goers, of course, wore regulation swimwear. For them the minor irritation of an itchy woollen bathing suit was nothing compared with the healthful experience of plunging into the sea. But for those who saw the beach as a site for pleasure as well as healthful leisure, and for those who followed the fashion pages of local magazines, it was clear that swimwear had to shrink. Their understanding of what was meant by a 'modest costume' was quite different from the wowsers' notion of modesty. Those differences only grew as bathing suits continued to shrink in the interwar years.

During the 1920s and 1930s swimwear shrank even further, but rather than being an unbearable scandal, beach-goers braved their opponents and enjoyed baring even more of their bodies on the beach. By the mid-1930s the consensus seems to have been that '[a]s bathing costumes grow less, so does the opposition to their styles shrink'.[26] Councils still clung to their bathing suit by-laws as members of a tight, puritanical society should, but they knew they had lost the battle of the beaches. Sun and sea bathers wanted a tight costume, not a tight society, and thanks to the wonders of a revolutionary new form of liquid elastic, Lastex, their wish was granted.

A stroll along the sands of New Zealand in the 1920s and 1930s offered the beachcomber a much more colourful sight than before the First World War. Alongside the swimmers in their regulation, dark one- and two-piece bathing suits were costumes of sea blue and sand yellow.[27] 'A beach thronged with bathers is as bright a spectacle as a ball-room', enthused one journalist in 1925.[28] Even those who continued to wear dark swimwear lightened their outfits with colourful accessories. A white cap with 'bright colored discs resembling confetti' turned a drab black bathing suit into a fun beach ensemble.[29]

Hollywood can take much of the credit (or blame) for New Zealand women sauntering along the sands of Sumner in a 'mimosa colored suit... with a woolen cape of the same shade, with white and black stripes to match the top of the costume'.[30] Locals flocked to films such as *The Venus Model*, which featured stars modelling the latest style of swimwear.[31] They pored over photographs of Hollywood stars in their bathing suits, reproduced in local newspapers.[32] They filled the theatre when Annette Kellerman, the champion swimmer and 'movie queen', dived into a glass-fronted tank on stages around New Zealand and 'performed wondrous feats in the water' clad in a 'tightly fitted golden costume'.[33] As *Truth* noted in 1929, 'where Hollywood leads the rest of the world soon follows'.[34]

On beaches around the Western world a new, post-war hedonism and consumerism clung to beach-goers in a way that no pre-war bathing suit could. The Portland Knitting Company deserves much of the credit for this. During the war this American company bought knitting machines that produced a lighter knit with good elasticity, allowing it to make swimwear that hugged the body. Relaunched in 1918 as the Jantzen Knitting Mills, they spearheaded the move to tighter, sleeker outfits.[35] Whether New Zealanders wore imported Jantzens or bathing suits made locally by Roslyn, elastic rib weave now clung snugly to their bodies.[36]

Fashionable bathing suits of the 1920s were one-piece sleeveless outfits. The necks were scooped, the legs inched ever higher and they came in a bright array of colours, often with a contrasting belt (helping to mark swimwear off from

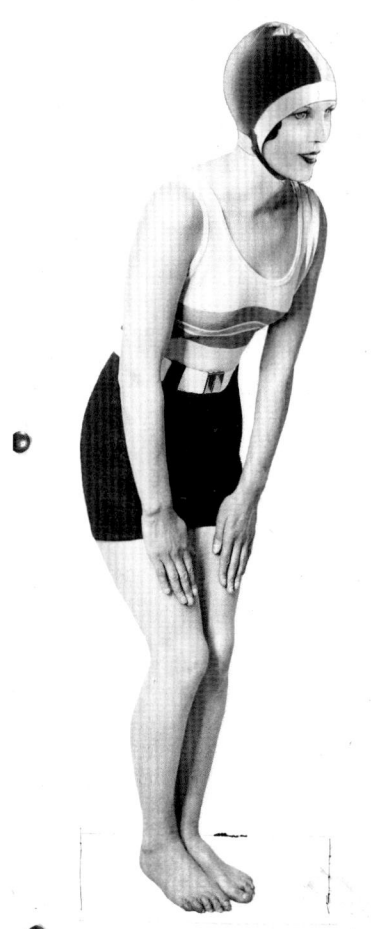

Photographed around 1930, this young model epitomised the modernity of interwar swimwear: her outfit was as streamlined as her body, and her cap matched her costume. 1/1-015770, GORDON BURT COLLECTION, ALEXANDER TURNBULL LIBRARY, WELLINGTON, NEW ZEALAND

combination underwear). These were the outfits worn by men and women alike.[37] As contemporaries and subsequent commentators have noted, the beach allowed women a 'freedom' that they were denied elsewhere.[38] On the beach women were able to bare more flesh, wear brighter colours and experiment with risqué fashions such as trousers and shorts. But what is often overlooked is that the beach also provided men with a welcome opportunity to throw off the shackles of the city. They wore bathing suits in a 'variety of colours and designs', some opting for 'creations' of 'crushed strawberry ... with mauve and orange stripes', others for green and yellow costumes. Such outfits led to speculation: 'one sometimes wonders if the costumes seen at the fashionable bathing places are family affairs, made to suit girls and boys alike. In some cases one sees a youth going down to the water with a party of girls, and if he wore a bathing cap he would certainly be the most gaudily-attired lady of the party.'[39] Within a couple of years the androgynous nature of modern bathing suits was being celebrated: 'The latest costume on the market consists of a smart pair of shorts, a colored belt and a smart, multi-colored top. This has the effect of lending trim boyishness to feminine figures and neatness to manly figures. It should be universally adopted.'[40] When Speedo was launched in Sydney in 1928 it adopted a universal, androgynous, knitted cotton suit. Men, women and children wore the same style.[41] On the beach, clearly demarcated gender roles and expectations were blurred, thanks to the universal one-piece.

Even the assumption that women bought into consumer culture in a way that their menfolk did not needs to be reassessed at the beach. Before the war women were encouraged to accessorise their seaside outfits. No self-respecting woman went down to the shore without shoes and stockings and a beach wrap, and many added hats and parasols to that list.[42] Through the 1920s they gradually discarded their stockings, only to replace them with 'fancy rubber shoes' in bright hues, colourful sleeveless towelling wraps and rubber caps adorned with roses.[43] They 'woke up' their faces with Palmolive soap and sea breezes, and soothed their sun-tinged skin with Sydal.[44] Along with changing her bathing suit each season – so that she was in the latest colour and design – the fashionable woman of the 1930s bought beach shoes, hats, bags, wraps and sun umbrellas and followed Hollywood's lead, putting 'liquid polish' on her toenails.[45] Some took to beach pyjamas and bathingjams (a combination of a bathing suit and beach pyjamas), only to replace them the next season with shorts; others preferred tight-fitting rubber suits.⁴⁶ But this consumerism was not limited to women. Advertisers also targeted beach-going men. Jantzen warned them that they would feel 'shabby' if they did not replace last season's bathing suit with the latest fashion.⁴⁷ Men's magazines noted that the modern man needed a beach wrap, sandals and a towel to match his new swimwear. And no self-respecting man could settle for only one bathing suit per season: the recommendation was three or four outfits, each with a matching beach shirt.⁴⁸ Even the Prime Minister, George Forbes, was spotted at mannequin parades, looking at the latest swimwear (next page).

Both men and women were consumed by the increasing commercialisation of the beach. Their purchases were part of the pleasure of beach-going but they were also motivated (and perhaps justified) by changes in technology and new scientific revelations about the healthful properties of sunlight. In the early 1930s the manufacture of elastic thread was revolutionised, thanks to the newly discovered properties of liquid latex. Manufacturers could now make elastic thread of the same fine gauge and length as other threads. In 1931 Lastex hit the market: a core of rubber was covered by at least two other yarns, allowing swimwear to be even more figure-hugging.⁴⁹ Jantzen renamed Lastex 'Sunsheen' and launch a new slogan: 'A Jantzen Fits as Though Painted on You'.⁵⁰ Lastex costumes cost more than most other knitted bathing suits, but for those who could not afford them new knit structures allowed for cheaper outfits with mesh and lace patterns. Sewing cotton bathing suits with elastic thread added stretch to these outfits and made them easier to mould to body contours.⁵¹ Consumers were told that buying at least one new bathing suit each season was essential given that the very fabric they were made of changed from year to year. For the fashion-conscious it was a poor show if, even in Depression-era New Zealand, you still had to knit your own backless swimwear.⁵²

Lastex is credited with helping to make topless suits for men popular; trunks made from Lastex held their shape and gave men support in ways that elastic knit weave could not.⁵³ But even more important than manufacturing know-how in this development was the growing awareness of the restorative powers of sunlight. Since the late nineteenth century a number of scientists and doctors

Despite the Depression, Bill was not prepared to 'pay in self-consciousness' when it came to his bathing suit. With his matching towel and confident hand on hip, he was perfectly suited in his Jantzen. TRUTH, 7 NOVEMBER 1934, P. 15

CORRECT BEACH ATTIRE

During a visit to London the Rt Hon. G. W. Forbes, Prime Minister, studied 'correct beach attire' at a fashion display. The new season outfit for 'Georgette', as Kennaway the cartoonist preferred to call him, was appropriately accessorised.
TOMORROW, 31 JULY 1935, P. 15

had argued for the healing properties of the sun, but it was not until the interwar era that deliberately getting a suntan became not just fashionable, but the mark of a responsible citizen. Alongside the health-giving properties of swimming and the sea air beach-goers now knew about the benefits of ultra-violet light and vitamin D. Sunbathers could tell themselves that they were not basking on the beach because they enjoyed the feeling of the sun on their skin; they were baking their bodies for the sake of the nation.[54]

Whatever rationale they used, through the 1920s and into the 1930s sunbathing became the norm on New Zealand's beaches just as it did in Europe, North America and Australia. In many places it was still an offence to 'loiter' on the beach in this way, but that did not stop the sunbakers. Their bathing suits and beach outfits, though, did prevent the rays from working their magic. Artificial silk stockings were recommended for women who still covered their legs on the beach, as they let in 'a fair proportion of the ultra-violet rays of the sun to the benefit of the wearer'. It was hoped that there would soon be artificial silk bathing suits to do likewise.[55] But for those wearing knitted swimwear, the solution was to shrink their outfit. By 1929 backless bathing suits were being worn. Following Hollywood's lead, local women exposed their backs to the sun, although whether this was prompted by health concerns or fashion sensibility is unclear. American film censorship restricted how much décolletage could be shown so Hollywood responded with backless evening gowns. Gown wearers did not want to ruin the effect with unsightly tan lines; swimming costumes thus joined evening gowns in their backless state.[56]

But going backless was not the only way that swimwear shrank in the 1930s. Early in the decade Jantzen's swimwear came with 'shouldaire strings', an innovation that allowed the straps of bathing suits to be slipped off. For women this meant shoulders could be tanned too; for men a whole new world of possibilities opened up.[57] Roslyn followed the lead and began to make swimwear with 'sunshine' backs, shoulder straps that could be dropped if the male bather wanted to tan his torso, front or back.[58] Then Jantzen advertised 'The Topper', which had a zipper band around the waist, allowing the top to be removed. 'The Sun-Suit' also had a detachable top, and its 'smart skirtless shorts' came with 'inside support'.[59] In 1935 Jockey bathing trunks appeared on the market.[60] By the end of the decade trunks had replaced the one-piece for men.[61] Men's bathing suits had not just shrunk; they had been cut in half.

 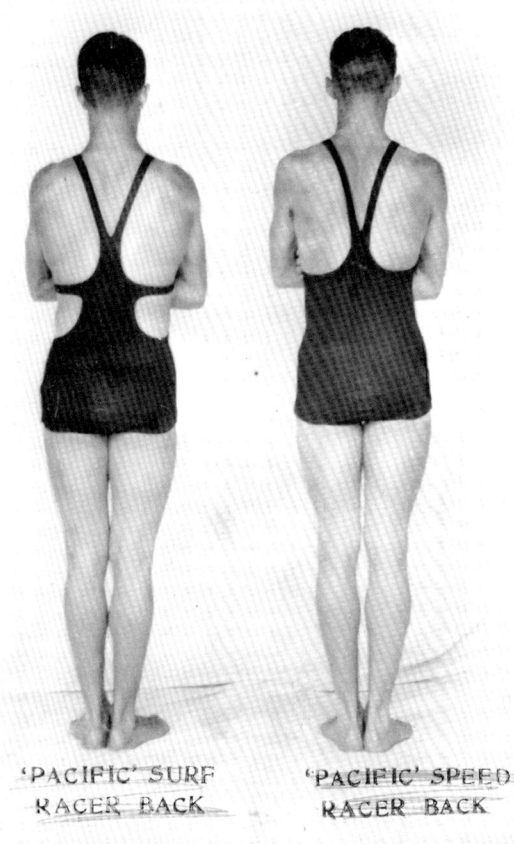

LEFT: As part of the shrinking process, holes began to appear in the sides of swimsuits, all the better to let the sun shine on the bodies of beach-goers. RIGHT: The names of the costumes indicate the vigorous, healthful exercise swimmers were encouraged to engage in, while the shoulder straps ensured that the wearers could pull down the tops of their costumes and bake their backs and chests a golden shade of brown. 1/1-015419 F AND 1/2-117909 F, GORDON BURT COLLECTION, ALEXANDER TURNBULL LIBRARY, WELLINGTON, NEW ZEALAND

Women's swimwear was also bisected. At the same time that Jockey bathing trunks appeared New Zealand women were beginning to wear shorts and brassiere tops to the beach, much to the chagrin of some local bodies.[62] The following year it was reported that women in France were wearing 'the tiniest of bassier's [sic] and brief shorts' this season. The next month a preview of new season swimwear noted that 'little two-piece suits, which don't make one ordinary garment in their entirety' were for sale locally, New Zealand manufacturers being praised for incorporating '[a]ll the latest ideas' in their costumes.[63]

The cost of these new costumes was not limited to their retail price. It had long been noted that 'men with the best figures wear well-fitting bathing raiment' unlike the 'human hairpin', who wore an old cotton costume that flopped below

Mr and Miss New Zealand 1940: the perfect beach couple. In the latest Jantzen suits (she with matching hat and shoes) this young pair radiated health and helped to restore the gender order. The androgynous suits of the past had been replaced by exposed manly chests and accentuated female breasts. In case the costumes did not speak loudly enough, the couple were posed so that his presence towered over her passive, reclining body.

1/2-036931 G, GORDON BURT COLLECTION, ALEXANDER TURNBULL LIBRARY, WELLINGTON, NEW ZEALAND

Young Greek Gods, running in a chariot race at a 1938 Piha Surf Club carnival. In late 1934 the New Zealand Surf Life Saving Association decided that trunks were acceptable beachwear, a decision these men clearly embraced. PACOLL-5469-003, ALEXANDER TURNBULL LIBRARY, WELLINGTON, NEW ZEALAND

his knees.⁶⁴ But in the days of the one-piece a man could hide a multitude of sins behind the protective shield of his bathing suit's top. Trunks, be they in new season stripes or checks, left manly bosoms permanently exposed, both to the sun and the critical gaze of other beach goers. If their bodies did not measure up, trunks wearers became the butt of jokes and cartoons. Echoing eugenic concerns about who was fit to marry whom, it was even suggested that a 'licensing' system should be put in place: only the 'Young Greek Gods' should be allowed to wear them.⁶⁵ Help was at hand though. Torso-toning exercises were offered to help men 'a little under the Apollo standard'.⁶⁶

Women's bodies had been under intense scrutiny long before two-pieces went on sale. Before the Great War the mayor of New Brighton had referred to women beach-goers as 'pigs', suggesting that their bodies were not a welcome sight. Once women adopted tighter, one-piece knit costumes, 'plump' girls were ridiculed for coming 'too far through their costumes'.⁶⁷ Expectations of bodily perfection grew as bathing suits shrank. Although women were said to enjoy looking at what other women were wearing on the beach, it was thought 'most men' relished the opportunity of seeing what women were not wearing.⁶⁸ Not wearing much meant that diets and exercise programmes were sold to women alongside

Louis Réard is said to have sold his bikinis in a matchbox, a marketing gimmick that emphasised how tiny they were. This 1974 outfit might have required a slightly larger box, but it was still many yards of fabric short of the outfits worn only 70 years before. 1/4-021883-F, ALEXANDER TURNBULL LIBRARY, WELLINGTON, NEW ZEALAND

mustard-coloured 'cute suits, with snappy little fastenings of tassels, bows or buttons' that set off their tan and showed off their bodies.[69]

The story of the shrinking bathing suit continued in the aftermath of the Second World War. 'Brief side-laced' trunks appeared in local shops and men took to wearing 'hippies' long before the word had counter-cultural connotations. The sides of men's trunks had shrunk to the width of shoulder straps on regulation costumes: 2 inches (5 centimetres).[70] Revelations continued in the 1950s as Speedo made swimwear from nylon. The immodest 'next-to-the-skin-fitting' trunks of the late 1930s seemed like modesty itself alongside the clinging properties of nylon.[71]

The shape of women's swimwear had long reflected the changing silhouette of women's outerwear. Boyish flappers wore androgynous one-pieces; when breasts became fashionable again bras were built into backless swimwear. The 'aggressive femininity' of 1950s fashion saw frilly, 'frankly frivolous' bathing suits from Cole of California and Jantzen on sale in local stores.[72] Nylon also clung to the body of 'Miss 1950', who got by 'with a minimum of orange nylon in a two-piece affair slashed up the sides of her very brief pants'.[73] But it was the 'French style' bathing suit that brought new attention to women's bodies and beach-going attire. In October 1945 Sydneysider Patricia Niland, a Tivoli showgirl, borrowed a bikini from a local department store and wore it downtown as a publicity stunt. Her actions were recorded across the Tasman.[74] The following month the footpath outside James Smith's in Wellington was 'blocked with curious, critical crowds', eager to see the 'French style' bathing suit they had previously only read about.[75] Few wore bikinis for the next decade though. Women seem to have agreed with the *Press* that most did not have the figure to wear such revealing outfits.[76] But gradually bikinis moved from the seclusion of the back garden to the public glare of the beach. *Australasian Post* offered readers its first of many bikini-clad cover girls in 1949.[77] By 1960 *Truth* noted that bikinis were being worn 'again' this summer, and began its own tradition of cover photographs of bikini wearers.[78] In 1964 the first official swimsuit issue of *Sports Illustrated* went on sale.[79] Lastex had now been replaced by 'Fiber K', Du Pont's working name for Lycra. Stronger and more durable than previous elasticised fabrics, Lycra revealed even more of beach-goers' bodies than nylon, as did its stable mate, Spandex.[80] By the 1970s and 1980s bodies were shrink-wrapped in Lycra and Spandex swimwear, their high-cut legs and plunging necklines suggestive of both athletic and sexual prowess.[81] There was nothing modest about a man in a thong or a woman experimenting with Rudi Gernreich's monokini.

Many who have written about the history of clothing have ignored swimwear. Few analytical studies of bathing suits have been published, even in the journals dedicated to the history of fashion.[82] Yet swimwear design is closely linked to changing general fashion. Bathing suit manufacturers rapidly adopted (and adopt) new techniques and fabrics, and some of the most famous names of twentieth-century western fashion designed swimwear.[83] The modest Bathing Suit of the *Graphic*'s 1904 story, with its 'retiring disposition', was hardly a high-fashion item but it deserves to be considered, along with Lastex, nylon and Lycra swimwear, as part of the evolving history of bathing suits.

The invention of new fabrics and techniques allowed for significant changes to swimwear through the twentieth century, but this does not explain why so many beach-goers were so quick to adopt the new, shrinking swimwear and why their shouldaire strings and side laces so outraged others. The rapidly shrinking swimsuit is intimately associated with the bodily fixations of the twentieth century. In the 'tight society' were those who opposed any bathing suit reform. New Zealand has a long record of passing legislation designed to bring moral order to the nation.[84] Not surprisingly, then, some councils appointed inspectors to patrol beaches and remove those wearing objectionable swimwear. In other instances the police were called upon to arrest those whose bathing suits had shrunk beyond the limits of local body tolerance. These are the stories we have come to expect from our history books. But for an increasing number of beach-goers shrinking swimwear was not an 'unbearable scandal': they enjoyed baring their bodies each summer, and the changing fashions and fabrics of swimwear meant that their 'tight' society came courtesy of Lastex and Lycra rather than legislation. In the name of good health and fun they flouted bathing suit by-laws and embraced the growing consumerism associated with the beach. These are not the accounts that historians have usually provided, which may tell us more about the authors than about the past.

Whether they endured or enjoyed the shrinking swimwear of the twentieth century, New Zealanders were not alone in these bathing suit debates. There is little that is 'national' about this story. Regardless of where in the world they were worn, bathing suits shrank, and shrank rapidly, over the twentieth century. An unbearable scandal to some, many down on the beach bore up under the glare of sun and public scrutiny, and enjoyed sashaying down the sands in the latest summer swimwear.

11. Dressing for War: Glamour and Duty in Women's Lives During the Second World War

Deborah Montgomerie

O**N 9 JULY 2005, AS PART OF THE CEREMONIES COMMEMORATING THE** sixtieth anniversary of the end of the Second World War, Queen Elizabeth unveiled a memorial honouring British women's contribution to the 1939–45 war effort. Located in central London, near the Cenotaph, the 7-metre-high bronze sculpture by John Mills features items of wartime clothing. The well-worn overalls, smocks and uniforms draped on pegs around a rectangular block evoke their owners obliquely. The memorial can be interpreted in many ways. It pays tribute to women's wartime efforts but also alludes to the facelessness and anonymity of home front labourers in standard war histories. Artistic conventions, which use a female body draped in classical robes to personify nationalist symbols and ideas – such as Britannia, Zealandia, the French Marianne, and America's Lady Liberty – are honoured only in the breach: here we have garments but no bodies, realism not abstraction. The monument could also be read as prefiguring the way in which the wartime generation, now elderly, is steadily passing away, leaving their old clothes and other material traces for their heirs to deal with. The Queen, herself the proud owner of an Auxiliary Territorial Service uniform, expressed the wish that the sculpted clothing would cause passers-by to ask themselves: 'What sort of women were they?' and look to history for answers. 'I love this monument', declared Baroness Betty Boothroyd, the former Speaker of the House of Commons and patron of the memorial fund. 'It depicts the women's working clothes and how they quietly took them off at the end of the day, hung them up and let men take the credit.'[1] The form of the memorial did not please all veterans. A statue of servicewomen, Georgina Hebb argued, would be 'much more appropriate than a line of coats and hats'. Eighty-year-old Jean Crawley, an ex-member of the British Auxiliary Territorial Services, disgustedly termed it a 'memorial for cloakroom attendants'.[2]

Memorialising the Second World War as a drab time misses the fact that many women, particularly those who were young in the early 1940s, associate the war with excitement and glamour not just duty and service. How one dressed for war was an important, consuming question. Tin hats, khaki uniforms and factory smocks capture part of the history of women at war – war was hard graft and women did their share – but alongside the workaday garb we need to peg up some other items: jaunty hats, evening skirts sewn from parachute silk or curtain material, bridal veils, fox furs and smartly tailored suits. What does it mean to acknowledge that the women remembered for wartime sacrifice, productivity and efficiency were investing considerable effort (and hard-earned cash) on millinery, ballgowns and bridal wear? Looking at some culturally loaded fripperies – stockings, hats, bridal wear, evening wear and military uniforms – shows how considerations of service and duty need to be balanced with ideas about glamour and duty if we are to fully understand the way women negotiated the terrain of war.

Dress was one of the most important ways women had of differentiating themselves from men and from each other. Clothes expressed a range of meanings. Most notably, they signalled social position and gender difference. The war did not erase class or racial difference – there continued to be considerable differences between the dress codes of Māori and Pākehā women, rural and urban women, working-class, middle-class and self-styled 'society' ladies – but this chapter's principal focus is on considerations uniting the various female dress codes. Even if few women could attain the fashionable heights of a society hostess or a Hollywood star, fashion in this period was aspirational. Dressing up indicated and showed off a woman's status, respectability and attractiveness; dressing down was seldom desirable. Keeping in mind wartime anxieties over men and women's respective social roles, fashion took on added importance as a primary marker of gender difference. Looking good, being serious about one's contribution to the war effort and expressing one's femininity through fashion were mutually reinforcing considerations shaping the way wartime women understood their clothing choices.

On the face of it, glamour is not an obvious entry point into the sartorial history of the Second World War. When the war is talked and written about, duty, scarcity and deferred gratification are more likely to come to mind than frills and frivolity.[3] Rationing, mending and making do were all central to the experience of war, yet they do not tell the whole story. Foregrounding glamour alongside duty brings into focus a set of questions about what fashion meant during a time of national emergency, about how young women presented themselves as feminine, functional and occasionally frivolous in order to cope with change, and about the ambivalence with which women's wartime activities were regarded in the wider culture.

The war generated a range of social activities for which one might want to be smartly dressed. Indeed, as a newspaper columnist noted, many household budgets suffered because women's 'outside-the-home-activities' created a 'special problem of clothes'. Dances were a perennial favourite for fundraising and entertaining the troops, but 'war fund bridge drives, sales and markets, group meetings, entertainment street collections, and clubs entertaining visiting troops' also made 'heavy demands on the woman who would appear well-groomed and appropriately dressed on all occasions'. Thoughtful planning, wise buying and careful laundering were advised, but not a relaxation of personal standards.[4]

Supply constraints and a sense that whims could not be indulged in a time of national emergency clearly affected wartime fashion, though the shortages here were never as severe as in countries like Britain or Germany. Nor were the ideological pressures as intense. In the early years of the war the British government proposed a complete ban on cosmetic manufacture, to the horror of its female population, who argued lipstick was a mainstay of morale. The Nazi regime embarked on a concerted programme to bring back the wholesome dirndl skirt, in preference to corrupt fashions sourced from Paris or Hollywood. By 1943 clothing shortages in Germany were so extreme that ration cards were virtually useless.[5] Still, New Zealand readers were told, wily women would find ways to manage. General Goering's wife, said to have commandeered the entire 1941 collection of the House of Molyneux, might be the object of bitter envy, but French women were busy knitting their own stockings in cotton, with 'a wide rib and very open mesh', in order to continue presenting nicely turned-out ankles. Sarah Churchill, the daughter of British Prime Minister Winston Churchill, proudly paired her classic tweed suit with a silk blouse printed with the text of one of her father's speeches. 'Adaptation is the keynote of many new fashions this year', a London correspondent enthused.[6]

In New Zealand rationing of clothing, footwear and household linen began in May 1942 and continued into 1947. Unrationed items like thread, elastic and paper patterns were also in short supply. Silk stockings, already scarce in the late 1930s after the introduction of import restrictions, became famously hard to procure, as did underwear, corsets and suspenders. The Finance Minister's statement in December 1940 that women might want to consider wearing hosiery made of fine wool rather than silk triggered panic buying.[7] When rationing was introduced in April 1942, stockings were the first item of clothing to be affected. Every woman over the age of sixteen received coupons entitling her to four pairs of fully-fashioned stockings each year, though finding stockings in the shops remained a personal challenge. Schoolgirls' time-honoured strategy of disguising holes in their black stockings by using their fountain pens to colour the flesh beneath could now be claimed as a war measure.[8] Some female employees were granted permission not to wear stockings in summer, a clever few experimented with paints and dyes to stain the legs brown (often to the detriment of furnishings and other clothing) and old silk stockings were mended and cherished. Despite repeated entreaties that women adapt to wartime conditions and wear locally made cotton, wool or rayon hose, throughout the war news that silk stockings had

Wartime fashions on display, DIC store, corner of Lambton Quay and Brandon Street, Wellington, 1944. F-1/4-015034, ALEXANDER TURNBULL LIBRARY, WELLINGTON, NEW ZEALAND

arrived in the shops would draw long queues of hopeful buyers. As the Australian parliamentarian Dame Enid Lyons wryly commented, the view persisted that 'the most undistinguished ankle became a thing of beauty in silken hose, and that even the most graceful without it deteriorates into a mere joint'.[9]

Under the rationing regulations, each individual was entitled to 52 clothing coupons a year. A man's three-piece suit required sixteen coupons, a women's two-piece eleven. Fur coats were calculated at fifteen coupons, a dress at four, a long dress or dressing gown at six; a petticoat, slip or corset at three; a brassiere, suspender belt or apron at one; gloves were worth two coupons and raincoats eight.[10] Rationing limited women's ability to augment their wardrobe at will, but most New Zealand women had always been constrained by a lack of ready cash: ways could be found around the rationing system. As a journalist reported from London, 'the solution – admitted by the rationing regulations – is to subtract the difference from your husband's ration book'. By deferring the purchase of a new suit for her man, a woman could find herself in possession of coupons sufficient for four new dresses. It was a lucky married man, the writer quipped, whose wife left him enough coupons to put a shirt on his back.[11] Coupons were officially transferable within families, and unofficially traded and gifted much more widely. Utilitarian clothing was not the only clothing they bought; evening dresses and the fabric to make formal wear remained in demand. Department stores like Wellington's DIC, whose Lambton Quay display windows continued to feature ballgowns and beautiful hats right through the war, still found a market for their wares. Most fabric purchases required coupons but some were excluded.

Ingenious uses were made of muslin, canvas, curtain material, chintz, linen and other furnishing fabrics and drycleaners did brisk business dyeing curtain netting for transformation into evening wear. Servicemen stationed in the Middle East sent back presents of dressmaking material, lingerie and stockings, knowing that those sort of 'feminine trifles' would please. After 1942, American soldiers stationed in New Zealand also supplied local women with hosiery and other treats.

Fabric shortages did not automatically translate into plain tailoring and nor did using less fabric in each garment necessarily create a frumpy silhouette. There were lots of ways clever dressmakers could use even small off-cuts of fabric to spice up an outfit, and styles tailored close to the body could look very feminine. Bodices tapered down from broadly cut shoulders to outline waists and breasts. The straight, short skirts that featured in many daytime ensembles flattered slim hips and showed off shapely legs. Eve Ebbett remembered women 'thumbing their noses at the solemnity of the times' by wearing bright colours and playfully detailing their attire:

> Dirndls with shirred waists, pinafore frocks with a sash at the back, and peplums were stylish variations. Shoulder yokes and shirring or gathering at the shoulders, neckline or bust featured prominently, and V-necks, round necks, square necks, even heart-shaped necklines were all acceptable. Small Peter Pan collars and revers were also fashionable.[12]

This is not a description of a consumer culture that has abandoned ornamentation but one in which aesthetic choices were being made within a framework of scarcity. Hats provide a good example of the maintenance of an inessential fashion. As Helen Laurenson has argued in her study of mid-twentieth-century department stores, 'Millinery represented consumption at its most conspicuous', and war or no war, hats and gloves remained essential parts of the well-dressed woman's turnout.[13] Indeed, as a reporter for the *Evening Post*'s women's page commented concerning the 'fantastic fairy-tale hats' featured at Trentham Racecourse's spring meeting, 'it almost seems as if the milliners consider as their special war effort the creating of amusing nonsensical hats, guaranteed to distract the mind, if only for a moment from the grim realities of the times and to bring a smile to the most serious-minded'.[14]

Women, young and old, knew the importance of a good hat. The insouciance of wartime headgear featured in Joy Eccles' recollection: 'Hats were very much "in". They were jaunty and decorated with wispy bits of veil, worn at provocative angles mimicking soldier's berets perhaps.'[15] Margaret Brown remembered how she and some of the other young Māori women living in wartime Wellington loved to go shopping. Dressing up was part of the fun: 'in those days you wore hats'.[16] They would stop in Willis Street to buy themselves pink carnations or violets from a street vendor to add a bit more colour to their outfit. Mabel Howard, the MP for Christchurch East, fought a losing campaign for standardisation of the quality, cut and size of bloomers, pyjamas, shirts, blouses, towels, blankets, sheets and other domestic goods, claiming that standards could save material and reduce prices by 5 to 50 per cent. But even she drew the line at standardising haberdashery. Asked if millinery could be included in her bill, she was forced to concede that there 'fashion would set the standard'.[17] Even servicewomen restricted to uniform headwear and hair at least an inch above the collar found ways to jazz up their look. 'Hats were supposed to be worn straight on, but girls will be girls and they still retained their individuality and femininity with face-framing curls . . . one way of "training" the stiff felt hats, was to wet the brim and slip it on to the edge of a dressing table drawer and close the drawer overnight. When dry it curled over the face most becomingly.'[18]

The idea that beauty and feminine grace should be maintained, even in challenging circumstances, is most apparent in the stories women tell about wartime weddings. Lavish weddings were not the norm, but nor were they prohibited. Three hundred people attended Yvonne Rapley's 1941 wedding in Palmerston North's All Saints' Church, including guests from all over the country. The bride wore white organdie and Valenciennes lace, a tulle veil flowed into a train behind her and her attendants were fitted out in ice-blue crepe with circular veils.[19] Some women chose not to marry in white, but still got a special wedding outfit. 'Like many wartime brides', the *Evening Post* reported, Nancy Blundell chose 'an afternoon ensemble' for her wedding costume yet 'dressed in deep forget-me-not blue wool crepe' with a coat in the same fabric trimmed with brown squirrel lapels, and her 'blue felt toque . . . veiled in blue', she was hardly a picture of austerity.[20] The daughter of a newspaper publisher, Nancy Blundell was a 'society' bride, but women from all sorts of social backgrounds wanted to look special for their wedding. The photograph of Rangi and Riria Utiku's 1941 wedding reception at the Ritz Tea Rooms in Wellington (overleaf) shows the bride in a smart suit with a floral spray and brooch at the neck. A fashionable hat worn at a rakish angle completed the outfit.

Many weddings were organised quickly, but that did not mean that ceremony was forsaken. Dressing correctly was an important part of establishing a wedding's propriety. Jean Frances did not marry in white but used her coupons for a new day dress trimmed in white, a white hat and two-toned pumps.[21] Nell Hartley's sister Betty made a speedy decision to marry after hearing her sweetheart was off overseas. Her mother considered it poor taste to spend money on a new frock in wartime. Yet though Betty married in a 'simple street frock', she had white accessories and, thanks to the efforts of members of the local Women's Institute and Patriotic Committee, the wedding was 'a major gala event', with streamers, balloons and ferns decorating the hall and a lavish meal for 250 guests.[22]

Some servicewomen chose 'civvies' for their big day, sartorially separating their identity as a war worker from their identity as a bride. Ruth Cederman

Rangi and Riria Utiku's wedding reception, Ritz Tea Rooms, Wellington, 29 March 1941. F-1/2-180901, ALEXANDER TURNBULL LIBRARY, WELLINGTON, NEW ZEALAND

joined the Women's Royal New Zealand Naval Service on the first day its ranks opened. She married in 1944, and proud as she was of her war service, she 'wore a proper wedding frock rather than a uniform'.[23] Yet uniformed weddings had their own glamour. Peg Robertson married in Italy while stationed there with the Women's Auxiliary Army Corps (WAAC). As a friend assured Peg's mother, the bride looked ravishing:

> [We] had arranged for Peg to have her hair done at 8.30 and so she sat in the hairdresser's out of everyone's way and sewed a new Africa Star [on] Jack['s uniform]. ... she returned from the hairdresser's with immaculate and shining hair.... Peg, attired in sweet floral voile undies, sheer silk stockings and super brown shoes from Cairo was meandering around the room at 10.30 with half an hour to go.... She made me carry her bouquet, which was of deep red carnations and arranged with greenery into a small sheaf, as it made her feel conspicuous. We got into the car and drove off to St. Luke's ... she looked lovely, her eyes particularly clear and shining and her skin perfect.[24]

Like Peg Robertson, Clementine McDonald married in uniform, though in her case it was a nurse's uniform. Little feminine touches adapted it for the occasion. Her wedding photograph shows her wearing white peep-toe sandals in place of the regulation issue shoes and carrying an elaborate bouquet.

Captain Wayne Smeeton and Sister Clementine McDonald on their wedding day. C24625, AUCKLAND INSTITUTE AND MUSEUM LIBRARY

A balance had to be found between the desire to celebrate a couple embarking on a new life together and the uncertain environment in which they were launching it. When wartime conditions meant weddings were rushed or the choice of partner disconcerting to friends and family, clothing rituals were incorporated into the event itself, and the way it was remembered afterwards created a sense of legitimacy. There was no shame in borrowing a dress from a friend; indeed it was authorised by the old tradition of wearing something old, something new, something borrowed and something blue. Lending a dress, or other bridal wear, was a gesture of female solidarity and support. After Evelyn Keenan announced she was marrying an American serviceman, and marrying him that very week, her father was sleepless with worry. The ceremony had to be organised in a great hurry. 'I would have got married in ordinary clothes,' Evelyn later reminisced, 'but a friend insisted that I wear her wedding dress. We had quite a wedding – proper cake, a case of wine. It was very nice.'[25] Similarly, another young war bride had only three days' notice of her wedding date, owing to her sailor-fiancé's departure orders. The couple got a special licence and dispensation to marry in church but, proudest of all, 'I married in full bridal regalia – gown, veil, bridesmaid, the lot, and had a lovely reception at home, a miracle brought about by the generosity and willing help of all our friends.'[26] In wartime, she remembered, 'weddings were happy diversions from day-to-day life' and dressing up helped mark them off as special. The flurries of female excitement accompanying them are indicative of one of the central reasons many women maintained an interest in fashion. Female clothing rituals were part of an important set of counterweights to war's potential to disrupt normal life. Doing something appropriately, whether it was setting a good tea table, giving someone a 'proper' send-off or marrying in correct attire, showed that traditions were observed and that the occasion was respectable.

Before the marrying came the courting. Here, too, memoirs written by women who were young during the war represent social life as coloured by considerations of glamour as well as austerity. Kathleen Hurley, who lived in the small Taranaki township of Ōpunake, remembered the thrill that went through her when war was declared: 'it conjured up all sorts of imaginings – soldiers, sailors dancing and generally romantic notions', ideas that her parents, well acquainted with the grief of the Great War, attempted to quash.[27] For some women the frisson of glamour conjured up by the image of dancing with a man in uniform was not just the stuff of girlhood dreams. Win Galland was working in a Dunedin department store when war was declared. Her social life, like that of many young girls of her era, centred on going to dances:

> They were held every Saturday night, sometimes mid-week as well. They were the place were 'Boy meets Girl'. Getting dressed for the dance was part of the fun. It took at least an hour to don that long frock, place that spray of flowers on the shoulder or in the hair.

She met her future husband at a dance in Central Otago. For three years she played 'the waiting game' while her man was overseas. She pared her dance attendance back, partly because 'the big balls' stopped and male dance partners were in short supply, but continued to attend smaller dances pressing her father – an unrivalled man for the waltz – into service as an escort. Even though she was spoken for, she still made the effort to look stylish: 'it was amazing what some ribbons or artificial flowers could do'.[28] Dressing for a dance became extra special if the working week was spent in utility clothing. As one land girl remembered, 'Many a sheep got a quick dose or a short clip on a dance night in the rush to finish up. It was a change to get dressed in a dress.'[29]

Freshening up an outfit through small alterations was a staple practice. Mihipeka Edwards, a regular attendee at wartime dances, detailed her strategy for making a few dresses go a long way:

> We girls learn to do the jive, and we're good at it. We wear lovely lacy panties and petticoats with a wide band of lace on the hem to look pretty. Our dancing shoes are a low, Cuban heeled type of sandal. I have a pair of silver shoes and a pair of black ones. I have three dresses suitable for dancing the jive. We girls team them with different colours and accessories. One of my dresses is black. I can do a lot

with that. I wear a white detachable lace collar with it on one night; the next time I stitch a wide band of mauve ribbon at the hem that I can remove; and the next time wear a long red chiffon scarf that trails as I dance.[30]

Throughout her memoir, dress is used as a symbolic language to express a range of emotions, from exultation at cutting loose on the dance floor, resignation when she reluctantly agrees to marry a serviceman going overseas with the Māori Battalion and hope for a new start when she begins her nursing training at the end of the war. The nurse's uniform is a 'nice pink and white' with white shoes and stockings, a white cap and a red cape, 'very glamorous, all spick and span'.[31]

Women wanted to look good for their men, but also for themselves. Jessie McClunie's husband-to-be was a prisoner of war for years. She spent the latter part of 1945 anxiously waiting for his repatriation. A friend with inside information tipped her off about the date of his return by telling her to go and get her hair done. On the big day Jessie was in such a rush to hug her fiancé that she ducked under a rope at the railway station and knocked her new hat off. Her memoir written 60 years later used his gallant retrieval of the hat as a symbol of their successful partnership. Another special costume completed their reunion. Their wedding photo shows her in a full-length white gown, flowing train and long veil, her husband resplendent in khaki.[32]

And what about some of the stories told by women about wearing uniforms? In the early 1940s a sizable number of New Zealand women were dissatisfied with the conventional female ways of contributing to the war effort. Patriotic organisations relied on women volunteers to fundraise; the Red Cross and the Emergency Precautions Scheme (a newly established civil defence organisation) trained women in first aid and emergency procedures; and New Zealand employers stepping up production in areas like food processing and clothing manufacture – long-time employers of large numbers of women – cried out for more women workers. Yet there was no formal enlistment process for women. Wanting to make a direct contribution to the war effort, and frustrated by the New Zealand government's reluctance to sign women up for uniformed war service, women began to demand formal recognition of their efforts. In July 1940, after muttering that he had no desire to see New Zealand women in trousers and that some women were unnecessarily fixated on getting into uniform, Prime Minister Peter Fraser agreed to set up the Women's War Service Auxiliary to coordinate civilian women's war work. Members would be entitled to wear uniforms, though they would have to purchase the khaki dresses and caps themselves, at a cost of £1.[33] Women's branches of the New Zealand Air Force, Navy and Army were established in 1941 and 1942 and the New Zealand Women's Land Corps reorganised as the New Zealand Women's Land Service.[34]

In 1942 Ruth Niblock joined the staff at New Zealand Army Headquarters assisting with the organisation of the Women's Auxiliary Army Corps (WAAC).

'Uniforms,' she recollected, 'seemed to be the main issue.' After researching what British women war workers were wearing, meeting with 'Mr Bedford on Lambton Quay', a 'respected tailor', and helping with the heady task of selecting an emblem for the corps badge, Ruth became one of the first WAACs to get an official uniform. She was pleased with the result:

> The hats were not becoming, but if worn with a dash the 'fore and aft' caps were fetching and easy to wear. I remember the first time I walked down Featherston St in full rig and ran into two senior officers. I swung my first salute. 'Come and have lunch,' said the Colonel. I knew I had passed the test.[35]

Gunner Billet recollected passing a different kind of test on her first day in khaki. Issued with men's battledress because the women's kit was still being manufactured, she and her fellow recruits struggled to get dressed on time and in a dignified manner:

> There were no brown boots my size so I was given a pair of men's boots, officers' issue. They were black with thick stiff soles and two sizes too big. After adding insoles and two pairs of thick woollen sox they were still too big and I walked with a rocking motion .... The first morning we were all late for parade as we hadn't counted on the time it would take to force all the thin metal buttons through the tight buttonholes of the men's new battledress. First on was a khaki shirt and tie, then braces which buttoned onto trousers, then fly buttons, the jacket was buttoned onto trousers and up the front and was over a khaki woollen jumper. Canvas spats and boots completed the outfit. There were broken fingernails and much panic before we turned up for parade.[36]

In each branch of the service careful consideration was given to how women would be uniformed. A recruiting device and a marker of the seriousness of the women's contributions, uniforms were a focus for building the corporate identity of each service. They had to project femininity while at the same time linking the women's branches of the services to the sartorial identity of their male counterparts. New designs were necessary because it was not regarded as appropriate or feasible, given different female body shapes and the expectations that women should be easily distinguishable from men, just to put them into cut-down versions of the male uniforms. The top half of the uniform issue was easier to settle than the bottom half. Jackets were cut along male lines with allowances for narrower female shoulders and waists and a more feminine line around the bust.[37] Trousers were out. In every case a skirt was commissioned as the bottom half of the dress uniform, to be paired with stockings and sensible shoes.

Over time regulations were formulated to deal with the minute detail of women's dress. During 1942 and 1943, for example, the Women's Auxiliary Air

Members of the Women's Auxiliary Army Corps saluting the Governor General's wife, Lady Newell, in suit and fox fur, September 1944. PACOLL-6203-19, ALEXANDER TURNBULL LIBRARY, WELLINGTON, NEW ZEALAND

Force (WAAF) commissioned a beret to replace one of the standard issue felt hats, a greatcoat for women drivers, summer dresses and 'sockettes'. Arrangements were made for issues of sanitary towels. Regulations allowed the wearing of discreet cosmetics on duty, but a handbag (plain black) could only be carried off duty and coloured nail varnish was prohibited. Cardigans could be worn over the summer dresses but not with the winter kit, gumboots could only be worn off duty and wedding and engagement rings were the only jewellery permitted. 'Customary attire' could be worn for sport and, with their commanding officer's approval, WAAFs were permitted to wear evening dress when attending dances, a 'highly appreciated' concession not felt necessary for male personnel.[38] It was a balancing act: women should not be garbed in so martial a manner that they looked masculine, but if they were dressed in styles which were too womanly they could look unmilitary.

Photographs that juxtapose uniformed women and women in civilian dress suggest some of the visual contrast between the two groups. In the photograph above an image of a group of army nursing sisters on final parade, the civilian woman watching them is individualised and feminised by her clothing; the uniformed women are more serious, more homogeneous and more masculine. Even when formally attired a civilian woman's dress marked her individuality and social background; the formalities of uniformed dress were designed to repress these markers in favour of corporate identity and military rank.

The dress issue highlighted some of the central paradoxes of integrating women into the military in a period when most people, male and female, believed that men and women were fundamentally different and that society was the better because of their differences. Military service was clearly defined as men's business. Even if that definition was widened to include women, sameness and the subjugation of self was at the heart of military culture – it is no accident that military clothing was called uniform. Yet women were meant to express individuality and allure through dress. The notion of a woman in uniform was paradoxical, a little threatening and sometimes even farcical. Cartoons showed military women in a variety of absurd situations. Older women were depicted as burly, unattractive and deluded, their petticoats hanging out on the parade ground, tattoos on their beefy forearms and false ideas of good looks in their heads. Younger women in uniform were more attractive but still out of place and the butt of jokes. Cartoons showed their husbands doing the housework while they touched up their make-up, pub owners calling 'time, gentlemen' on their carousing, and real (male) soldiers distracted by their wasp-waisted figures.[39]

Claims that servicewomen got better treatment, easy jobs and soft billets abounded. Military spokesmen and journalists vacillated about whether women got special treatment and whether special conditions were a good thing. WAACs stationed outside Christchurch were initially allowed twice the living space of male recruits: 'We realise girls need more room and more privacy than men . . . extra space to keep their clothing and effects'.[40] WAAFs manning Auckland's anti-aircraft stations, *Herald* readers were told, would not be required to sleep in their gun positions like men: 'the women have a house although it is still barely furnished'.[41] The army's public relations officers felt obliged to assure people that women were being treated well, partly to ensure a steady supply of female recruits, but also in deference to prevailing opinion that women soldiers had different needs from men. In a military camp outside Auckland, the *Herald* reported, 'Waacs have their own well-equipped regimental aid post, staffed by an Army girl . . . . swimming, organised games and rest periods are all worked into the busy programme and so that feminine morale will not suffer there is even a WAAC hairdresser.'[42] Women in uniform reacted angrily to implications of special treatment, which often involved the suggestion that women's concern with appearance set them apart from men. Forty years after the end of the war, Betty, a former staff sergeant who had been stationed on Wellington's Mount Victoria, was still fuming about accusations made in the newspapers that she and her fellow servicewomen were 'Glamour Girls' living in luxurious accommodation.[43]

The charge of glamour was an insult in this context, partly because of a history of conflict over women's right to uniform. Women who wanted to join the New Zealand armed forces had not had an easy time. Even after initial opposition to the setting up of women's branches of the armed services was overcome, women still battled a series of stereotypes that cast aspersions on their motives for volunteering. Some women, it was widely believed, were rushing to volunteer for the military in order to avoid industrial conscription. By mid-1942 'manpowering', as industrial conscription was known, had become a bugbear. The government had to compel women to undertake certain kinds of paid work precisely because so much essential 'women's work' was poorly paid, low status and outright unpleasant.[44] For a large number of women, uniformed service was a more attractive option than working in a factory, a mental asylum or a hospital laundry – all possible destinations for a manpowered worker. Women, some disgruntled employers suggested, were being lured away from more worthy employments by the glamour of uniform. Even the editor of the *New Zealand Woman's Weekly*, a backer of women war workers' claims to official status, warned of the dangers of forming a Women's Air Force Auxiliary:

> One can easily imagine how youth in its eagerness will enrol in droves, anxious to wear the uniform, anxious to co-operate with that branch of the fighting service most in the public eye, anxious to work side by side with the boys and, apart from patriotic motives, also attracted by the glamour of this proposed work which on the surface seems so much more exciting than work in a factory or an office.[45]

Articles in the *Mirror* and the *Listener* lauding civilian women's war work also worried that some women might join the armed forces out of a hare-brained fascination with the allure of uniformed service.[46]

Another related finger-pointing exercise claimed that young women in uniform were making a mockery of the garments if they looked too feminine in them, or making a mockery of themselves if they looked too masculine. This surfaced first in reports from Britain that a 'lipstick and uniform controversy' dogged the incorporation of women into British auxiliary services. According to the *New Zealand Woman's Weekly*'s London reporter, a rumour that servicewomen would not be allowed to use cosmetics had ruffled many young women's feathers. Some had declared they would not join up if powder and lipstick were banned, while 'women commandants, as a whole, showed no anti-make-up bias, but were united against the girl who made herself conspicuous by the too lavish use of it'.[47] In December 1940 a *Woman's Weekly* article in favour of uniforms conceded that 'the mere dressing up of women in uniforms might become a senseless mannequin show', while a *Listener* columnist defending New Zealand women's desire to look attractive in uniform felt obliged to add the proviso that it was important not to glamorise war or turn in into a fashion parade: 'Even worse than the dowdy uniform is the oversmart uniform'.[48] It was hard to get the balance right between the seriousness of participating directly in the war effort and the need to look feminine while doing so. Dowdiness had its risks too. Writing to the editor of Wellington's *Dominion*, 'A Woman' worried that women's organisations which mimicked military titles, spent large sums on uniforms and assumed 'an expression of grim masculinity' put women's true nature at risk.[49]

In sizing up the military, women often considered how they would look in uniform. Barbara Grierson and her twin sister Daphne chose the service they would join partly on the relative merits of the various uniforms – 'that was a big thing for young girls'. June Fear was unimpressed by the WAAC's khaki stockings and 'terribly dull brown shoes' but joined anyway, consoling herself with the

Models wearing Women's Land Service uniforms, c.1943. F-37125-1/2, ALEXANDER TURNBULL LIBRARY, WELLINGTON, NEW ZEALAND

thought that she could wear civilian clothes in the evenings.[50] The absence of a smart dress uniform was one of the reasons cited for the New Zealand Women's Land Corps' slow rates of recruitment. MPs Mary Grigg and Mary Dreaver attempted to rectify the situation. After getting approval for an upgraded uniform, they toured the country during October and November 1942 kitted out in dress uniforms, addressing meetings in more than 40 localities.[51] Publicity photographs showed good-looking women posed in the land girls' gear.

At the heart of most of the discussions of military women's appearance was the notion that women had to preserve their femininity as insurance against peacetime redundancy. Deploying women in the military was an emergency measure; few contemporaries foresaw a future in which women would be an integral part of New Zealand's peacetime armed services. As Major Eleanor Manning of the Australian Women's Auxiliary Services told a New Zealand audience in September 1942, 'it was not desired that women in the Army should become hardened. There was no reason why they should lose their femininity and home-making instincts.... They would return to homes when the war ended.'[52] Fashion sense and the ability to make oneself attractive to men was not a superficial attribute of a uniformed woman's femininity, it was an important marker of her capacity to deal with the

WAACs at Maadi camp, Egypt, c.1943.
C26724, AUCKLAND INSTITUTE AND MUSEUM LIBRARY

post-war world. Just as advocates of women's suffrage had earlier deployed stylish attire to upset the stereotypes about feminine women as decorative and non-political, and political women as masculine and unattractive, mid-twentieth-century advocates of the expansion of female citizenship to include uniformed service insisted that well-turned-out women could make a substantial, direct contribution to the war effort without losing their femininity.[53] The WAACs posed against the sign declaring their section of Cairo's Maadi camp out of bounds to all male ranks offered lipsticked smiles to the photographer capturing their neatly pressed, nicely coiffed and stockinged selves.

The association between women's wartime morale-bolstering duties and their appearance was most clearly expressed in advertisements. Victory Red lipstick would help to spur the country on to glory; Monterey Cosmetics told WAACS, WAAFs and Wrens that it was their ally in the campaign for charm. Manufacturers of cosmetics and toiletries depicted women as paragons of usefulness by day and visions of elegance by night. 'Putting on a brave face', Cashmere Bouquet advised, meant using its lipstick, powder and rouge to transform 'the Girl at the Wheel's' charming efficiency into evening glamour.[54] Ponds ran a whole series of advertisements for their popular cleansing products featuring titled British beauties, with the clear implication that New Zealand's uniformed women should see 'feminine loveliness' as compatible with uniform service. Ponds Vanishing Cream kept Lady Diana Stuart-Wortley's complexion glorious while she drove ambulances and entertained troops. It helped Lady Cecelia Smiley dig for victory and Lady Carolyn Howard work day and night in the Transport Service.[55] Photographs of real New Zealand women looking glamorous in uniform ran alongside the advertisements in the press, suggesting that the combination of good looks and patriotic service was more than an advertising writer's fantasy.

New Zealand Red Cross transport driver, c. 1943. C31573, AUCKLAND INSTITUTE AND MUSEUM LIBRARY

Other advertisements ignored wartime changes in women's roles and kept up a steady stream of images in which themes of feminine indulgence, often centred on evening glamour, were used to encourage women to maintain an interest in fashion and make-up despite the shortages. The makers of the deodorant ODO-RO-NO counselled against shortcuts in personal grooming, illustrating its advertisements with a line drawing of a radiant woman in an off-the-shoulder evening gown.[56] Prestige Hosiery promised the wartime Cinderellas reading the *New Zealand Farmer's Weekly* that they would get to the ball. A time would come 'when the right to live gracefully shall be restored, when austerity will depart' and they would 'step into dream dresses and the exquisite adornment of such perfect silk stockings'.[57] That war involved austerity and sacrifice on the part of women as well as men was generally accepted, but the loss of women's desire for nice, new things (and their wish to provoke desire in others) was neither commercially nor socially acceptable.

If we look at wartime clothing in both its functional and frivolous manifestations and ask ourselves the question posed by the Queen when she opened the London memorial, 'What sort of women were they?', we get some clear answers. These women prided themselves on the ingenuity with which they overcame shortages of materials and money to ring the changes in their wardrobes and to mark special occasions. They also prided themselves on their femininity and saw dress as a key arena for expressing that femininity. Wartime femininity was not drab and nor were wartime women blind to the personal and cultural significance of dress. Given a choice, it is likely that at least some of these women would have hung toques, evening stoles and white wedding gowns up alongside the work wear John Mills used to symbolise the women's war effort in his sculpture.

Women's wartime dress was shaped by a complex set of material constraints and cultural considerations. They wanted uniforms because uniforms signified seriousness, but they also continued to aspire to forms of non-uniform dress that they equated with femininity because these signified other aspects of the old gender order they wished to maintain: attractiveness to men, access to consumer pleasures, and clear differentiation between men and women in matters of dress. Many, if not most, agreed with the popular sentiment that maintaining morale was as much about putting a brave, Victory Red smile on adversity, as it was about patriotic sentiment. 'Working for Victory', a 1941 article about women in the *Weekly News*, New Zealand's widely circulated illustrated magazine, speculated that the discomfort many New Zealanders felt when confronted by wartime's images of new womanhood was rooted in the fear of masculine women. In women's dress preferences, the writer saw clear evidence that women could contribute to the war effort without losing their femininity: 'Don't worry Mr Man! "Frills and Furbelows" are too near a woman's heart for a change of occupation to alter her'.[58]

12. Moving in Unison, Dressing in Uniform: Stepping Out in Style with Marching Teams

Charlotte Macdonald

SHORT SKIRTS, WHITE BOOTS, HIGH HATS: THIS IS THE CHARACTERISTIC uniform of 'marching girls'. Loved by some, admired by many, reviled by others, it stands out as a distinctive element in New Zealand's dress culture. Worn by girls as young as six or seven years, but more often by team members in their early teens to early twenties, marching uniforms first appeared in the 1920s and 1930s. Over the next four decades the sight of teams of girls and young women marching in precision formation attired in striking outfits was increasingly common on sportsgrounds and streets throughout the country, particularly during the summer. Although less prominent from the 1980s, marching teams and the uniforms they wore with pride were major features of post-war life and have become notable elements in New Zealand's cultural lexicon. In 2005–06 alone, marching teams have featured in two television advertisements, a novel, a major dramatic production and in museum exhibits.[1] What was the origin of this style of uniform and how was it produced and worn? Why did it sometimes provoke sharp public criticism and how might it be understood in the wider history and dress culture of the twentieth century?

As it developed in New Zealand, marching represented a unique transformation of military-style parade ground drill into a civilian, competitive display sport performed by girls and young women. In the transition, highly decorative features of historical and ceremonial military dress uniform – close-fitting tunics, braid, epaulettes, lanyards, busbys, cockades and strong contrasting colours – were combined with short skirts and white boots to produce a dramatic visual mixed metaphor. Exposed legs and short skirts emphasised the femininity of the wearers, while tunics, hats and a rigid posture conveyed a strong sense of the masculine and military.

From about 1945 to the 1970s marching became a major sport in which thousands of girls and young women participated and hundreds of adults – as parents, coaches, judges, chaperones and supporters – were also involved. The competitive

Championship-winning Wellington team, the Sargettes, led by Flo McLeod, demonstrating their routine at Tanera Park, Brooklyn, in Wellington, April 1951. Medals worn by team members indicate their success, though it became customary for these not to be worn while teams were competing. EVENING POST COLLECTION, ALEXANDER TURNBULL LIBRARY, WELLINGTON, NEW ZEALAND

season extended from October to its culmination in regional, island and national championships in early March. In addition, marching teams performed in anniversary and holiday parades, at Agricultural & Pastoral Association shows and civic receptions for visiting royalty and other dignitaries, where they were watched by thousands of spectators. Successful marching teams spent many hours perfecting the execution of elaborate drill routines. These were performed to music, the leader issuing whistle commands to teams of seven to ten attired in uniforms worn in exact conformity – down to the last detail in skirt length, hat angle, glove seam and boot heel. The aim was to produce the effect of a single body moving as one, a vision of precision and order, a display both ceremonial and disciplined. To dress in uniform and perform in unison was the goal.

Only in New Zealand has precision marching by girls and young women developed and thrived as a sport and a spectacle, performed and competed for by teams as an end in itself. While sharing some of the features of American cheerleading and phenomena such as drum majorettes, New Zealand 'girls' marching' (as it was universally termed) stands alone as a codified competitive sport, and an autonomous activity rather than one performed as an auxiliary to another event.[2] It is one of the few wholly local sporting inventions, an indigenous 'body culture'.[3] The uniforms worn by marching teams are similarly unique. Short skirts and boots may be seen in some other team displays but nowhere else is the particular vocabulary of New Zealand marching uniforms in evidence. Marching outfits exist in marked contrast to other uniforms in New Zealand's culture. At once both costume and uniform, worn in a highly technical sporting contest and public pageant, by adults and children, marching teams present a highly specialised and striking form of dress.

Recognising the place marching and its attire have come to occupy in New Zealand life is not to suggest any kind of agreement about its meaning. Far from being inconspicuous or mundane elements in New Zealand's cultural history, marching teams have, at times, drawn hostile public commentary.[4] At other points they have been dismissed as kitschy, or disdained as unsophisticated, even embarrassing; the frequent use of diminutives in team names – for example, Benmorettes, Skodaettes, Nevilettes – a sure sign of lack of taste.[5] To their detractors, marching teams gave the impression of strident militarism (even fascism), or at the very least, of an unhealthy preoccupation with conformity, regimentation and the suppression of individuality, made worse through being enacted by young women. The teams' subordination to exacting command and show of obedience in gaudy uniforms was at once a disturbing (and stirring) display of order and unnerving exhibitionism. The post-war decades have often been characterised as dull and conformist. For some contemporaries, marching teams were clear signs of conformity gone too far, display that had become ostentation.

That marching outfits proved controversial is not surprising. Women in uniforms of authority have always been perceived as anomalous; a challenge to, if not an inversion of, the usual order.[6] However innocent the intentions of the wearers or the administrators and coaches, this style of dress carried powerful social and political messages, which were never singular or static. Marching outfits were a source of pride and self fashioning for those who wore them, as well as making their wearers objects of fascination for others. They were highly regimented yet highly creative; those who wore them commanded attention while themselves being subject to a minutely detailed set of commands. Such tensions underlie the discussion that follows.[7]

It is also important to identify the broader historical circumstances in which marching enjoyed a strong following, while recognising the risk of a simplistic reading of fashion and dress as a cultural barometer of social change. The popularity of uniformed youth movements and mass recreation between the wars in many parts of the world; the imperatives and exceptional conditions of the Second World War; the relieved return to 'normality' and the advent of the

The Woolworths (NZ) Ltd marching team competing in the third annual sports meeting of the Wellington Inter-House Girls' Association at the Basin Reserve, Wellington, November 1935. The uniforms were relatively simple but the key elements of hat and white footwear – sandshoes as worn by this team – were already established.
NEW ZEALAND FREE LANCE COLLECTION, ALEXANDER TURNBULL LIBRARY, WELLINGTON, NEW ZEALAND

Cold War with its lurking menace in the ever-present possibility of conflict; and, in the changed conditions of world power, New Zealand's renegotiation of its alliances – all these were vital. Alongside the old ties to Britain, reinforced in sentiment if shaken in power, and a surge of enthusiasm for the British monarchy under young Queen Elizabeth, there existed a newly vital relationship with the United States. Individual and local identities were shaped by, and in turn shaped, the contest of national, racial and gender interests on the wider stage.

Teams of young women dressing in uniform and marching in formation were reported in New Zealand as early as 1928, though they did not feature on a regular basis until the early 1930s.[8] Most of these early teams were workplace-based with groups of factory or shop workers, attired in simple costumes and marching under a business banner. In several centres, interhouse associations, along with the Young Women's Christian Association (YWCA), organised sports days where teams representing different workplaces competed against each other in a range of athletic events.[9] In the third sports day held by the Wellington interhouse association in 1935, for example, marching teams from James Smiths and Woolworths department stores were among those competing.[10] Marching teams in Taranaki competed for a prize of £30 in the New Year Mardi Gras organised by a committee of municipal and business representatives at Ngāmotu Beach between Christmas and New Year 1938 and 1939.[11] Massed formations or 'march ons' and 'march offs' at the beginning and end of such occasions provided the impetus for display marching, some groups discovering that they enjoyed these items on the sports days' programmes more than the athletic events in between. By the late 1930s, marching displays and competition were taking place on a regular basis at several centres around the country.[12] Although the outfits worn by these teams were simple compared with those of later teams, the distinguishing elements – sharp contrasts, white footwear, tailored top, hat and bare legs – were visible. Marching competitions were often held in conjunction

The Woolworths team, Nelson, 1939. Department stores encouraged team activities such as marching, providing the uniforms, organising studio portraits like this one and supporting 'their' girls in competition against those from rival stores. More elaborate than the outfits worn by the Wellington team in 1935, these uniforms show that interest in the costume aspect of marching developed quickly. 158841/6, KINGSFORD COLLECTION, TASMAN BAYS HERITAGE TRUST/NELSON PROVINCIAL MUSEUM

with performances by Highland pipe and brass bands. Popular in New Zealand, but an exclusively male arena at the time, the regalia of the pipe bands was an inspiration for the girls' marching teams.[13]

Joyce Simpson was working at Woolworths in New Plymouth when a marching team was started up in 1938 with the support of the branch manager and assistant manager. 'Seven enthusiastic members of our staff volunteered and we had some great times', she later recalled.[14] In early 1940 Simpson's team was one of a number which travelled to Wellington to take part in a marching display at the Centennial Exhibition.[15] Team sports encouraged loyalty and worker camaraderie which employers were keen to foster, and reflected a heightened interest in healthy recreation. Debilitating diseases such as tuberculosis, polio and rheumatic fever could still darken the door of households, whether rich or poor, while underlying eugenic concerns over the falling birth rate and levels of maternal mortality had also given physical fitness for young women a particular priority in the 1920s and 1930s.[16] The advertising of a firm's name in the banner and uniforms was an additional bonus, though these were not primarily commercial endeavours.

Marching gained momentum with the outbreak of war in 1939. Maintaining physical fitness and labour force morale was emphasised all the more, while the pervasiveness of military disciplines and uniforms made drill a normal rather than exceptional activity. New Plymouth's thriving marching competition grew during the war years, encompassing teams from the McKenzies, Woolworths and McDuffs retail stores, another under the banner of Boon Brothers (a timber and building company) and a team from the Post Office. They competed against each other and regional rivals in Wanganui and Taumarunui, including appearing at the fifth annual championships held at Cooks Gardens, Wanganui, on 27 February 1943 (with other teams including Hansell's Laboratories, Masterton, DIC department store and Wellington Woollen Mills).[17]

When her McKenzies' team did not re-form after four years together, Peggy Jones called together other young women to form the New Plymouth Kilties team in 1944. Their demanding schedule of twice-daily practice sessions at the height of the season and exacting coaches soon won them competitive success and an enviable reputation. (Their key rivals were the Roebuck's team.)[18] Around the same time, the success of the New Plymouth teams (including the prospect of an Australian tour) prompted Mrs Peggy Klenner to start something in her town, Inglewood. She put a notice in her shop window: 'Wanted. 16 smart girls to form an Inglewood Marching Team. Only girls without glasses will be eligible. Please apply within.' She was overwhelmed by over 100 local girls and young women keen to try marching.[19]

Rather than fading into obscurity after 1945, girls' marching thrived in the post-war era, becoming a major sport. In many ways this went against trends elsewhere that saw the pre-war enthusiasm for mass movements quietly forgotten in the wake of Nazi revelations, and military uniforms and practices packed away with the end of hostilities. In New Zealand ceremonial marching had proved genuinely attractive to groups of young, working women, to the surprise of the many men conscripted into the armed services and subjected to the discipline of parade ground drill. Marching won the political support and organisational entrepreneurship of the Department of Internal Affairs, notably Minister W. E. (Bill) Parry and Assistant Under Secretary Arthur Harper.[20] Critically, the marching routine was modified to fit a civilian, peacetime and distinctly feminine model. Teams of ten replaced teams of seven, now organised in three rows and a leader; march plans deliberately departed from the pattern set by the *Army Manual of Elementary Drill*, and the newly defined recreation of marching was firmly described as a sport rather than training, something designed to 'put colour, laughter and fellowship back into everyday living'.[21] In this reconfiguration, it was hoped that marching was clearly differentiated from its wartime and militarist associations.

The change was described as making marching 'more feminine and technical'.[22] March plans were to emphasise skill and pageantry – the display element rather than straight parade ground manoeuvre. Uniforms clearly signalled the shift: short skirts became an obligatory part of team outfits. Shorts and long trousers, which had been worn by a number of teams in the 1930s and war years, were no longer to be seen. Dargaville's Warrington team of 1946 was one of the last to

Marching teams assembled on the Ōtaki Domain during the 1955–6 season. Ōtaki marchers quickly gained a top reputation when the first local team, Bandoliers, won honours at the North Island and New Zealand Championships in 1950–1. By the 1955–6 season a new team, the Casualairs, was in competition with other local and visiting teams from Wanganui and Levin. EDNA SNOWDON, WANGANUI

appear in long trousers.[23] The skirts worn by marching teams were considerably shorter than those worn as conventional or fashionable garb by adolescent or adult women until at least the mid-1960s. But the femininity conveyed by the wearing of skirts was problematic. On the one hand, the skirt was provocative in its revealing brevity; on the other hand, it was worn with a severe and all-covering jacket and hat. Marching teams presented an intriguing confusion of gender and sexual identities.

Representatives from eight existing regional organisations formed the New Zealand Marching Association (NZMA) at a meeting convened by officers of the Physical Welfare Branch, Department of Internal Affairs, in Wellington on 15 August 1945, VJ (Victory over Japan) Day.[24] A national structure was quickly followed by codification: the first handbook was published in 1946. Over the next decade, in what can be thought of as the classic era, marching enjoyed the support of state patronage and flourished in popularity. Enthusiasm for marching quickly spread from places where it was already established to other centres. In Ashburton women working for the railways started up their own team, NZR Ashburton, after watching a demonstration by a team from Timaru. To travel to competitions in Temuka and Timaru they worked the night shift, sometimes having to swap team members depending on who was rostered on or off. Their white uniforms with red braid were made by the mother of a team member.[25] Similarly impressed by the demonstrations put on by visiting teams – this time from Levin and Wanganui – Ōtaki girls formed their first team in October 1947. The original Bandoliers team was joined the following season by a junior team, the Tuis, and a midget team the following year. By 1949 further teams formed at Waikanae (Huias) and in Ōtaki where Raukawa, a Māori girls marching team, and the Troubadours, competed in

The Midhirst Spic-n-Span midget marching team, Taranaki, 1957–8. The team made a clean sweep of all competitions they entered including the Taranaki and North Island championships. Team members pictured are, left to right: L. Blick, J. Mortlock, N. Fawcett, D. Copeland, H. Kendrick (leader), C. Blick, J. Hoffman, D. Hart, A. Caskey and S. Horgan (marker), with their instructor Mr N. Mitchell and chaperone Mrs M. Kendrick. PHO2006.064, SWAINSON'S STUDIOS, PLUMB COLLECTION, PUKE ARIKI, NEW PLYMOUTH

the 1949–50 season. By 1954 a number of the original members of the Bandoliers and Troubadours had left the district but the remaining members formed a new team, the Casualairs. Much later, Ōtaki produced successful junior teams under the names Featherettes and Teensetters.[26]

In 1951 *Quick March*, the NZMA's magazine, reported well over 300 teams in 80 associations spread over 20 centres affiliated to the national organisation, representing around 4500 people.[27] The national profile of the sport was also in the ascendant. Dunedin's Blair Athol team travelled to Britain in 1952 and marching teams were prominent in both the 1953–4 Royal Tour of the young Queen Elizabeth II and the Duke of Edinburgh, and again in 1958 during the visit of the Queen Mother.[28] Prime ministers, governors-general, leaders of the opposition and members of cabinet attended national championships, annual luncheons, and served as patrons of the sport.[29] Numbers remained around 4000–5000 through the 1960s and 1970s, as teams came and went, and as generations of marchers, some in the same family, graduated from team members, to leaders, instructors and judges. In 1980 there were 350 teams representing 6000 marchers, chaperones and officials (in a larger population) but, as with other organised sports, marching found it hard to attract new participants and the many volunteers needed to maintain the sport at its earlier levels. By 1998 the number of members had dropped to 2000 and the sport's profile had declined.[30]

Terms and conditions for competition – the march plan, judging criteria, appointment of judges, allocation of points and penalties – were, from the outset, highly specified and grew exponentially to constitute a minutely detailed set of

V. E. Wheeler, instructor of the Wellington Sargettes team, measuring the distance between the rows, 1951. March plans and judging criteria set by the New Zealand Marching Association made highly exacting demands on teams and instructors in regard to appearance, demeanour and routine to be performed.
EVENING POST COLLECTION, ALEXANDER TURNBULL LIBRARY, WELLINGTON, NEW ZEALAND

rules.³¹ Marching teams were assessed by a panel of judges and separate awards went to teams, team leaders and different phases in performance – appearance, fall in, and march routine – within each of several grades, at first junior and senior, later midget. The spectacle relied very much on the uniform. In the general notes to the NZMA's handbook, instructors and leaders were advised that the contents would provide sufficient guidance to prepare a team for the standard they were likely to meet in competition, at the same time allowing scope for teams' creativity 'to ensure novelty and spectacle at competitions'.³²

Teams were responsible for designing and producing their own uniforms. Peggy Nelson described how the very first uniform worn by the Inglewood Vanguards 'was made by Betty Charteris (O'Sullivan) [a member of the team] and it was a very beautiful uniform – pleated skirts, dress Stewart . . . the tartan was, a red waistcoat – velvet waistcoat – long sleeved white blouse and we're not sure who made the hats but they were just little berets on the back of our heads of the same tartan . . . . And we had white boots, we were lucky.'³³ They were lucky to have boots rather than sandshoes which many teams, especially in the early years, wore with spats to create the effect of an ankle boot. While Colleen Eagles and Joan Lander loved the black and white satin and velvet uniforms they wore as members of the Roebuck's team, complete with white gloves, and feathered conductor's caps with the entwined letters 'RCC' (Roebuck's Construction Company) embroidered on the front,³⁴ they sighed at the memory of spats. 'It used to take us hours to get these spats on cos we had one button hook. At least an hour to get dressed. One button hook for the whole team.'³⁵ For her Kilties team Peggy Jones knitted 'a strip of green woollen [fabric] . . . and we put those underneath our spats so they looked like socks'. But they too struggled to do up all 20 tiny white buttons with an old-fashioned button hook and had to whiten the spats 'every time we marched'.³⁶ Boots were expensive, not always easy to get and hard to manage among groups with growing feet.³⁷

In the 1950s, and starting at a much younger age, Bev Nickson (later Pui) was easily able to recount the sequence of uniforms she wore through her marching career in the Pleiades team, Waitara, from the age of seven to sixteen years:

> I can remember the one [uniform] we started off when I was 7, it was royal blue and white. When we went to juniors we went to pink and white, a red and white, and then it was lavender and black our last uniform . . . . The red and white was the white skirt and red jacket. The pink one was like a flared skirt and when we swung our arms the white would show on the skirt . . . . Somebody made them. And before we could go on a marching championship everything had to be, not even a button out of place, not a speck of dirt on our boots, the heels had to be black and our boots had to be absolutely white, we weren't allowed to have a hair out of place. The uniforms just had to be immaculate.³⁸

Wearing Stewart tartan skirts with yellow hats and jackets, the Inglewood Vanguards team, 1956–7, continued the winning tradition established by the team under instructor Bernie Plumb. Taranaki champions, the team was also consistently either second or third in the New Zealand Championships from 1953 to 1957. Pictured, from back left: B. R. Plumb (instructor), B. Benny, L. Herlihy, S. V. Cramer (chaperone), N. Cranefield, M. Robinson, V. Smith, Rachel Josephs (leader), J. Curd, D. Corney, Y. Austin, V. Scott, D. Tunnicliff, E. Benny and C. Curd (marker). PHO2006.063, SWAINSON'S STUDIOS, PLUMB COLLECTION, PUKE ARIKI, NEW PLYMOUTH

Two costume judges made up part of the panel of judges.[39] Rules for competition emphasised that what mattered was 'suitability' rather than a 'lavish' uniform.[40] The underlying principle for judging was set down as follows: 'Uniforms are judged, not for their elaborateness, but for neatness, cleanliness, simplicity, fit – and uniformity. Skirt length, tunic length, sock length, hat angle, all come in for the judges' critical glance.' At the same time costume judges had 'to declare their complete lack of bias or prejudice "against the suitability of any particular material, colour, combination of colours, style of uniform, or type of uniform"'.[41] Judging took place at the halt, before teams took part in the competition march. Judges passed along the team standing in rank, then inspected the team as it marched a short distance of fifteen paces. During the short march the team's uniform was assessed for 'suitability'. Marks were awarded for meeting standards set while deductions were made on the basis of one point 'for each case of lack of neatness, cleanliness, fit, and uniformity'. Up to five points could be deducted for 'unsuitability', and a crippling ten points if any member of the team was absent during the costume judges' inspection. Judges were prohibited from walking through the rank, conversing with any team member and were enjoined not to 'handle the uniform or person' of anyone in the team.[42]

Materials for uniforms were drawn from what was at hand. In the straitened circumstances of war and the years of shortages that followed there was not a great choice. Creativity and inventiveness were often called on, as well as dressmaking skill.[43] Pleated tartan and plain skirts worn with white or contrasting shirts, often with waistcoats, were common. In the early years girls wore berets (often with

The Inglewood Vanguard team in formation at Pukekura Park, New Plymouth.
PHO2006.104, CRAGO STUDIOS, PLUMB COLLECTION, PUKE ARIKI, NEW PLYMOUTH

the front raised), glengarry hats (Highland caps), 'lieutenant' and air force style caps (also known as fore-and-aft or garrison caps). Teams often improvised: at least one adapted lightshade frames for early tall hats.[44] White gloves and boots drew attention to the extremities of the body in marching stride and gave a pleasing effect to a team moving on a green field or on a dark grey road. Timaru's championship team, Balmoral, Wellington's Sargettes, Whāngārei's Grenadiers, Dunedin's Blair Athol and Inglewood's Vanguards all displayed the characteristic varieties of marching uniform of the 1950s. Colours remained largely black and white with contrasting blue, red and yellow, or were chosen to complement a tartan. Jewellery, apart from wedding and engagement rings, was not permitted and could attract penalties from costume judges. Make-up was conventional among senior teams and later adopted among midgets.[45]

Purchasing uniforms, especially expensive boots and hats, meant energetic fundraising by most teams. The sixpenny tickets sold by a member of the Kilties team who lived in the railway settlement (now Coronation Avenue), New Plymouth, for a prize of a dozen beer, sold 'like hot cakes', but more often the money came from dances, stalls, demonstration marches and, later, march-a-thons and newspaper circulation.[46] Maintaining the uniforms, including having them in pristine condition when travelling away for competition, involved a good deal of labour and care. Keeping pleats sharp could require tacking them in after each outing and drawing the thread only as the team was about to enter the field, while the lace frills at the end of the Kilties' sleeves had to be taken off, starched and resewn after each wearing. Nonetheless, their leader reported: 'We never had one person that didn't look after their uniform properly, you know. They took pride in their uniform really.'[47] Joan Black, chaperone to the Auckland Convairs team in the late 1960s, was not unusual in doing the weekly laundry for the team, but noted that she had 'to press them on Saturday night so that they don't go limp before the parades' on Sunday.[48]

In their military styles and adaptation of regimental forms, marching uniforms were neither glamorous in a conventional sense nor a product of contemporary fashion trends. They were anachronistic yet drew on the recognition that twentieth-century warfare had made civilian society the battleground. They exploited the prestige uniforms had acquired in wartime and drew on the pageantry associated with outfits worn by men in the Highland pipe and, to a lesser extent, brass bands, that were a common feature in most New Zealand communities in the mid-twentieth century.

Marching team uniforms made a symbolic rather than a direct link with the wartime uniform culture and the qualities of respect and service with which it was associated. In their ceremonial form marching teams set themselves apart from both the modified service dress worn by the Women's War Service Auxiliary, the Women's Land Service and the women's branches of the army, navy and airforce (Women's Auxiliary Air Force, Women's Royal New Zealand Naval Service and Women's Auxiliary Army Corps), and the utilitarian uniforms worn by men in the contemporary army, navy and air force. Marching teams did not seek to emulate the function or purpose of these bodies, but rather conveyed a similar preparedness to undertake training that was of both social and individual benefit: to enhance physical health, to learn how to work in a team and to contribute to public culture, through displays. Although clearly defined as a competitive sport from its formal establishment in 1945, the NZMA saw its work within a wider realm of service. The formula 'Marching is a way of life; Marching is a service to the community; Marching is a competitive sport' was widely promulgated.[49]

The outfits designed and worn by members of such teams as the Inglewood Vanguards, led by Nyla Downs and later Rachel Josephs, Balmoral in Timaru or Blair Athol in Dunedin, had style and panache; they were a decorative, attractive and grown-up form of dress. In contrast to the body-disguising dark grey, black, brown and navy blue box-pleated gym frocks worn by schoolgirls, netball and hockey teams, or the more utilitarian and muted colours of Girl Guide, Brownie and Girls' Brigade uniforms, marching outfits stood out. As uniforms, but also as costumes in which to perform, marching outfits offered many young New Zealand women a form of recreation in which they could develop skill and win recognition for their hard work. This was an arena of achievement that did not rely on academic, occupational or conventional sporting disciplines. Marching offered an opportunity for self-invention and independence – it was at once adventurous in its novel attire and legitimate in its sporting purpose. The appeal of uniforms was felt beyond the straitened material circumstances of the late

Davina Tait (Prattley), leader of the Cavaliers senior team, Gore, 1959. The dove grey uniform with contrasting buttons and detail in lavender was newly made for the 1959 season by Esther Richmond, with assistance from Elsie Tait, Davina's mother. A long zip in the centre back gave the dress a fitted shape while the heavily gored skirt emphasised movement. PC003904-07, MUSEUM OF NEW ZEALAND TE PAPA TONGAREWA

1940s or 1950s. Talking to members of the Auckland Swift Foote team in 1969, Linda Brady reported: 'Ask the team what they think about the uniforms and they will say, "they're neat," in perfect unison and quickly reel off, "Princess pleated tartan skirt, red jacket and tartan cap."' [50]

By the late 1950s, when Davina Tait's Gore Cavaliers team began competing in the Eastern Southland Association, some new trends were evident. Busby hats, modelled on the bearskin hats worn by the Queen's guards, and drum majors at the head of pipe bands, had become popular. So, too, had Sam Browne belts, which wrapped around the waist and then ran an additional strap diagonally across the upper body from left hip to right shoulder (front and back). The championship Auckland team, the Scottish Hussars, wore black Sam Browne belts over white jackets with tartan skirts and black glengarries at the civic reception for the Queen Mother in February 1958. The influence of fashion on colours worn by teams is also apparent. The Gore Cavaliers wore a mauve and dove grey uniform, picking up on the preference for pastels in the late 1950s and early 1960s. Their uniform also showed the trend among some teams for a one-piece uniform, which could be easier to maintain, and, from later in the 1960s, of the fashion for shift dresses. The skirts were heavily gored, allowing the wearers plenty of swirl as they stepped through their routines. The uniforms' emphasis on the two lines of buttons allowed easy adjustment to produce an impression of conformity more easily than a waist belt, while the fore-and-aft caps carried the colour contrast through to mauve buttons and insets against the grey. The

The Ingleguards team competing at Rugby Park, New Plymouth, in the 1970s. The blue and white shift-style dress, longer hair (tied in pig-tails) and sporty hats reflect a more contemporary and casual style than teams of the 1940s and 1950s. PH2006-109, PLUMB COLLECTION, PUKE ARIKI, NEW PLYMOUTH

one-piece was also more comfortable.[51] In designing outfits teams had to choose carefully between uniforms that offered something novel, but might be judged 'unsuitable', those which stood out on the field and those in which it was possible to achieve complete team conformity. Sam Browne belts, for example, made for a striking effect but could draw the judges' attention to uneven shoulder height and movement.

In the 1970s, variations on the uniforms such as shallow busbys, and busbys with brims, allowed a greater range of attire to be worn, especially by younger competitors, as well as styles more suited to senior adult teams. Colours in the 1960s and 1970s indicated a growing sense of inventiveness. The NZMA's October 1973 bulletin carried advertisements for sets of team uniforms in white and maroon (white wrapover skirt, maroon jacket, white busby for senior team); feather yellow jackets and tartan skirts with berets (midget team); a set of pillbox hats in orange with black and white trim and gold chin straps (junior team); black jackets and Beatrice tartan skirts, red cowboy hats and red gloves (for a junior or senior team), among others. New fabrics were also in evidence: crimplene skirts and jackets and busby-style hats made from poodle cloth.[52] The advent of easy-care fabrics, including washable jackets and skirts with permanent pleating, plus fastenings in Velcro, revolutionised the production and maintenance of uniforms.

In the 1978–9 season, the range of uniforms available for sale included a set of senior uniforms, 'tailor made' kingfisher blue jackets, orange pleated skirts, black gloves, black Sam Browne belts and busbys in white with orange stripes in front;[53] sets of midget uniforms in lime green and silver with pillbox hats, or powder blue with white epaulettes and mandarin collars along with white fur fabric hats, royal blue feather and white chin straps; junior uniforms from Ōtorohanga in royal blue jackets, citrus yellow skirts, matching hats with yellow and white plumes and white Sam Browne belts and gloves, and a set of blue check tartan skirts with Velcro fastenings from Hawera.[54] Innovations of the 1980s included Lycra pantyhose instead of leg paint, and what became a very popular form of hat known as the 'pancake'. This was a circular shape sitting on a round band where the main plane of the hat lay at a slight angle to the back of the head.[55]

Marching teams drew on a range of patterns and symbols familiar from the vocabulary of ceremonial and decorative cultures. In these could be seen some of New Zealand's links with the wider world in the mid-twentieth century, such as American service uniforms (especially hats worn by marines) and Hollywood depictions of smart dressing represented by sharply contrasting revers and chevrons. More prominent however, were elements of British, especially royal, pomp and the London ceremonial calendar – the trooping of the colour, the changing of the guard, the opening of Parliament – and details from dress regimental uniforms. While affiliated to local, regional and national organisations, teams were not bound to adopt the colours or insignia of clubs or provinces. Each was largely autonomous in its choice of name and outfit, which were the key to identity and reputation. When a team-mate of Peggy Jones visited Australia in the 1940s and wore her New Plymouth Kilties blazer to the Easter Show, she was instantly identified as a member of the team though not known by name.[56] Much later, in the 1980s, former members of the Westlanders team, and the marching community as a whole, were indignant that the uniforms worn by the 'Taita Supremes', the fictional (and inexpert) marching team in Fiona Samuel and Steve La Hood's television drama series, *The Marching Girls*, were those that had been worn by the champion winning team a few years earlier. To see the uniforms worn by a team falling well below the competitive proficiency achieved by the original wearers was a deep slight on the team's identity and reputation.[57]

Scottish emblems and themes constitute a prominent and enduring component not only of the outfits but also of the names adopted, the accessories used and the settings for performance.[58] Tartans, widely used from the beginning, have remained a perennial favourite. Tartan skirts worn with plain coloured tunics or as contrasting detail in hats, sashes and cuffs, have proven the most popular combinations in team uniforms. The most successful and best known team in recent years, Lochiel, wears uniforms in a series of variations on tartan in contrasting skirt, hat, tunic and decorative detail. Blair Athol, Lochiel, the Scottish Hussars, the Kilties, the Pioneer Gordons, Gordonaires and Gordonettes (seniors, juniors and midgets), the Glen Gordans [sic] and Balmoral are only some of the

Timaru's Balmoral team competing in the South Canterbury championships at the Caledonian Ground, 2 December 1953. Rita McLeod is in the lead with team members Colleen McKenna, Denise Foley, Margaret Broadhead (front row), Madelene Kaveney, Elenor Schedel, Doreen McKerrow (middle row), Marie Lloyd, Beverley Bradley and Marie Bradley (back row). PACOLL-7171-13, ALEXANDER TURNBULL LIBRARY, WELLINGTON, NEW ZEALAND

many who adopted Scottish names. Marching teams participated at Caledonian sports at Turakina and elsewhere on regular occasions, while Caledonian grounds were commonly used as places for practice and performance, as was the case for the Balmoral team in December 1953.[59] Scottish borrowings are not surprising, given the close connections with pipe bands in the early years of marching. Nonetheless, Scottish names have persisted long after the link with bands was lost. Is this evidence of the cultural legacy of Scottish settlement in New Zealand society? Rather than attributing it in a simple way to the strong Scottish element in New Zealand's migrant past, it might more usefully be thought of as part of the making of a local Scottishness. Cultural markers are more prominently found in displaced or diasporic societies: the strong New Zealand 'tradition' of pipe bands and marching, both wearing tartans, is a local invention of Scottish culture.[60]

The elements were put together liberally – with more regard for innovation and achieving a winning edge than any adherence to correct military forms. Prominent elements included tall busby style hats, sometimes worn with chin straps in the same style as Buckingham Palace Guards, and in decorative cockades rising from the centre of berets or other styles of hats (glengarries, balmorals, modified berets and, later, 'pancakes'). The great surge in the popularity of the monarchy stirred by the coronation of Queen Elizabeth and her lengthy visit to New Zealand over the summer of 1953–4 should not be underestimated. Although the reaction to the tour cannot be read as a simple expression of

Teams assembled for the national marching championships, Pukekura Park, New Plymouth, c.1951. The judges' table is in the foreground while the pipe bands providing music to which teams performed can be seen on the far side. PH 2006-107, PLUMB COLLECTION, PUKE ARIKI, NEW PLYMOUTH

patriotism, the ubiquity of Union Jacks, pervasive reporting about the Royal family, continued reference to Britain as 'home' and the dominance of British goods in the New Zealand market, cannot be discounted. Royal ceremonial provided an ornamental culture largely lacking in New Zealand Pākehā culture. Some marching team leaders carried a mace, using it in a similar manner to a drum major in spectacular feats of spinning, twirling and throwing. Peggy Jones's plumber father fashioned her mace from materials at hand, crafting the stave in such a way that one end was weighted with lead in order to assist it in flight.[61] The danger of mixing agricultural displays with impeccable grooming was brought home to the team the day Jones dropped the mace in what the prize bulls had left behind on the showground grass. Not skipping a beat she retrieved the mace but her Kilties team-mates behind were pelted with fresh dung.[62]

Marching uniforms were entirely decorative, devoid of other symbolic meanings, divorced from the spaces, institutions or articulations of their wider meaning. Highly local in nature, they were constructed from found elements, but assembled in a unique way – not quite nostalgia, and certainly not parody, but freely eclectic.[63] There was also, perhaps, a sense that in a 'young' country like New Zealand, ceremony could be reinvented, that it was appropriate for ceremonies performed by military men in the metropolitan centres to be enacted by young civilian women in the 'new' society of a recent daughter dominion. This was suggested by the inclusion of performances by marching teams at such events as local stops on Royal tours, and in trooping of colour ceremonies in front of the British High Commissioner at Pukekura Park in March 1944 and April 1956, where sixteen teams took part.[64]

Marching uniforms owed little to modernist design principles of simplicity, clean lines, low relief and absence of decoration. Instead, they emphasised embellishment, formality and sharp contrasts. Although the short skirts and boots drew attention to marchers' legs and feet – the exposure of women's legs representing movement and modernity[65] – the aesthetic was one of order and rigidity rather than freedom. Marching outfits did not so much produce a 'modern' female form as a body clothed for the performance of an adapted historical tradition, an outfit that also enabled a particular form of self fashioning, drawing on costume and ceremonial elements (allowing for fantasy and agency). Between the height-extending hats and white boots, marching uniforms encased the body of the wearer to create a vertical plane rather than accentuating a curving female shape as contemporary fashions did. Shoulders, arms and feet moved while the body was held rigidly straight. Marching emphasised appearance, but it was not a traditional contest for feminine beauty: the face was not accentuated, held in a serious rather than a smiling pose.[66]

The rejection of modernity represented by marching lies behind much of the critical comment it attracted. In the July 1952 issue of the left-leaning periodical *Here and Now*, poet A. R. D Fairburn answered the question posed on the cover alongside a caricature of a marching girl in burlesque pose: 'Are marching girls decadent?'. A sign of western civilisation's malaise, the 'cult' of marching, Fairburn suggested, arose from totalitarian tendencies and should be substituted by activities of a 'more organic' and 'less mechanical nature'.[67] Six years later a stir of debate was aroused by a *New York Times* story reporting denunciation of the sport of marching as 'unnatural' and 'a sign of hidden fascism'. Writing in the mass circulation *New Zealand Listener* in 1976, playwright Bruce Mason was both disturbed and impressed by the scene he had observed on his local Kilbirnie Green where the Wellington marching championship was taking place. There 'is something skewed about it all,' he mused, 'some quirk in the national psyche which bids girls ape men at their least attractive'.[68] Mason's questions drew firm retorts. On all these occasions, and at other times when marching has been criticised as undesirable or lacking in discernment, the outfits were the focus. For Fairburn, marching teams wore 'fantastically *recherché* uniforms'; for Mason the uniforms were 'amazing, quite amazing. Some of these girls, if their rig be the criterion, could have fought at Waterloo . . . . Some teams were arrayed in the gear of bellhops at the Savoy Hotel, and others had a Scottish whiff, but two factors were constant: white boots to mid-calf, and a cockaded hat or busby.' [69] What marching dress signified about New Zealand, about women and about social tendencies was worrying. Dress was anything but neutral.

When Joyce Simpson and so many other young women stepped out onto Pukekura and other parks around the country they did so with pride and confidence. White boots cleaned to the last inch, skirts hemmed precisely to the same length as their fellow team members, tunics pressed and perfectly

Not everyone was enamoured with marching. Readers of the left-leaning *Here & Now* magazine were provoked to consider local marching girls a decadent 'cult' at a time when Cold War tensions gave militarist tendencies a raw edge. The cartoon was probably the work of Dennis Knight Turner. ALEXANDER TURNBULL LIBRARY, WELLINGTON, NEW ZEALAND

proportioned, arms swinging, gloved hands held to form a straight line from the shoulder to the backs of fisted knuckles, heads erect and berets sitting with the cockade centred exactly in line with the bridge of the nose, they were smart figures: unmistakeably New Zealand marching girls. Attired precisely as she was, Simpson, like the others, was ready to lead her team out before the scrutinising eyes of the judges and the crowds of people lining the steep banks of the park on three sides. The power of the spectacle she and other teams helped to create was one of an intriguing mixed metaphor, which exercised a strong hold over its exponents and viewers. The spectacle of a highly feminised body performing a masculine routine was a major element in New Zealand's culture for over four decades, drawing its power from the period in which the Cold War shaped international security (and insecurity). The polarities in geo-political power were echoed in the polarities around which gender identities were formed, nowhere more visibly, and variably, than in dress. New Zealanders, like others, grew into manhood or womanhood by learning how to dress the part. Being a member of a marching team was one way to learn.

13. Engaging in Mischief: The Black Singlet in New Zealand Culture

Stephanie Gibson

Certain items of dress sneak into cultural consciousness and end up bearing a much greater burden than originally intended. The black singlet is such a garment. At first manufactured as a practical item of menswear for manual work and sport in the early twentieth century, it quickly came to represent hard work and rural values in New Zealand culture. By the 1970s, the black singlet had become an instantly understood shorthand for the archetypal 'Kiwi bloke' – a strong, independent, no-nonsense, hard-working man. At the same time, the black singlet took on other, more subversive wearings, and has been creating mischief ever since.

Whatever versions of it are worn – from workwear to fashion, from underwear to outerwear, in wool, cotton or synthetic fibre – the black singlet appears in a diverse range of visual expressions, including art, postage stamps, advertising, comedy and cartoons. When joined by other iconic items of clothing (or 'Kiwiana') such as the Swanndri jacket, gumboots and jandals, the black singlet becomes part of our wardrobe of national dress. In this chapter I offer a history of the black singlet and some of its key manifestations in New Zealand culture over the last century.

Creating the mischief

The black singlet is particularly prevalent in New Zealand humour. Comedians and cartoonists have long used clothing for purposes of satire and ridicule or to express social comment, creating their work within an environment of shared opinions or one that is ripe for manipulation.[1] The wearing of black singlets by working men and athletes became widespread after the First World War, and by the 1930s, the black singlet was familiar enough for cartoonists to use it as a strong visual code for proletarian work and sport. Over the next few decades, characters dressed in black singlets increasingly appeared in newspaper and magazine cartoons as workers, athletes, trade unionists and even politicians.[2]

'The Paper Chase' by Gordon Minhinnick is an early example of cartoon characters dressed in singlets. 'Hard earned income' is wearing a black athlete's singlet while being chased by devilish characters in white singlets with the names of various taxes. Gordon Minhinnick, *Cartoons: Political and Otherwise*, Wilson & Horton, Auckland, 1935.
PUBL-0222-047, DION MINHINNICK AND THE ALEXANDER TURNBULL LIBRARY, WELLINGTON, NEW ZEALAND

From the 1970s they began appearing on television and film. Both rural and urban commentators, Māori and Pākehā, used such characters to disseminate ideas and opinions about New Zealand society, politics and culture. They ranged from the banal ('Ches and Dale' of the Chesdale cheese advertisements) to the deceptively simple characters created by humorists John Clarke and Billy T. James, and cartoonists Murray Ball and Burton Silver. They all tapped into, and played with, the archetype of the 'Kiwi bloke', which had taken its cue from the rural landscapes and economies familiar to New Zealanders since the late nineteenth century (namely, meat, dairy products, crops and wool).

The most famous and enduring manifestation of this archetype was the satirical character, farmer Fred Dagg, created by John Clarke in the early 1970s for the stage and then formalised with a name and look for television in 1973. Clarke had wanted to create a character that was amusing and endearing, and recognisably from New Zealand – 'you can only do what you know'.[3] He was able to create the look and sound of Fred Dagg based on experience, having spent time on farms while growing up and worked in shearing gangs after leaving school. With only a quarter of New Zealanders living in rural areas by

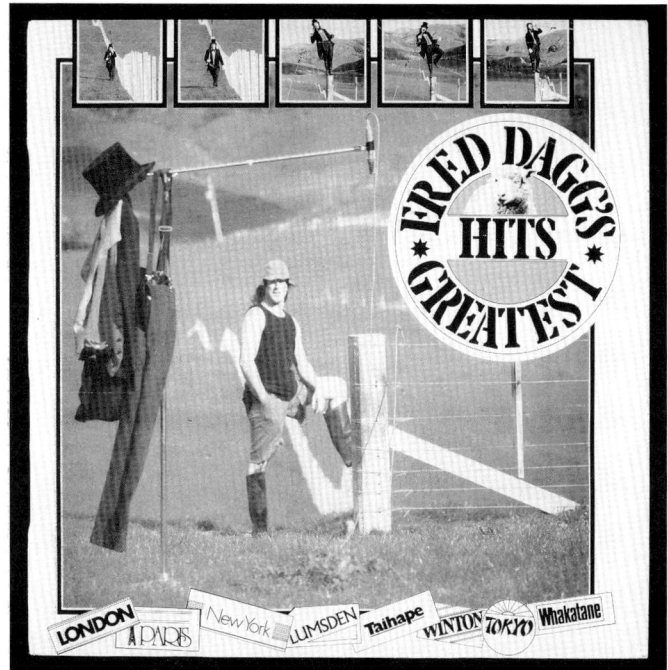

Fred Dagg's Greatest Hits album cover, EMI (New Zealand), 1975. One of the most memorable songs on this album is about stupidity: 'We Don't Know How Lucky We Are'. GH005615, JOHN CLARKE AND THE MUSEUM OF NEW ZEALAND TE PAPA TONGAREWA

the 1970s, Clarke could safely use Fred Dagg as a vehicle to parody the values remaining at the heart of New Zealand's identity as a farming nation.[4] Like many rural workers at the time, he wore a hat, black singlet, shorts and gumboots. He appeared simple, almost rustic, both in dress and speech, but had a smart, satirical and surreal view of New Zealand culture and politics. As Clarke noted, 'He was fair-minded in all things, graceful under pressure and was capable of developing strong opinions unspoilt by knowledge or formal logic'.[5] His humour was subtle, allowing the audience to meet him halfway: 'I was aware how people could engage in mischief'.[6]

Clarke assembled Fred's outfit over his first few television appearances. Most of it was recycled. The shorts were trousers ripped off at the knees, taken from the wardrobe of his employer, the New Zealand Broadcasting Corporation. The gumboots were a mismatched pair 'found somewhere'. The black woollen singlet was inspired by sheep shearers and therefore 'obligatory'. Clarke actually had three black singlets to choose from: two cotton ones for summer and a woollen one for winter. However, he usually wore the cotton ones as the wool became scratchy when performing under hot stage lights.[7]

Fred Dagg's immediate popularity with New Zealanders meant that once Clarke had established his outfit, he felt that he could not change it even if he had wanted to. But the strength and safety of the image allowed him to talk about 'whatever I wanted to bend'.[8] As art historian Anne Hollander notes, 'visual clarity means more than beauty, and costumes might be rudimentary as long as they helped show what kind of character was meant and what the audience ought to think of him'.[9] Since local audiences understood that Clarke was dressed as a farmer, his black singlet and gumboots became 'like a wink'; by seeming so familiar, he could slyly critique New Zealand society and politics.[10] Only three hours of screen-time were recorded over a three-year period, but Fred Dagg struck a deep chord with New Zealanders and is still instantly recognisable. Although Clarke moved to Australia in 1977, Fred Dagg has endured in New Zealand memory and continues to be a cultural icon of the 1970s, as seen by the acquisition and display of his outfit by the Museum of New Zealand Te Papa Tongarewa.[11]

More blokes in black singlets

The Fred Dagg archetype influenced others. In 1975 cartoonist Murray Ball created the hugely popular cartoon series *Footrot Flats*, with Wal Footrot as the central character. He and his mate Cooch were drawn from Ball's observations of the Manawatū rural scene. Like other cartoonists, he developed his characters through clothing.[12] For most of his career Wal wore a simple farmer's outfit (or 'uniform'): hat, black singlet, shorts and gumboots.[13] He covered up only when it was cold or wet, or dressed up in the presence of women, namely his Aunt Dolly and girlfriend 'Cheeky' Hobson. Occasionally, and very reluctantly, Aunt Dolly was allowed to 'scrape Wal's singlet off him to give it a wash', but much to Wal's shame and horror the result could be scented.[14]

In Wal's world, the black singlet symbolised a particular type of masculinity – men who work hard, live simply, have no airs or graces and see themselves as being free from 'civilising' women. When a school class visited his farm, Wal put on his hat to be more presentable, but the female schoolteacher saw his black singlet as underwear: 'Would you mind . . . er . . . your underclothes . . . ?! It's a mixed class, both sexes, you understand . . . ?'[15] But where Wal went, so did his

'What's the matter with the dog?' *Footrot Flats Three* by Murray Ball, INL Print Limited, Lower Hutt, 1978, p. 43, #FF 445.
MURRAY BALL

'Good morning trees', 1981. Bogor loved to pretend, using the forest around him to create various scenarios. Even his singlet was useful in these games, becoming an executioner's hood. *The Best of Bogor*, by Burton Silver, Silverculture Press, Wellington, 1994.
BURTON SILVER

singlet. He and Cooch even wore their singlets to bed, but Wal swapped his for an All Black rugby jersey in his dreams. In the 1986 film *Footrot Flats – The Dog's Tale*, half a dozen black singlets hung in Wal's wardrobe and nothing else. The black singlet was also important to Cooch, but he would 'give up his Jacky Howe to a slug with a sniffle', or swap it with a white singlet to box or play cricket ('Jacky Howe' was a popular name for shearers' singlets in Australia).[16]

Another black-singleted character born in the 1970s was the whimsical, lone woodsman Bogor created by cartoonist Burton Silver.[17] Initially he was bare-chested, but Silver redrew him in a black singlet as it was 'appropriate wear for a character out in the bush' and the scooped neck of the singlet helped to define Bogor's jawline. The simplicity of the black singlet fulfilled Silver's need as a cartoonist for a strong graphic image that framed the character's body. Over time, Bogor's singlet became longer and more prominent until it swathed much of his body. However, it never exceeded the hem of his shorts – to do so might have implied a dress, and the character's masculinity would have been undermined.[18]

Māori comedian Billy T. James actively subverted this rural archetype. In the mid-1980s, he used the black singlet to create a different type of 'Kiwi bloke' – one who was urbanised, politicised and anti-authority. On television he could be seen wearing a ripped and worn black singlet, tucked into shorts held up with string, mocking the image of the proud working man.[19] In cartoon form, he appeared as 'Nippy' from 'Jamestown', wearing either a rugby shirt or a close-fitting black singlet, shorts, cap and sunglasses, whatever the occasion. His character was deceptively naive and gullible – a seemingly ordinary bloke trying to make sense of the world but fully aware of racism and double standards. Like Fred Dagg, Billy T. James satirised the topics of the day, from the Fiji coup of 1987 to taxation, particularly revelling in generous-hearted stereotypes of Māori at a time of growing public and political debate about Māori rights and grievances.[20]

John Clarke moved to Australia in 1977, Billy T. James died in 1991 and Burton Silver and Murray Ball stopped drawing their cartoons in 1994. However, the residue of their characters remains, and any figure dressed like them in black

'What are you doing?' Hard-Case Book II, by Billy T. James and Chris Slane, Beckett Publishing, Auckland, 1987.
CHRIS SLANE AND HODDER MOA BECKETT PUBLISHERS LTD

singlets, shorts and boots will be recognised wherever they appear and would be read as symbols of masculinity.[21]

The black singlet as icon

Much of New Zealand culture is 'saturated with interest in the nature of masculinity', from cartoons to scholarly publications, resulting in a 'shared cultural environment rich with ideas about and images of masculinity'.[22] The black singlet is part of this environment, but takes on more than its share of representing work, masculinity, and even pioneering myths of the nineteenth century.

As a symbol of men's work, the black singlet has become most closely identified with farming and shearing, regardless of other occupational groups who wear it. This is partly due to romantic notions about the farmer in New Zealand culture, reinforced by the overwhelming number of sheep on the land. By the time Britain, New Zealand's largest export market, had entered the European Economic Community in 1973, rural workers were a minority. Their image, however, had become a major icon in Pākehā culture. Unpretentious, but 'looked upon from the city with a degree of benign contempt as well as sneaking respect', this archetype became increasingly clothed in a black singlet as the twentieth century progressed.[23] The black-singleted man offered an easily read image of 'male physical prowess'. It conjured up hard physical work, the toughness and loneliness of outdoor life and possibly even suggested the process of nation-building through 'taming' the land and making it productive. By the end of the twentieth century the black singlet had become the most popular image of New Zealand rural dress, arguably a 'vital ingredient of national identity'.[24]

The black singlet can be identified as Kiwiana, objects and images widely adopted and agreed upon as symbols or icons of national identity. Nostalgia and Kiwiana are very closely aligned and help to create a fictional history through myth making.[25] The black singlet, which is a twentieth-century phenomenon, is sometimes used to represent an earlier stage of Pākehā history when the land was being cleared and 'settled'. An example of this myth-making can be seen in New

Final artwork for the Kiwiana stamp issue, by Dave Gunson, 1994. The final issue did not date the black singlet.
NEW ZEALAND POST MUSEUM COLLECTION, MUSEUM OF NEW ZEALAND TE PAPA TONGAREWA/NEW ZEALAND POST

Zealand Post's popular 1994 Kiwiana stamp issue, which it described as 'items that are affectionately regarded by New Zealanders themselves as important and familiar parts of their national culture'. The stamp images included a black singlet and pair of gumboots, which New Zealand Post observed would be unlikely to 'approximate the status of an icon elsewhere!'[26] One of the earlier drawings for this issue anachronistically depicted a 'Singlet and Gumboots from the 19th Century'. A black singlet and gumboots alone were intended to conjure up a century of rural labour before they even existed. Because myths act economically to be generally understood, historical accuracy, such as period and dress, becomes less important.[27]

At the opposite end of the scale, towns throughout New Zealand have created large public sculptures or billboards to confirm their particular identities and contributions to nation-building. In Te Kuiti, 'The Shearing Capital of New Zealand', visitors are welcomed by a 6-metre-high reinforced concrete statue of a black-singleted shearer by sculptor Denis Hall. The statue's 'absolutely obvious' black singlet helps to tell the story of local shearer David Fagan, who has been world champion five times since 1988, but also shows the key role played by sheep farming in the building of New Zealand. The town relies on rural ways of life, but it also wants to attract tourists and share in symbols of national identity.[28]

Product advertising also claims such symbols of masculinity and national identity. The 'Southern Man' advertising campaign for Speight's beer makes a regional claim for the black-singleted man, though in the cold far south of New Zealand he usually wears a weather-proof Swanndri jacket. Accompanied by his dog and horse, the Southern Man is usually positioned in remote Otago landscapes as part of his work, such as sheep mustering. These images appear to be timeless and evoke nostalgia for the 'man alone' archetype, where a man can be in charge of 'unspoiled' nature and unfettered by women and society.[29]

Artists, like cartoonists, understand the 'cultural importance of clothing' in their work.[30] In 1948, Colin McCahon painted himself as a worker wearing a black singlet, set within bleak and stylised New Zealand landscapes in The

The big shearer statue in Te Kuiti, created by sculptor and balloonist Denis Hall from a model by fellow sculptor George Hanratty in 1994. The size of the statue increases its physical and emotional impact. Many locals regard it as art but Hall prefers to see it simply as a signpost.
PHOTOGRAPH BY PETER BUSH

Promised Land.[31] Since the 1970s, Nigel Brown has painted many male figures clothed in black singlets, their mournful faces and powerful arms framed by the three deep scoops of the neck and arm holes. They wear their singlets with the power of an icon, even when in bed. One work, *The Black Singlet* (1982), shows the upper body of a man wearing a black singlet inside a house with his arms crossed in either despair or frustration (overleaf). He could be an 'agent of land-rape, destruction and suppression of the female principle in history. But he also is an heroic builder embodying the pathos of his limitations ... Life is paradoxical: killer and lover both live in the black-singletted body of the pioneer axeman.'[32] This interpretation again points to the heavy burden borne by the black singlet – that of symbolising the nineteenth-century 'pioneer' without actually having been there.

Off the sheep's back

A singlet is a close-fitting garment, usually sleeveless and seamless (apart from at the shoulders) and worn underneath or instead of a shirt. As an undergarment, the singlet serves to keep the torso and its vital organs warm and comfortable, and so is usually made from soft, washable fabrics such as knitted wool or cotton.

The Black Singlet, silkscreen after woodcut, by Nigel Brown, 1982.
NIGEL BROWN AND THE WARWICK HENDERSON GALLERY, AUCKLAND

When worn as an outer garment, the singlet allows for airflow under the arms and across the neck and shoulders, while protecting the torso and preserving 'decency', thus making it an ideal garment for hard physical labour and sport.

Like New Zealand workers, Australians also adopted the singlet as practical workwear. In the 1890s, renowned Australian shearer Jacky Howe was considered the first shearer to wear sleeveless undershirts as singlets. Like other shearers of the period, he wore flannel undershirts but found the sleeves restrictive while shearing. He reputedly tore out the sleeves of his undershirt and converted all his shirts into singlets, thereby 'inventing' a practical work shirt. His innovation influenced others.[33] Since then, many Australian shearers and rural workers have called their singlet a 'Jacky Howe' in his honour.[34] The annual flow of shearers and labourers back and forth across the Tasman around the turn of the twentieth century meant that some New Zealanders also came to call their singlets by this name.[35]

From visual evidence, it appears that New Zealand men began wearing singlets, black and otherwise, as practical workwear in the early twentieth century, when occupational dress codes had started to relax.[36] Early working singlets may have been customised undershirts with the sleeves removed, or made at home by the needle workers of the family, usually women. Local production of practical clothing had became possible with the establishment of woollen mills throughout New Zealand in the late nineteenth century and by the 1920s many New Zealand workers were wearing mass-produced woollen singlets like a uniform.[37] These generally had high, collarless necklines and tight armholes to provide protection and maintain decency. They were knitted from wool dyed black or dark navy blue, serviceable colours for the grime of labour.[38]

By the 1940s and 1950s black dominated and the shape of the singlet had relaxed into a deeply scooped neck with looser armholes, allowing for more airflow and mobility, and had been adopted by a broad range of manual occupations and pursuits – shearers, farmers, hunters, trampers, labourers, railway workers, truck drivers, freezing workers, forestry workers, miners and fishermen. Some occupational groups named it for themselves, such as the 'bush singlet' for hunters and the 'slaughter singlet' for freezing workers.

The key characteristics of this now classic black woollen singlet are its length (sometimes almost to the knees) and its coarse heavy wool. The strength of wool and its ability to keep the lower back warm after a day of hard manual labour make it a particularly ideal garment for shearers, who can be prone to lower back trouble. Champion shearer Laurie Keats, who has shorn since the late 1940s, has always worn a black woollen singlet. He believes that wearing wool has kept his back strong because it soaks up sweat but stays warm and helps to regulate body temperature. A shearer can work comfortably all day in a sweaty singlet. Like other shearers in the mid-twentieth century, Keats wore his singlet with woollen tweed trousers and moccasins made from sacking or wool felt. Over time, the coarse

Queen Elizabeth II and the Duke of Edinburgh chatting with champion shearers and brothers Godfrey (left) and Ivan Bowen during a Royal Command Performance in McLean Park, Napier, 1954. Regardless of the proximity of royalty, urban and rural dress codes are different and are generally not seen side by side. Photograph by Edward P. Christensen.
F 19828 ½ (AAQT 6538, 15/C/8), COURTESY OF ARCHIVES NEW ZEALAND TE RUA MAHARA O TE KĀWANATANGA WELLINGTON OFFICE, NATIONAL PUBLICITY STUDIOS COLLECTION, AND ALEXANDER TURNBULL LIBRARY, WELLINGTON, NEW ZEALAND

wool of his singlet would capture stray bits of wool, which would mat together to become almost 'bullet-proof'. When the wool stretched, he would 'hitch' up the shoulders. Laurie bought his singlets from farm suppliers or army surplus stores where they were 'stacked to the ceiling'. He remembers that 'you could have any colour you wanted as long as it was black'. To Keats, the black singlet is like a uniform, but is also iconic in that it represents 'pretty hard work'.[39]

Godfrey Bowen, a renowned shearer who established a national shearing instructor scheme in 1953, is remembered for saying that a man not wearing a wool singlet was not a real shearer, but just a man shearing a sheep.[40] Wherever he travelled in New Zealand or around the world to demonstrate his technique, Bowen usually wore the traditional shearer's uniform: black woollen singlet, tweed trousers and sacking moccasins. Bowen was profiled by newspapers,

Slaughtermen at the Waipāoa freezing works, East Coast, c.1920, photographer unknown.
TAIRAWHITI MUSEUM TE WHARE TAONGA O TE TAIRAWHITI

magazines and television, and was even photographed several times alongside British royalty, wearing his black singlet.

Freezing workers also embraced the black singlet. When Rangi Paenga began working at the Kaiti freezing works in Gisborne in 1952, the slaughtermen all wore black woollen singlets with dark blue denim trousers, as their predecessors had done since the First World War. Initially the men bought their own singlets, and needed at least two to rotate during the day, with a clean singlet at home for the next day. During their breaks, they would change into their dry singlets, then swap back again at mid-shift. These singlets were dyed black to hide staining from dirt, blood and grease, and were made from wool, which helped prevent ill-health by soaking up perspiration and keeping the torso dry and warm. The workers 'did the best they could' to stay clean, even washing their singlets when taking showers. The black woollen singlet was not a uniform, but was 'virtually compulsory' because it was practical and safe.[41] Most workers liked wearing their black singlets and would wear them off-season at other jobs such as shearing or at home. Some in the industry considered the black singlet a status symbol.[42] Even though Paenga retired in the mid-1990s, he wears black singlets 'all the time and can't live without them'.[43]

However, black woollen singlets suffered a dramatic decline in the slaughtering industry in the early 1970s when new hygiene regulations were introduced to meet the higher standards required by American and British markets. The purchase, care and maintenance of the black singlet had been up to the individual, which did not sit well with the new standards of cleanliness required in meat handling. Black singlets were replaced with standard issue white singlets, shirts, trousers, aprons and hats, which were laundered on site every day.[44]

There were also changes in the shearing singlet. With the influence of American sportswear and underwear on the New Zealand market in the 1960s, many shearers came to see the classic black woollen singlet as too hot and heavy, and started wearing lighter wool and cotton versions, which also came in other colours. When shearers began wearing cotton singlets, Laurie Keats noticed an increase in back injuries and complaints. Once cotton is wet with sweat, it stays cold. During breaks, shearers would take their cotton singlets off and wring them out, but the cotton never warmed up, so they were prone to 'getting chills'.[45] However, fashions prevailed, and most shearers today wear cotton singlets in a vast array of colours and styles, and are specifically catered for by small manufacturing companies. Depending on the needs of the customer, male or female, these singlets can come in different colours, have contrasting edgings around the neck and armholes, wide or narrow backs and logos printed onto the fabric.[46]

Yet sturdy woollen clothing for rural workers has continued to be made and sold in New Zealand, regardless of fashion and technology. Norsewear, which has made black woollen singlets for rural workers, shearers and freezing workers since its establishment in 1963, continues to manufacture a traditional black woollen 'Shearer's Singlet' for those who 'just want something old and really durable to last the season'. Norsewear's singlets are made from heavyweight wool or a slightly finer worsted-based version for wearers with more sensitive skin. However, 'back country farmers are bullet-proof' and prefer the hard-wearing rough black singlets worn for generations. The 'Shearer's Singlet' is still popular among rural workers and sold all year round: over 1000 were sold in the year from July 2005. However, sales at Norsewear's Wellington city store went against the expected trend in the same year, when most of its black singlets were sold to women who wore them as dresses over leggings or trousers, with fashionable belts slung around their hips.[47]

Beyond the farm

The wearing of a black singlet is usually a sign of rural competence and familiarity with hard work. It allows the exposure of a manly chest and muscled arms (and can hide a growing stomach).[48] But urban manifestations of the black singlet have little to do with the rural archetype. In 1940, when the New Zealand government published a pictorial series called *Making New Zealand*, it noted that 'farm workers and country people have greater liberty in dress than city dwellers', showing an image of a farmer in a singlet which was 'suitable for open-air work'.[49] Even now with more relaxed dress codes, some would consider it odd, even unsettling, for a man in a black singlet to walk through the central business district of a major New Zealand city on a weekday, unless he was a labourer on a nearby building site. Such underdressing may be seen as uncouth or even aggressive. The black singlet can acquire menacing connotations when taken away from its work setting, best expressed in the violent character of 'Jake the Muss' in the 1994 film *Once Were Warriors*. His black singlet accentuated his muscled body, signifying working-class strength, but this admirable feature was negated in its manifestation as domestic violence.[50]

In the context of sport, a black singlet indicates athletic competence and achievement, particularly when combined with the silver fern. Sportsmen began wearing singlets, black and otherwise, in the late nineteenth century for athletics, rowing, cycling, boxing, wrestling, weightlifting and wood chopping. The now famous black singlet with silver fern patch was worn as part of the uniform for New Zealand's first Olympic teams, beginning with Antwerp in 1920.[51] Since then, several of our national sports teams, male and female, have embraced both the word and colour, and wear black singlets as part of their uniforms. In élite sport, the black singlet has an aura of strength and power: 'when you put on the Tall Black singlet you do what's asked of you . . . it's a New Zealand symbol'.[52] Function, fashion and symbolism are always held in balance with sportswear – the athletic black singlet allows freedom of movement and airflow, but looks smart, and when combined with the silver fern becomes another item in our wardrobe of national dress.[53]

Fashion statement

Popular All Black Dan Carter took the black singlet one step further when he launched his new Jockey product, 'Dan's Singlet', in October 2006. With its high neck and armholes, this was essentially a throwback to earlier versions and Jockey observed that 'over the years the classic singlet has become something of a style icon . . . Like many modern garments, what was originally intended for underwear has come out from under and today is regarded as a stand-alone item.' Carter, 'a sporting, living legend', could make this transition easier for urban men.[54] The media was quick to position the new Jockey product within the context of the popular history of the classic black singlet: 'the humble singlet is a kiwi icon worn by Fred Dagg and "rugby legend" Wal Footrot'. But, the media asked, 'can an endorsement by Dan Carter really make the singlet cool?' The answer came from a *Woman's Day* magazine editor, 'I think men are going to look at Dan in that singlet and secretly they want to be him, and women secretly want their men to be like Dan Carter as well'.[55]

'Wananga Heads Feather Own Nests!' by Tom Scott (1947–), 2005. The Māori character wearing a black singlet is mute and almost buried in the trench, lending comic poignancy to cartoonist Tom Scott's message of corruption. However, he is not a figure of derision: his black singlet indicates hard, honest labour.
DCDL-0000521, ALEXANDER TURNBULL LIBRARY, WELLINGTON, NEW ZEALAND/TOM SCOTT

The black singlet has been worn as a fashion item since the 1980s. As a vernacular garment, the woollen singlet became an attractive image and many aspired to own one regardless of whether they would be doing any work while wearing it. In the 1980s, many young New Zealand women saw the possibilities of the black woollen singlet as a fashion item. It was relatively inexpensive, practical and warm. And it was a versatile garment, long enough to be worn as a dress over shirts and tights, skirts or trousers and belted at the waist. Many found the clean lines of the black silhouette flattering. For one woman it felt like a 'security blanket'; for another it was an alternative feminist fashion statement, and a chance to dress like a 'pseudo-punk'.[56] For Rachael Hadwen, a young student in Wellington in the 1980s, the black singlet was warm, comfortable and practical. It was shapeless, could hide stains and was a gender non-specific garment: 'I love black singlets because they're so androgynous. They're like comfort food – the macaroni cheese of clothing. They're dark and cosy – a safe little place when against your skin.'[57]

For gay men, however, the black singlet is quite a different garment. Tight-fitting, short (stopping at the hips), made from cotton or synthetic fibres, with a constantly changing style, the gay man's black singlet is about fashion and physical attraction. The look for each season will be dictated by fashionistas in centres such as Sydney or London. White and black are preferred, with black in particular slimming the torso and framing arm and back muscles. The cut, make and styling of a singlet will clearly indicate who the wearer is. For example, women and gay men will generally wear a singlet to their hips, whereas a straight man is more likely to wear it below his belt or tucked in.

James Laverty, Mr Gay Wellington for 2005–06, says that 'a singlet sells a gay man' and is part of a 'gay man's uniform . . . It flatters more, and gives you a powerful, strong and confident feeling.' A styled singlet provides decency while being fashionable and shows enough flesh to attract without being obvious. However, revealing a styled, tight-fitting black singlet is a conscious and careful act for a gay man – while expected on the dance floor, it may not be appropriate at a dinner party or family event. That said, Laverty has noticed New Zealand society relaxing about what men can wear and how they choose to wear a garment like a singlet.[58]

The history and use of the black singlet reveals a powerful intersection between pioneer mythology, the wool economy, national identity, the archetypal Kiwi bloke, sexual politics and fashion. After a century of existence, the black singlet is still being worn – either on the farm or in city streets – and male and female characters dressed in black singlets still appear in cultural representations whenever a manual worker, athlete, rural archetype or anti-authority figure needs to be evoked. The uniformity of the black singlet, and its role as a signifier of work, generally protects such characters from censure. New Zealanders trust the black singlet, allowing fashion to dictate its 'coolness', and humorists using it to get away with daring comments on culture, sexuality, politics, race and the environment. The black singlet is still very much with us.

14. One Man's Fantasy: The Eden Hore Collection of High and Exotic Fashion Garments

Jane Malthus

Collectors come in all shapes, sizes and disguises, but James Eden Hore (1919–97) was perhaps one of the least predictable.[1] A sheep and cattle farmer near the tiny rural settlement of Naseby in Central Otago, he collected deer antlers, Jim Beam whiskey decanters, miniature horses, peacocks and other exotic animals, and amassed a startling collection of 1970s New Zealand designer women's fashion. An early proponent of rural diversification into tourism, he converted a tractor shed on his property, Glenshee, into a display room, where visitors could see what he called the 'high and exotic fashion' and the whiskey bottles, then tour the yards and house paddocks petting and feeding the birds and animals. At times peacock feathers were procurable and visitors were treated to the playing of the 21-jet fountain in his extensive and colourful garden. In 1976–7 Hore was host to 'more than 4,000 visitors . . . most of them from overseas'.[2] Many factors conspired to propel Hore into the role of collector and preserver of some of the more elaborate clothes produced in the 1970s.

The collector

Hore grew up at Kyeburn and worked as a musterer and shepherd before serving in the Second World War. He was employed on his family's farm from 1945 and purchased the nearby Glenshee Station in 1948, with clear plans to develop its potential as a sheep and cattle rearing and finishing farm. His success in this endeavour became part of New Zealand farming history: in 1973 a television documentary was made about the largest single sale offering of cattle in the South Island. Hore's short marriage had ended by 1960, so he hired a woman from Millers Flat, via Dunedin, as a housekeeper. A part-time model and very fashion conscious, she stayed at Glenshee for twelve years, introducing Hore to the fashion world, and possibly also to Joe Brown, of the Peppermint Lounge in Dunedin, organiser of Dunedin's famous town hall dances.[3] A promoter of

Finalists in the Miss New Zealand contest, 1972, with Eden Hore at his ranch at Kyeburn. From left: Miss Horowhenua (Lauren Ryan), Miss Taranaki (Linda Laursen), Miss Manawatū (Susan Connell), Miss Auckland (Sandra Hansen), Miss Coromandel Peninsula (Kristine Allan), Miss Hawke's Bay (Gaynor Saxon), Miss Otago (Dreana Bowman), Eden Hore, Miss Wellington (Vivienne Hamlin), Miss Tourist Diamond (Denise Marton), Miss Southland (Wanda Copland) and Miss Canterbury (Inese Berzins). OTAGO DAILY TIMES, 16 MAY 1972, P. 5

fashion and music, and owner of the franchise for the Miss New Zealand beauty pageants from 1960 to 1973 and 1979 to 1986, Andrew Joseph Francis Brown, known as Joe, was born in Naseby in 1907, but had left the area before Hore was born.[4] In January 1963 Brown staged a variety concert and talent quest as part of the centennial celebrations for the Naseby district. A young man, apparently too shy to enter, was pushed forward by his mates at the end of this competition, and performed. Brown clearly saw potential in this singer, as well as the irony of finding such a talent in his old hometown, and became his manager.[5] Two years later, John Hore – later John Denver Hore, now John Grenell – made his name as a country and western singer, his first album enjoying record sales in New Zealand.

A keen music fan, Eden Hore (no relation) took on the role of supporter and companion to this young local musician as he was trying to break into the big time as a country singer. Eden Hore accompanied John on tours with Joe Brown's beauty pageants, finding backstage and administrative work to do, and in the process becoming fascinated by the high fashion evening dresses and daywear

Advertisement for a showing of Eden Hore's collection. MOUNTAIN SCENE, 16 JUNE 1977, P. 16

the contestants wore in parades.[6] He did not start collecting garments until 1970, however, and purchased first those that had transformed the wool or skin products from farms like his into glamorous outfits. Hand-spun, hand-woven fashions and leather and suede designs, both one-off and commercial productions, were initially collected to show to overseas cattlemen and their wives who visited Glenshee.[7] But Hore was soon collecting evening wear and other award-winning fashion outfits. Once his intention to preserve such garments for posterity became known, outfits made specifically for the Benson & Hedges Fashion Awards or the Australian or New Zealand Gown of the Year were gifted or offered for purchase by their makers. The collection is unique evidence of an emerging couture and high fashion industry in New Zealand as well as a reminder of the quality of the local dressmaker trade.

Having amassed garments, which were at first kept in a room in his house, Hore liked to see them being worn as well as admired. Housekeepers were known to wear garments from the collection to local events, and for a few years Hore took

Photograph from one of the 1970s fashion parades as displayed at Glenshee.
JANE MALTHUS

parts of his collection to various cities for fundraising fashion shows. Finalists in the Miss New Zealand contest visited his farm in May 1972, but it is not known if they modelled any garments while there.[8] Over the summer of 1975 fashion parades were held picnic style in the garden at Glenshee and in 1976 North Island shows were held.[9] On 24 June 1977, J. Eden Hore 'Cattleman Extraordinary and Fashion Fancier' proudly presented his collection of unique and outstanding fashion garments to the people of Queenstown for the first time at the Lakeland Resort Hotel. Tickets cost $4.50 and included champagne and cocktail snacks.[10] He also did private shows in Queenstown for conference 'wives', and at least two parades in Invercargill in 1977 in support of the Plunket Society, the first having sold out in a matter of days. Interviewed by the *Southland Times*, he indicated that he had 'twenty shows lined up, including three in Australia'. Hore transported 80 separate outfits to Invercargill, some of which were for sale, as they had been made specifically for this purpose. He bought 'exclusive' fabric lengths and had them made into garments by Te Kuiti's Kevin Berkahn or Alexandra designer Pat Hewitt.[11] The Gore Garden Club hosted his collection in July 1977 and in August the Dunedin Plunket Society raised money for the Plunket-Karitane Hospital by showing 90 outfits from Eden Hore's collection. In 1978 Hore took part of the garment collection to Australia to show alongside those of Australian contemporary fashion designers at the Royal Randwick Racecourse in aid of the Air Ambulance and Royal Flying Doctor Services.

The collection

The garments in Eden Hore's collection are a testament to some key fashion influences of the late 1960s, 1970s and early 1980s. The particular flamboyances of colour, design and fabric are well represented. Pattern and decoration such as sequins, lurex, glitter, fringing, feathers, heat transfer prints, embroidered cottons, printed and sculptured velvets and metallised fabrics were all part of good and bad taste 1970s fashion. Synthetic fabrics and other textile innovations, acid and neon colours, nostalgia, folkloric and glam themes can all be noted.[12] But their designers never intended to be part of mainstream fashion. They were creating 'couture' or costume, designed for particular wearers or events, competitions or shows, and made to high standards. Most of the garments were part of a 'legitimate parallel fashion universe'.[13] These designers had, for the most part, resisted the shift to mass production and ready-to-wear, preferring to follow the example of 1950s European couturiers, even if they could not aspire to the wealth or status accorded their northern hemisphere counterparts. Their existence in this collection is a testament to how far from everyday the garments were. Street fashion and the hippie movement had moved clothes away from the high fashion and etiquette patterns of the early to mid-1960s. Hats, matching shoes, gloves and handbags, and fancy evening dresses were becoming obsolete as young people adopted long dresses for day and night wear, long hair, and denim jeans for any occasion.[14] The increasing casualness and individuality of clothing was emphasised in a speech to the New Zealand Retailers Federation in 1976 by L. P. Mechan of Lane Walker Rudkin. There was 'no longer a standard fashion' and young people were dressing to feel good rather than dressing for particular occasions or places. The lifestyles of consumers were now more important, he stressed, urging retailers to begin the process of niche marketing that has developed since the mid-1970s.[15]

Eden Hore's collection of high and exotic fashion contains 228 garments, mostly from the 1970s. Some of New Zealand's best-known fashion designers of the time are represented, such as Colin Cole, Kevin Berkahn, Vinka Lucas and Barbara Herrick. But the converted tractor shed also houses more individualistic garments: those entered in various fashion competitions through the 1970s. Some of these are designed by veterans of many such entries, such as Susan Holmes, others by people who entered only once or twice, while pursuing very different careers. The collection is idiosyncratic; some designers prominent in New Zealand during the 1970s are hardly represented or completely missing from this collection. For instance, there is only one outfit from Michael Mattar, who worked from a workroom and shop in Taumarunui, opened an Auckland boutique in the refurbished Parnell houses in 1976, won 'every major New Zealand fashion award' and became well known as an adjudicator.[16] There are none from Peter Homan of Auckland, who won the Benson & Hedges Gown of the Year in 1973 and the Supreme Award in 1974.[17] Presumably their garments were not offered to Hore, and he did not seek them out.

The designers

The oldest dress in the collection, though not the first one Hore collected, is the 1970 winner of the Australian Gown of the Year Award (Plate 13). Made from hand-spun merino blended with a metallic yarn and hand woven by Pauline Kingston, the full-length gown is empire line with an inverted pleat at the centre front. The fabric of the skirt section is ivory-coloured, striped horizontally with brown and orange, although two vertical welts on the front at about waist level interrupt the stripes. The bodice and short sleeve sections are bordered by wide ivory-coloured fabric bands and are richly embroidered and beaded in a pattern of circles. The empire line, named for the high-waisted style made in delicate cotton fabrics in France during and after the French Revolution, had returned to late 1960s fashion in the form of lacy baby-doll dresses. Kingston's design subverted the style by making it in such a heavy-looking and weighty fabric.

Pauline Kingston was originally from Auckland but was living in Australia at Cootamundra in New South Wales. She was 'a non-professional designer from the country, in the heart of a wool growing district', and the dress 'present[ed] a home craft that was becoming immensely popular and shedding its homely look . . . . The skilled work in this gown was further proof of how well our creative designers, at all levels, were using their multi skills to create fabrics of their own at an *haute couture* standard.'[18] The choice of this garment as winner of the award for 1970 provoked 'an unprecedented and unwarranted public outburst of pique from a handful of ill-informed, disappointed professional designers', which may have contributed to it ending up in Hore's collection, rather than remaining in Australia.[19]

Other award-winning garments in the collection came from Rosalie Gwilliam, Susan Holmes, mother and daughter Eleanor and Miranda Joel, and Maritza Tschepp. Contact initiated through a mutual friend allowed Hore first to purchase garments made from wool and later to have first option on all of Gwilliam's competition output.[20] Gwilliam was a textiles teacher and dress designer for a manufacturer. She began entering New Zealand Gown of the Year and Wills Award (the precursor of the Benson & Hedges) competitions in the early 1960s, gaining a third place in the Gown of the Year, and a fourth in the Wills Award in 1964. Her successes in the Benson & Hedges Fashion Awards began in 1970 with a Merit Award in the futuristic design category for a dress called 'The Puritan

– Year 2000'.[21] In 1971 she went to the United States to study the sewing of stretch knit fabrics. Most of her gowns in Hore's collection are made from knitted fabric such as Aqualana (a washable wool fabric) or Qiana (a du Pont nylon fabric), both heavily promoted for high fashion clothing in advertisements during the 1970s.[22] A camel-coloured wool jersey trouser suit with flared trousers and a hand-embroidered cape featuring New Zealand ferns won Gwilliam first prize for needlework at the 1974 Sydney Easter Show. She gained a Highly Commended Award the same year with an entry in the Benson & Hedges Fashion Awards inspired by butterflies, named 'Papillon'. This black Aqualana evening dress had a centre front cut out in the shape of a butterfly, which was edged with multi-coloured sequins, and a multi-coloured cape trimmed with sequins formed butterfly wing-like sleeves. A helmet completed the illusion. Applying sequins and beads and piecing fabrics became distinctive characteristics of Gwilliam's designs. From 1975 a spectacular padded cape-sleeved coat made from jewelled and sequinned black lace mounted over gold fabric was designed to cover a brief dance outfit (Plate 14). This consisted of a bikini top of gold metal cones held in place by chains, gold knickers, and a short black net skirt with fishtail hemline and a yoke of the multi-coloured jewelled and sequinned black lace over gold fabric. A coronet, partly made by a jeweller, completed the outfit, which cost $3,500 just for the materials.

Hore also purchased Gwilliam's wedding dress from 1961. In a letter offering it, she described it as made of:

> delustered off white satin mounted over Vilene and hand embroidered by me in a traditional Elizabethan scroll design with the centre of each scroll having a simple bead design in it in pearl, crystal, silver or gold. Gown has a train to it. Very simple style with full skirt, pearl coronet and cathedral length 10 [foot] long pure silk tulle veil . . . with machine embroidered edge. Took 1000 hours to make, how's that for dedication.[23]

In a very different style, a Hawaiian inspired one-shoulder, one-sleeved dress with red, purple and green flounces on skirt and sleeve, called 'Tropicana', was highly commended in the 1978 Benson & Hedges Fantasy Section. It featured multi-coloured artificial flowers that were perfumed with a tropical floral fragrance. Several Rosalie Gwilliam evening gowns from 1980 are part of the Hore collection, while one of the youngest outfits is Gwilliam's 1989 strapless evening dress in cream dupion silk matched with a black velvet jacket.[24] The dress has a richly embellished bodice featuring lace, braid, pearls and ribbons and the collarless long-sleeved jacket with flaring peplum is also decorated with cream braid, lace and pearls. Gwilliam stopped making entries for fashion competitions in the late 1990s, when her interest in photography left her little time for designing and sewing.

'Cloud with a silver lining' won the 1978 Benson & Hedges Fashion Awards Fantasy Section for Susan Holmes and is the only one of her many spectacular outfits in Hore's collection. Featuring her trademark hand dyeing, it is a trouser and pinafore-like cape in grey silk with pink and blue borders and floating panels, and a grey silk cloud-shaped mask headdress. An Aucklander by birth, Holmes studied home science at the University of Otago, completing a master's degree in human nutrition.[25] Dyeing and printing fabric was her passion, however, developed through producing and selling ready-to-wear garments at Brown's Mill market craft cooperative in Auckland throughout the 1970s, and entering her work in fashion and wearable art competitions.[26] In 1977 three entries in different categories in the Benson & Hedges Awards all gained highly commended awards.[27] She has won four Mohair Awards, the 1988 New Zealand Wool Board Handcrafts in Wool Premier Award, and the 1996 Supreme Award at the New Zealand Wearable Art Awards.[28] A number of her elaborate design costumes are held at WOW: The World of Wearable Arts Museum in Richmond, Nelson. Susan Holmes continues to teach and make wearable art, as well as working as a costume designer and maker.

Eleanor Joel (*née* Norman), who grew up near Winton in Southland, was a keen and gifted amateur painter throughout her life. Although she probably made clothes for herself and her daughter Miranda, and was described as a part owner of an Auckland boutique, her entry in the 1978 Benson & Hedges Fashion Design Awards seems to have been her only foray into competition. The black silk marquisette, hand-screenprinted with a bold arabesque border design, was fashioned into a dress with layered full circle skirts on a waistband and two over-the-shoulder bodice panels.[29] The dress was worn with a black velvet belt with gold braid and embroidery and the model carried a gold fabric rose as an accessory. The outfit won Joel the 1978 Benson & Hedges New Zealand Gown of the Year Section. She said at the time that 'she was really too old to be entering fashion competitions – let alone winning them'.[30]

Miranda Joel was in the top ten prize winners at the Cleo Awards in 1977. *Cleo* magazine launched these awards to encourage young designers either in tertiary education or work, and presumably also to raise their own profile. Rosaria Hall was also in that year's top ten and Patrick Steele took out the Supreme Award.[31] Miranda Joel's entry 'Birth of Venus', now in Hore's collection, was created from a crystal sheer fabric as a strapless shirred bodice above a short bubble skirt with elastic to give it shape and create a frill. Self-fabric ribbons, bias tape trims and small 'virgin' paua shells hang from the dress.

As a 'young struggling designer' working freelance after studying fashion design at Wellington Polytechnic, Maritza Tschepp, originally from Oamaru, had to 'sneak in late' to the Benson & Hedges Fashion Awards event she had entered in 1977, because she could not afford the ticket price. She went home with the Supreme and Gown of the Year awards, for her 'shimmering evening gown' in 'gold lace and organza'. She also gained Highly Commended awards for entries in women's daywear and young designer categories that year.[32]

Designed under her Kasphara label, Tschepp's winning dress had a golden lace underskirt gathered to a hipline yoke, which was visible beneath a chiffon striped dress with elasticised waist, circular yoke and full long sleeves. A triangular gold lace shawl completed the outfit. Hore's collection also contains two of her highly commended entries. The daywear entry was a very stylish cream single knit jersey day dress with long cuffed sleeves and draped tubular collar, worn with a cream and brown jacquard weave jacket trimmed with cream and brown plaid and gold, orange, cream and brown braid, a triangular plaid shawl and a cream knitted fabric hat trimmed with mink. In the young designer category Tschepp had entered red satin trousers with a red paisley printed silk knee-length tunic with full sleeves and a plain red sash.

Maritza Tschepp's designs were part of the extravagant 'new wave of ethnic [and oriental] fashions' triggered by Yves Saint Laurent's 1976 Ballets Russes collection.[33] She clearly enjoyed this style of design: the six other Kasphara label outfits in the Hore collection include an Egyptian-inspired tunic dress in green, orange and yellow, and a cream tunic trimmed with striped fabric and a twisted sash reminiscent of an ancient Greek youth.

The suede and leather garment showcase at Glenshee.
JANE MALTHUS

Early 1970s Berg label suede coat with opossum fur trim, by John West. JANE MALTHUS

The 'anti-consumerist hippie ideology' spawned interest in vernacular clothing, which in New Zealand included that made using products of the hunting and farming traditions.[34] Hore's collection started with some of these items but he continued adding outfits when they took his fancy. Jo Dunlap, David Dunlap, Beverley Horne, James Jaye, June Mercer, Skin Things, Wapiti Handcrafts, and John West are represented in the collection by garments showing how stylishly wool or skin could be used in designing and making.[35] From 1970 to 1972 five ensembles by Beverley Horne showcase elegant use of locally produced wool fleece. For each the breed of sheep is known (Perendale, Merino, Romney, Corriedale), and the wool has been hand spun and hand woven and some of it hand dyed. Beverley Horne became a spinner and weaver in her early twenties and wrote *Fleece in Your Hands* to encourage others to take up these crafts.[36] The full-length dresses include combinations of subtle beading, woven fabric strips, fringing, yarn tassels, peacock feathers, fancy weaves and colour (Plate 15). John West's Berg label cashed in on the fashion for 'Afghan' coats, producing fitting and supple deer skin suede versions, here represented by one each in black, orange and fawn from 1971. They are slightly different, with the black version having a hood and crystal beading, and the fawn fur koru designs on the fronts.[37] These two are opossum fur trimmed, while the orange one is plainer and has a wide belt with large 'bronze' buckle.

The Dunlaps were keen amateur leather garment designers. Jo Dunlap had trained as a nurse and teacher and worked as a photographer, display artist, fashion designer and dressmaker, while her husband David was an aircraft engineer.[38] David Dunlap's outfits in this collection are crafty. 'Midas Touch' consists of a light brown and bright gold yellow suede and leather jacket trimmed with white rabbit and flared trousers that Velcro apart at the knee to leave matadors, while the flares can be reassembled into a skirt. 'Ensenada' is a four-piece creation with a calfskin jacket and skirt worn with soft leather laced shirt and brief shorts.[39] Jo Dunlap's deerskin trimmed four-piece leather suit in brown (jacket, gauchos, hat and satin bodysuit), entered in the coordinates section of the 1979 Benson & Hedges Fashion Awards, is relatively traditional, but two outfits from 1978 entered into the Australian Gown of the Year competition are rather less so. 'Solar Flare' has a body section of flame shapes made of New Zealand leather, hand dyed red and machine embroidered in yellows and oranges, with sleeves and culottes of three layers (red, pink and yellow) of nylon chiffon cut very full and edged with ruffles.[40]

In 1977 a Woolgrowers' Award for hand-crafted wool fashion, with a prize of $750 donated by the New Zealand Wool Board, was added to the Benson & Hedges awards list, and 1978's winning outfit of this section and the Supreme Award was snapped up by Eden Hore.[41] Created by June Mercer, described as 'a Palmerston North engine driver's wife and mother of six', who had been spinning and weaving for less than three years, it was a natural grey Irish-crocheted jumpsuit, wrap skirt, jacket and shawl with appliquéd clover motifs made from a hand-spun Romney cross fleece.[42] Suede or leather skirt and vest outfits by Wapiti Handcrafts, James Jaye of Dunedin and Skin Things of Wellington in Hore's collection also show innovative cutting, piecing and fringing.

Kevin Berkahn, Colin Cole and Vinka Lucas designed many of the most eye-catching evening dresses in the collection. They were independent and entrepreneurial designers known throughout the 1970s for their spectacular evening and wedding gowns. At least 30 dresses or outfits made by Berkahn are part of Hore's collection, prompting Hore to believe he was one of Berkahn's best customers.[43] He purchased off the peg, but also occasionally commissioned garments. Berkahn, whose father came from German and Scandinavian stock, was raised during the 1940s on a dairy farm near Dannevirke. After getting an off-farm job at Jenkins' jewellers shop at sixteen, he started sewing clothes for his sister. He moved from Hawke's Bay to Auckland at the age of seventeen with the Jenkins family and made extra clothes for their new boutique in Takapuna. With a growing reputation for outfitting bridal parties, Berkahn went into business for himself at the end of the 1950s.[44]

These 1970s photographs of four Kevin Berkahn outfits were taken in the Glenshee garden.
JANE MALTHUS

As an Auckland designer of high fashion women's garments, he thought New Zealand garments sufficiently world class to organise a travelling show in 1971 aimed at letting other countries know of the quality fashion design produced here. Called New Zealand's World of Fashion, the show gained sponsorship from Pan-Am, and Berkahn toured Australia, the United States and England with selected couture and ready-to-wear. Hore subsequently purchased a number of Berkahn's garments from this touring show. One was cut as a straight full-length sleeveless dress from a floral sheer nylon fabric. In purples, green and blue with couched threads outlining the leaf and flower shapes, Berkahn lined the dress with teal blue acetate, and teamed it with a poncho edged with lilac-coloured feathers at the neck and shaped hemline.[45] A Berkahn pure wool crepe sleeveless empire-line gown with a more than full circle skirt created from gores cut in red, orange, yellow, and green was worn at St James Palace, London as part of a Commonwealth show organised by Princess Margaret.[46] The vertical, flaring rainbow effect Berkahn fashioned was possibly inspired by a similar

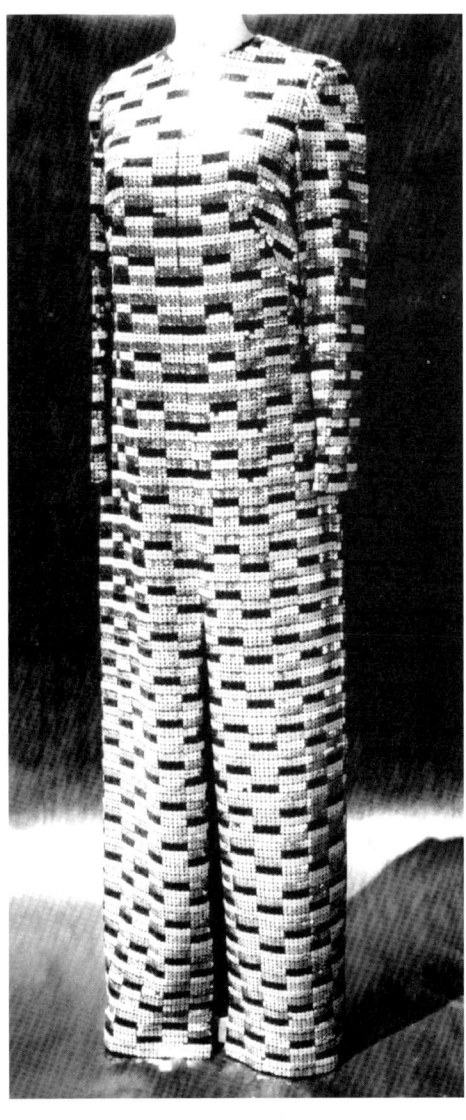

Kevin Berkahn evening dress, 1974.
JANE MALTHUS

effect in mini-dresses worn by Aretha Franklin and her backing singers in the late 1960s, but his elegant full-length version with its plaited girdle was also reminiscent of a Greek chiton.

Three of the Berkahn garments in the Hore collection were first shown at a fashion parade at the 1973 opening of the Sydney Opera House, which Hore attended, where they won an award as the best collection of three by one designer. Berkahn was able to participate in what was otherwise an all-Australian show because that same year he opened a shop in prestigious Double Bay, Sydney, stocked with his special occasion designs. David Jones, an Australian department store, also carried a Berkahn wedding dress range at the time.[47] The three full-length gowns were striking: one had a black velvet bodice and sleeves with a skirt made from many tiers of black Swiss lace, the edges of which were finished with large rhinestones. Another resurrected the tradition of the opera cape, with a white chiffon full-circle empire line dress with pleated bodice and shoulder straps covered by a dramatic green velvet cape edged with white feathers. The third outfit was a black empire line dress with fine shoulder straps in a double knitted fabric, worn with a bolero jacket covered in poppies made from red silk. Hore could not wait to buy at least the green opera cape and white chiffon dress for his growing collection and did not baulk at the $3000 price Berkahn nominated since he was not ready to sell. Hore immediately went off and got the cash.[48] The Hore collection also displays Kevin Berkahn's replica of Princess Anne's 1973 wedding dress, and a 1974 evening dress created in a simple sheath style from a Swiss all-over sequinned fabric, which was made to be shown at the opening of the Intercontinental Hotel in Auckland (left).

Spectacular quality fabrics also appealed to Colin Cole, another Auckland designer, and Hore's collection contains dresses in the same fabric by Cole and Berkahn.[49] Cole, 'tall, inclined to the dramatic and very romantic', began his career in clothing design by undertaking a five-year apprenticeship as a cutter-designer and taking sewing and pattern drafting lessons in his own time. He gained further experience in companies specialising in coats, lingerie and children's wear before setting up on his own in 1958 in Karangahape Road. He subsequently moved to

Queen Street, then on to Parnell as it was revitalised.[50] In 1961 he won a Golden Shears award. He established a reputation as one of New Zealand's leading high fashion designers in the 1960s, always producing one-off designs rather than ready-to-wear, and women travelled from all over the country to his studio for orders and fittings. This evening dress in a sheer synthetic fabric printed with large floral motifs in apricot, green, blue, brown and purple, which are outlined with couched apricot and gold thread, is a highlight of Hore's collection. The dress has a long straight skirt attached to a wide waistband with an apron bib bodice, and yoke and dolman sleeves cut from a plain apricot satin.[51] In 1975, Cole diversified slightly as the market changed (having recently designed the new uniforms for New Zealand Railways), by moving into larger business premises in Parnell and advertising to manufacturers as a design consultant and pattern maker. In the 1980s he sent a range of 50 outfits to a salon in Muscat, Oman.[52]

Evening dress by Colin Cole, 1973–4.
JANE MALTHUS

Dress by Vinka Lucas, c.1973. A hip-length feather-trimmed cape is part of the outfit.
JANE MALTHUS

Hore purchased some of his Vinka Lucas dresses through the shop Vanity Walk in Dunedin, and many still have their price tags attached. All feature ornate, decorative brocades, laces or sequin-covered fabrics combined with plainer sheers or opaques.[53] Vinka Lucas grew up in Yugoslavia and attended the Academy of Dress Design in Zagreb. After emigrating to New Zealand she established a business specialising in evening and bridal dresses using elaborate fabrics imported from Europe, as well as local fabrics. Vinka's husband David Lucas, described in *Apparel Manufacturing* as a bridal magnate, operated the textile side of their business.[54] Vinka Lucas sold her designs under Maree de Maru, After Five and Vinka Lucas labels depending on the style or intended use of the product. In 1973 Lucas-designed Air New Zealand uniforms were unveiled: blue-green ensembles with touches of gold.[55] In the mid-1970s, the Lucas group of textile-related companies extended to two bridal retail outlets in Auckland, three other 'salons' and production of a *Modern Bride* magazine featuring Vinka Lucas's designs.[56] A 1976 fire in the City Chambers Building in Auckland, where Lucas had her production house, destroyed or damaged a large collection of finished orders for her salons and a quantity of exclusive imported fabrics, but interrupted expansion of the Lucas empire only briefly.[57]

Although for a time Vinka Lucas produced ready-to-wear ranges for the New Zealand market, the demand from the Middle East for her particular styles led to her tailoring production for this market by the end of the 1970s.[58] The Vinka Lucas Designer Collections Salon opened in 1980 in partnership with Suzan Trading and Contracting in Jeddah. Evening and wedding gowns retailed there for between $1000 and $10,000, and since shops were staffed by men, and had no fitting rooms, potential buyers were allowed to take a garment home for one hour to try it on.[59]

In Hore's collection a $199.95 ($1848 today) Maree de Maru dress has a hip-length bodice cut from metallic brocade featuring a design of paisley shapes and wavy bands, with coffee-coloured sheer fabric gathered and flared skirt and sleeves. Another dress priced at $169.95 uses a bold printed paisley border design as the skirt and sleeves, and has a plain black bodice with roll collar. Floating panels of chiffon hanging down the back from the shoulders create an Isadora

Satin dress with printed velvet coat and belt, by Vinka Lucas.
JANE MALTHUS

Duncan effect. One of the most expensive ($395 or $3225 today) is a dress and full-length cape. The dress has been created in a straight through style from a daisy embroidered dark red and cream net fabric, with the scalloped edges of this lace positioned down the centre front and godets of cream wool crepe inserted from thigh level to allow for movement. The slightly flared hooded cape is made from cream wool crepe with long ties at the front and is edged with the daisy embroidered net lace (see over).

There is only one Babs Radon dress, the trade name of a 'fashion partnership' set up by Don and Barbara Penberthy.[60] Barbara Penberthy had long designed clothes, and her husband Don was a precision engineer before they established their workshop and salon in Mount Eden. Other retail outlets also sold their garments. By 1969 Babs Radon had a retail salon in the new high-rise 246 building on Auckland's Queen Street, and a workroom in Emily Place, which

Daisy embroidered net lace and wool crepe dress and cape, c.1975, by Vinka Lucas. JANE MALTHUS by the late 1970s was considered Auckland's fashion centre. As Chapter 5 noted, her label regularly featured in *New Zealand Vogue*.[61] From 1971, the dress in Hore's collection is the new midi length, long-sleeved and low-waisted. Made from a floral patterned silk in orange, cream, tan, black and white, it has a two-layered skirt and a sash belt. During the 1970s, as Barbara Herrick, she altered her manufacturing style from *haute couture* features such as bound buttonholes, silk linings and self-covered buttons to one that accommodated the demand of the market for 'two garments for the price of one', introducing the Miss Babs and Katie labels.[62]

By the end of the 1970s, the designers represented in Eden Hore's collection, whether commercially oriented or competition contenders, were an endangered breed. The general economic depression of the late 1970s affected many of them, while New Zealand's clothing and textile industries generally felt that they were under siege from various government measures designed to create freer trade access across the country's borders. Apparel imports began to increase from 1979, and closer economic relations (CER) with Australia became a reality in 1983, even though apparel was initially excluded. Redundancies and increased unemployment in the sector reflected these influences as well as fluctuating consumer clothing preferences and export market potentials. The viability of the whole sector was questioned.[63] In the 1980s the Industry Development Commission (IDC), while ostensibly supporting the apparel industry, recommended a transfer of resources into apparel growth areas that would improve efficiency and enable fewer units with larger turnovers. It urged the industry to purge production of those lines for which the domestic market was too small to support economic production. The country needed larger businesses than single-designer operations if it was to have a more efficient apparel industry that could compete with imports as well as export to Australia and beyond.[64] The government extended this transfer of resources over a much longer time frame than the IDC preferred, but small apparel designer businesses did suffer, especially after the 1987 stock market crash.

The collection today

Eden Hore bequeathed his collections to his niece and nephew, Margaret and John Steele, who now live at Glenshee, run the farm and look after the contents of the old tractor shed. Not much has changed. They have added to the collection of Jim Beam decanters, and many of Hore's beloved exotic animals, such as the yak bull, coyote, peacock and rabbits, have been mounted as a static display in the foyer. When visitors walk into the gallery, they are first greeted by the tableau of animals on their right and displays of some of the other photographic memorabilia on their left. Then, through further doors, a long, rectangular, carpeted split-level room appears, with glass-fronted, closed-in wardrobes

Part of a showcase at Glenshee featuring feather-edged outfits by Kevin Berkahn and Vinka Lucas.
JANE MALTHUS

around the walls and across the lower portion. Inside the wardrobes most of the garments are on padded hangers, some grouped according to designer, or style, but mostly arranged in a somewhat random order. Labels provide information as to designer and date, and for some a photograph of the garment being worn allows for a better idea of how the outfit looks on the body. Not all of the collection is on show at once: rotations are allowed for by having some garments stored in a room off to one side, also in glass-fronted wardrobes, but hanging more closely. The wardrobes also contain shoes and boots of the period, the accessories for particular garments, some of the Jim Beam decanters and the Franklin Mint collectible dolls Hore purchased more recently, while around the room on top of the wardrobes the rest of the decanters are displayed. A showcase of Hore's travel and Miss New Zealand souvenirs is positioned at one end of the room. There is a lot to see.

Hore was a man of vision and grand plans, although not all of them were realised. In 1975, he was planning to hold fashion shows of the dresses, using the raised section of the gallery as a stage, and envisaged tourists would undertake a five-hour safari taking in his collection, some local gold mining history and the Dansey's Pass Hotel.[65] His energy and enthusiasm have now gone, but others are still inspired by what they find at Glenshee. In 2003 artist Scott Eady visited and subsequently created 'Honeymoon on the Pigroot', a sculptural installation comprising a male mannequin dressed in a dinner suit made from oilskin (by designer Nicholas Blanchet), a pink miniature pony named Dahlia and close-up photographs of dahlias.[66] It left the Steeles slightly nonplussed but I think Hore would have loved it.

His garments were out on 'fashion's fringe', mostly created for one-off events such as the Benson & Hedges Fashion Awards, using hand techniques that ruled them out of commercial production.[67] They were never meant to be mainstream. Eden Hore was not interested in the everyday: he preferred a certain flamboyance in the garments he collected, and he wanted uniqueness. His collection, presented as hanging objects, offers the viewer opportunity to reflect on the ambivalences of fashion's many functions: a creative product of artistic genius, or gimmick; frivolity and fantasy or economic fuel; an expression of individuality or convention, or just body protection; cultural icon or homogenous status symbol.[68] And because they have been kept out of the way, safe in Naseby, these remarkable garments have survived as they may not have otherwise. For this we should all be grateful.

List of Contributors

David Butts is Senior Lecturer in and Programme Coordinator of the Museum Studies Programme in the School of People, Environment and Planning at Massey University, Palmerston North. He has an MA in archaeology from Otago University and a PhD from Massey in Museum Studies. His thesis is entitled 'Māori and Museums: The Politics of Indigenous Recognition'.

Valerie Carson has recently retired from her position as Conservator of Textiles at the Museum of New Zealand Te Papa Tongarewa. A graduate of the Textile Conservation Centre in London, she has held this position for 25 years, and has also taught the history of textiles, at the (then) School of Design, Wellington Polytechnic and embroidery at adult evening classes.

Caroline Daley is an Associate Professor in the Department of History at the University of Auckland. She is the author of *Girls and Women, Men and Boys: Gender in Taradale 1886–1930* (Auckland University Press, 1999) and *Leisure and Pleasure: Reshaping and Revealing the New Zealand Body 1900–1960* (Auckland University Press, 2003), from which this chapter stems. She is co-editor of *Suffrage and Beyond: International Feminist Perspectives* (Auckland University Press, 1994), *The Gendered Kiwi* (Auckland University Press, 1999), and the *New Zealand Journal of History*.

Stephanie Gibson is a Curator History, at the Museum of New Zealand Te Papa Tongarewa. Previously she was part of the redevelopment team for the Museum of Wellington City and Sea, and the first Collection Manager of the Adam Art Gallery, Victoria University. She has exhibited clothing in numerous exhibitions, including, most recently, *Kiri's Dresses*. She has written on the museum's relationship with its communities through a case-study of the development of the Indian community gallery at Te Papa.

Bronwyn Labrum is a Senior Lecturer in the School of Visual and Material Culture, Massey University, Wellington. She was a Curator History at the Museum of New Zealand Te Papa Tongarewa from 1996 to 2000, where she was responsible for the textile and clothing collection and exhibitions based on them. She is the co-editor of *Fragments: New Zealand Social and Cultural History* (Auckland University Press, 2000) and has published widely on the history of women, welfare and museums, contributing to a number of the key collections and reference works in these areas.

Rosanne Livingstone is a PhD candidate at Monash University in Melbourne, studying the textiles from Kellis, a Roman period village in Egypt. She worked at the Museum of New Zealand Te Papa for sixteen years; for most of this time she was employed as a collection manager, caring for the museum's collection of historical clothing and textiles.

Charlotte Macdonald is an Associate Professor of History at Victoria University. Her publications include *Women Writing Home: Female Correspondence Across the British Empire, Volume 5: New Zealand* (Pickering and Chatto, 2006), '*My Hand Will Write What My Heart Dictates*': *The Unsettled Lives of Women in Nineteenth-Century New Zealand as Revealed to Sisters, Family and Friends* with Frances Porter (Bridget Williams Books and Auckland University Press, 1996), *The Book of New Zealand Women/Ko Kui Ma Te Kaupapa* with Merimeri Penfold and Bridget Williams (Bridget Williams Books, 1991), and *A Woman of Good Character* (Allen & Unwin, 1990). She has written articles in the fields of women's and gender history and the cultural history of leisure and sport.

Jane Malthus is Honorary Curator for Dress at the Otago Museum, a part-time teacher of dress history at the School of Fashion, Otago Polytechnic, and an artist. Her PhD thesis was on colonial women's dress and she is the author of several key articles on the history of clothing, including 'Dressmakers in Nineteenth Century New Zealand', in *Women in History 2* (Bridget Williams Books, 1992).

Fiona McKergow has been a researcher for Anne Else's *Women Together: A History of Women's Organisations* (Daphne Brasell Associates Press, 1993) and an editorial officer for the *Dictionary of New Zealand Biography*. From 1998 to 2001 she was Social History Curator at the Science Centre & Manawatu Museum (now Te Manawa), where she developed and promoted the institution's clothing collection in a range of exhibitions. A contributor to *Fragments: New Zealand Social and Cultural History* (Auckland University Press, 2000), she is an independent researcher and writer.

Deborah Montgomerie is a Senior Lecturer in the Department of History at the University of Auckland. The author of *The Women's War: New Zealand Women 1939–45* (Auckland University Press, 2001) and *Love in Time of War*

(Auckland University Press, 2005), she co-edited *The Gendered Kiwi* (Auckland University Press, 1999) with Caroline Daley and is currently co-editor of the *New Zealand Journal of History*.

Katie Pickles is a Senior Lecturer in the School of History at the University of Canterbury. She is the author of *Transnational Outrage: The Death and Commemoration of Edith Cavell* (Palgrave, 2007) and *Female Imperialism and National Identity: Imperial Order Daughters of the Empire (IODE)* (Manchester University Press, 2002) and co-editor with Myra Rutherdale of *Contact Zones: Aboriginal and Settler Women in Colonial Canada* (University of British Columbia Press, 2005) and with Lyndon Fraser co-editor of *Shifting Centres: Women and Migration in New Zealand History* (University of Otago Press, 2002). She is currently writing a book about Kiwi heroines.

Jennifer Quérée is Senior Curator of Canterbury History at Canterbury Museum, where she has been responsible for the curation, research and exhibition of the extensive dress collection since 1980. An anthropology graduate from Otago University, Jennifer is a member of the International Council of Museums Costume Committee and a founding member of the New Zealand Costume and Textile Section. Her current research interests include the myths and realities of men's clothing in colonial New Zealand.

Awhina Tamarapa (Ngāti Kahungunu, Ngāti Ruanui, Ngāti Pikiao) is a Curator Māori, at the Museum of New Zealand Te Papa Tongarewa. She has over ten years of museum experience. Her previous positions include Concept Developer Māori, and Collection Manager Māori for Te Papa. Her publications include: *Nga Puna Roimata o Te Arawa* (National Museum catalogue, 1993); 'Curatorship: Indigenous Perspectives in Post-Colonial Societies', Canadian Museum of Civilisation Conference Proceedings, 1996; and *Taiāwhio: Conversations with Contemporary Māori Artists* (Te Papa Press, 2002).

Patricia Te Arapo Wallace (Ngāti Porou) is a Research Fellow in the Macmillan Brown Centre for Pacific Studies and Associate Lecturer in Pacific Studies at the University of Canterbury. Her primary research interest is in Māori material culture, traditional textiles and dress and the recovery of early Māori technology. Her PhD thesis was an analysis of pre-1820 Māori dress. She represents Ngā Puna Waihanga (Māori Artists and Writers Association) at national level, and currently edits the national Māori weavers' newsletter for Te Roopu Raranga Whatu o Aotearoa.

Notes

I. DRESSING HISTORY UP: INTRODUCTION

1. Linda Gill, 'Introduction', *Letters of Frances Hodgkins,* Auckland University Press, Auckland, 1993, p. 6, cited in Linda Tyler, 'Fanny's Frocks: Exploring Frances Hodgkins' Fashion Sense', *Context: Dress/Fashion/Textiles,* no. 5, 2004/2005, p. 10.
2. Ibid. Eight of Hodgkins' textile designs are now in the collection of the Museum of New Zealand Te Papa Tongarewa. See the chapter on her designs in Douglas Lloyd Jenkins, *40 Legends of New Zealand Design*, Random House New Zealand, Auckland, 2006, pp. 66–9.
3. Tyler, p. 15. See also Juliet Ash, 'The Aesthetics of Absence: Clothes without People in Paintings', in Amy de la Haye and Elizabeth Wilson (eds), *Defining Dress: Dress as Object, Meaning and Identity*, Manchester University Press, Manchester, 1999, pp. 128–42.
4. Tyler, p. 14.
5. Susan Vincent, *Dressing the Elite: Clothes in Early Modern England*, Berg, Oxford and London, 2003, pp. 3, 4. In the huge literature that has developed, useful introductory texts include: de la Haye and Wilson (eds), *Defining Dress*; Lou Taylor, *The Study of Dress History*, Manchester University Press, Manchester, 2001 and *Establishing Dress History*, Manchester University Press, Manchester, 2004; Barbara Burman and Carole Turbin (eds), *Material Strategies: Dress and Gender in Historical Perspective*, Blackwell, Oxford, 2003; Valerie Cummings, *Understanding Fashion History,* Batsford, London, 2004. Good studies of fashion include Elizabeth Wilson, *Adorned in Dreams: Fashion and Modernity*, revised edition, I. B. Tauris, 2003; Jennifer Craik, *The Face of Fashion: Cultural Studies in Fashion*, Routledge, New York and London, 1994; Valerie Steele, *The Corset: A Cultural History*, Yale University Press, New Haven, 2001. For men and masculinity, see Christopher Breward, *The Hidden Consumer: Masculinities, Fashion and City Life 1860–1914*, Manchester University Press, Manchester, 1999. Studies in different national contexts include Jane Ashelford, *The Art of Dress: Clothes and Society 1500–1914*, National Trust, London, 1996; Margaret Maynard, *Fashioned from Penury: Dress as Cultural Practice in Colonial Australia*, Cambridge University Press, 1994; Katie Pickles and Myra Rutherdale (eds), *Contact Zones: Aboriginal and Settler Women in Colonial Canada*, University of British Columbia Press, 2005; Berg Publishers has a large range of studies in its important 'Dress, Body, Culture' series. The long-standing journals *Costume, Dress* and *Textile History* have been supplemented recently by *Fashion Theory: The Journal of Dress, Body and Culture* and *Textile: The Journal of Cloth and Culture.*
6. Taylor, *The Study of Dress History*, p. 64.
7. Ibid., p. 2.
8. Cited in ibid., p. 70.
9. Ann Smart Martin, cited in ibid., p. 72.
10. See fn 5 above.
11. Taylor, *The Study of Dress History*, p. 83.
12. Suzanne Küchler and Daniel Miller (eds), *Clothing as Material Culture*, Berg, Oxford and New York, 2005, p. 1.
13. Ibid., p. 1.
14. Designer Karen Walker, quoted in Pamela Stirling, 'The Way We Wore', *New Zealander Listener* (NZL), 18 December 1999, p. 18, cited in Bronwyn Dalley, *Living in the Twentieth Century: New Zealand History in Photographs*, Bridget Williams Books/Craig Potton Publishing in association with the Ministry for Culture and Heritage, 2000, p. 176.
15. Richard Wolfe, *The Way We Wore: The Clothes New Zealanders Have Loved*, Penguin Books, Auckland, 2001, p. 118.
16. A point made by Danielle Sprecher in 'Clothes are Good Business: Consumption and Appearance in the Office, 1918–1939', in Caroline Daley and Deborah Montgomerie (eds), *The Gendered Kiwi*, Auckland University Press, Auckland, 1999, p. 141. Overviews include Doris McIntosh, 'Dress', *Making New Zealand: Pictorial Surveys of a Century*, vol. 2, no. 23, 1940; Eve Ebbett, *In True Colonial Fashion: A Lively Look at what New Zealanders Wore*, Reed, Wellington, 1977; Jenny Lynch, *Ready to Wear: The Changing Shape of New Zealand Fashion*, Random House, Auckland, 2004. Good exhibition catalogues include: Claire Regnault, *The New Zealand Gown of the Year*, Hawke's Bay Museum, Napier, 2003.
17. Sandra Coney, *I Do: 125 Years of Weddings in New Zealand*, Hodder Moa Beckett, 1995; Hamish Keith, *Reader's Digest New Zealand Yesterdays*, David Bateman, Auckland, 2001; Wolfe; Lynch; Rosemary McLeod, *Thrift to Fantasy: Home Textile Crafts of the 1930s–1950s*, HarperCollins, 2005.
18. Sidney Moko Mead, *Traditional Maori Clothing: A Study of Technological and Functional Change*, Wellington, Reed, 1969; Amiria Henare, 'Nga Aho Tipuna (ancestral threads): Maori cloaks from New Zealand', in Küchler and Miller, pp. 121–38; Jane Malthus, ' "Bifurcated and Not Ashamed": Late Nineteenth Century Dress Reformers in New Zealand', *New Zealand Journal of History* (NZJH), vol. 23, no. 1, 1989, pp. 32–46 and 'Dressmakers in Nineteenth Century New Zealand', in Barbara Brookes, Charlotte Macdonald and Margaret Tennant (eds), *Women in History 2*, Bridget Williams Books, Wellington, 1992, pp. 76–97. It is important to note that broader historical accounts have some material on clothing. See Nancy Taylor,

The New Zealand People at War: The Home Front, Historical Publications Branch, Department of Internal Affairs, Wellington, 1986; Jeanine Graham, 'Settler Society', in Geoffrey W. Rice (ed.), *The Oxford History of New Zealand,* second edition, Oxford University Press, Auckland, 1992; Sandra Coney, *Standing in the Sunshine: A History of New Zealand Women Since they Won the Vote,* Viking, Auckland, 1993; Dalley; Jane Malthus and Chris Brickell, 'Producing and Consuming Gender: The Case of Clothing', in Barbara Brookes, Annabel Cooper and Robin Law (eds), *Sites of Gender: Women, Men and Modernity in Southern Dunedin, 1890-1939,* Auckland University Press, Auckland, 2003, pp. 123–50; Fiona McKergow, 'Opening the Wardrobe of History: Dress, Artefacts and Material Life of the 1940s and 1950s', in Bronwyn Labrum and Bronwyn Dalley (eds), *Fragments: New Zealand Social and Cultural History,* Auckland University Press, Auckland, 2000; Heather Nicholson, *The Loving Stitch: A History of Knitting and Spinning in New Zealand,* Auckland University Press, Auckland, 1998; Sprecher; Frazer Andrewes, 'The Man in the Grey Flannel Suit: White-Collar Masculinity in Post-War New Zealand', in Daley and Montgomerie, pp. 191–212; Barbara Brookes, ' "When Dad Was a Woman": Gender Relations in the 1970s', in ibid., pp. 235–50 and Barbara L. Brookes, 'A Germaine Moment: Style, Language and Audience', in Tony Ballantyne and Brian Moloughney (eds), *Disputed Histories: Imagining New Zealand's Past,* Otago University Press, Dunedin, 2006, pp. 191–294.

19 For more on contemporary designers, see Maureen Molloy, 'Cutting Edge Nostalgia: New Zealand Fashion Design for the New Millennium', *Fashion Theory,* vol. 8, no. 4, 2004, pp. 477–90; Alison Goodrum, Wendy Larner, and Maureen Molloy, 'Wear in the World? Fashioning Auckland as a Globalising City', in Ian Carter, David Craig and Steve Matthewman (eds), *Almighty Auckland?,* Dunmore Press, Palmerston North, 2004, pp. 257–74; Alison Goodrum, Wendy Larner and Maureen Molloy, 'Auckland as a Globalising Fashion City', in Linda Welters and Abby Lillethun (eds), *The Fashion Reader,* Berg, Oxford, 2007, pp. 185–90.

20 For an illuminating discussion of this as it applies to the former British Dominions, including New Zealand, see Jennifer Craik, review of Margaret Maynard, *Out of Line: Australian Women and Style,* University of New South Wales Press, Sydney, 2001, in *Fashion Theory,* vol. 6, no. 4, pp. 457–62.

2. HE WHATU ARIKI, HE KURA, HE WAERO: CHIEFLY THREADS, RED AND WHITE

1 Turnbull, n.d., cited in Hirini Moko Mead and Neil Grove (eds), *Ngā Pēpeha a ngā Tīpuna,* Victoria University Press, Wellington, 2001, p. 35.
2 Ibid.
3 S. M. Mead, *Traditional Maori Clothing: A Study of Technological and Functional Change,* A. H. & A.W. Reed, Wellington, 1969. An detailed study of the garments in the British Museum's collection is in Mick Prendergast, 'The Fibre Arts', in D. C. Starzecka (ed.), *Maori Art and Culture,* David Bateman in association with the British Museum, Auckland, 1996, pp. 114–46. See also Mick Pendergrast, *Kakahu: Maori Cloaks,* David Bateman in association with the Auckland Museum, Auckland, 1997.
4 Aubrey Cannon, 'The Cultural and Historical Contexts Of Fashion' in Anne Brydon and Sandra Niesson (eds), *Consuming Fashion: Adorning the Transnational Body,* Berg, Oxford, 1998, pp. 23–5.
5 According to H. W. Williams's *Dictionary of the Maori Language* (1971), p. 84, this kākahu kura is not the same as the kahu kura which is a flax cape covered with red ochre, but both kahu whero (red) and kākahu kura had red feathers; H. W. Williams (ed.), *Nga Mahi a Nga Tipuna,* Wellington, Reed, 1971, p. 129; Mohi Turei, 'Tu-whakairi-ora', *Journal of the Polynesian Society (JPS),* vol. 20, no. 77, 1911, pp. 17–34.
6 Although varieties of garments are not specified, weapons and clothing are similarly found inside the taniwha in the story of the slaying of Te Kaiwhakaruaki, the taniwha in the Parapara Stream at Collingwood, Tasman Bay. Te Whetu, 'The Slaying of Te Kaiwhakaruaki', *JPS,* vol. 3, 1894, pp. 18–19.
7 Roger Neich, 'New Zealand Maori Barkcloth and Barkcloth Beaters', *Records of the Auckland Institute and Museum,* no. 33, 1996, pp. 111–58.
8 For example waka huia have been found wrapped in tapa. Testing of this tapa wrapping, with samples of hoheria (lacebark) cloth from Otago, hoheria fibre samples from the Dunedin region and Marquesas Island paper mulberry barkcloth, indicated that the sample bore closer comparison to the paper mulberry barkcloth than the other fibres. Jennifer A. Rowley, 'Note on the Tapa Covering Found with a Box of Huia Feathers on the Talla Burn, Central Otago,' *JPS,* vol. 75, 1966, p. 108.
9 J. C. Beaglehole (ed.), *The Journals of Captain James Cook On His Voyages of Discovery, Volume 1,* Cambridge University Press, Cambridge, 1955, p. 218.
10 John Stack, *South Island Maoris, A Sketch of their History and Legendary Lore,* Kiwi Publishers, Christchurch, 1984, pp. 72–3.
11 '…quelques pannes … des peaux de Chins [sic] cousues l'une contre l'autre ….une peau d'oyseau ….' in Isabel Ollivier and Cheryl Hingley (compilers), *Extracts from Journals Relating to the Visit to New Zealand of the French ship St Jean Baptiste in December 1769,* Alexander Turnbull Library Endowment Fund/National Library, Wellington, 1982, pp. 66–7.
12 Ibid., p. 73.
13 Andrew Sharp (ed.), *Duperrey's Visit to New Zealand in 1824,* Alexander Turnbull Library, Wellington, 1971.
14 See Roger Duff, *The Moa Hunter Period of Maori Culture,* Government Printer, Wellington, 1977, p. 217.
15 They were found on Cottesmore Station near Middlemarch, Central Otago and are now held at the Otago Museum.
16 It is now in the collection of the Auckland Museum, registration number MHE 23.2.
17 'Double' probably meant 'double-sided', indicating that the cloak was reversible.

18 Te Rangi Hiroa (Sir Peter Buck), *The Coming of the Maori*, Whitcombe & Tombs, Wellington, 1949, pp. 64, 171.
19 Its registration number is A 79.966. Other names identifying such garments include tāpahu, see Augustus Hamilton, *The Art Workmanship of the Maori Race in New Zealand*, Board of Governors, Dunedin, 1901, p. 287 and Edward Tregear, *The Maori Race*, A. D. Willis, Wanganui, 1904, p. 236. It was also apparently called tahi uru on the West Coast, see Ernst Dieffenbach, *Travels in New Zealand: With Contributions to the Geography, Geology, Botany and Natural History of that Country*, J. Murray, London, 1843, vol. 2, pp. 53–4 and Tregear, p. 236. However, there is no evidence that the southern dogskin garment had a similar name.
20 Hamilton, p. 287 and Mead, p. 46.
21 Some records appear to suggest the cloak was covered literally with dog tails, so I have chosen to be very specific in describing the tail hair of white dogs. Williams's dictionary translates kahu waero as a 'cape covered with skin of dogs' tails', p. 84.
22 William Colenso, *Notes on the Ancient Dog of the New Zealanders*, 1877, URL: http://www.nzetc.org/tm/scholarly/tei-ColNote-t1-body.html, accessed 20 November 2006.
23 Hamilton, p. 286 and Mead, p. 47.
24 Hamilton, p. 286.
25 See Beaglehole and Isabel Ollivier (eds), *Extracts from Journals Relating to the Visit to New Zealand in May-July 1772 of the French Ships Mascarin and Marquis de Castries Under the Command of M.-J. Marion du Fresne*, Alexander Turnbull Library Endowment Trust with Indosuez New Zealand Limited, Wellington, 1985.
26 John Liddiard Nicholas, *Narrative of a Voyage to New Zealand Performed in the Years 1814 and 1815, in Company with the Rev. Samuel Marsden, Principal Chaplain of New South Wales*, James Black & Son, London, 1817, p. 107.
27 I have seen rediscovered maroon-red kākā feathers used as mattress stuffing.
28 E. G. Turbott (ed.), *Buller's Birds of New Zealand: A New Edition of Sir Walter Lawry Buller's A History of the Birds of New Zealand*, Whitcombe & Tombs, Christchurch, 1967.
29 Elsdon Best, *Tuhoe: The Children of the Mist*, Board of Maori Ethnological Research, Wellington, 1925, vol. 1, p. 101.
30 Best, pp. 452–5.
31 Sir Joseph D. Hooker (ed.), *Journal of the Right Hon. Sir Joseph Banks, During Captain Cook's First Voyage in H.M.S. Endeavour in 1768–71 to Terra del Fuego, Otahite, New Zealand, Australia, the Dutch East Indies, etc*, London, Macmillan, 1896, pp. 233–4.
32 G. Forster, *A voyage round the world in His Britannic Majesty's sloop*, Resolution, *commanded by Capt. James Cook, during the years 1772, 3, 4, and 5*, B. White, in Fleet-Street, J. Robson, in Bond-Street, and P. Elmsly, in the Strand and G. Robinson, Pater-Noster Row, London, 1777, vol. 1, pp. 218–9.
33 Anderson in Beaglehole, vol. 3, part 2, p. 810.
34 John White, *The Ancient History of the Maori*, 13 volumes [computer file], University of Waikato Library, Hamilton, 2001, vol. 2, Maori Text, p. 37; vol. 2, English text, p. 38.
35 Ibid., vol. 5, p. 63.
36 Mohi Tūrei, dictated by Pita Kapiti, 'Kumara Lore', *JPS*, vol. 22, 1913, pp. 36–9; translated by H.W. Williams, pp. 62–5.
37 J. H. Mitchell, *Takitimu*, A. H. & A.W. Reed, Wellington, 1944, p. 104.
38 Tūrei, p.37.
39 The definitions of the garments as translated by W. L. Williams give a pūeru as a coarsely woven garment of dressed flax, a tarahau as a shaggy cloak of kiekie fibres, māhiti as a cloak covered with long white hairs of dogs' tails, and aronui, paepaeroa, puhoro and pātea as finely woven garments of dressed flax differing from one another in their ornamentation. Tūrei, p. 37.
40 Best, pp. 294–5.
41 Patricia Burns, *Te Rauparaha – A New Perspective*, Reed, Wellington, 1980, pp. 53, 98.
42 Material for this paragraph is from The Maori Land Court Minute Books for Wellington: 1, pp. 31, 38; 1C, pp. 53, 140-5.4; 1H, p. 327, 10, p. 109; Mairatea Tahiwi & Cushla Parekowhai, 'Ruhia Porutu', in Charlotte Macdonald, Merimeri Penfold and Bridget Williams (eds), *The Book of New Zealand Women Ko Kui Ma Te Kaupapa*, Bridget Williams Books, Wellington, 1991, pp. 533–6; Dinah Priestly, *Old Thorndon*, Anchorage Press, Wellington, 1988; Obituary, *New Zealand Times*, 10 December 1886.
43 William Colenso, *The Authentic and Genuine History of the Signing of the Treaty of Waitangi, New Zealand, February 5 and 6, 1840*, George Didsbury, Government Printer, Wellington, 1890, p. 15.
44 T. Lindsay Buick, *The Treaty of Waitangi*, Thomas Avery & Sons, New Plymouth, 1936, p. 136.
45 Colenso, 1890, pp. 24–5.

3. UNPICKED FOR THE VOYAGE? HEIRLOOM DRESSES IN COLONIAL NEW ZEALAND
We would like to thank the Greenwood and Burnett families for their generosity and assistance with the project, especially Joanna Douglas and the late Anne Burnett. We would particularly like to thank Ann Atkinson, textile designer, for carrying out weave analysis on the Te Papa textiles. Collection information was provided by staff at the following institutions in New Zealand: Otago Museum, Otago Settlers Museum, Dunedin Public Art Gallery, Olveston, Hocken Library, South Canterbury Museum, Canterbury Museum, Nelson Provincial Museum, Alexander Turnbull Library, Te Manawa, Whanganui Regional

Museum, Puke Ariki, Hawke's Bay Museum, Tairāwhiti Museum, and Auckland War Memorial Museum; in Australia: the Migration Museum, Adelaide; National Gallery of Victoria, Melbourne; Benalla Museum, Victoria; Tasmania Museum and Art Gallery, Hobart; and the Powerhouse Museum, Sydney. Others who assisted include Sandra Troon, textile conservator, Oregon; Edward Maeder, Historic Deerfield, New England; Margaret Maynard, University of Queensland and Charlotte Macdonald, Victoria University of Wellington. And special thanks to the editors and our colleagues at Te Papa for their ongoing support and encouragement.

1. Family information acquired with accession, Burnett Collection, History Department, Te Papa.
2. Charlotte Macdonald, *A Woman of Good Character: Single Women as Immigrant Settlers in Nineteenth-Century New Zealand*, Allen & Unwin/Historical Branch, Wellington, 1990, p. 77. Single women immigrants were 'required to have a minimum stock of clothing before they embarked: six shifts, two flannel petticoats, six pairs of stockings, two pairs of shoes, and two strong gowns (one of which had to be warm)'.
3. Te Papa holds approximately seven eighteenth-century dresses, some other eighteenth-century garments and fabric pieces.
4. Philippa Scott, *The Book of Silk*, Thames & Hudson, London, 1993, p. 7.
5. Brocade is produced by 'A supplementary weft introduced into a ground weave. Its movement is limited to the width of the area where it is required by the pattern. It does not travel from salvage to selvage.' Dorothy K. Burnham, *Warp and Weft: A Textile Technology*, Royal Ontario Museum, Toronto, 1980, p. 18. In damask 'The pattern is distinguished from the ground by contrasting luster and is reversible. In two-color damask, the colors reverse on either side.' Phyllis G. Tortora and Robert S. Merkel (eds), *Fairchild's Dictionary of Textiles*, 7th edition, Fairchild Publications, New York, 2000, p. 162.
6. Eric Broudy, *The Book of Looms*, Brown University Press, Hanover, 1979, p. 124.
7. Natalie Rothstein, *The Victoria and Albert Museum's Textile Collection: Woven Textile Design in Britain to 1750*, Victoria and Albert Museum, London, 1994, pp. 10, 13; Jane Ashelford, *The Art of Dress: Clothes and Society, 1500–1914*, The National Trust, London, 1996, p. 154.
8. Natalie Rothstein, *Silk Designs of the Eighteenth Century in the Collection of the Victoria and Albert Museum*, Thames & Hudson, London, 1990, p. 18.
9. Ibid., pp. 9–23 passim; Ashelford, p. 154.
10. Rothstein, *Silk Designs*, pp. 37–58 passim.
11. Deborah E. Kraak, 'Eighteenth-Century English Floral Silks', *Antiques*, 1 June 1998, p. 845.
12. Ibid., pp. 845–46 passim.
13. Judy Wentworth, 'Spitalfields Silk', *Antique Collecting*, vol. 23, no. 2, June 1999, p. 27.
14. Janet Arnold, *A Handbook of Costume*, Macmillan, London, 1973, pp. 144, 146.
15. Notes from interview with Anne Burnett, September 1990, Burnett collection, History Department, Te Papa.
16. Dress, GH007353, Collection of the Museum of New Zealand Te Papa Tongarewa.
17. Ann Atkinson, textile designer, personal comments, 12 December 2006: 'Ivory plain weave with undulating stripes of varying blocks (1, 2, 4, 8) of floating wefts, 1.25cm apart. The larger, more detailed floral posies are brocade, woven with supplementary wefts in four different colourways. Each posy (two per row), is reversed in mirror image and in a different colourway in the following row. There is a total of 11 hues and tints. The smaller, simpler and more numerous brocaded sprigs in three colours (in three different colourways) are scattered irregularly with four consecutive rows facing one way and the next four being mirror imaged. The sett of the fabric is 144 ends per 2.5cm. The width of the repeat is 50.2cm and the length of the repeat is in excess of 152.5cm (none of these pieces show the pattern in one full repeat). The multi-striped selvedges have the same sett as the fabric field, and have frequent distortions and a line of stretcher nail holes where the fabric has been held on-loom.'
18. Dr J. D. Greenwood, Memoranda, 7 July 1887, in 'Greenwood Letters 1', unpublished, 1948, p. 88–9.
19. Janet Paul, 'Greenwood, Sarah 1809?–1889', *Dictionary of New Zealand Biography* (DNZB), updated 7 April 2006, URL: http://www.dnzb.govt.nz/, accessed 14 December 2006.
20. Examples of Sarah Greenwood's drawings and watercolours are held at the Nelson Provincial Museum and ATL.
21. Sarah Greenwood to Mrs Lyon, September 1842, 'Greenwood Letters 1', p. 1.
22. An eighth child was left behind because of poor health, and a ninth was born during the voyage. See June E. Neale, *The Greenwoods: A Pioneer Family of New Zealand*, General Printing Services Ltd, Nelson, 1984, pp. 7, 92.
23. A number of Greenwood family heirlooms are held at Nelson Provincial Museum and Te Papa.
24. See Greenwood family papers, 1803–1942, MS Papers 98, ATL. For published extracts, see Frances Porter and Charlotte Macdonald (eds), *My Hand Will Write What My Heart Dictates: The Unsettled Lives of Women in Nineteenth-century New Zealand*, Auckland University Press/Bridget Williams Books, Auckland, 1996.
25. Carrie Rebora, Paul Staiti, Erica E. Hirshler, Theodore E. Stebbins and Carol Troyen, *John Singleton Copley in America*, Metropolitan Museum of Art, New York, 1996, p. 269.
26. Wentworth, p. 26.
27. Neale, p. 88.
28. Anne Greenwood to Sarah Greenwood, 12 August 1870, 'Greenwood Letters 2', unpublished, 1952, p. 41.
29. John Greenwood to Isabelle Greenwood, 19 June 1890, 'Greenwood Letters 2', p. 53.
30. Neale, p. 93.
31. Dress, PC002090, donated by Anne Burnett, 1982, Collection of Te Papa. Edward Maeder, Los Angeles

County Museum of Art, personal communication, 1985. Bradfield, p. 4.
32 Anne Atkinson: 'On the obverse the solid blue warp face ground contrasts beautifully with the ivory weft and multicoloured supplementary weft brocades which together form a lively overall floral pattern, woven in left-handed twill. The design has a strong central motif with a secondary design area on the selvedges. When two repeat lengths are matched at the selvedge a single motif is formed from the two (mirrored) halves on the edges of the fabric. The pattern repeat is 41cm selvedge to selvedge, and 106.7cm vertically. The sett is 120 ends per 2.5cm.'
33 Dress, PC002091, donated by Anne Burnett, 1982, Collection of Te Papa. Ann Atkinson: 'The fabric is warp-dominant plain weave with warp stripe and floating weft design elements. A delicate meandering foliate pattern is formed by blocks of floating wefts over 4-30 warp ends in vertical blocks from 1-8 rows high. Supplementary wefts in 7 shades and tints of red and green plus ivory form floral posies. The smaller sprigs have 4 of the same colours plus ivory. The brocade posies are woven with 3 rows facing one way and the next 3 rows facing the opposite direction. The pattern repeats are subtly different for each posy and sprig in both vertical and horizontal directions. The yellow stripes are 1.4cm and the blue stripes 2mm wide. The sett is 2.5cm. There are continuous ends along the selvedge due to stretching during weaving. Unpicked running stitches are still present along the selvedge.'
34 Rothstein, *The Victoria and Albert Museum's Textile Collection*, pp. 91–3.
35 Dress, PC002089, donated by Anne Burnett, 1982, Collection of Te Papa.
36 Ann Atkinson: 'Brown silk satin damask in 7/1 warp faced weave. Three loose posies of 4 different flower heads face one direction in one row, and the opposite direction in the following row. Between and around the posies are small buds facing one way for 2 rows and the other way for the next 2. The sett is 175 ends per 2.5cm, the repeat 15.85cm across and 19.65cm vertically. Selvedge to selvedge measures 48.25cm. The selvedge is undifferentiated, remarkable only for the clear nail holes from the on-loom stretcher.'
37 Personal communication, Anne Burnett, 17 April 1996.
38 Henry Brett, *White Wings: Fifty Years of Sail in the New Zealand Trade, 1850–1900*, vol. 1, Brett Printing Co. Ltd, Auckland, 1924, p. 351.
39 Martha Burnett to her mother, 4 September 1852, Burnett Family Papers MS-Papers-4773, ATL.
40 Personal communication, Anne Burnett.
41 Burnett family information acquired with accession, History Department, Te Papa.
42 Personal communication, Truus Gribben, Benalla Museum, 3 May 2005. The dress was donated to the museum in 1995.
43 PC003958, donated by Mrs. A. Williamson, great-granddaughter of the Reverend Vicesimus Lush, 1991, Collection of Te Papa.
44 A New Zealand Historic Places Trust property.
45 Personal communication, John Webster, Supervisor, Ewelme Cottage, Auckland, 8 December 2006.
46 Personal communication, Louis Le Vaillant, Curator Applied Arts, Auckland War Memorial Museum, 3 September 2006. Gift of Mrs Betty Brookes Clouston. Collection of Auckland War Memorial Museum, T696.
47 Silk dress, c.1760, 84/49/1. Gift of Mr. Compton-Smith. Collection of the Hawke's Bay Cultural Trust, Napier.
48 Personal communication, Jennifer Quérée, Senior Curator, Canterbury Museum, 27 October 2005. Canterbury Museum, EC147.137.
49 Neale, p. 81.
50 *Wises New Zealand Directory*, 1872–3, pp. 178, 186.

4. KILTS AS COSTUMES: IDENTITY, RESISTANCE AND TRADITION
I would like to thank the School of History at the University of Canterbury for funding the research for this chapter, Karen Fox for her excellent research assistance and Kathryn War and Ann Corry for their insightful comments. The knowledge, expertise and support received from the editors of this collection are greatly appreciated.
1 Katie Pickles, 'Sherry Party', *Christchurch Girls' High School Magazine*, 1985, p. 39.
2 Margaret Maynard, *Fashioned From Penury: Dress as Cultural Practice in Colonial Australia,* Cambridge University Press, Cambridge and Melbourne, 1994, p. 6.
3 Hugh Trevor-Roper, 'The Invention of Tradition: The Highland Tradition of Scotland', in Eric Hobsbawm and Terence Ranger (eds), *The Invention of Tradition*, Cambridge University Press, Cambridge and New York, 1983, pp. 15–42.
4 Tom Brooking and Jennie Coleman (eds), *The Heather and the Fern: Scottish Migration and New Zealand Settlement*, University of Otago Press, Dunedin, 2003, p. 15; James Belich, *Paradise Reforged: A History of the New Zealanders From the 1880s to the Year 2000*, Allen Lane & Penguin, Auckland, 2001, p. 221.
5 Robin Nicholson, 'From Ramsay's Flora MacDonald to Raeburn's MacNab: The Use of Tartan as a Symbol of Identity', *Textile History*, vol. 36, no. 2, 2005, pp. 146–67, p. 147.
6 James D. Scarlett, *Scotland's Clans and Tartans*, Lutterworth Press, Guildford and London, 1975, pp. 40–1.
7 S. M. Mead, *Traditional Maori Clothing: A Study of Technological and Functional Change*, A. H. & A. W. Reed, Wellington, 1969, pp. 119, 140.
8 Hugh Cheape, *Tartan: The Highland Habit*, National Museums of Scotland, Edinburgh, 1991, 2nd edition 1995, p. 7.

9. URL: http://www.kilts.co.nz/mitartans.htm, accessed 31 January 2005.
10. Trevor-Roper, pp. 18–19.
11. URL: http://www.kilts.co.nz/mitartans.htm, accessed 31 January 2005.
12. Trevor-Roper, pp. 20, 22.
13. Ibid., p. 23.
14. Roddy Martine, *Scottish Clan and Family Names: Their Arms, Origins and Tartans*, John Bartholomew & Sons Ltd, Edinburgh, 1987, p. 26.
15. Trevor-Roper, p. 15.
16. W. A. Thorburn, 'Military Origins of Scottish National Dress', *Costume,* no. 10, 1976, p. 29.
17. Trevor-Roper, p. 25.
18. Thorburn, p. 40.
19. Nicholson, p. 160.
20. Martine, p. 38 and Tom Brooking, *Lands for the People? The Highland Clearances and the Colonisation of New Zealand: A Biography of John MacKenzie*, University of Otago Press, Dunedin, 1996, p. 17.
21. *Sunday Star Times (SST)*, 23 April 2006, C11. In *Lands for the People?* Tom Brooking raises the paradox of Scots settlers dispossessing Māori of land.
22. Margaret Maynard, 'Blankets: The Visible Politics of Indigenous Clothing in Australia', in Wendy Parkins (ed.), *Fashioning the Body Politic: Dress, Gender and Citizenship*, Berg, Oxford and New York, 2002, pp. 189–204, p. 194. See also Maynard, *Fashioned From Penury*, pp. 59–73.
23. Trevor-Roper, p. 20.
24. *New Zealand Herald (NZH)*, 18 June 1996, Section 3, p. 1.
25. Chris Laidlaw, *Rights of Passage: Beyond the New Zealand Identity Crisis*, Hodder Moa Beckett, Auckland, 1999, pp. 38–9.
26. Trevor-Roper, p. 15; Peter Womack, *Improvement and Romance: Constructing the Myth of the Highlands*, Macmillan, London, 1989, p. 15.
27. Womack, p. 25.
28. Trevor-Roper, pp. 29, 35; Cheape, p. 72.
29. Thorburn, p. 40.
30. Scarlett, p. 43.
31. Tom Brooking offers an alternative reading of these politicians as 'radicals'. Tom Brooking, 'Introduction', pp. 11–15 and 'Sharing out the Haggis: The Special Scottish Contribution to New Zealand History', pp. 49–65 in Brooking and Coleman.
32. *SST*, 14 September 2003, A17.
33. *Southland Times (ST)*, 14 April 2000, front page; *Press*, 5 May, 2000, front page, 'Hurt MP kits out in kilt'.
34. Dover Samuels, Minister of Māori Affairs, 3 May 2000. URL: http://www.vdig.net/ hansard/archive, accessed 21 October 2005.
35. John M. MacKenzie, 'A Scottish Empire? The Scottish Diaspora and Interactive Identities', in Brooking and Coleman, p. 28.
36. Stephen Ladanyi, 'The New Zealand Scottish Regiment: A Brief History 1939–1982', MA thesis, University of Canterbury, 1982, pp. iv, 29.
37. Jock Phillips, *A Man's Country?: The Image of the Pakeha Male – A History*, Penguin, Auckland, Revised edition, 1996, pp. 82–130.
38. Ladanyi, pp. 32–3.
39. Thomas S. Abler, *Hinterland Warriors and Military Dress: European Empires and Exotic Uniforms*, Berg, Oxford and New York, 1999, p. 78.
40. Ladanyi, pp. 6–10.
41. Ibid., pp. 16, 20.
42. Thorburn, p. 34.
43. Eve Ebbett, *In True Colonial Fashion: A Lively Look at What New Zealanders Wore*, A. H. & A. W. Reed, Wellington, 1977, p. 58.
44. See Shiobhan O'Donnell, 'Dancing at the Auld Cale: A History of Highland Dancing in Dunedin between 1863 and 1900', BA Hons Thesis, University of Otago, 1998; Jennie Coleman, 'Ceol Mor of the South: Theme and Variations on an Immigrant Music Culture', in Brooking and Coleman, pp. 133–52.
45. Maureen Molloy, *Those Who Speak to the Heart: The Nova Scotian Scots At Waipu 1854–1920*, Palmerston North, Dunmore Press, 1991, pp. 123, 132.
46. Personal communication, Karen Fox to Ann Corry, 27 October 2005 and Helean Kiltmakers pamphlet.
47. *Metropol*, Issue 15, 13 May, 1999, p. 19; advertisement for Highland Kilt Hire, Kildonan Highland House Ltd, 33 New Regent Street, Christchurch, http://www.kilts.co.nz/ mitartans.htm, accessed 31 January 2005; Ira Von Furstenberg with Andrew Nicholls, *Tartanware: Souvenirs from Scotland*, Pavilion Books, London, 1996, p. 22.
48. Michael King, *Being Pakeha: An Encounter with New Zealand and the Maori Renaissance*, Auckland, Hodder & Stoughton, 1985, and Michael King, *Being Pakeha Now: Reflections and Recollections of a White Native*, Penguin, Auckland, 1999, 2004.
49. *New Zealand Woman's Weekly*, 6 March 2006, p. 40.
50. Theresa M. Winge and Joanne B. Eicher, 'The American Groom Wore a Celtic Kilt: Theme Weddings as Carnivalesque Events', in Helen Bradley Foster and Donald Clay Johnson (eds), *Wedding Dress Across*

     Cultures, Berg, Oxford and New York, 2003, pp. 207–18, p. 209.
51 *Press*, 30 December 2000, p. 8.
52 Ibid., 8 February 2001, p. 14.
53 Scotch Kiwi advertisement, *New Zealand Adventure*, April–May 1996, p. 24.
54 *Press*, 4 February 2005, p. 5.
55 *NZH*, 18 July 1996, Section 3, p. 1.
56 Scarlett, p. 48.
57 *SST*, 23 April 2006, C10.
58 Barbara Peddie, *Christchurch Girls' High School 1877–1977*, Christchurch Girls' High School Old Girls' Association, Christchurch, 1977, p. 50.
59 Villa Maria College introduced a kilt in 1966. *Villa Maria College: 75 Years, 1918–1993*, 75th Jubilee Magazine, Villa Maria College, Christchurch, 1993, p. 74. Mollie F. Chalklen, *The School at the Terminus: A Jubilee History of Papanui High School 1936–1986*, Raven Press and the Papanui High School Old Students' Association, Christchurch, 1986, p. 97.
60 See also Charlotte Macdonald, 'Putting Bodies on the Line: Marching Spaces in Cold War Culture', in Patricia Vertinsky and John Bale (eds), *Sites of Sport: Space, Place, Experience*, Routledge, London and New York, 2004, pp. 85–100.
61 Interview, Karen Fox with Kathryn War, Buyer/Manager at 'Ballantynes studentbody', 2 November 2005; J. Garnham and G. Cowlrick (eds), *Ad Lucem: Napier Girls' High School, 1884–1984*, Central Hawke's Bay Printers and Publishers, Waipukurau, p. 91; *Press*, 7 January 2000, p. 25.
62 Judy Mason, *A Venture of Faith: The Story of St Hilda's Collegiate School, 1896–1996*, St Hilda's Board of Trustees and University of Otago Printing Department, Dunedin, 1996, p. 148.
63 Personal communication, Karen Fox with Lauren Holroyd, Burnside High School Uniform Committee, November 2005.
64 Interview, Karen Fox with Kathryn War, 2 November 2005; Anne Denniston, *School by the River: Avonside Girls' High School Celebrates 75 Years of Independence*, Avonside Girls' High School, Christchurch, 2003, p. 65.
65 Interview, Karen Fox with Kathryn War, 2 November 2005, Peddie, pp. 191, 102; Sarah Lees-Jeffries, *Christchurch Girls' High School 1977–2002*, Christchurch Girls' High School, 2002, p. 16, URL: http://www.rangiruru.school.nz/studentcommunity-clans.shtml, accessed 21 October 2006.
66 Interview, Karen Fox with Kathryn War, 2 November 2005.
67 Personal communication, Karen Fox with Pauline Moore, Deputy Principal, Mairehau High School, November 2005.
68 Lees-Jeffries, p. 16.
69 *Press*, 27 May 2005, front page.
70 Atholea Ramsay, Helen Stead and Elspeth Ludemann, *The Honour of Her Name: The Story of Waitaki Girls' High School 1887–1987*, Waitaki Girls' High School Centennial Committee and John McIndoe Ltd, Dunedin, 1987, p. 177; New Zealand Press Association, 25 August 2004, Factiva, Dow Jones and Reuters.
71 M. N. Broome (ed.), *Cashmere High School: 40 Year Celebration: 1956–1996*, Souvenir Publication, Cashmere High School, Christchurch, the '1980' page; *Press*, 27 May 2005, A1; *Press*, 28 May 2005, A4.
72 On queer clothing and comfort see Ruth Holliday, 'Fashioning the Queer Self', in Joanne Entwistle and Elizabeth Wilson (eds), *Body Dressing*, Berg, Oxford and New York, 2001, pp. 215–31.
73 Shaun Cole, 'Don We Now Our Gay Apparel': *Gay Men's Dress in The Twentieth Century*, Berg, Oxford and New York, 2000, p. 187; *New York Times*, 4 July 1993, p. 3; *Globe and Mail*, 30 December 1993, A14.
74 *Evening News Scotland*, 7 February 2001, p. 1.
75 See Steve Garlick, 'Men, Clothing and Identity: Fashioning Masculine Subjectivities', *Sites*, no. 37, 1999, pp. 64–82.
76 Sandra Coney, *I Do: 125 Years of Weddings in New Zealand*, Hodder Moa Beckett, Auckland, 1995, p. 101.

5. EVERY GARMENT TELLS A STORY: EXPLORING PUBLIC COLLECTIONS

1 In 1982 I accepted the position of curator at the museum and for five years I had the privilege of working with all the collections in the museum. Although I left the museum to work in Wellington in 1987 I have always maintained my connection with the museum and the staff who work there. In recent years, as a Senior Lecturer in Museum Studies at Massey University, I have regularly taken students to the museum in Napier and the directors and staff (including the honorary curators of archaeology and textiles) have generously given time to speak to the students and given us access to the wonderful collections that have been developed and maintained by the people of Hawke's Bay.
2 D. Butts, 'Nga Tukemata: Nga Taonga o Ngati Kahungunu (The Awakening: The Treasures of Ngati Kahungunu)', in P. Gathercole and D. Lowenthal (eds), *The Politics of the Past*, Unwin, London, 1994, pp. 107–17.
3 Preventive conservation standards ensure that collections are stored and exhibited in appropriate climatic conditions and that each item is handled with care and packed in appropriate materials. Textiles, for example, are damaged when folded and unfolded because the fibres break along the folds, so modern museum practice requires textiles to be stored in big flat drawers, on large rolls, in acid-free boxes or hung on coathangers, where the garments are strong enough to bear their own weight, to avoid having to fold the garments. In order to achieve these improved standards, museum storage now takes up far more room than

in the past and this is an ever increasing expense.

4   Exhibitions including items from the clothing collection include: 'Cocktail Couture' (1997), 'Marine Parade: Real and Imagined' (2000), 'A New Land' (2000), 'Avis Higgs: Joie de Vivre' (2000), 'Stepping Out: Napier and the Art Deco Maori' (2002), 'Bother the Servants: A Year in the Life of Anna Spencer' (2004), 'Red Cross' (2006).

5   Although there is no surviving list of the items in the collection of the Hawke's Bay Philosophical Institute museum in 1890, there are photographs of the displays and a number of Māori garments can be seen (R. Fea and E. Pishief, *Culture of Collecting*, Hawke's Bay Cultural Trust, Napier, 1996, p. 15). However, by the time the remaining elements of the Athenaeum collection were transferred to the Hawke's Bay Art Gallery and Museum in 1936, only one kākahu Māori was recorded. Hamilton removed his own collection of taonga Māori from the Institute's museum and eventually deposited the collection in the Dominion Museum in Wellington.

6   The range of honorary keepers appointed during the early years of the museum's development indicate the areas of the collection that were developing most actively: art, botany, zoology, entomology, geology, history, archives, ethnology, prints, etchings, ceramics, antiques, coins and stamps. In 1949 the museum decided to stop collecting natural history material and the existing natural history displays were reduced and eventually removed (Fea and Pishief, pp. 35–6).

7   Ibid., p. 36. See also Robert McGregor, 'Bestall, Leonard Delabere 1895–1959', *DNZB*, updated 7 April 2006, URL: http://www.dnzb.govt.nz/.

8   Fea and Pishief, p. 63.

9   Ibid., p. 87.

10 David Kuchta, 'The Making of the Self-Made Man: Class, Clothing, and English Masculinity, 1688–1832', in Victoria de Grazia (ed.), *The Sex of Things: Gender and Consumption in Historical Perspective*, University of California Press, Berkeley, 1996, p. 55.

11 Susan Upton, 'Spencer, Anna Elizabeth Jerome 1872–1955', *DNZB*, updated 7 April 2006, URL: http://www.dnzb.govt.nz/.

12 These figures are approximate as not all such garments have yet been included on the computerised collection database.

13 Unfortunately, despite strenuous efforts, I was unable to arrange a suitable image of the christening gown in time to meet the publication schedule.

14 Details from Bessie Thompson's birth certificate, Folio No. 1911/5300, Births, Deaths and Marriages, Department of Internal Affairs. This was kindly supplied by Fiona McKergow.

15 Information provided by Patricia Teunon, daughter of Hinemoa Harvey (née Collison), 14 September 2006.

16 Hamish Keith, *New Zealand Yesterdays*, Reader's Digest, Auckland, 1984, p. 186.

17 Margaret Maynard, *Out of Line: Australian Women and Style*, University of New South Wales Press, Sydney, 2001, pp. 22–5.

18 Douglas Lloyd Jenkins, 'Babs and the Trouser Girls', *NZL*, vol. 195, 16 October 2004. See also Claire Regnault, *The New Zealand Gown of the Year*, Hawke's Bay Museum, Napier, 2003.

19 For publications arising from these exhibitions see Claire Regnault, Douglas Lloyd Jenkins and Ingrid Dubbelt, *Mason Handprints*, Hawke's Bay Cultural Trust, Napier, 1998; Douglas Lloyd Jenkins, *Avis Higgs: Joie de Vivre*, Hawke's Bay Museum, Napier, 2000; Douglas Lloyd Jenkins, *Frank Carpay*, Hawke's Bay Museum, Napier, 2003; and Regnault, ibid.

20 This was the number of taonga Māori and kākahu Māori recorded on the Hawke's Bay Art Gallery and Museum's computerised collection database in April 2005. It is also recorded that the museum exchanged at least one kahu kiwi in 1952 with an American museum (Fea and Pishief, p. 37).

21 The largest collection of kākahu Māori held in a regional museum is at the Whanganui Regional Museum. There are 110 cloaks in its collection in 2005.

22 This is because these kākahu no longer have their original accession numbers attached and therefore cannot be related to an entry in the accession register or because they were not recorded when they entered the museum. It is reasonable to assume, however, that most of the undated acquisitions entered the museum during the early years of the institution and that subsequently their accession tags have become detached. Further research matching kākahu to descriptions in the accession register may reassign some kākahu to particular acquisitions, though this may not provide any further provenance.
Kākahu Māori acquisitions at Hawke's Bay Art Gallery and Museum by decades:

Decade	Number of cloaks & capes	Number of piupiu/rāpaki
1930–9	13	7
1940–9	15	1
1950–9	8	6
1960–9	7	5
1970–9	4	5
1980–9	11	3
1990–9	1	0
2000–	0	2
Accession date unknown	32	16
Total	91	45

23 Fea and Pishief, pp. 26–7. The McLean Collection numbers over 850 items including taonga Māori, historical archival material and material from the Pacific Islands, the Mediterranean and Europe.
24 Future research in the Donald McLean archival resources may enable some of the cloaks to be identified. See also Alan Ward, 'McLean, Donald 1820–1877', *DNZB*, updated 7 April 2006, URL: http://www.dnzb.govt.nz/.
25 The McLean Collection can be compared with the Sir Walter Buller Collection now held by Te Papa. Because a catalogue was made of this collection while Buller was alive he was able to provide provenance information. Of the 45 kākahu in the Buller collection, 18 are identified to their source.
26 L. D. Shepard, 'Ancient DNA Studies of New Zealand Avifauna', PhD thesis, Massey University, 2005, ch. 5.
27 Haplotypes are antigenic phenotypes determined by closely linked genes linking a unit and providing a distinctive genetic pattern.
28 S. M. Mead, *Traditional Maori Clothing: A Study of Technological and Functional Change*, A. H. & A. W. Reed, Wellington, 1969, p. 189.
29 Ibid., p. 168. 'The replacement of Maori clothing by European clothes and the subsequent emphasis on costume for ceremonial occasions was probably the main cause for the development . . . towards the modern piupiu. . . .'
30 Rangi Te Kanawa is the daughter of nationally renowned weaver Diggeress Te Kanawa and granddaughter of Rangimārie Hetet, who was an important leader in the movement to revive the customary Māori art of weaving.
31 Physical access to the collection is problematic because of the limited museum storage facilities. The cloaks are stored in large flat drawers, as appropriate for kākahu, but the limited number of drawers means there is often more than one cloak in each drawer. Access to one cloak may mean moving another, and each movement of these fragile garments can cause damage. Some of the larger kākahu have been rolled to avoid folding them into the drawers. The museum is very conscious of this problem and is planning additional cloak storage in the proposed facility redevelopment.
32 The paepaeroa is 2880 mm wide by 1650 mm long, including kaupapa and tāniko border (accession number 39/38).
33 Mead, p. 130.
34 Rangi Te Kanawa, Conservation Assessment Report, Paepaeroa (39/38), 2002.
35 While travelling with James Cook in 1769, Sydney Parkinson observed a kaitaka with tāniko in black, red and white in Hawke's Bay, though it is not known whether the kaitaka paepaeroa in the Hawke's Bay Art Gallery and Museum came from this region (Mead, p. 55).
36 *Hawke's Bay Today*, 23 October 2002, p. 17.

6. 'WHAT ARE THESE, SO WITHERED, AND SO WILD IN THEIR ATTIRE?': CASTAWAYS' CLOTHING FROM THE AUCKLAND ISLANDS

1 The title quotation is from William Shakespeare, *Macbeth*, Act 1, Scene 3. For a full discussion of the clothing of the *Dundonald* castaways see my 'Seabirds, Seals and Sailcloth: The Clothing of the *Dundonald* Castaways', *Costume*, no. 37, 2003, pp. 75–94.
2 *Lyttelton Times* (*LT*), 2 December 1907, p. 7.
3 The name of the earliest ship is unconfirmed but may have been the *Rifleman* in 1833. Others were the *Grafton* (1864), *Invercauld* (1864), *Minerva* (1864), *General Grant* (1866), *Derry Castle* (1887), *Compadre* (1891), either *Stoneleigh* or *Marie Alice* (1895), *Sally* (recorded on maps for 1896 but unsubstantiated) and *Anjou* (1905). The *Dundonald* was the last ship wrecked on these islands.
4 *Otago Witness* (*OW*), 4 April 1868, p. 11.
5 The remains of the huts and other historic sites on the Auckland, Campbell/Motu Ihupuku, Bounty and Antipodes Islands are now cared for by the New Zealand Department of Conservation under the management plan for these islands (plus the Snares/Tini Heke) as a World Heritage site.
6 R. Bartra, *Wild Men in the Looking Glass: The Mythic Origins of European Otherness*, University of Michigan Press, Ann Arbor, 1994, pp. 206–7.
7 Thomas Musgrave and J. J. Shillinglaw (eds), *Castaway on the Auckland Isles*, Lockwood & Co., London, 1866.
8 Ibid., pp. 73–4.
9 François E. Raynal, *Wrecked On A Reef; or Twenty Months Among the Auckland Islands*, Thomas Nelson & Sons, London, 1892, p. 123.
10 Ibid., p. 122.
11 Ibid.
12 The remaining two crew were rescued by the *Flying Scud*, piloted by Captain Musgrave, in August 1865.
13 Raynal, p. 297.
14 W. Rogers, *A Cruising Voyage Round the World*, 1712. Extract in *Alexander Selkirk*, 2005, URL: http://academic.brooklyn.cuny.edu/english/melani/novel_18c/defoe/selkirk.html, accessed 24 December 2005.
15 Keith Eunson, *The Wreck of the General Grant*, A. H. & A. W. Reed, Wellington, 1974, p. 103. Eunson does not quote his source but it is likely to have been a local newspaper such as the *Southland Times* or the *Otago Witness*.
16 Joseph Jewell, *An Authentic Narrative of the Loss of the American Ship, "General Grant," On One of the Auckland Islands, The 13th May, 1866*, Ross, Westland, 16 July 1868, (2005), URL: http://homepage.ntlworld.

17 James Teer, *OW*, 25 January 1868, p. 3.
18 The *General Grant* survivors referred to both 'hair seals' (the New Zealand fur seal, *Arctocephalus forsteri*) and sea lions (the New Zealand sea lion, *Phocartos hookeri*). Later castaways (and writers) seemed to have used the terms 'seals' and 'sealskin' rather indiscriminately for both species, probably because they did not know the difference. Charles Eyre of the *Dundonald*, who dictated *The Castaways of Disappointment Island*, admitted to reporters that he had never seen such creatures before.
19 Jewell.
20 Between 11 July and 8 December 1866 the *General Grant* castaways separated into two groups, to spread their meagre resources. One group lived in the hut erected in 1864 at Carnley Harbour by the *Grafton* castaways, and the other remained in repaired huts that had survived from the former Hardwicke settlement at Port Ross.
21 *OW*, 25 Jan 1868, p. 3. In the entry for 26 May 1866, Teer also recorded their attempts to make a sail from the New Zealand flax which 'grows in small quantities at the old settlement [of Hardwicke]'.
22 'The Lost Ship, General Grant', *OW*, 18 January 1868, p. 4.
23 Mary Louise Ormsby, 'Teer, James 1826/1827?–1887', *DNZB*, updated 7 July 2005, URL: http://www.dnzb.govt.nz/.
24 Collection of Southland Museum and Art Gallery Niho Te Taniwha, Invercargill.
25 A reproduction of this image in the *Otago Witness*, 24 May 1905, identifies this man as 'Mr. W. Ganquilly' [*sic*: W. M. Sanguilly], but this is almost certainly incorrect as the image is on p. 83 has the hand-written inscription 'Aaron Hayman', and is from an album originally owned by the family of David Ashworth.
26 *OW*, 25 January 1868, p. 3.
27 Jewell.
28 Eunson, pp. 120–1.
29 Ormsby.
30 H. Escott-Inman, *The Castaways of Disappointment Island*, S. W. Partridge & Co. Ltd, Victoria, 1911. Escott-Inman authored the book, but notes that he has recounted 'Mr Charles Eyre's story just as he told it to me' (p. 6).
31 In late 1906, a deputation from the Philosophical Institute of Canterbury approached the Honourable R. McNab, Minister of Lands, with a proposal to extend the Magnetic Survey of New Zealand to the sub-Antarctic Islands, and to additionally study their flora, fauna and general geology. The proposal was supported initially by the Otago Institute and then by the main body, the New Zealand Institute (known today as the Royal Society of New Zealand). The government agreed, allowing the use of the *Hinemoa* during its annual trip south in November 1907. Among the vast amount of scientific knowledge acquired was the first accurate positioning of the Auckland Islands.
32 Other items are the remains of the fragile 'canvas boat' or coracle made from the twisted branches of *Hebe elliptica*, three wooden paddles, a twiggy meat hook and two spoons of rata wood, and a canvas water bag. Other clothing – a sealskin jacket and blanket owned by George Ivimey, and a jacket and trousers of sailcloth – was photographed at the time, but was seemingly retained elsewhere and has not been located. The Southland Museum and Art Gallery Niho Te Taniwha (Invercargill) holds a pair of sealskin moccasins.
33 Eyre records Peters's death as occurring twelve days after the wreck. However, the cross on his grave states that he died on 26 March 1907. McLaughlin and Knudsen quote the inscription on the cross as '6th March', which is patently wrong. It is likely that Eyre also made a mistake. *LT*, 14 December 1907. The *Lyttelton Times* secured publishing rights to the so-called 'Diary of the Second Mate', which was published in three successive Saturday editions in December 1907. This 'diary' appears to have been a collaborative recollection by McLaughlin and Knudsen, who both signed the final episode. It was possibly an elaboration of the statements prepared by them for the Magisterial Inquiry into the loss of the ship, held in Invercargill on 4 December. No actual ship's log or diary of any sort exists, as all the records went down with the ship, and the men certainly had nothing on which to write during their eight and a half month ordeal; Daniel McLaughlin to Mr & Mrs Pattie, 23 Dec 1907, p. 9. Photocopy supplied by Baden Norris.
34 Escott-Inman, p. 101.
35 Elizabeth Wilson, 'Bohemian Dress and the Heroism of Everyday Life', *Fashion Theory*, vol. 2, no. 3, 1998, pp. 225–44.
36 *LT*, 14 December 1907, p. 6.
37 Escott-Inman, pp. 111–12.
38 Ibid., p. 120.
39 *LT*, 14 December 1907.
40 Escott-Inman, p. 128.
41 Albert Roberts, 'The Wreck of the *Dundonald*', *Spectrum* documentary, Radio New Zealand, 1976.
42 Escott-Inman, p. 130.
43 Ibid., p. 136.
44 Ibid., pp. 192, 193–4.
45 *LT*, 21 December 1907, p. 6.
46 Escott-Inman, pp. 237–8.
47 Ibid., pp. 248–50.
48 Ibid., p. 256.

49 Ibid., p. 272; McLaughlin to the Patties, p. 11.
50 McLaughlin–Knudsen, *LT*, 21 December 1907, p. 6.
51 Escott-Inman, pp. 278–9.
52 Ibid., pp. 275–6.
53 Ibid., pp. 289–90.
54 Ibid., p. 311.
55 Roberts, 1976.
56 Escott-Inman, pp. 316–17.
57 Joanne Entwhistle, 'Fashion and the Fleshy Body: Dress as Embodied Practice', *Fashion Theory*, vol. 4, no. 3, 2000, pp. 323–48.

7. WEAVING A JOURNEY: THE STORY OF A UNIQUE CLOAK
    I wish to acknowledge the following people and institutions: Auckland War Memorial Museum Tāmaki Paenga Hira: Chanel Clarke, Paul Tapsell, and Roger Neich; Te Papa: Matiu Baker, Kate Button, Valerie Carson, Arapata Hakiwai, Ross O'Rourke, Huhana Smith, and Te Taru White; the New Zealand Film Archive Ngā Kaitiaki o Ngā Taonga Whitiāhua: Bronwyn Taylor; Hilda Inia, Huhana (Aunty Bubbles) Mihinui and Wihapi Te Amohau Winiata (all three have sadly passed away); Audrey McCaull; Shirley-Marie Whata-Coffin; Ngahuia Te Awekotuku; Patricia Wallace; Jeremy Coote; Dunbar Sloane senior. To the editors, Stephanie, Bronwyn and Fiona, thank you.
1   For the principle of mana taonga, see Museum of New Zealand Te Papa Tongarewa, *Statement of Intent 2005/2008*, p. 2 and *Icons Nga Taonga: From the Museum of New Zealand Te Papa Tongarewa*, Te Papa Press, Wellington, 2004, p. 2.
2   David Williams, 'Matauranga Maori And Taonga: The Nature and Extent of Treaty Rights Held by Iwi and Hapu in Indigenous Flora and Fauna, Cultural Heritage Objects, Valued Traditional Knowledge', Waitangi Tribunal Research Report, Wellington, 2001, pp. 13–26.
3   R. K. Dell outlines significant collectors of taonga Māori collections and their year(s) of acquisition by the Museum in 'The First Hundred Years of the Dominion Museum', unpublished manuscript, Dominion Museum, Wellington, [196–?], pp. 219–21.
4   See the annual reports of the Colonial Museum from 1865 for evidence of these exchanges. See also D. C. Starzecka, 'The Maori Collections in the British Museum', in D. C. Starzecka (ed.), *Maori Art and Culture*, British Museum Press, London, 1996, p. 156.
5   Moira G. Simpson, *Making Representations: Museums in the Post-Colonial Era*, Routledge, London and New York, revised edition, 2001, p. 192.
6   Statistics gathered in 2003 by the Mātauranga Māori Team at Te Papa.
7   Janet Davidson, *The Prehistory of New Zealand*, Longman Paul Ltd, Auckland, 1984, p. 129.
8   Puke Ariki, New Plymouth, has one such cloak in their collection.
9   H. Ling Roth, *The Maori Mantle*, Bankfield Museum, Halifax, England, 1923, pp. 7–15, 50–1.
10 J. C. Beaglehole (ed.), *The Endeavour Journal of Joseph Banks*, vol. 2, Angus & Robertson, Sydney, 1962, p. 15.
11 Cited in Roth, p. 95.
12 Jeremy Coote, *Curiosities From the Endeavour: A Forgotten Collection*, Captain Cook Memorial Museum, Whitby, 2004.
13 Valerie Carson notes that the thread for this area may also be black cotton.
14 Tāniko is the finger twining process that created geometric patterns with multi-coloured muka threads.
15 Exhibition catalogue, *Nga Puna Roimata o Te Arawa*, Museum of New Zealand Te Papa Tongarewa, Wellington, 1993, p. 6. At the time the cloak was described as a 'mahiti' and Tamihana Korokai of Ngāti Whakaue was identified as the elder wearing the cloak at the welcome for the American Fleet to Rotorua in 1908 (photograph taken by James McDonald negative number B.19347, Te Papa).
16 *Taiāwhio: Continuity and Change*, an exhibition exploring Māori visual arts at Te Papa, June to December 2002. Exhibition catalogue: Huhana Smith (ed.), *Taiāwhio: Conversations with Contemporary Māori Artists*, Te Papa Press, Wellington, 2002.
17 Ross B. O'Rourke, 'S. Dannefaerd, Jeweller, Lapidary, and Curio Merchant: The Collection and Associated Correspondence in the Museum of New Zealand Te Papa Tongarewa: A Chronological Document Bank', Museum of New Zealand Te Papa Tongarewa, 1997.
18 S. Dannefaerd to A. Hamilton, 26 October 1909, MU (Museum series), Series 2, 2/16, Te Papa Archives, Wellington.
19 For an account of this visit, see Ranginui Walker, *He Tipua: The Life and Times of Sir Āpirana Ngata*, Viking, Auckland, 2001.
20 *American Fleet Officers' Visit to Rotorua 1908*, DVD from original movie, filmed by James McDonald for the Department of Tourist and Health Resorts, F3033, New Zealand Film Archive Ngā Kaitiaki o Ngā Taonga Whitiāhua. Photographs of the reception for the American Fleet can be found at: B.1260, B.1261, B.1258, B.1259, B.19347, B.1705, Te Papa Image Library.
21 Te Wharetoroa Tiniraupeka to James McDonald, 30 October 1921, MU2, 2/16.
22 George Graham to James McDonald, date unknown, MU2, 2/16. I am grateful to Te Papa for allowing extensive quotation from these letters.
23 Elsdon Best, 'The Art of the Whare Pora: Notes on the Clothing of the Ancient Maori', *Transactions and Proceedings of the New Zealand Institute*, 1898, pp. 625–58; Elsdon Best, *The Maori as He Was: A Brief*

Account of Maori Life as it was in Pre-European Day, New Zealand Board of Science and Art Manual No.4, Dominion Museum, Wellington, 1924.
24 James McDonald to George Graham, 17 November 1921, MU2, 2/16.
25 George Graham to James McDonald, 18 November 1921, MU2, 2/16.
26 James McDonald, Memorandum to the Under Secretary of Internal Affairs, 27 April 1922, MU2, 2/16.
27 George Graham to James McDonald, 3 May 1922, MU2, 2/16.
28 Roger Neich, *Carved Histories: Rotorua Ngati Tarawhai Woodcarving*, Auckland University Press, Auckland, 2001, p. 34.
29 Hilda Inia, interview with author, 9 October 2005, transcript, p. 4.
30 Ibid., p. 1.
31 Ibid., p. 5.
32 Personal communication from Ngahuia Te Awekotuku, 25 March 2004.
33 For more information about Tene Waitere, see Roger Neich, 'Waitere, Tene 1853/1854?–1931', *DNZB*, updated 7 April 2006. URL: http://www.dnzb.govt.nz/.
34 And following quotes, Hilda Inia interview, pp. 5, 7, 8.
35 For more information see Jenifer Curnow and Edward Rahiri Graham, 'Graham, George Samuel 1874–1952', *DNZB*, updated 31 July 2003, URL:http:// www. dnzb. govt. nz/.
36 'He was a nice man, very nice to Kiri and I, he was lovely. He actually spoilt us . . . he fulfilled his life by spoiling Kiri and I. We were always the best dressed, the best fed. When we'd come back to Rotorua, he'd come down and he always had something nice.' Hilda Inia interview, p. 10.
37 Ibid.
38 Ibid., p. 12.

8. HAND-ME-DOWNS AND RESPECTABILITY: CLOTHING AND THE NEEDY

I am grateful to Margaret Tennant for information and conversations about second-hand clothing and to Fiona McKergow for finding Elizabeth Smither's poem. Research for this and related projects was funded by the Faculty of Arts and Social Sciences, University of Waikato and the Massey University Research Fund. Many thanks to research assistants Deborah Powell and Deborah Salter for their help.

1 'Oamaru Victorian Heritage Celebrations', URL: http://www.tourismwaitaki.co.nz /index.cfm/default/ Service/ServiceID/109/Menu/False, accessed 13 December 2006.
2 Gavin McLean (ed.), *Oamaru 1878: A Colonial Town: K. C. McDonald*, Oamaru, Publication Group of the Waitaki District Council, 2006, pp. 82–5, 119.
3 'Victorian Heritage Week – A Huge Success', URL: http://www.tourism waitaki.co.nz /index.cfm/news/ Victorian/, accessed 13 December 2006.
4 Cited in Margaret Tennant, *Paupers and Providers*, Bridget Williams Books, Wellington, 1989, p. 192.
5 See also in the North American context: Susan Porter Benson, 'What Goes 'Round Comes 'Round: Secondhand Clothing, Furniture, and Tools in Working-Class Lives in the Interwar United States', *Journal of Women's History*, vol. 19, no. 1, 2007, pp. 17–31; Katrina Sigley, 'Consumption, Identity, and Desire in Depression-Era Toronto', *Journal of Women's History*, vol. 19, no.1, 2007, pp. 82–104.
6 Jane Malthus and Chris Brickell, 'Producing and Consuming Gender: The Case of Clothing', in Barbara Brookes, Annabel Cooper and Robin Law (eds), *Sites of Gender: Women, Men & Modernity in Southern Dunedin 1890–1939*, Auckland University Press, Auckland, 2003, p. 145.
7 *Icons Nga Taonga: From the Museum of New Zealand Te Papa Tongarewa*, Te Papa Press, Wellington, 2004, p. 223.
8 Karen Sayer, '"A Sufficiency of Clothing": Dress and Domesticity', *Textile History*, vol. 33, no. 1, 2002, p. 12. See also the other articles in the special issue of *Textile History* on 'The Dress of the Poor', edited by Steven King and Christiana Payne, vol. 33, no. 1, May 2002.
9 David Thomson, *A World Without Welfare: New Zealand's Colonial Experiment*, Auckland University Press/Bridget Williams Books, Wellington, 1998, p. 83.
10 Tennant, p. 105. See also Anne Brogden, 'Clothing Provision in the Liverpool Warehouse', *Costume*, no. 36, 2002, pp. 50–5 and 'Clothing Provision by Liverpool's Other Poor Law Institutions: Kirkdale Industrial Schools', *Costume*, no. 37, pp. 71–4.
11 Tennant, p. 93.
12 Cited in Jeanine Graham, 'Settler Society', in Geoffrey W. Rice (ed.), *The Oxford History of New Zealand*, 2nd edition, Oxford University Press, Auckland, 1992, p. 121.
13 Ibid.
14 Miles Fairburn, *Nearly Out of Heart and Hope*, Auckland University Press, Auckland, 1995, p. 39.
15 Ibid., p. 43.
16 Ibid., p. 48.
17 Ibid., p. 56.
18 Ibid., p. 132.
19 John E. Martin, 'Slattery, Edmond 1839/184?–1927', *DNZB*, updated 7 July 2005, URL: http://www.dnzb.govt. nz/.
20 Details in this and following paragraphs from Tennant, ch. 8.
21 Tennant, p. 156.
22 See for example, Bronwyn Dalley, 'From Demi-Mondes to Slaveys: Aspects of the Management of the Te

Oranga Reformatory for Delinquent Young Women, 1900–1918', in Brookes et al (eds), *Women in History 2*, Bridget Williams Books, Wellington, 1992, pp. 48–67; Margaret Tennant, '"Magdalens and Moral Imbeciles": Women's Homes in 19th Century New Zealand', in Barbara Brookes et al (eds), *Women in History 2*, pp. 49–75.

23 Bronwyn Labrum, 'Gender and Lunacy: A Study of Women Patients at the Auckland Lunatic Asylum, 1870–1910', MA Thesis, Massey University, 1990; Barbara Brookes and Jane Thomson (eds), *'Unfortunate Folk': Essays on Mental Health Treatment 1863–1992*, University of Otago Press, Dunedin, 2001; Bronwyn Labrum, 'The Boundaries of Femininity: Madness and Gender in New Zealand, 1870–1910', in Wendy Chan, Dorothy E. Chunn and Robert Menzies (eds), *Women, Madness and the Law: A Feminist Reader*, Cavendish Publishing Limited, London, 2005, pp. 59–77.

24 Annual Report on the Lunatic Asylums of New Zealand, *Appendix to the Journals of the House of Representatives (AJHR)*, 1895, H-10, p. 3.

25 Erving Goffman, *Asylums: Essays on the Social Situation of Mental Patients and Other Inmates*, Harmondsworth, Middlesex, Penguin, 1968.

26 Names in all cases quoted have been changed to preserve anonymity. Case 1637, Carrington Hospital Auckland (YCAA) 1048/5, Archives New Zealand (ANZ), p. 468.

27 R. M. Hunter, 'Historical Notes on the Auckland Psychiatric Hospital', *The New Zealand Nursing Journal*, February 1957, p. 19.

28 The Eighth Annual Report on the State of the Auckland Provincial Lunatic Asylum, 1874, *Auckland Provincial Government Gazette*, 1875, p. 208.

29 'A term for converted warp sateen, jean, or five-harness warp-faced twill made in white and printed color stripes and solid colors. 2. A good grade of British cotton shirting made in equal blue and white stripes'. URL: http://www.fabrics.net/define.asp, accessed 15 December 2006; Hunter, p. 19.

30 M. A. Crowther, *The Workhouse System 1834–1929: The History of an English Social Institution*, Batsford Academic and Educational, London, p. 7.

31 Stephen Garton, *Medicine and Madness: A Social History of Insanity in New South Wales 1880–1940*, NSW University Press, Kensington, 1988, p. 181.

32 Tennant, 'Magdalens and Moral Imbeciles', p. 59.

33 Dalley, 'From Demi-mondes to Slaveys', p. 161.

34 Tennant, *Paupers and Providers*, p. 132.

35 Ann Rosalind Jones and Peter Stallybrass (eds), *Renaissance Clothing and the Materials of Memory*, Cambridge University Press, New York, 2000, p. 3.

36 Robert Chapman, 'From Labour to National' in Rice (ed.), *Oxford History*, p. 352.

37 For more on this see Bronwyn Labrum, 'The Material Culture of Welfare in Aotearoa/New Zealand: A Case Study of Clothing', *History Australia: The Journal of the Australian Historical Association*, vol. 2, no. 3, December 2005, pp. 81.1–81.12.

38 Margaret McClure, *A Civilised Community*, Auckland University Press, Auckland, 1998, p. 141.

39 Memo for registrars and district agents on War Pension and Social Security Emergency Funds, 14 February 1952, Social Security (SS), Series 7, 7/7/13, ANZ.

40 Case 1956, Child Welfare (CW), Series 1, 4/7/4, ANZ.

41 Sally K. Parker, 'A Golden Decade? Farm Women in the 1950s', in B. Brookes et al (eds), *Women in History 2*, pp. 217–18.

42 Bronwyn Dalley, 'The Golden Weather 1949–1965', in Bronwyn Dalley and Gavin McLean (eds), *Frontier of Dreams: The Story of New Zealand*, Hodder Moa Beckett, Auckland, 2005, p. 331.

43 CW 1, 4/16. See also my 'Persistent Needs and Expanding Desires: Pakeha Families and State Welfare in the Years of Prosperity', in Bronwyn Labrum and Bronwyn Dalley (eds), *Fragments: New Zealand Social and Cultural History*, Auckland University Press, Auckland, 2000, pp. 188–210.

44 Graeme Dunstall, 'The Social Pattern', in Rice (ed.), *Oxford History*, p. 467.

45 30 December 1954, District child welfare officer, Wellington, to Superintendent, 21 January 1953, CW 1, 4/7/2.

46 Dominique Jean, 'Family Allowances and Family Autonomy: Quebec Families Encounter the Welfare State, 1945–1955' in Bettina Bradbury (ed.), *Canadian Family History: Selected Readings*, Copp Clark Pittman, Toronto, 1992, p. 422.

47 Janet Frame, *To the Is-land*, Hutchinson Group, Auckland, 1989, p. 39.

48 Ibid., p. 71.

49 Ibid., pp. 80, 90, 133.

50 For more on this see my 'Developing "The Essentials of Good Citizenship and Responsibilities" in Maori Women: Family Life, Social Change and the State in New Zealand, 1944–1970', *Journal of Family History*, vol. 29, no. 4, October 2004, pp. 446–65.

51 Headmaster of — School to Mrs H. Ross, 27 October 1951, Maori Affairs (MA), Series 1, 36/11, part 2, ANZ.

52 Assistant district officer, Palmerston North, to Head Office, 9 September 1966, MA 1, 36/5/7.

53 Miles Lambert, '"Cast-off Wearing Apparell": The Consumption and Distribution of Second-hand Clothing in Northern England during the Long Eighteenth Century', *Textile History*, vol. 35, no. 1, 2004, pp. 1–26.

54 Peter Jones, 'Clothing the Poor in Early-Nineteenth-Century England', *Textile History*, vol. 37, no. 1, May 2006, pp. 17–37.

55 Helen Dollery, 'Social Service, Social Justice, or a Matter of Faith? The Palmerston North Methodist Social

Service Centre 1963–2000', MA Thesis, Massey University, Palmerston North, 2005, pp. 2–21, 42–3.
56 Ibid., p. 42.
57 Rita Snowden, *The Sun is High*, Hodder & Stoughton, London, 1974, p. 69.
58 Dollery, p. 42.
59 Loyal J. Gibson, *A Stitch in Time*, Methodist Social Service Centre, Palmerston North, 1999, p. 16.
60 Ibid.
61 Ibid.
62 Ibid., p. 77.
63 Ibid., p. 78.
64 Ibid., p. 16.
65 Elizabeth Smither, *Professor Musgrove's Canary*, Auckland University Press, Auckland, 1986, p. 15. Reproduced with kind permission of the author.
66 For the notion of 'retro-chic' see Raphael Samuel, *Theatres of Memory, Vol. 1 Past and Present in Contemporary Culture*, Verso, London and New York, 1994. For vintage clothing see Alexandra Palmer and Hazel Clark (eds), *Old Clothes, New Look: Second-Hand Fashion*, Berg, London, 2004 and Nicky Gregson and Louise Crewe, *Second-Hand Cultures*, Berg, London, 2003.
67 Jock Phillips, 'Generations 1965–1984', in Dalley and McLean (eds), *Frontier of Dreams*, p. 342. See also Barbara L. Brookes, 'A Germaine Moment: Style, Language and Audience', in Tony Ballantyne and Brian Moloughney (eds), *Disputed Histories: Imagining New Zealand's Past*, Otago University Press, Dunedin, 2006, pp. 191–294.

9. 'JUST THE THING': SHOPPING FOR CLOTHES IN PALMERSTON NORTH
    I would like to thank the following people for their contribution to this chapter: Cindy Lilburn and Tony Rasmussen of Te Manawa made collection items available and willingly sharing their knowledge; Richard and Geraldine Mildon generously gave access to family papers; Carina Hickey provided valuable help with newspaper research; Anne Else made useful comments on earlier drafts; and Graeme Brown kindly took photographs.
1   *Manawatu Times* (*MT*), 3 January 1877, p. 1. The title's quotation is from an advertisement by 'W. H. Wilson, The New House, The Square, For Ladies' Wear', *Manawatu Evening Standard* (*MES*), 18 September 1922, p. 6.
2   Wellington Provincial Directory, *Wises New Zealand Directory*, 1875–6, p. 28; Ian Matheson, *Community and Council: 125 Years of Local Government in Palmerston North, 1877–2002*, Palmerston North City Council, Palmerston North, 2003, p. 5.
3   At present there is no comprehensive history of shopping in New Zealand. Useful studies include Helen B. Laurenson, *Going Up Going Down: The Rise and Fall of the Department Store*, Auckland University Press, Auckland, 2005; Julia Millen, *Kirkcaldie & Stains: A Wellington Story*, Bridget Williams Books, Wellington, 2000; Jane Malthus and Chris Brickell, 'Producing and Consuming Gender: The Case of Clothing', in Barbara Brookes, Annabel Cooper and Robin Law (eds), *Sites of Gender: Women, Men & Modernity in Southern Dunedin, 1890–1939*, Auckland University Press, Auckland, 2003, pp. 123–50; Danielle Sprecher, 'Clothes are Good Business: Consumption and Appearance in the Office, 1918–1939', in Caroline Daley and Deborah Montgomerie (eds), *The Gendered Kiwi*, Auckland University Press, Auckland, 1999, pp. 141–62. For a summary of shopping in Australia, see Beverley Kingston, *Basket, Bag, Trolley: A History of Shopping in Australia*, Oxford University Press, Melbourne, 1994.
4   Jane Malthus, 'Dressmakers in Nineteenth Century New Zealand', in Barbara Brookes, Charlotte Macdonald and Margaret Tennant (eds), *Women in History 2*, Bridget Williams Books, Wellington, 1992, pp. 91–2; Jane Malthus, 'The Sewing Trades in the Nineteenth Century', in Norma Bethune (ed.), *Work 'n' Pastimes: 150 Year of Pain and Pleasure, Labour and Leisure. Proceedings of the 1998 Conference of the New Zealand Society of Genealogists*, New Zealand Society of Genealogists, Dunedin, 1998, p. 158; 'A General Summary of the Import, Export & Shipping Returns . . . of the Colony of New Zealand for the Year 1869', *AJHR*, 1870, D-1, pp. 3–5.
5   For more on New Zealand department stores, see Laurenson; Millen; Evan Roberts, 'From Mail Order to Female Order? The Work Culture of Department Store Employees in New Zealand, 1890–1960', BA (Hons) research essay, University of Victoria, 1999; Louise Shaw, 'Hallenstein Brothers and Company, 1876–1906', PGDip research essay, University of Otago, 1994. For Australian department stores, see Gail Reekie, *Temptations: Sex, Selling and the Department Store*, Allen & Unwin, St Leonards, NSW, 1993. On dressmakers and tailoresses, see Malthus, 'Dressmakers', pp. 76–97; Malthus, 'The Sewing Trades', pp. 157–74; Erik Olssen, *Building the New World: Work, Politics and Society in Caversham, 1880s–1920s*, Auckland University Press, Auckland, 1995, esp. ch. 4; Lee Duncan, '"A New Song of the Shirt"?: A History of Women in the Clothing Industry in Auckland, 1890–1939', MA thesis, University of Auckland, 1989; Penelope Harper, 'The Dunedin Tailoresses Union, 1889–1914', PGDip research essay, University of Otago, 1988. For a more general account see Malthus and Brickell.
6   Asa Briggs, *Victorian Things*, University of Chicago Press, Chicago, 1989, ch. 10, pp. 369–425.
7   Peter Stearns, *Consumerism in World History: The Global Transformation of Desire*, Routledge, London and New York, 2001, ch. 5, pp. 44–60.
8   A pioneering study is Neil McKendrick, Colin Brewer and J. A. Plumb, *The Birth of a Consumer Society: The Commercialisation of Eighteenth-Century England*, Indiana University Press, Bloomington, 1982. More recent work includes John Brewer and Roy Porter (eds), *Consumption and the World of Goods*, Routledge,

9. Kathryn Morrison, *English Shops and Shopping: An Architectural History*, Yale University Press, New Haven and London, 2004, pp. 125–43 passim; Stearns, pp. 16, 23.
10. Anne Salmond, *Between Worlds: Early Exchanges Between Maori and Europeans, 1773–1815*, Viking/Penguin, Auckland, 1997, pp. 175, 395–7. For the Australian context, see Margaret Maynard, *Fashioned from Penury: Dress as Cultural Practice in Colonial Australia*, Cambridge University Press, Cambridge, 1994.
11. For the range of commodities, see 'Summary of the Import, Export & Shipping Returns', *AJHR*, 1870, E-1, and subsequent annual reports.
12. James Belich, *Making Peoples: A History of the New Zealanders From Polynesian Settlement to the End of the Nineteenth Century*, Allen Lane/The Penguin Press, Auckland, 1996, pp. 148–52.
13. 'Reports on the Social and Political State of the Natives in Various Districts at the Time of the Arrival of Sir G.F. Bowen', *AJHR*, 1868, A-4, p.18. For further information, see Gabrielle Mary Bettany, 'A Quantitative Analysis of the Adoption of European Dress by Maori Women, 1850–1910', BCApSc research essay, University of Otago, 1994.
14. Hazel Petrie, *Chiefs of Industry: Maori Tribal Enterprise in Early Colonial New Zealand*, Auckland University Press, Auckland, 2006, pp. 9, 39, passim.
15. For instance, kits were extensively used for trading produce with settlers, see 'Native Produce Imported into the Ports of Auckland and Onehunga', *AJHR*, 1865, E-12, pp. 1–20.
16. Malthus & Brickell, p. 126. In Palmerston North the drapers McDowell Bros sold 'Best Clothing for Men's and Boy's wear, including Geelong, Kaiapoi and Mosgiel Tweed suits', see *MT*, 2 January 1883, p. 3.
17. Malthus & Brickell, p. 125. A branch was formed in Palmerston North in 1883, see *The Cyclopedia of New Zealand*, The Cyclopedia Publishing Co., Christchurch, 1897, p. 1181.
18. 'Royal Commission Appointed to Inquire into Certain Relations Between the Employers of Certain Kinds of Labour and the Persons Employed Therein ("The Sweating Commission")', *AJHR*, 1890, H-5, passim; Melanie Nolan, *Breadwinning: New Zealand Women and the State*, Canterbury University Press, Christchurch, 2000, pp. 41–2.
19. Report and Evidence of the Royal Commission on the Cost of Living in New Zealand, *AJHR*, 1912, Session ii, H-18, pp. 163–4.
20. Typewritten copy of Stewart's handwritten manuscript of 1902, J. T. Stewart Papers, Series 1, Folder 2, Palmerston North City Library Archive, p. 2.
21. On provisioning the surveying party Stewart wrote: 'The nearest supply of provisions was then down the Manawatu at Hartley's at Te Maire (near where Shannon now is) at Kebbell's a little lower down, and at T.U. Cook's at Te Awa Hou (now Foxton) and at Scott's at mouth of the Rangitikei River. Native produce and potatoes could be got at several small Maori settlements along the river banks of the Manawatu and along the Oroua as far up as Te Awahuri (a few miles below where Feilding now is).' Ibid., p. 2.
22. Obituary, Mr G. M. Snelson, *MES*, 1 November 1901, p. 2; 'A Tribute to the Late Mr G. M. Snelson', *MES*, 4 November 1901, p. 2; Obituary, Mrs G. M. Snelson, *MES*, 15 December 1919, p. 5.
23. See for instance, the following photographs: Roe & Green's General Store, The Square, Bc20, and H.T. Flyger's 'Terrace End Colonial Produce Store', Main Street, Bc42, Palmerston North City Library.
24. See photographs of The Square, such as 'Square – North, c.1888', SQ3, 'Square – West, c.1889' and 'Square – Palmerston North – Southwest, c.1893', SQ101, Palmerston North City Library.
25. Matheson, p. 12.
26. Papers Relating to Immigration II. Introduction of Scandinavian Immigrants, *AJHR*, 1871, vol. 1, D-3A, p. 12.
27. Ibid., p. 11.
28. Ibid., p. 13.
29. Val Burr, *Mosquitoes & Sawdust: A History of Scandinavians in Early Palmerston North & Surrounding Districts*, Scandinavian Club of Manawatu, Palmerston North, 1995, p. 50.
30. Ibid., pp. 50–1.
31. *MT*, 10 February 1877, p. 3.
32. Malthus, 'The Sewing Trades', p. 164.
33. *MT*, 2 February 1878, p. 1.
34. *MT*, 28 March 1877, p. 3.
35. *MT*, 24 March 1877, p. 3.
36. Malthus, 'The Sewing Trades', p. 158.
37. *Feilding Star* (*FS*), 14 January 1983, p. 3; *FS*, 18 March 1893, p. 3.
38. *MT*, 10 April 1883, p. 2. J. C. Fowler sold Jones & Co. sewing machines, which allegedly 'gained more first prizes at the Melbourne Exhibition, than all the other exhibitors put together', see *MT*, 4 January 1883, p. 3. Thompson Bros, Feilding, were agents for Home Shuttle and Wertheim sewing machines, see *FS*, 5 July 1882, p. 3.
39. Palmerston Electoral Roll, 1893. These figures exclude men and women involved in the clothing trades in the nearby settlements of Ashhurst, Awahuri, Bunnythorpe, Linton and Longburn. Note that electoral rolls do not include male and female employees under the age of 21.
40. Entries for provincial towns in nineteenth-century directories were organised alphabetically by name, rather than by business or street location. See for instance, *Wises New Zealand Post Office Directory*,

41. Malthus & Brickell, p. 132.
42. *Cyclopedia*, 1897, p. 1181; *New Zealand Post Office Directory*, 1890–1, p. 349.
43. *Cyclopedia*, 1897, p. 1181.
44. Wendy Gamber, *The Female Economy: The Millinery and Dressmaking Trades, 1860–1930*, University of Illinois Press, Urbana and Chicago, 1997, p. 27.
45. Palmerston North electoral roll, 1905. Later electoral rolls list women by marital status not occupation.
46. For more on this, see Barbara Burman (ed.), *The Culture of Sewing: Gender, Consumption and Home Dressmaking*, Berg, Oxford and New York, 1999.
47. Margaret Walsh, 'The Democratization of Fashion: The Emergence of the Women's Dress Pattern Industry', *Journal of American History*, vol. 66, no. 2, September 1979, p. 313.
48. *MES*, 19 January 1904, p. 4.
49. *MES*, 13 January 1915, p. 6.
50. *The New Zealand Draper, Clothier and Boot Retailer* (*NZD*), vol. 1, no. 4, 30 December 1920, p. 9.
51. Collinson & Cunninghame Ltd was purchased by the Farmers' Trading Company in 1983. C. M. Ross Co. Ltd was purchased by Milne & Choyce in 1959, and the DIC in 1967. The PDC emerged from a takeover of W. F. Durward & Co., and remained a private company until it was sold to the Consumer Co-operative Society in 1956. See Roberts, pp. 126, 130; *MES*, 9 July 1915, p. 3.
52. *NZD*, 30 December 1920, p. 11.
53. Ibid.
54. *MES*, 7 June 1922, p. 6.
55. *FS*, 21 June 1882, p. 2; *MT*, 2 January 1883, p. 3.
56. *FS*, 21 June 1882, p. 2.
57. *FS*, 9 August 1882, p. 2.
58. *MES*, 17 January 1922, p. 9.
59. *MT*, 3 January 1877, p. 2.
60. Millen, p. 19; for a local advertisement see, *FS*, 7 January 1893, p. 2.
61. See catalogues, 'Spring & Summer Fashions, 1913–14', 86/133/109; 'Summer, 1922–23', 86/135/160; 'Christmas, 1924', 86/133/111; 'December 1925', 86/133/112; 'Winter, 1928', 86/133/113; 'Spring & Summer, 1929–30', 86/133/114, Collinson & Cunninghame Collection, Te Manawa.
62. 'Spring & Summer 1929–30' catalogue, 86/133/114, Collinson & Cunninghame Collection, Te Manawa.
63. Gamber, pp. 96–124 passim.
64. *MES*, 29 March 1915, p. 2.
65. 'Conduct a sewing week and sell more dress goods', *Draper of Australasia*, 31 July 1915, p. 227.
66. Claude Dixon Scrapbook, 86/135/124, p. 1, Collinson & Cunninghame Collection, Te Manawa.
67. *Draper of Australasia*, 31 July 1915, p. 227.
68. *Draper of Australasia*, 30 June 1921, p. 10; *MES*, 13 March 1922, p. 2; quote from *MES*, 20 June 1922, p. 16.
69. Programme for 'Mannequin Parade', 17–19 May 1928, in scrapbook 86/135/105, Collinson & Cunninghame Collection, Te Manawa.
70. Ibid.
71. Gamber, p. 124.
72. *Cyclopedia of New Zealand*, Cyclopedia Company Ltd, Christchurch, 1908, p. 677; *New Zealand Post Office Directory*, 1920, pp. 744, 753.
73. *MT*, 30 September 1922, p. 1.
74. Gamber, p. 97.
75. Arthur de Luen appears to have left Palmerston North by 1922, see Palmerston North electoral rolls, 1919 and 1922. New Zealand death registers from 1920 to 1925 do not record his name.
76. Regarding 'her unhappy marriage . . . it probably wasn't noticeable to outsiders or even close acquaintances who she considered to be her social equals, because even their casual socialising was conducted along formalised lines of behaviour that concealed all this sort of stuff from one another.' Email from Richard Mildon, 21 December 2006.
77. *MT*, 21 June 1922, p. 6.
78. Richard Mildon, *Kairanga: More Than One Hundred Years*, The Heritage Press, Waikanae, 1989, p. 150.
79. Chris Brickell, 'The Politics of Post-War Consumer Culture', *NZJH*, vol. 40, no. 2, October 2006, p. 133.

10. ON THE BEACH: OR THE 'UNBEARABLE SCANDAL' OF SHRINKING SWIMWEAR

1. *New Zealand Graphic*, 6 August 1904, p. 14.
2. Legend has it that Louis Réard, one of the French men who designed the bikini, claimed that a 'true' bikini was small enough to fit into a matchbox and should be able to be threaded through a wedding ring. James Cockington, *Itsy Bitsy Teeny Weeny: A Brief History of the Bikini*, Manly Art Gallery and Museum, Sydney, 2004, p. 3.
3. James Laver, *Taste and Fashion: From the French Revolution Until To-Day*, George G. Harrap & Company Ltd, London, 1937, p. 220; Carrie A. Hall, *From Hoopskirts to Nudity: A Review of the Follies and Foibles of Fashion, 1886–1936*, Caxton Printers, Idaho, 1938, p. 197; Alexandra Joel, *Best Dressed: 200 Years of Fashion in Australia*, Collins, Sydney, 1984, p. 31; Fiona McKergow, 'Bodies at the Beach: A History of Swimwear', *Bearings*, vol. 3, no. 4, 1991, p. 18.

4   Naming beaches rather than swimming pools here is not accidental. Although many of the developments and concerns surrounding bathing suits were the same on beaches and at swimming pools, it was much easier to enforce swimwear regulations at council-run swimming pools than it was at the beach. The discussion in this chapter centres on bathing suits at the beach. For more on swimwear at council pools see Caroline Daley, *Leisure and Pleasure: Reshaping and Revealing the New Zealand Body 1900–1960*, Auckland University Press, Auckland, 2003, pp. 146–59.
5   Douglas Booth, 'Healthy, Economic, Disciplined Bodies: Surfbathing and Surf Lifesaving in Australia and New Zealand, 1890–1950', *NZJH*, vol. 32, no. 1, 1998, pp. 51–8; Emma Joyce, 'The Pursuit of Sun, Sand and Surf: Beach-going in New Zealand, 1910–1970', MA thesis, The University of Auckland, 2006, ch. 1.
6   These ideas are more fully explored in Daley, especially pp. 117–26.
7   This was suggested in Auckland (*Graphic*, 21 November 1903, p. 12) and imposed in Dunedin (*Truth*, 16 April 1910, p. 4).
8   For mixed-sea bathing at Napier see *Truth*, 21 December 1907, p. 1; for New Brighton see *Truth*, 1 January 1910, p. 6 and *LT*, 1 March 1910, p. 7.
9   Richard Rutt, 'The Englishman's Swimwear', *Costume*, no. 24, 1990, p. 72.
10 Stephen Barnett and Richard Wolfe, *At the Beach: The Great New Zealand Holiday*, Hodder & Stoughton, Auckland, 1993, p. 57.
11 This was a new by-law at New Brighton in 1910: *Truth*, 1 October 1910, p. 6.
12 The most recent exponent of this view is James Belich, *Paradise Reforged: A History of the New Zealanders From the 1880s to the Year 2000*, Allen Lane/The Penguin Press, Auckland, 2001, especially ch. 5.
13 For local knowledge of these international restrictions see *Truth*, 5 November 1910, p. 4.
14 *Truth*, 11 January 1908, p. 1. Trilby was a fictional character who posed in the nude without shame.
15 *Truth*, 17 October 1908, p. 1.
16 *Truth*, 2 January 1909, p. 6; *LT*, 1 March 1910, p. 7; *Truth*, 1 October 1910, p. 6.
17 *LT*, 1 March 1910, p. 8.
18 *Daily Telegraph* [Napier] (*DT*), 30 January 1911.
19 *NZH*, 21 April 1913, p. 4.
20 *DT*, 24 January 1911.
21 *Graphic*, 11 January 1908, p. 61.
22 *NZH*, 18 January 1910, p. 7.
23 *DT*, 30 January 1911.
24 *Dominion*, 5 February 1910, p. 13.
25 *DT*, 31 January 1911.
26 *Truth*, 2 January 1936, p. 12.
27 *Truth*, 13 January 1927, p. 3.
28 *Auckland Star* (*AS*), 23 January 1925, p. 9.
29 *Truth*, 15 September 1923, p. 14. 'American' spelling in the original has been retained in this and subsequent quotations.
30 *Truth*, 31 October 1929, p. 10.
31 The film screened in New Zealand in the summer of 1919. *Truth*, 11 January 1919, p. 2.
32 See, for example, *Truth*, 13 October 1937, p. 32. For more on this phenomenon see Richard Martin, *Splash! A History of Swimwear*, Rizzoli, New York, 1990, p. 49; Gloria Ricci Lothrop, 'A Trio of Mermaids – Their Impact Upon the Southern California Sportswear Industry', *Journal of the West*, vol. 25, no. 1, 1986, pp. 73–82.
33 *Press*, 14 November 1921, p. 11. Kellerman was later immortalised by Esther Williams in the film *The Million Dollar Mermaid*.
34 *Truth*, 31 October 1929, p. 10.
35 Mary E. Allender, 'The Jantzen Company: A Classic Case of Marketing Success', *Essays in Economic and Business History*, vol. 14, 1996, p. 222.
36 Roslyn claimed their costumes were 'Strongest Where Most Costumes Are Weakest' thanks to the reinforced seat, but reassured buyers that they were also fashionable and a perfect fit. *Truth*, 15 December 1927, p. 12.
37 By the first decade of the twentieth century women had joined men and children in wearing combination underwear. Elizabeth Ewing, *Dress and Undress: A History of Women's Underwear*, Drama Book Specialists, New York, 1978, p. 118.
38 *Truth*, 13 January 1927, p. 3. For subsequent work that makes claims about freedom through swimwear see Maxine James Johns and Jane Farrell-Beck, '"Cut Out the Sleeves": Nineteenth-Century U.S. Women Swimmers and Their Attire', *Dress*, no. 28, 2001, pp. 53–63.
39 *AS*, 23 January 1925, p. 9. New Zealand men resisted swimming caps, unlike the men of Australia and the United States.
40 *Truth*, 22 December 1927, p. 1.
41 Joel, p. 70.
42 As *Vogue* noted, after 1914 a beach parasol was an essential accessory. Christina Probert, *Swimwear in Vogue Since 1910*, Abbeville Press, New York, 1981, p. 9.
43 *Truth*, 13 January 1927, p. 3.
44 *Truth*, 13 January 1922, p. 8; 19 January 1924, p. 14.

45. *Truth*, 1 January 1931, pp. 7; 3 March 1937, p. 28. For international parallels to this consumerism see Felicity Robinson, *Fashion*, Murdoch Books, Sydney, 2005, p. 35; Martin, p. 29.
46. *Truth*, 19 November 1931, p. 16; 3 December 1921, p. 18; 18 April 1934, p. 13.
47. *Truth*, 7 November 1934, p. 15.
48. *Man*, November 1937, p. 85; October 1938, p. 145. An Australian magazine, *Man* was widely available in New Zealand.
49. Ewing, p. 146; Robinson, p. 35; Patricia Cunningham, 'Swimwear in the Thirties: The B.V.D. Company in a Decade of Innovation', *Dress: Annual Journal of the Costume Society of America*, no. 12, 1986, p. 22.
50. Allender, p. 223.
51. Cunningham, p. 22; Michael Colmer, *Bathing Beauties: The Amazing History of Female Swimwear*, Sphere Books, London, 1977, p. 14.
52. Knitting books as early as 1930 contained 'recipes' for one-piece backless costumes for men and women. Heather Nicholson, *The Loving Stitch: A History of Knitting and Spinning in New Zealand*, Auckland University Press, Auckland, 1998, p. 102.
53. Colin McDowell, *The Man of Fashion: Peacock Males and Perfect Gentlemen*, Thames & Hudson, London, 1997, p. 156.
54. Daley, pp. 126–43.
55. *Evening Post* (*EP*), 2 January 1926, p. 11.
56. Elizabeth Wilson, *Adorned in Dreams: Fashion and Modernity*, Virago Press, London, 1985, p. 92; Yhe-Young Lee, 'Controversies about American Women's Fashion, 1920–1945: Through the Lens of *The New York Times*', PhD thesis, Iowa State University, 2003, p. 15; Laver, p. 221; *Truth*, 31 October 1929, p. 10; 5 February 1931, p. 9.
57. *Truth*, 1 January 1931, p. 7.
58. *Truth*, 3 December 1931, p. 18; 26 September 1934, p. 7.
59. *Truth*, 28 November 1934, p. 13.
60. McDowell, p. 156.
61. By 1938 men under 50 who went to buy swimwear were offered trunks rather than one-piece suits. *DT*, 12 February 1938, p. 9.
62. *Truth*, 2 January 1935, p. 1.
63. *Truth*, 16 September 1936, p. 9; 14 October 1936, p. 22.
64. *AS*, 23 January 1925, p. 9.
65. *AS*, 27 December 1934, p. 8.
66. *Health and Physical Culture*, 1 December 1937, p. 38. A Sydney-based magazine, *HPC* had many New Zealand contributors and subscribers.
67. *LT*, 1 March 1910, p. 7; *Truth*, 22 February 1922, p. 2.
68. *Truth*, 4 December 1930, p. 11.
69. *Truth*, 14 October 1936, p. 22.
70. *Press*, 26 December 1946, p. 3.
71. *Man Junior*, November 1938, p. 125; Joel, p. 141.
72. Martin, p. 105; *Truth*, 11 September 1956, p. 36.
73. *Truth*, 5 April 1950, p. 27.
74. Cockington, pp. 3–4; *Press*, 13 October 1945, p. 6; *Truth*, 31 October 1945, p. 5.
75. *Truth*, 14 November 1945, p. 5.
76. *Press*, 13 October 1945, p. 6.
77. Cockington, p. 7.
78. *Truth*, 5 January 1960, p. 1.
79. Laurel R. Davis, *The Swimsuit Issue and Sport: Hegemonic Masculinity in Sports Illustrated*, State University of New York Press, Albany, 1997, p. 10. But as Davis notes, photographs of attractive young women in swimsuits had featured in the magazine since its launch in 1954.
80. Colmer, p. 13; Allender, p. 221.
81. Martin, p. 131.
82. *Fashion Theory*, for example, has yet to publish an article on swimwear and few studies have appeared in either *Costume* or *Dress*. An index search of most major works in the field also disappoints those wanting to learn more about the social and cultural history of bathing costumes. An exception is Margaret Maynard, *Out of Line: Australian Women and Style*, University of New South Wales Press, Sydney, 2001.
83. For example, Coco Chanel designed swimwear in the 1920s; in 1955 Cole of California signed Christian Dior to design for it. Rutt, p. 74; Colmer, p. 14.
84. For more on this see Caroline Daley, 'Puritans and Pleasure Seekers', in Allison Kirkman and Pat Moloney (eds), *Sexuality Down Under: Social and Historical Perspectives*, Otago University Press, Dunedin, 2005, pp. 47–62.

11. DRESSING FOR WAR: GLAMOUR AND DUTY IN WOMEN'S LIVES DURING THE SECOND WORLD WAR

1. *Guardian*, 29 June 2005, URL:http://www.guardian.co.uk/uk_news/ story/ ,,1516819,00.html, accessed 30 June 2005; *Observer*, 10 July 2005, URL:http://observer.guardian.co.uk/uk_news/story/0,,1525283,00.html, accessed 30 June 2006. It was initially intended that a statue of a female air raid warden sheltering a child

stand on top of the rectangular block. The design was modified after objections that there was a poor artistic fit between the base arrayed with clothing and the statue on top. The monument was funded partly by public donation but also received a grant of UK£1 million from the National Heritage Memorial Fund. Ministry of Defence, WW2 60th Anniversary Commemorations, 'The Story Behind the Women's Monument', URL: http://www.mod.uk/aboutus/history/ww2/ womensmonument.htm, accessed 6 June 2006. The Queen's ATS uniform featured in the Kensington Palace, 2005 exhibit, 'The Queen's Working Wardrobe'. It was the only piece of wartime clothing included.

2   Don Wall, 'Women's Memorial Cloaked in Controversy', *City Parent* (Toronto), 28 June 2005, URL: http://www.cityparent.com/foreveryoung/archive/ 0050628/ 5683.html, accessed 30 June 2006. According to Crawley some women who had donated money to the memorial fund asked for and received their money back, see URL:http://www.thewrens.com/memorial/guestbook.shtml, accessed 30 June 2006.

3   See for example the chapter on wartime shortages, 'The Shoe Pinches', in Nancy M. Taylor, *The New Zealand People at War: The Home Front*, Government Printer, Wellington, 1986, or Richard Wolfe's *The Way We Wore: The Clothes New Zealanders Have Loved*, Auckland, 2001, esp. pp. 9–10. The chapter in Sandra Coney, *I Do: 125 Years of Weddings in New Zealand*, Auckland, Hodder Moa Beckett, 1995, on wartime weddings is titled 'Hasty Marriages and Fabric Shortages'.

4   *EP*, 17 October 1941, p. 8.

5   On Britain see Ina Zweiniger-Bargielowska, *Austerity in Britain: Rationing, Controls, and Consumption 1939–1955*, Oxford University Press, New York, 2000; on Germany, Irene Guenther, *Nazi Chic: Fashioning Women in the Third Reich*, Berg, Oxford and New York, 2004.

6   *EP*, 1 November 1941, p. 1; 13 December 1941, p. 13.

7   *NZH*, 7 December 1940, p. 10; 14 December 1940 p. 15; *Press*, 7 December 1940, p. 12.

8   'Girls' College', in Lauris Edmond (ed.), *Women in Wartime: New Zealand Women Tell Their Story*, Government Printing Office, Wellington, 1986, p. 164.

9   Taylor, pp. 758–61, Lyons quote on p. 761.

10 Ibid., pp. 792–3.

11 *NZL*, 3 September 1941, p. 12.

12 Eve Ebbett, *When the Boys Were Away: New Zealand Women in World War II*, Reed, Wellington, 1984, p. 95.

13 Helen Laurenson, *Going Up, Going Down: The Rise and Fall of the Department Store*, Auckland University Press, Auckland, 2005, pp. 65–6.

14 *EP*, 24 October 1941, p .8.

15 Don Taylor (comp.), *Everyone's War: A Collection of Tales from World War II*, Zenith Publishing, New Plymouth, 2005, p. 50.

16 Edmond, p. 101. The photograph accompanying her account shows her wearing a little feather-trimmed hat pinned on at an angle.

17 *EP*, 1 September 1941, p. 3.

18 Iris Latham (ed.), *The WAAC Story: The Story of the New Zealand Women's Army Auxiliary Corps*, n.p. , Wellington, 1986, p. 77.

19 *EP*, 6 November 1941, p. 12.

20 *EP*, 12 November 1941, p. 10.

21 Taylor, *Everyone's War*, p. 67.

22 Nell Hartley, *Swagger on Our Doorstep*, Moana Press, Tauranga, 1987, p. 211.

23 Jim Sullivan (ed.), *Doing Our Bit: New Zealand Women tell their Stories of World War Two*, HarperCollins Publishers, Auckland, 2002, p. 69.

24 June to Mrs G. Robertson, 27 August 1944, private collection, copy in author's possession.

25 Sullivan, p. 127.

26 'A War Bride's Story', in Edmond, p. 40.

27 Taylor, *Everyone's War*, p. 143.

28 Bracy Gardiner, *It Wasn't Easy: Memoirs of Women of the Wartime South*, Craig Printing Co., Invercargill, 1990, pp. 96–7. On dances and girls social identity see Emma Dewson's excellent, 'Off to the Dance: An Exploration of New Zealand Women and Social Interaction at Community Dances and Balls, 1870s to the 1930s', BA Hons research essay, Victoria University of Wellington, 2000.

29 M. L. Paterson in Gardiner, p. 27.

30 Mihi Edwards, *Mihipeka: Time of Turmoil Nga Wa Raruraru*, Penguin, Auckland, 1992, p. 126. The other jive dresses were coloured 'wine' and cyclamen pink. In the same passage she also mentions a long dress more suitable for formal dancing and a 'lovely dress' made from unrationed furnishing material.

31 Ibid., pp. 90, 135–6, 151.

32 Sullivan, p. 168.

33 Deborah Montgomerie, *The Women's War: New Zealand Women 1939–45*, Auckland University Press, Auckland, 2001, pp. 45–8.

34 The Women's Auxiliary Air Force, set up in January 1941, reached peak strength of 3746 in August 1943, with a total of 4753 women serving at some point in the war. The Women's Auxiliary Army Corps established in late 1941, peaked in strength in July 1943 with 4489 members. The Women's Royal New Zealand Naval Service was established in May 1942 and its staff peaked at 519 in October 1944. Many more women volunteered than could serve. The National Service Department estimating that there were 15,000 volunteers for the armed services and 75,000 members of the Women's War Service Auxiliary, *AJHR*, 1946,

       H-11A, pp. 28–9.
35. Ruth Flashoff, *With a Pen in My Hand: Memoirs of Ruth Flashoff*, Steele Roberts, Wellington, 2000, p. 79.
36. Gunner S. Billet, New Zealand Women's Army Auxiliary Corps narrative, URL:http://www.geocities.com/nzwrac/Billett1.html, accessed 30 June 2006.
37. D. O. W. Hall, *Women at War*, Whitcombe & Tombs, Christchurch, 1948, p. 26.
38. Bathia Mackenzie, *The WAAF Book: A Scrapbook of Wartime Memories*, Whitcoulls, Christchurch, 1982, p. 26.
39. For a discussion of the depiction of uniformed women in wartime cartoons see Deborah Montgomerie, 'Reassessing Rosie: World War II, New Zealand Women and the Iconography of Femininity', *Gender and History*, vol. 8, no. 1, April 1996, pp. 108–32.
40. *NZH*, 18 August 1942, p. 2.
41. *NZH*, 26 August 1942, p. 4.
42. *NZH*, 25 January 1943, p. 4.
43. Latham, p. 88.
44. Montgomerie, *The Women's War*, chs 4–5.
45. *New Zealand Woman's Weekly (NZWW)*, 13 February 1941, p. 1; *NZH*, 26 September 1942, p. 8; 1 April 1943, p. 5.
46. *Mirror*, January 1941, pp. 6–7; *NZL*, 11 September 1942, p. 12.
47. *NZWW*, 1 July 1939, p. 14.
48. *NZWW*, 5 December 1940, p. 15; *NZL*, 1 September 1942, p. 12.
49. *Dominion*, 14 October 1940, p. 9; *NZH*, Saturday Supplement, 25 November 1939, p. 7, 'You can only be a woman or a soldier. You can not be both!'
50. Sullivan, pp. 77, 103.
51. Dianne Bardsley, *The Land Girls: In a Man's World, 1939–46*, Otago University Press, Dunedin, 2000, pp. 13–30.
52. *NZH*, 19 September 1942, p. 4.
53. Kate Sheppard is the classic example of a New Zealand suffragist regularly praised for her feminine demeanour, see for example Judith Devaliant, *Kate Sheppard: A Biography*, Penguin, Auckland, 1992, pp. 134, 136. On the use of fashion by British suffragettes see Wendy Parkins, '"The Epidemic of Purple White and Green": Fashion and the Suffragette Movement in Britain, 1908–14', in Wendy Parkins (ed.), *Fashioning the Body Politic: Dress, Gender and Citizenship*, Berg, Oxford, 2002.
54. *EP*, 10 November 1941, p. 5.
55. These kinds of advertisements were carried by a wide range of publications including the major newspapers, the *New Zealand Woman's Weekly* and the *Listener*. For other examples see the London House Beauty Preparations promotion, 'Beauty Enhances Morale These Days', *NZWW*, 12 October 1944, p. 34; examples of the Ponds advertisements can be found in *NZWW*, 23 January 1941, p. 31; *NZL*, 14 March 1941, p. 15; 17 March 1944, p. 6; 8 August 1944, p. 15; *EP*, 8 November 1941, p. 15.
56. *EP*, 20 October 1941, p. 8.
57. *New Zealand Farmer's Weekly*, 30 November 1944, p. 44. For other hosiery advertisements overlaying wartime austerity with images of well-earned peacetime luxury, see *New Zealand Home Journal*, 10 March 1944, p. 5; 10 October 1944, p. 16.
58. *Weekly News*, 31 December 1941, p. 10.

12. MOVING IN UNISON, DRESSING IN UNIFORM: STEPPING OUT IN STYLE WITH MARCHING TEAMS

I would like to thank the donors of materials and papers relating to marching without which this research would not have been possible; current and former members of marching teams and Marching New Zealand, especially Dianne Bond, Lorraine Simpson, Edna Snowdon and Jan Hoad; Shirley Adams and interviewees in the Puke Ariki oral history project; the staff at Puke Ariki, New Plymouth; Auckland Public Library and Te Papa; the School of History, Politics, Philosophy and International Relations, Victoria University of Wellington, for a small research grant to assist with travel to New Plymouth, and the editors of this volume for useful suggestions and their patience.

1. One of the two television advertisements was for New Zealand Insurance; Maggie Rainey-Smith, *About Turns*, Random House, Auckland, 2005; Marie Adams and Mike Mizrahi (dir.), *Holy Sinners*, New Zealand International Festival of the Arts, Wellington, Westpac St James (10–13 March 2006); 'Golden Days', Museum of New Zealand (Te Papa); 'Taranaki Experience', Puke Ariki, New Plymouth. In earlier years marching teams have featured on a stamp (November 1993), and were the subject of a major television drama series, *The Marching Girls* (written by Fiona Samuel, produced by Steve La Hood and directed by Melanie Read, Lex Van Os, John Anderson, Tony Wilson), screened October–November 1987. With the sport now in decline it has become part of the nostalgic vocabulary of things deployed to signify what New Zealand is, or rather what it once was.
2. Mary Ellen Hanson, *Go! Fight! Win! Cheerleading in American Culture*, Bowling Green State University Popular Press, Bowling Green, 1995. Unlike cheerleading, New Zealand marching used few accessories, and never pompoms.
3. Henning Eichberg, *Body Cultures: Essays on Sport, Spaces and Identity*, Routledge, London and New York, 1998. See also 'Marching Teams', A. H. McLintock (ed.), *An Encyclopaedia of New Zealand*, Government

Printer, Wellington, 1966 (now available at URL: www.TeAra.govt.nz/1966/M/MarchingTeams/en). N. Mangos and J. Stayt, *Marching Down Under*, New Zealand Marching Association (NZMA), Wellington, 1984; Jill Williams, Val Browning and Charlotte Macdonald, 'New Zealand Marching Association 1945–', in Anne Else (ed.), *Women Together: A History of Women's Organizations in New Zealand*, Historical Publications Branch/Daphne Brasell Associates, Wellington, 1993, pp. 437–9; 'Military Precision, Chorus Line Glamour', Sandra Coney, *Standing in the Sunshine*, Viking, Auckland, 1993, pp. 250–1, and under 'History' on the website for Marching New Zealand, URL:www.marching.co.nz. See also Charlotte Macdonald, 'Putting Bodies on the Line: Marching Spaces in Cold War Culture', in Patricia Vertinsky and John Bale (eds), *Sites of Sport: Space, Place, Experience*, Routledge, London and New York, 2004, pp. 85–100.

4   Among the most prominent are A. R. D. Fairburn, 'Marching Girls', *Here and Now*, vol. 2, no. 10, July 1952, pp. 9–10. 'Girl Marching Teams in New Zealand Arouse Controversy and Draw Crowds', *New York Times*, 25 February 1958, p. 3; Bruce Mason, 'Stepping it out, stepping it high', *NZL*, vol. 82, no. 1899, 1 May 1976, p. 9. Subsequent issues carried indignant responses to Mason's article, see S. Williams, Napier, to editor, *NZL*, vol. 82, no. 1902, 22 May 1976, p. 9; Beverley Cameron (aged fifteen), Wellington, and Betty Veale, Westport, to editor, *NZL*, vol. 82, no. 1903, 29 May 1976, pp. 6–7.

5   Ann Hardy captures this attitude in her review of the 1987 drama series, *Marching Girls*: 'Boring, vulgar, kitsch and pointless, practised, for good reason, only in this country and America, women's marching has, until now, hardly rated highly in the educated New Zealander's hierarchy of the social arts. It's always seemed to me to be a rather embarrassing reminder of how low the non-School-Cert-achiever can sink in the time when the telly's off and there are no soap operas to fill the day.' 'The Marching Girls: A Small Step for Woman', *Illusions*, no. 7, 1988, pp. 36–40. Irene, the central character in Maggie Rainey-Smith's novel, *About Turns*, hides her youthful marching past in the Hutt Valley as a secret not to be revealed to her Kelburn/Karori middle class book club years later. The Benmorettes, one of several teams formed in the early 1960s at Otematata, the hydro-electric construction village for the Benmore dam; the Waitara Skodaettes, a 1970s team; the Nevilettes, a midget team in the Roebuck's club, New Plymouth, c.1958–9 to 1965–6, named after Neville Roebuck, the team's sponsor. *Quick March*, no. 148, October 1963; Avonette Marching Records, ARC 2002-335, Puke Ariki; Roebuck's Marching Team Records, ARC 2002-143, Puke Ariki.

6   Elizabeth Wilson, *Adorned in Dreams: Fashion and Modernity*, University of California Press, Berkeley, 1985; Jennifer Craik, *The Face of Fashion: Cultural Studies in Fashion*, Routledge, London, 1994, ch. 9; Jennifer Craik, *Uniforms Exposed: From Conformity to Transgression*, Berg, Oxford, 2005; Nathan Joseph, *Uniforms and Nonuniforms: Communication through Clothing*, Greenwood Press, Connecticut, 1986.

7   See works by Wilson and Craik; Fiona McKergow, 'Opening the Wardrobe of History: Dress, Artefacts and Material Life of the 1940s and 1950s', in Bronwyn Dalley and Bronwyn Labrum (eds), *Fragments: New Zealand Social and Cultural History*, Auckland University Press, Auckland, 2000, pp. 163–87; Carole Turbin, 'Refashioning the Concept of Public/Private', *Journal of Women's History*, vol. 15, no. 1, Spring 2003, pp. 43–51; Christine Boydell, 'Review Article. Refashioning Identities: Gender, Class and the Self', *Journal of Contemporary History*, vol. 39, no. 1, January 2004, pp. 137–46; Barbara Burman and Carole Turbin, 'Material Strategies Engendered', *Gender and History*, vol. 14, no. 3, November 2002, pp. 371–81; Christopher Breward, Becky Conekin and Caroline Cox (eds), *The Englishness of English Dress*, Berg, Oxford and New York, 2002.

8   *Quick March*, no. 1, November 1951, p. 1.

9   Sandra Coney, *Every Girl: A Social History of Women and the YWCA in Auckland, 1885–1985*, Auckland YWCA, Auckland, 1986; Clare Simpson, 'The Social History of the Christchurch Young Women's Christian Association', MA thesis, University of Canterbury, 1984; Miriam Clark, ' "Be Fit and Add Something to the Person": The Sport and Physical Recreation Programme of the YWCA in Wellington 1918–1939', BA (Hons) research essay, Victoria University of Wellington, 1993; Williams, Browning and Macdonald.

10 Photographs of the James Smith team can be found at PAColl-3332-1-2, and of the Woolworths team at 1/2-C-016178-F, ATL.

11 New Plymouth Mardi Gras Carnival Committee, 1939–43, ARC 2002-439, Puke Ariki. The prize in 1939 also included a framed coloured photograph of the winning team and individual smaller photographic prints for each member of the team, a prize donated by E.W. Crago, a local photographer. See also Peggy Jones (b. 3 January 1927, Hawera) interviewed by Shirley Adams, 4 July 2002, ARC 2002-918, Puke Ariki (hereafter Jones, ARC 2002-918, Puke Ariki).

12 Coney, *Every Girl*; Mangos and Stayt; Williams, Browning and Macdonald. Photographs of some of the early teams can be found as follows: Wellington McDuff store Marching Team, 1937, C.021135, Te Papa (unusually the team is wearing high heels). A team from the Wellington General Motors factory was photographed by Gordon Burt in 1935. The eight women are wearing dark silk overalls over white silk shirts with rolled up sleeves and white caps, on each of which is embroidered a name of an automobile model: Pontiac, Vauxhall, Chevrolet, Oldsmobile, Buick, etc., C.002654, Te Papa. A photograph of the Grenadiers marching team, Te Kuiti, c.1939–41, supplied by N. J. Waite, Te Kuiti, appeared in the 'Over the teacups' page, *NZWW*, 29 August 1994, p. 91. All six members of the Grenadiers team, attired in long white trousers and dark tunic tops, are named. The Bryant and May championship marching team led by Florence Cunningham (born Smith), c.1933, probably in Wellington, appeared on the 'Those were the days' page, *NZWW*, 1 December 1997, p. 68. The photograph was supplied by Florence's daughter Heather Bevan. The magazine appealed to readers who might also have been members of the team (none other than Florence were identified). The Ross and Glendining team photographed by the *Evening Star* marching in Dunedin's Octagon, 1945, was

13   reproduced on the back cover of *Quick Step*, no. 193, September 1994.
13   Stanley P. Newcomb, 'Girls and Marching – New Zealand Style', *Instrumentalist*, vol. 25, no. 2, September 1970, pp. 84–5. Allan Thomas, *Music is Where You Find It. Music in the Town of Hawera, 1946. An Historical Ethnography*, Music Books New Zealand, Wellington, 2004.
14   Joyce Simpson to Ron Lambert, September 2002, Joyce Simpson Papers, ARC 2002-1029, Puke Ariki. The Woolworths managers who supported the team were Matt Mathews and Jim Ramsay.
15   Ibid.; New Plymouth Mardi Gras Carnival Committee, ARC 2002-439, Puke Ariki; *New Zealand Free Lance*, 10 January 1940.
16   The oral history interviews with former marchers reveal a number of comments on the health benefits of marching along with serious conditions. Rae Boulter, a member of the Roebuck's team, died at the age of 25 after suffering bouts of unconsciousness after exertion. Joan Lander interviewed by Shirley Adams, 17 August 2002, ARC 2002-912, Puke Ariki.
17   Programme excerpt, Girls Marching Championship 5th Annual Competition 1943, Roebuck's Reunion booklet, p. 20, ARC 2002-143, Puke Ariki. Three bands were in attendance at the championships. The Hansell's team wore white and red; Roebuck's were in black and white, DIC wore white pleated skirts, military hats and blue military tops, while Wellington Woollen Mills were in white with white cap and blue band.
18   Jones, ARC 2002-918, Puke Ariki. Peggy Jones was an employee at McKenzies store, New Plymouth. The exacting standards demanded by the Kilties' instructors, Ralph Buckham and E. ('Jumbo') Rowe, were accepted by the team, though they shocked some other members of the community. Peggy recalled an occasion when the team was out practising between 6.30 and 7.30 a.m. at Pukekura Park. The instructor was up on the terraces 'to see if our lines were straight, our arms were straight you know and things like that. They used a few military swear words sometimes . . . there were houses by Pukekura Park there and one morning a woman came running over in her nightie and she says, "Go home girls, go home" and we says, "What for?" and she said, "I wouldn't have a man talking to me like that". She was quite upset. Cos both of them had very loud voices, and they were wanting perfection, really perfection.' The Roebuck's team was formed in 1941 by Dot Eden (Andrews) and Nola Pentecost (Paul). Their first instructor was army officer Bill Groombridge. Roebuck's Marching Team records, ARC 2002-143; Joan Lander interviewed by Shirley Adams, 17 August 2002, ARC 2002-912; Colleen Eagles (Arden), interviewed by Shirley Adams, 17 August 2002, ARC 2002-914, Puke Ariki.
19   Peggy Nelson (b. 5 October 1928, New Plymouth) interviewed by Shirley Adams, 15 August 2002, ARC 2002-916, Puke Ariki. Inglewood teams went on to enjoy a long and illustrious history, with Bernard Plumb and other members of the Plumb family at the centre of activities. The Miltonettes Club celebrated its twenty-fifth anniversary in 1994, *Quick Step*, November 1994, p. 8 (two members of the team at that time, Debby Bendall and Deborah Gyde, had been marching for all 25 years). When life member of the Inglewood Miltonettes Marching Club Audrey Longstaff died in February 1994, members of the club formed an honour guard at her funeral service. *Daily News* (New Plymouth), 23 February 1994.
20   The sport's most prestigious trophy, for the senior team winning the national championship, was the Parry Cup, donated by W. E. Parry, Minister of Internal Affairs in the 1935–49 Labour administration. A list of winners can be found in 'Marching Teams', in McLintock.
21   Mangos and Stayt, p. 3.
22   'History', Marching New Zealand website, URL:www.marching.co.nz/history.html; Mangos and Stayt.
23   A photograph of the team can be seen at 1/4-091101-F, ATL.
24   *Quick March*, no. 1, March 1951; Representatives (all but one of whom were men) came from Wellington, Timaru, Wanganui, Wairarapa and Martinborough, Hastings, Hastings and Napier, Pahiatua and Palmerston North. Arthur Harper, Assistant Under Secretary for Internal Affairs, conveyed the minister's apologies for unavoidable absence but was at pains to express his 'great interest . . . in the sport of marching and intimated that every possible assistance would be gladly given by the Department'. Mangos and Stayt, p. 1. All the office holders in the NZMA were men until the first women were elected in the late 1950s. The sport was described with pride rather than apology as 'a girl's sport . . . run for girls by men'. Morgan, 'The Girls are Marching', *New Zealand Magazine*, no. 1, 1951, p. 5a. The NZMA became Marching New Zealand in 1998.
25   Michael Roche to author, 11 and 22 October 2004, including photograph (Michael Roche's mother, Marjory Hunter, was the marker in the team).
26   Edna Snowdon, 'Girl's Marching', *Otaki Historical Society Historical Journal*, vol. 9, 1986, pp. 21–7. Membership of marching teams shows both Māori and Pākehā participants. The Ōtaki Māori girls' team was an exception in its specific Māori membership and name. Rachel Josephs, a champion winning leader with the Inglewood Vanguards, remarked that it 'was not normal for Maoris to march' but thought her example had 'encouraged other Maori into marching' when interviewed in the early 1990s, Coney, *Standing in the Sunshine*, p. 51.
27   *Quick March*, no. 1, November 1951, p. 1.
28   Photographs of the marching display put on as part of the civic welcome in Auckland can be found at F-19846-1/4 (QM39), F-42658-1/2 (QM44), F-42439-1/2 (QM59), F-42441-1/2 (QM61), F-42657-1/2 (QM45), National Publicity Studios Collection, ATL. See also 'Bright Marching at Basin Reserve', *Dominion*, 7 February 1958, p. 11.
29   Mangos and Stayt; *Women in Sport*, vol. 1, no. 11, December 1948; *N.Z. Sportswoman*, vol. 1, no. 7, October

1949, p. 35; Morgan, pp. 5–6.
30. *Quick March*; *Quick Step*; Mangos and Stayt; Matt Philp, 'March Past. Marching Girls – Are they History or Can the Sport Survive?, *NZL*, vol. 165, no. 3040, 15 August 1998, pp. 30–1.
31. By the 1970s costume judging reflected the extremely fine-grained judging schedules applied to teams in competition. Uniformity was expected in all aspects of appearance. The march plans came to specify more and more of the criteria to be applied. Among the definitions of how cleanliness of uniforms would be judged, for example, it was noted that: 'Grass clippings from a newly mown marching area, if adhering to footwear, will not be treated as uncleanliness', NZMA, *Marching Plans and Drills*, 1987, p. 240. Jan Hoad to author, 13 December 2006.
32. *Handbook of Marching*, p. 2.
33. Nelson, ARC 2002-916, Puke Ariki.
34. Lander, ARC 2002-912; Eagles, ARC 2002-914; Roebuck's Team Records, ARC 2002-143, Puke Ariki. Neville Roebuck, the owner of the company (and neighbour of Nola Pentecost, one of the founders of the team), paid for all the team's expenses: travel, as well as separate sets of performing and travelling uniforms.
35. Eagles, ARC 2002-914, Puke Ariki.
36. Jones, ARC 2002-918, Puke Ariki.
37. Bowerco, a Wellington company, was initially the main supplier of white leather boots to marching teams. In 1963 a pair of boots cost 83s 6d (close to £50 for a team). By the 1990s 'Strida Marching Boots' were supplied by Simpsons in Auckland in two styles, 'traditional' at $79.50 and 'budget' at $69. Legs were painted with a brown fluid to create a uniform appearance ('Paul Duval' was the preferred product in the 1950s). *Quick March*, 1963; *Quick Step*, 1994; Jan Hoad to author, 13 December 2006.
38. Bev Pui (born Beverley Nickson, 6 September 1946, Waitara), interviewed by Shirley Adams, 12 June 2002, ARC 2002-921, Puke Ariki.
39. *Handbook*, 1956, p. 53 specified two costume judges, 'preferably a lady and a gentleman'. The two costume judges at the championships held in Wanganui in February 1943 were Mrs H. M. Armitage and Mrs Newton Hood, Roebuck Marching Team Records, booklet, p .20, ARC 2002-143, Puke Ariki.
40. *Handbook*, 1956, p. 3.
41. *Quick March*, no. 1, 1951. 'Suitability' in uniforms was emphasised consistently. As early as 1939 the New Plymouth Mardi Gras Committee was prepared to leave choice of costumes to the members of the marching teams, deciding only 'to impress on them the necessity for suitability in this costume'. New Plymouth Mardi Gras Festival Committee Records, 18 October 1939 minutes, ARC 2002-439, Puke Ariki.
42. *Handbook*, p. 54.
43. Betty Charteris and Peggy Jones both made the first uniforms worn by their teams, the Inglewood Vanguards and Kilties, respectively. Colleen Eagles and two other members of the Roebucks team worked at Carter Brothers, a men's tailoring business in New Plymouth where they made men's suits, air force uniforms and 'stuff like that' so they were sometimes applying occupational skills to their marching outfits. Eagles, ARC 2002-914, Puke Ariki.
44. Two companies prominent in supplying hats to marching teams were the Team Hats company, and Hills Caps in Wellington, Jan Hoad to the author, 13 December 2006.
45. Ibid.
46. Jones, ARC 2002-918; Snowdon, p. 23. In 1986 the City Gate Marching Club in New Plymouth ran a housie night every Thursday at the West End Bowling Club, organised a March-a-thon from New Plymouth Post Office to Oakura on 26 January and every fortnight members inserted a Motor Market supplement in the local newspaper between 1 and 3 a.m., to support the activities of their three marching teams, Avonette Marching Team Records, ARC 2002-335, Puke Ariki.
47. Jones, ARC 2002-918, Puke Ariki.
48. Linda Brady, 'Whatever Happened to Marching Girls?', *Thursday*, 16 October 1969, p. 60.
49. NZMA, Information Bulletin, No. 7 April 1974, p. 3, NZMA Records, Box 1, NZMS 856, Auckland Public Library.
50. Brady, p. 60.
51. Several uniforms worn by the Gore Cavaliers team are now in Te Papa's collection, see PC3904-3907.
52. NZMA, Information Bulletin, October 1973, 'For Sale' section, p. 10, NZMA Records, Box 1, NZMS 856.
53. *Quick Step*, no. 2, October 1978, p. 16. 'Tailor-made' uniforms were exceptional, most outfits being made by parents and team supporters. The experience of those who did employ tailors to make team jackets was often one of frustration – on both sides, Jan Hoad to author, 13 December 2006.
54. *Quick Step*, nos. 9 & 11, May and July 1979.
55. Several examples of teams wearing 'pancake' hats can be seen on the home page of Marching New Zealand, URL:www.marching.co.nz.
56. Jones, ARC 2002-918, Puke Ariki.
57. Nicola Legat, 'Marching Girls', *Metro*, vol. 7, no. 81, March 1988, pp. 124–30. See also Pamela Stirling, 'When a Girl's Gotta March', *NZL*, vol. 118, no. 2488, 24 October 1987, pp. 20–2.
58. The Lochiel team was invited to perform as part of the Edinburgh Tattoo in 1978, and has done so on a number of occasions since. In 2002 the Edinburgh Tattoo was performed for the first time outside Scotland, at the Westpac Stadium in Wellington as part of the New Zealand International Festival of the Arts. Every performance was sold out well in advance.
59. The Pioneer Gordons, Gordonaires and Gordonettes were Wanganui teams of the early 1960s, *Quick*

March, no. 148, Octoer 1963, pp. 7, 10; the Glen Gordans were an Auckland team established in 1958 and still competing in the late 1960s, Brady, p. 59.
60 Tanja Bueltmann, paper presented at the Scots Abroad Conference, July 2006; 'Plenty of "Kilties"? Patterns of Scottish Settler Identities in New Zealand, c.1860–1910', paper presented at New Historians Conference, Victoria University of Wellington, 1–2 September 2006; 'Anchoring the Old Home in the New: Representations of "Scottishness" in New Zealand, c.1860 to 1930', seminar presented at Stout Research Centre, Victoria University of Wellington, November 2006.
61 Jones, ARC 2002-918, Puke Ariki.
62 Ibid.
63 See Wilson's discussion of pastiche and the interesting parallel of bricolage in the postmodern context, Wilson, ch. 8.
64 This event comprised a grand march and march past performed in front of the Commissioner Sir Harry Battersbee, Lieutenant-Colonel J. K. Irving, Army Area Commander and E. C. Gilmour, Chairman of the New Plymouth Borough and Taranaki County Patriotic Committee. An admission price raised £425 for the Patriotic Fund. The ceremony was prepared by A. D. Lynch of Napier, who acted as marshall, with incidental music being supplied by the band of Royal New Zealand Air Force. *Taranaki Daily News*, 6 March 1944, clipping in Roebuck's Marching Team Records, ARC 2002-143, Puke Ariki. For the 1956 ceremony see Roebuck's records, ARC 2002-143, Puke Ariki. On the appeal of ceremony see *Evening Post* 1 March 1958, p. 12 (editorial). The artifacts deposited as part of the Plumb/Avonette Marching Records at Puke Ariki contain a very large Union Jack and standard on which it was carried.
65 Wilson quoting Hollander, p. 165.
66 Judges had to be able to see the eyes of team members, Jan Hoad to author, 13 December 2006.
67 Fairburn, p. 9.
68 Mason, p. 9.
69 Fairburn, p. 9; Mason, p. 9.

13. ENGAGING IN MISCHIEF: THE BLACK SINGLET IN NEW ZEALAND CULTURE

I am grateful for John Clarke's input and advice, including inspiration for the title. Many people kindly offered their thoughts and experiences of wearing and observing the black singlet in New Zealand culture. In particular I would like to thank Burton Silver, Murray and Pam Ball, Tom Scott, Laurie Keats, Rangi Paenga, James Laverty, Rachael Hadwen, Denis Hall, Del Bettridge, Heather Macaulay, Gabi Rosenstreich, Prudence Stone, Stephen Munro, Hocken Library, Norsewear New Zealand, the Cartoon Archive (Alexander Turnbull Library) and Greta Larmer of the Olympic Museum.
1 Lou Taylor, *The Study of Dress History*, Manchester University Press, Manchester, 2001, p. 140. Seren Wendelken, 'Visual Constructs of Wealth in the *Maoriland Worker*, 1911–12: Cartoon and Intertext', in Miles Fairburn and Erik Olssen (eds), *Class, Gender and the Vote: Historical Perspectives from New Zealand*, University of Otago Press, Dunedin, 2005, p. 193.
2 Consecutive prime ministers Rob Muldoon and Bill Rowling even appeared together dressed in singlets in the 1970s cartoon series 'Rob-n-Bill', created by Bob Kerr and Burton Silver. Cartoon Archive, ATL.
3 'Dag' means amusing on this side of the Tasman Sea and John Clarke added another 'g' to give it the respectability of a surname. John Clarke, interviews with author, 6 May 2002 and 25 May 2006. Fred Dagg appeared on *Gallery*, *Nationwide*, *Country Calendar* and *Buck House*, which were locally made programmes screened by the New Zealand Broadcasting Corporation in the mid-1970s.
4 Malcolm McKinnon (ed.), *New Zealand Historical Atlas: Visualising New Zealand*, David Bateman Ltd, Auckland, 1997, Plate 65.
5 John Clarke, *A Dagg at My Table*, Text Publishing, Melbourne, 1998, p. 1.
6 Clarke interview, 6 May 2002.
7 Ibid. The cotton singlets were made by Lane Walker Rudkin Ltd under the American *Jockey* licence, and were intended to be worn as underwear. The woollen singlet was made by Mosgiel Woollens Limited in the early 1970s.
8 Clarke interview, 25 May 2006.
9 Anne Hollander, *Seeing Through Clothes*, University of California Press, Berkeley and Los Angeles, 1993, p. 263.
10 Clarke interview, 6 May 2002.
11 Clarke took the character of Fred Dagg to Australia, but appeared only in writing and on radio: Australians did not see him. James Belich, *Paradise Reforged: A History of the New Zealanders Since the 1880s*, Allen Lane/The Penguin Press, Auckland, 2001, p. 221. The Museum of New Zealand Te Papa Tongarewa (Te Papa) collected Dagg's outfit in 2002, and displayed it in the 2005 exhibition *Out On the Street: New Zealand in the 1970s* in the context of humour. His black woollen singlet is currently on display in *Blood Earth Fire* within a wider context of sheep farming and the wool industry in New Zealand. Even though the black singlet is considered iconic in its own right, the three singlets worn by Fred Dagg are the only black singlets held in Te Papa's collections.
12 Taylor, p. 142.
13 Ball describes his characters' outfits as a uniform. He originally intended their singlets to be dark navy blue. 'Obviously, working in black and white, the nearest I could get was black.' Personal communication from Murray Ball, 16 October 2006.

14 Murray Ball, *Footrot Flats*, Inprint Ltd, Lower Hutt, 1991, pp. 77, 84.
15 Murray Ball, *Footrot Flats*, INL Print Publication, New Zealand, 1982, p. 63.
16 Ball, *Footrot Flats*, 1991, p. 7. Ball himself didn't wear a 'Jacky Howe' as they were 'as itchy as knitted barbed wire', personal communication.
17 Published in the *New Zealand Listener* magazine from 1973 to 1994.
18 Burton Silver, personal communication, 15 September 2006.
19 *The Billy T. James Show* screened from 1984 to 1986 on Television New Zealand.
20 On a holiday trip to America, Nippy (still dressed in a black singlet) takes his family to see a rundown Indian reservation, observing; 'So, this is an Indian reservation? It's just like home, only the cars are bigger!' (Billy T. James, *Billy T. James: Hard-Case Book II*, Beckett Publishing, Auckland, 1987).
21 Claudia Bell, *Inventing New Zealand: Everyday Myths of Pakeha Identity*, Penguin, Auckland, 1996, pp. 163, 165.
22 Robin Law, 'Masculinity, Place, and Beer Advertising in New Zealand: The Southern Man Campaign', *New Zealand Geographer*, vol. 53, no. 2, 1997, p. 23. In the academic literature, Jock Phillips's *A Man's Country?* is a prime example and even features a cover image of two rural workers in black singlets (Penguin Books, Auckland, revised edition, 1996).
23 Belich, p. 148.
24 Bell, p. 35. Lou Taylor, *Establishing Dress History*, Manchester University Press, Manchester and New York, 2004, p. 252. See similar positioning from an Australian perspective in Margaret Maynard, *Fashioned From Penury: Dress as Cultural Practice in Colonial Australia*, Cambridge University Press, Cambridge, 1994, pp. 170–6.
25 Claudia Bell, 'Kiwiana Revisited', in Claudia Bell and Steve Matthewman (eds), *Cultural Studies in Aotearoa New Zealand: Identity, Space and Place*, Oxford University Press, Melbourne, 2004, pp. 175, 178, 180–1.
26 New Zealand Post, Kiwiana, 1994, URL:http://stamps.nzpost.co.nz/Cultures/en-NZ/Stamps/StampsHistoricalIssues/1994/Kiwiana, accessed 27 March 2006.
27 Bell, 'Kiwiana Revisited', p. 181.
28 Denis Hall, personal communication, 29 May 2006. Shear Discovery Centre, Masterton, personal communication, 6 October 2006. Bell, *Inventing New Zealand*, pp. 103, 116, 124. On the other hand, some might consider such massive 'civic imagery' as crudely comic (Peter Walker, 'Maori War', *Granta*, 58, 1997, p. 228).
29 Law, p. 25. Others have traversed this territory through fiction, for example John Mulgan's *Man Alone* (Selwyn & Blount, London, 1939) and Barry Crump's *A Good Keen Man* (A. H. & A. W. Reed, Wellington, 1960).
30 Taylor, *The Study of Dress History*, p. 144.
31 Gordon H. Brown, *Colin McCahon: Artist*, revised edition, Reed Books, Auckland, 1993, pp. 207–8.
32 Denys Trussell, 'Paintings for the Earthly Predicament' in Nigel Brown, *Black Frame*, Earl of Seacliff Art Workshop, Auckland, 1988.
33 Halina Ogonowska-Coates, *Boards, Blades & Barebellies*, Benton Ross Publishers Ltd, Auckland, 1987, p. 84. The Jackie Howe singlet, URL: http://or.essortment.com/ legendsshearing_rvha.html, accessed 4 Jan 2006.
34 The term 'Jacky Howe' is now generally only heard in rural areas of New South Wales and Queensland. Personal communication, Bruce Moore, Australian National University, Canberra, 29 September 2006.
35 John Wilson, 'Australians', Te Ara – the Encyclopedia of New Zealand, updated 26 Sept 2006, URL: http://www.TeAra.govt.nz/NewZealanders/NewZealandPeoples /Australians/en. The term 'Jacky Howe' is no longer common in New Zealand but a few references can be found, for example in Murray Ball's *Footrot Flats*, 1991, p. 7.
36 Rural workers such as gumdiggers, tree fellers and farm workers wore a mixture of garments ranging from undershirts to singlets.
37 The first woollen mill to be established in New Zealand was at Mosgiel, Dunedin in 1871.
38 Richard Wolfe, *The Way We Wore: The Clothes New Zealanders Have Loved*, Penguin Books, Auckland, 2001, p. 112.
39 Interview with Laurie Keats, Chairman of the Shear History Trust and co-founder of the Shear Discovery Centre, Masterton, 5 February 2006.
40 Ibid.
41 Rangi Paenga worked at the Kaiti works until 1994. He was a union delegate for many years, and the national president of the New Zealand Meat Workers Union in 1975. Rangi Paenga, personal communication, 1 October 2006.
42 Terry Perriam, *Where It All Began: A History of the Waitaki-Pukeuri Freezing Works, Oamaru, 1914–1989*, Waitaki International Limited, 1989, p. 127.
43 Paenga, personal communication.
44 Sheridan Gundry, *Making a Killing: A History of the Gisborne-East Coast Freezing Works Industry*, Tairawhiti Museum, Gisborne, 2004, pp. 55, 119.
45 Keats interview.
46 Such as Rangitikei Cotton Products Ltd which produces about 1000 cotton singlets for shearers and farmers each year, of which 700 are exported to Wales. Del Bettridge, Rangitikei Cotton Products Ltd, personal communication, 18 August 2006.
47 Norsewear New Zealand, personal communications, 30 January 2006 (with staff at the Norsewear store in Wellington, the factory at Norsewood, and the head office in Petone, Wellington). Other companies make

48 Silver, personal communication.
49 Department of Internal Affairs, *Making New Zealand: Dress*, Wellington, 1940, vol. 2, no. 23, p. 31.
50 Such a singlet is sometimes referred to as a 'muscle shirt' or more disturbingly, the slang term 'wifebeater'. URL: http://en.wikipedia.org/wiki/Wifebeater_(shirt), accessed 31 August 2006.
51 Personal communication, Greta Larmer, Olympic Museum, Wellington, 25 September 2006. Ron Palenski and Terry Maddaford, *The Games*, Moa Publications Ltd, Auckland, 1983, p. 20.
52 Basketball player Pero Cameron on playing for New Zealand at the Commonwealth Games, Melbourne, 2006. 'Mackinnon moves on', *The Age*, 26 March 2006, URL: http://www.theage.com.au/news/basketball/mackinnon-moves-on, accessed 14 September 2006.
53 The uniform for the Commonwealth Games athletes in 2006 featured 'traditional black' and a wide-shouldered, high-necked 'performance' black singlet made from lightweight synthetic fibres. 'Uniform a hit', *Dominion Post*, 24 January 2006, p. C14.
54 'Dan's singlet revealed', Jockey Press Release, 9 October 2006, URL: http://www.scoop.co.nz/stories/BU0610/S00150.htm, accessed 10 October 2006.
55 TV3 News, 6 p.m., 9 October 2006, URL: http://www.tv3.co.nz/News/tabid/67/article ID/14117/Default.aspx, accessed 10 October 2006.
56 Gabi Rosenstreich and Heather Macaulay, personal communication, 13 and 30 January 2006 (respectively). Both women were remembering their student days at the University of Otago in Dunedin during the mid-1980s.
57 Rachael Hadwen interview, 20 April 2006.
58 James Laverty interview, 26 January 2006.

14. ONE MAN'S FANTASY: THE EDEN HORE COLLECTION OF HIGH AND EXOTIC FASHION GARMENTS

1 *One Man's Fantasy* was also the title of an exhibition of a selection of garments from the Eden Hore collection, held at the Otago Museum in 1989, curated by Rae Vernon and Jane Malthus.
2 Lynne Wenden, 'Glenshee Ranch draws tourists to Maniototo', *ODT*, 15 November 1980, p. 19; *ST*, 10 February 1977, p. 6.
3 'A Fashion Oasis on Farm', *ODT*, 31 May 1975, p. 17; Arlene Griffin, *NZWW*, 12 July 1976, p. 24; Richard Worrall, 'Fashion on the Farm', *New Zealand Geographic*, no. 29, January–March 1996, p. 118.
4 Rachel McDermott, 'Entertaining Ideas: The Enterprises of Joe Brown, H.S.O.E', BA (Hons) long essay in history, University of Otago, 1998; Jim Sullivan, 'Brown, Andrew Joseph Francis 1907–1986', *DNZB*, updated 7 April 2006, URL: http://www.dnzb.govt.nz/; Richard Worrall, *Pacific Way*, no. 82, April 1995, p. 20.
5 Programme for Miss New Zealand Contest, 1965, n.p., Joe Brown Enterprises, Dunedin; *Evening Star*, 22 September 1966, p. 4.
6 From evidence at Glenshee, Eden Hore was involved with Miss New Zealand shows 1963–72.
7 *ST*, 10 February 1977, p. 6.
8 *ODT*, 16 May 1972, p. 5.
9 *ST*, 10 February 1977, p. 6.
10 *Mountain Scene*, 16 June 1977, p. 16; 23 June 1977, p. 16.
11 *ST*, 10 February 1977, p. 6; 12 March 1977, p. 6. Pat Hewitt produced her designs for Hore under the One Only label, and later became an expert patchworker and quilter.
12 Valerie Steele, 'Anti-fashion: The 1970s', *Fashion Theory*, vol. 1, no. 3, 1997, pp. 279–95; see Gerda Buxbaum (ed.), *Icons of Fashion: The 20th Century*, Prestel Verlag, Munich, 1999; *Making Textiles: Some Recent Developments in Machines and Methods*, Papers presented at the Seventh Shirley International Seminar, 8–10 October 1974, Shirley Publication S 11, Manchester, 1974. Textile production innovations of the 1970s included texturing of polyesters and other heat-settable fibres to create fabrics with more thickness and spring, and computer-aided design especially in weft and warp knitting, and textile printing.
13 Janice Breen Burns, 'Fifty Years of Fabulous', *The Age*, 20 June 2003, Section A3, p. 7, writing about the Australian Gown of the Year.
14 Jenny Lynch, *Ready to Wear: The Changing Shape of New Zealand Fashion*, Random House, Auckland, 2004, p. 17. By 1978 evening wear was also considered a 'shrinking market' in the United States, according to *The Market for New Zealand Apparel and Textiles in the United States*, Export Opportunity Team Report, Department of Trade and Industry, Wellington, June 1978, p. 32.
15 *Apparel*, vol. 8, no. 3, March 1976, p. 20.
16 *Apparel*, vol. 6, no. 8, August 1974, p. 1; *Apparel*, vol. 7, no. 2, February 1975, p. 4; *Apparel*, vol. 8, no. 11, November 1976, p. 11. The Michael Mattar outfit is a fitting daywear dress of black double-knit wool, waisted with long sleeves, with matching waist length jacket in cream and black plaid, featuring black cuffs and frog closures. It is pictured in an *ODT* 'Fashion at Vanity Walk' feature, 3 May 1972, p. 11. Hore probably purchased it from Vanity Walk.
17 *Thursday*, 8 November 1973, p. 13; *Apparel*, vol. 6, no. 10, October 1974, p. 3.

18 Barbara Permezel, *A Crucible of Creative Fashion Talent: Australian Gown of the Year 1953–1993*, Shop, Distributive and Allied Employees' Association, Melbourne, 1993, p. 32.
19 Ibid. The Australian Gown of the Year competition had begun in 1953 and was run by the Mannequins and Models Guild, who entrusted a panel of judges to select one evening gown with 'visual appeal' for its elegance, beauty, decorative detail, superb fabric, high standard of workmanship and creative design as the winner each year. One rule stated that gowns had to be made in Australia, and the competition focused on nurturing Australian design talent, but contestants' nationality was not explicitly mentioned in the rules, allowing a number of New Zealanders to enter over the years.
20 He bought most of her garments produced for competition at cost price, not usually including her labour costs. Hore and Gwilliam (b. 1938) corresponded intermittently for the rest of his life (Rosalie Gwilliam, personal communication, 24 October 2006).
21 This dress does not appear to be in Hore's collection, but another from the same year is. Called 'Aphrodite – Goddess of Love' and made from cream pure wool crepe, it consists of a long tabard with gold beads and crystal sequins applied to its empire-line bodice.
22 See, for example, *Thursday*, 19 April 1976, p. 25; *Apparel* and *AFF*, 1970s issues; Phyllis G. Tortora and Robert S. Merkel (eds), *Fairchild's Dictionary of Textiles*, 7th edition, Fairchild Publications, New York, 1996, p. 453.
23 Letter/notes from Rosalie Gwilliam to Eden Hore, no date, at Glenshee.
24 This outfit was entered in the 1989 Benson & Hedges Fashion Awards.
25 Susan Holmes, 'The Effects of Changes in Meal Pattern on the Metabolism of Two Women', MHSc thesis, University of New Zealand, 1966.
26 *Thursday*, 9 February 1976, p. 17, featured a kimono-inspired top and skirt 'designed and hand-printed by Susan Holmes, Browns Mill' and retailing for $50.
27 *Apparel*, vol. 9, no. 10, October 1977, p. 25; Jane Malthus and Rae Vernon, *New Zealand Fashion Flair of the 70s*, Otago Museum, 1989, p. 8. A catalogue accompanied the exhibition *One Man's Fantasy – A Selection from the Eden Hore Collection of High and Exotic Fashion Garments of the 1970s*; URL: www.textiles.org.nz/profiles/susanh, accessed 8 August 2006.
28 Twenty-three according to Ann Packer, *Stitch: Contemporary New Zealand Textile Artists*, Random House, Auckland, 2006, p. 107.
29 Mark Joel, personal communication, 25 September 2006. *Apparel*, vol. 10, no. 10, October 1978, p. 5. Although this entry is credited as Eleanor's work, it may have been a team effort. Miranda has subsequently claimed that she did the screen-printing. (Margaret Steele, personal communication, 18 August 2006).
30 *Apparel*, vol. 10, no. 10, October 1978, p. 5.
31 *Apparel*, vol. 9, no. 5, May 1977, p. 10; *Apparel*, vol. 9, no. 8, August 1977, pp. 1, 4. The overseas judge was Carla Zampatti of Australia.
32 *Apparel*, vol. 9, no. 10, October 1977, pp. 3, 25.
33 Steele, p. 292.
34 Ibid., p. 286.
35 I am uncertain if James Jaye was a label or the designer's name.
36 Beverley Horne, *Fleece in Your Hands*, New Zealand Spinning, Weaving and Woolcrafts Society, 1976 (US Revised edition, Interweave Press, Loveland, Colorado, 1979). The text encouraged spinners to try a broad range of sheep's wool breeds, and always to turn their yarn into some end product.
37 The fawn version at least was part of Kevin Berkahn's New Zealand World of Fashion show in 1971, Malthus and Vernon, 1989, p. 10.
38 Malthus and Vernon, 1989, p. 5. For some of the 1970s at least the Dunlaps lived in Australia, and designed and made some of their outfits there.
39 Both 'Midas Touch' and 'Esenada' were entered in the Australian Gown of the Year and the Benson & Hedges Coordinates Sections, in 1977 and 1978 respectively.
40 Jo Dunlap worked with fabrics other than leather too, and two of these creations are in the collection at Naseby: 'Cosmic Gold' (1978) and 'Electra' (1976).
41 *Apparel*, vol. 9, no. 6, June 1977, p. 3.
42 *Apparel*, vol. 10, no. 10, October 1978, p. 5. It took her 400 hours to create the yarn and design and crochet the pieces. Malthus and Vernon, p. 9.
43 The exact numbers of garments from any one designer are difficult to state, because some dresses are unlabelled, although they may be credited to a particular designer (orally or case label).
44 Kevin Berkahn with Maggie Blake, *Berkahn Fashion Designer*, HarperCollins, Auckland, 1999, pp. 23–32.
45 The collection also contains a similarly styled and feather-trimmed dress in greens and gold floral fabric, with a deep circular frill from the knee, and from the touring show a green and gold Lurex brocade jumpsuit with knee-length breeches and corded girdle, covered by a full-length cape whose hood was edged with a gold and Lurex frill.
46 Malthus and Vernon, 1989, p. 4. The dress is dated as from 1971. However, Berkahn's autobiography states that this dress was commissioned by the New Zealand Wool Board for Miss New Zealand 1973, Pam King, to wear representing her country. Berkahn and Blake, p. 61.
47 Berkahn and Blake, pp. 38–40.
48 Ibid., p. 56. It is unclear whether the other two gowns were purchased at the same time, or later.
49 A painterly floral spring-summer sheer, printed in green, blue, brown, yellow and white colours, was made into a knee-length dress with flared skirt, round neckline and two layer flared sleeves by Kevin Berkahn, and

into a full-length, waisted, long-sleeved dress with a square neckline yoke and cuffs in green satin, by Colin Cole (1931–87).
50. James Allan, 'From Bags to Bitches: The Passion of Fashion', *Auckland Metro,* April 1985, pp. 106–17; Wynsome Marshall, 'Do you get fun from your clothes?', *NZWW,* 14 September 1959, p. 17; *ODT,* 9 June 1987, p. 23; Allan, pp. 106–17.
51. Cole is also represented by a full-length halter neck dress featuring a gored skirt of Taiwanese border printed and sculptured velvet, with a matching red shawl-collared jacket and a purple waisted evening dress with a shantung silk gored skirt and silk marquisette sleeveless fitted bodice. Four layers of ruffles around the neckline create a cap sleeve effect and are balanced by a knee-to-floor deep ruffle on the skirt.
52. *Apparel*, vol. 7, no. 2, February 1975, p. 4; *Appare*l, vol. 7, no. 9, September 1975, p. 2. Deauville International was one company that contracted Colin Cole to design for their three ranges (Deauville International, dile, and Lady Lana) as part of a four-person team. *Apparel*, vol. 8, no. 9, September 1976, p. 16; *ODT,* 9 June 1987, p. 23.
53. Margaret Farry-Williams, personal communication, 17 November 2006. At least nineteen Vinka Lucas creations are part of the Eden Hore Collection. Favoured colours are black, gold, silver and salmon pink, although typically 1970s orange, teal and purple are to be found. Floral and paisley designs predominate. Eden Hore may have purchased some of the fabrics and commissioned Vinka Lucas to design and make up the dresses, with the intention of selling them. *ODT,* 31 May 1975, p. 17.
54. URL: www.vinkabrides.com/aboutvinka, accessed 8 August 2006; *Apparel Manufacturing*, vol. 1, no. 1 March 1970, p. 17, *Apparel*, vol. 8, no. 9, September 1976, p. 29.
55. *Apparel*, vol. 8, no. 7, July 1976, p. 12. These were worn until 1976 when designs from Nina Ricci of Paris were commissioned for Air New Zealand.
56. *Apparel*, vol. 8, no. 9, September 1976, p. 29. Yardage and garment specifications allowed local amateur dressmakers to more or less copy the design. Atkins Textiles also generously offered a cutting service for their fabrics. One could send purchased fabric and pattern and have the gown professionally cut.
57. *Apparel*, vol. 8, no. 2, February 1976, p. 32.
58. Malthus and Vernon, 1989, p. 9.
59. *Apparel*, vol. 12, no. 9, September 1980, p. 28. In 1984 Vinka Lucas launched a collection in front of 100 guests at an Auckland television studio, so that the occasion could be filmed for overseas advertising in her European, United States and Middle Eastern markets. Max Cryer compered the show, in which seventeen models paraded 145 garments. *Apparel,* vol. 16, no. 4, April 1984, p. 10.
60. Barbara Penberthy was born Georgina Barbara Lewis and was later Barbara Herrick.
61. Marie Studdard, 'Man and Wife in Fashion Partnership', *NZWW,* 14 September 1959, p. 18; *Thursday*, 17 April 1969, pp. 8-13 in feature on Wool; *Apparel*, vol. 9, no. 1, January 1977, p. 4; Douglas Lloyd Jenkins, 'Babs and the trouser girls', *NZL*, 16 October 2004, pp. 56–7.
62. *Apparel*, vol. 9, no. 1, January 1977, p. 4.
63. For example *Textile News*, vol. 4, no. 1, April 1979, p. 7; *Clothing Press*, vol. 1, no. 3, August 1980, p. 1.
64. *IDC Interim Report on the Review of the Textile Development Plan*, Wellington, 1985, p. 96.
65. *ODT,* 31 May 1975, p. 17.
66. Courtney Johnston, Scott Eady, 'Honeymoon on the Pigroot, 2003', URL: www.telecomprospect2004.org.nz/artist/eadyscott.asp, accessed 8 August 2006.
67. Burns.
68. See Joanne Finkelstein, 'Chic – A Look That's Hard to See', *Fashion Theory*, vol. 3, no. 3, 1999, pp. 363–85.

Further Reading

Andrewes, Frazer, 'The Man in the Grey Flannel Suit: White-Collar Masculinity in Post-War New Zealand', in Caroline Daley and Deborah Montgomerie (eds), *The Gendered Kiwi*, Auckland University Press, Auckland, 1999, pp. 191–212
Breward, Christopher, *The Hidden Consumer: Masculinities, Fashion and City Life 1860–1914*, Manchester University Press, Manchester, 1999
Breward, Christopher, Becky Conekin and Caroline Cox (eds), *The Englishness of English Dress*, Berg, Oxford and New York, 2002
Brickell, Chris, 'Through the (New) Looking Glass: Gendered Bodies, Fashion and Resistance in Post-war New Zealand', *Journal of Consumer Culture*, vol. 2, no. 2, 2002, pp. 241–69
Brookes, Barbara L., 'A Germaine Moment: Style, Language and Audience', in Tony Ballantyne and Brian Moloughney (eds), *Disputed Histories: Imagining New Zealand's Past*, Otago University Press, Dunedin, 2006, pp. 191–214
Brookes, Barbara, '"When Dad Was a Woman": Gender Relations in the 1970s', in Caroline Daley and Deborah Montgomerie (eds), *The Gendered Kiwi*, Auckland University Press, Auckland, 1999, pp. 235–50
Brydon, Anne and Sandra Niesson (eds), *Consuming Fashion: Adorning the Transnational Body*, Berg, Oxford, 1998
Burman, Barbara (ed.), *The Culture of Sewing: Gender, Consumption and Home Dressmaking*, Berg, Oxford and New York, 1999
Burman, Barbara and Carole Turbin (eds), *Material Strategies: Dress and Gender in Historical Perspective*, Blackwell, Oxford, 2003
Colchester, Chloë (ed.), *Clothing the Pacific*, Berg, Oxford and New York, 2003
Cole, Shaun, *'Don We Now Our Gay Apparel': Gay Men's Dress in The Twentieth Century*, Berg, Oxford and New York, 2001
Coney, Sandra, *Standing in the Sunshine: A History of New Zealand Women Since They Won the Vote*, Viking, Auckland, 1993
Coney, Sandra, *I Do: 125 Years of Weddings in New Zealand*, Hodder Moa Beckett, Auckland, 1995
Craik, Jennifer, *The Face of Fashion: Cultural Studies in Fashion*, Routledge, London, 1994
Cummings, Valerie, *Understanding Fashion History*, Batsford, London, 2004
Daley, Caroline, *Leisure and Pleasure: Reshaping and Revealing the New Zealand Body 1900–1960*, Auckland University Press, Auckland, 2003
Dalley, Bronwyn, 'Appearances: Hair and Clothing', in *Living in the Twentieth Century: New Zealand History in Photographs*, Bridget Williams Books/Craig Potton Publishing in association with the Ministry for Culture and Heritage, 2000, pp. 172–211
de la Haye, Amy and Elizabeth Wilson (eds), *Defining Dress: Dress as Object, Meaning and Identity*, Manchester University Press, Manchester, 1999
Ebbett, Eve, *In True Colonial Fashion: A Lively Look at What New Zealanders Wore*, A. H. & A. W. Reed, Wellington, 1977
Entwistle, Joanne and Elizabeth Wilson (eds), *Body Dressing*, Berg, Oxford and New York, 2001
Garlick, Steve, 'Men, Clothing and Identity: Fashioning Masculine Subjectivities', *Sites*, no. 37, 1999, pp. 64–82
Goodrum, Alison, Wendy Larner, and Maureen Molloy, 'Wear in the World? Fashioning Auckland as a Globalising City', in Ian Carter, David Craig, and Steve Matthewman (eds), *Almighty Auckland?*, Dunmore Press, Palmerston North, 2004, pp. 257–74
Joel, Alexandra, *Best Dressed: 200 Years of Fashion in Australia*, Collins, Sydney, 1984
Jones, Ann Rosalind and Peter Stallybrass (eds), *Renaissance Clothing and the Materials of Memory*, Cambridge University Press, New York, 2000
Küchler, Suzanne and Graeme Were (eds), *The Art of Clothing: A Pacific Experience*, UCL Press, London, 2004
Küchler, Suzanne and Daniel Miller (eds), *Clothing as Material Culture*, Berg, Oxford & New York, 2005.
Laurenson, Helen B., *Going Up Going Down: The Rise and Fall of the Department Store*, Auckland University Press, Auckland, 2005
Leota-Ete, Jakki, Shigeyiki Kihara, and Rosanna Raymond, 'Body Beautiful: New Zealand fashion – Pacific style', in Sean Mallon and Pandora Fulimalo Pereira (eds), *Pacific Art Niu Sila: The Pacific Dimension of Contemporary New Zealand Arts*, Te Papa Press, Wellington, 2002, pp. 91–101
Lloyd Jenkins, Douglas, *Avis Higgs: Joie de Vivre*, Hawke's Bay Museum, Napier, 2000
Lloyd Jenkins, Douglas, *Frank Carpay*, Hawke's Bay Museum, Napier, 2003
Lynch, Jenny, *Ready to Wear: The Changing Shape of New Zealand Fashion*, Random House, Auckland, 2004
Malthus, Jane, '"Bifurcated and Not Ashamed": Late Nineteenth Century Dress Reformers in New Zealand', *New Zealand Journal of History*, vol. 23, no. 1, 1989, pp. 32–46
Malthus, Jane, 'Dressmakers in Nineteenth Century New Zealand', in Barbara Brookes, Charlotte Macdonald and Margaret Tennant (eds), *Women in History 2*, Bridget Williams Books, Wellington, 1992, pp. 76–97
Malthus, Jane, 'European Women's Dress in Nineteenth-Century New Zealand', PhD Thesis, University of

Otago, 1996

Malthus, Jane and Chris Brickell, 'Producing and Consuming Gender: The Case of Clothing', in Barbara Brookes, Annabel Cooper and Robin Law (eds), *Sites of Gender: Women, Men & Modernity in Southern Dunedin 1890–1939*, Auckland University Press, Auckland, 2003, pp. 123–50

Maynard, Margaret, *Dress and Gloablisation*, Manchester University Press, Manchester, 2004

Maynard, Margaret, *Fashioned From Penury: Dress as Cultural Practice in Colonial Australia*, Cambridge University Press, Cambridge and Melbourne, 1994

Maynard, Margaret, *Out of Line: Australian Women and Style*, University of New South Wales Press, Sydney, 2000.

McIntosh, Doris, 'Dress', *Making New Zealand: Pictorial Surveys of a Century*, vol. 2, no. 23, 1940

McKergow, Fiona, 'Opening the Wardrobe of History: Dress, Artefacts and Material Life of the 1940s and 1950s', in Bronwyn Dalley and Bronwyn Labrum (eds), *Fragments: New Zealand Social and Cultural History*, Auckland University Press, Auckland, 2000, pp. 163–87

McLeod, Rosemary, *Thrift to Fantasy: Home Textile Crafts of the 1930s–1950s*, HarperCollins, Auckland, 2005

Mead, S. M., *Traditional Maori Clothing: A Study of Technological and Functional Change*, A. H. & A.W. Reed, Wellington, 1969

Millen, Julia, *Kirkcaldie & Stains: A Wellington Story*, Bridget Williams Books, Wellington, 2000

Molloy, Maureen, 'Cutting Edge Nostalgia: New Zealand Fashion Design for the New Millenium', *Fashion Theory*, vol. 8, no. 4, 2004, pp. 477–90

Montgomerie, Deborah, *The Women's War: New Zealand Women 1939–45*, Auckland University Press, Auckland, 2001

Nicholson, Heather, *The Loving Stitch: A History of Knitting and Spinning in New Zealand*, Auckland University Press, Auckland, 1998

Parkins, Wendy (ed.), *Fashioning the Body Politic: Dress, Gender and Citizenship*, Berg, Oxford and New York, 2002

Prendergast, Mick, *Kakahu: Maori Cloaks*, David Bateman in association with the Auckland Museum, Auckland, 1997

Regnault, Claire, *The New Zealand Gown of the Year*, Hawke's Bay Museum, Napier, 2003

Sprecher, Danielle, 'Clothes are Good Business: Consumption and Appearance in the Office, 1918–1939', in Caroline Daley and Deborah Montgomerie (eds), *The Gendered Kiwi*, Auckland University Press, Auckland, 1999, pp. 141–62

Steele, Valerie, *The Corset: A Cultural History*, Yale University Press, New Haven, 2001

Taylor, Lou, *Establishing Dress History*, Manchester University Press, Manchester, 2004

Taylor, Lou, *The Study of Dress History*, Manchester University Press, Manchester, 2001

Wallace, Patricia, 'Traditional Maori Dress: Rediscovering Forgotten Elements of Pre-1820 Practice', PhD Thesis, University of Canterbury, 2002

Welters, Linda and Abby Lillethun (eds), *The Fashion Reader*, Berg, Oxford and New York, 2007

Wilson, Elizabeth, *Adorned in Dreams: Fashion and Modernity*, Virago Press, London, revised edition, I. B. Tauris, 2003

Wolfe, Richard, *The Way We Wore: The Clothes New Zealanders Have Loved*, Penguin, Auckland, 2001

Index

References to illustrations are in **bold**.

Abrahams, Samuel, 133
Akuhata, Kiharoa, **101**
Alderson, Miss M., 137–8
Amherst (brig), 76, 78, 82
Anderson, William, 22
Ashworth, David, 81, **82**
asylums: clothing worn in, 119–21, **120**
Auckland City Mission, 127
Auckland Islands: shipwrecks on, 76–93
Auckland Lunatic Asylum, 119–20, **120**
Avonside Girls' High School, 55

Babs Radon (designer label), 68–70, **69**, 237–9; *see also* Herrick, Barbara
Baker, Matiu, 100
Baker family, **plate 2**
Ball, Murray, 207, 209–10, 219
Banks, Joseph, **13**, 22, 97, 98
barkcloth, 15
bathing suits *see* swimwear
belts, Sam Browne, 199–200, 201
benevolent institutions: clothing worn in, 117–21, **118**; *see also* charitable aid; poor
Benson & Hedges Fashion Awards, 224, 227–8, 229, 232, 241
Berg (designer label), 231–2, **231**
Berkhahn, Kevin, 225, 226, 232–4, **233**, **234**
Best, Elsdon, 103, 104
Bestall, Leo, 61
bikinis, 166–7
Billet, Gunner, 178
bird skins: in Māori clothing, 15–16
Black, Joan, 198
black singlet *see* singlet, black
Blandford, Henry, 152
Blundell, Nancy, 173
Bogor, 207, 210, **210**
Bowen, Godfrey, 216–17, **216**
Brady, Linda, 199
Brown, Joe, 222–3
Brown, Margaret, 172
Brown, Nigel, 213, **214**
Burnett, Anne, 38
Burnett, Barbara, 37–8
Burnett family, 28–9; heirloom dresses, 35–9, **36**, **37**, **plates 4–6**
Burnside High School, 54–5

Carroll, Carmel, 57–8
Carson, Valerie, 63, 98
Carter, Dan, 219
Cashmere High School, 56–7
castaways: clothing of, 8, 76–93
Catholic Cathedral College, 54
Cave, Augustus, 71
Caversham: clothing in, 113–14
Cederman, Ruth, 173–4
charitable aid, 115; *see also* benevolent institutions; poor; welfare state
Charteris, Betty, 195
christening gown, 66
churches: and second-hand clothing shops, 127–30
Clarke, John, 207–9, **208**, 210, 219
cloaks, Māori, 8, 12; feathered, 21–3, 72–3, **plate 2**; in Hawkes Bay Museum, 59–60, 71–4; kaitaka paepaeroa, 73–4, **74**, **plate 11**; kahu waero, **13**, 18–20, **19**, 94–110, **97**, **100**, **101**; materials used in, 15–21; modern, 27, 73; of Ruhia Pōrutu, 25, **plate 12**; status and, 13–14, 20, 23; weaving styles, 14, 20–1, 98–9, **99**; whakapapa and, 95, 104–11
clothing and dress: as heirlooms, 7, 28–40, 66; clothing trades in Palmerston North, 140–2; decline of fashion industry in 1980s, 239; gender issues and, 3, 155, 169, 179–85, 188, 205; Highland costume, 41–58; historiography of study of, 1–5; history of clothing trade, 133–5; identity and, 1, 7, 8, **26**, 41, 54, 58, 77–8, 81–3, 93, 114–15, 152–3, 179–85, 198–9, 201, 205; in art, 1, 168, 185, 212–13, **213**, **214**, **plate 1**; in benevolent institutions, 117–21; in maintaining respectability, 77–8, 91–3, 114–15, 117, 123, 131, 154–5; in wartime, 9, 168–85; international dimension of, 11, 155, 159, 167, 230; iconic Kiwi clothing, 206, 207, 221; modernity and, 155, 157–8, 204; poor and, 8, 113–26; rationing coupons, 170–2; remade clothing, 39, 66, 115; second-hand, 8, 126–31; shopping for, 8–9, 132–53; social change and, 11, 154–67; status and, 13–14, 20, 45, 169–70; used as punishment, 121; *see also* Māori clothing; men's clothing; second-hand clothing; women's clothing; work clothes; and names of specific types of clothing
clothing materials: harakeke, 70–1, 98–9, **99**, **plate 10**; hippie-inspired fabrics, 231–2; knit fabrics, 228; in Art Deco dress, 67; in black singlets, 213–14; in christening gown, 66; in Māori clothing, 15–21; in marching uniforms, 196–7; in 1960s–1980s high fashion, 226, 227; in swimwear, 154–5, 159, 161, 166–7; in wartime, 169, 171–2; in waistcoats, 62–3; *see also* bird skins; dog skins; sea lion skins; seal skins; silk; tartan; weaving
Cole, Colin, 226, 232, 234–5, **235**
Colenso, William, 25–6
collectors: in museums, 7–8, 60–1, 67, 70, 95; *see also* Dannefaerd, Sygvard; Hore, Eden
Collinson & Cunninghame Ltd, 142, 143–4, **144**, **145**, **146**, 146–7
Collison, Hinemoa, 67–8, **plate 9**
comedians: and black singlet, 206–10
consumerism: and clothing, 2, 123–4; anti-consumerist hippie ideology, 231; civilising influence of, 134; in wartime, 172–3; swimwear and, 159–61, 167; *see also* shopping
Cook, James, **13**, 15, 22–3, 98
Coote, Jeremy, 98
cosmetics: in wartime, 170, 181, 183

Cox, James, 115–17

Dagg, Fred, 207–9, **208**, 210, 219
dances: dressing for in wartime, 176–7, 179
Daniels, John, 57
Dannefaerd, Sygvard, 100–1, 103, 104
Davies, Guy, 53
De Lu, Katia, 57
de Luen, Madame Elizabeth, 150–2
de Maru, Maree, 236–7
Denholm, Jess, 57–8
Devereux, Mrs Humphrey, painting of, **34**, 35
DIC (shop), 171, **171**
Dixon, Claude, **146**
dog skins: in cloaks, 16–20, **17**, **19**, 96–7; kahu waero (white dog skins), **13**, 18–20, **19**, 94–110, **97**, **100**, **101**
Downs, Nyla, 198
dresses, **30**, **138**, **149**; Art Deco 21st dress, 67–8, **67**, **plate 9**; as heirlooms, 66; eighteenth-century heirloom dresses, 7, 28–40; in marching uniforms, 199–200; 1960s–1980s dresses, 68–70, **69**, 222, 224, 226–39, **231**, **233**, **234**, **235**, **236**, **237**, **238**
dressmakers, 137–8, 140–1, 142, 150–2; *see also* home sewing; names of individual dressmakers
Dunedin Female Refuge, 121
Duncan, Antony, 52
Dundonald, shipwreck, 76, 84–93
Dunlap, David and Jo, 231, 232

Eady, Scott, 241
Eagles, Colleen, 195
Eccles, Joy, 172
Edwards, Mihipeka, 176–7
Ellis, Bob, 88, 89, **91**
Eyre, Charles, 84–93 *passim*, **91**

fabrics *see* clothing materials
Fairburn, A. R. D., 204
fashion designers, 226–39; *see also* names of individual designers and design labels
fashion parades, 147–8; of Eden Hore's collection, 224–6
Fear, June, 181–2
femininity: and marching uniforms, 186, 191–2, 204–5; and uniforms, 182–5; *see also* masculinity
Footrot Flats, 207, 209–10, **209**, 219
footwear: 'austerity' shoes, 114, **114**; bootmakers, **141**, 142; castaway clothing, 81, 86–7, **87**, 88; 1920s shoes, **plate 9**
Forbes, George, 161, **162**
Forster, Johann, 22
Fowler, J. C., 139
Frame, Janet, 125
Frances, Jean, 173
Fraser, Peter, 45, **46**
freezing workers: clothing of, 217–18, **217**

Galland, Win, 176
gays: and black singlets, 221; and kilts, 57–8
gender: and clothing, 3; kilts and, 53–4, 56–7, 57–8
General Grant, shipwreck, 78–85
George, Elizabeth, 140
Gilroy, Captain Paddy, 78
Ginn, Elsie, 152

Glenshee, Naseby, Hore's museum at, 222, 224–5, **225**, **230**, 239–41, **240**
Gore Cavaliers (marching team), 199, **199**
Grafton, shipwreck, 76, 77–8
Graham, George Montrose, 96, 105, **107**, 111
Graham, George Samuel, 102–4, 105, 109–11, **110**
Graham, Margaret *see* Tiniraupeka, Te Wharetoroa
Graham, Rangihuia, 105
Grattan, John, 89, 90, **91**
Greenwood, John and Sarah, 32–5, **33**
Greenwood family, 28–9, 39–40; heirloom dress, 31–5, **32**, **plate 3**
Grenell, John Hore, 223–4
Grierson, Barbara and Daphne, 181
Gundersen, Torkil and Kari, **136**, 137
Gwilliam, Rosalie, 227–8, **plate 14**

Hadwen, Rachael, 220
Hakitara, 26, **plate 12**
Hall, Denis, sculpture by, 212, **213**
Hall, Rosaria, 229
Hallensteins, 48, 135
Hamilton, Augustus, 60–1, 101–2, 104
Hamilton, J. B., 143
Hansen, Mrs C. J., 140
Hanson, John, 133
Hapi, Mary Magdalene, 105, 110
Hardwick-Smith, Alison, 35
Harper, Arthur, 191
Harris, Edwin, 115
Hartley, Betty, 173
Hawkes Bay Art Gallery and Museum: clothing collections, 7–8; European clothing, 61–70; history of museum, 60–1; Māori clothing, 71–5
Hayman, Aaron, 81, **83**
Hector, Dr James, 95
Helean Kiltmakers, 51
Hellier, Patrick, **52**
Henley, Elizabeth Dandridge Aylett, **30**
Herrick, Barbara, 68–70, 226, 237–9; *see also* Babs Radon (designer label)
Hewitt, Pat, 225
Highbury House, 128–30
Highland Kilt Hire, 51
Hinemoa (ship), 84, 92, 93
Hodgkins, Frances, self-portrait, 1, **plate 1**
Holmes, Susan, 226, 227, 229
Homan, Peter, 227
home sewing: drapery shops for, 135, 142, 146–7; needles used by castaways, 86–7, **86**; women's dressmaking skills, 79; *see also* sewing machines
Hore, (James) Eden, 9–10, 222–6, **223**; dress collection of, 226–41
Hore, John, 223–4
Horne, Beverley, 231, **plate 12**
Hosking, Mary Susan, **138**
Howard, Mabel, 172–3
Howe, Jacky, 215
Hurley, Kathleen, 176

identity: after shipwreck, 77–8, 81–3, 93; clothing and, 1, 7, 8, **26**, 41; kilts, 54, 58; Kiwi identity and clothing, 206, 207, 221; loss of in uniform, 179–85; marching uniforms and, 198–9, 201, 205
Imrie, Mr and Mrs, **3**
Inglewood Vanguards (marching team), **196**, **197**,

198, **200**
Inia, (Iritana) Hilda, 105–11 *passim*
Inia, Kirihuruhuru, 105, 107
Iti, Tama, 44
Ivimey, George, 87, **88**, 88, **90**, **91**

James, Billy T., 207, 210, **211**
Jaye, James, 231, 232
Jenkins, Douglas Lloyd, 70
Jenkins, J., **2**
Jewell, Joseph, 78, **80**, 81, 84
Jewell, Mary Ann, 78, 79, **80**, 81, 83–4
Joel, Eleanor, 227, 229
Joel, Miranda, 227, 229
Johansen, F. & Co., bootmakers, **141**
Jones, Peggy, 191, 195, 201, 203
Josephs, Rachel, 198

Kahuka, 22
Kaiapoi High School, 55
kākahu kura, 21–3
kākāpō skins: used in clothing, 15
Kapiti, Pita, 24
Kapu, 23
Kasphara (design label), 230
Keats, Laurie, 215–16, 218
Keenan, Evelyn, 175
Kemp, Charlotte (née Greenwood), 35
Kiharoa, 101, 103, 104
kilts, 7, 41–58; as mark of status, 45; as symbol of hegemonic authority, 43, 45; as symbol of resistance, 43–4; as working clothes, 53; gays and, 57–8; history of, 41–5; in military uniforms, 45–9; in school uniforms, 53–7; in uniforms for dancing and pipe-bands, 49–51; sports uniforms, 53; *see also* tartan
Kingston, Pauline, 227, **plate 13**
Kiripūia, 12
Kiu, Rangi, 73
Kiwiana, 206, 211–13; on stamps, 212, **212**
Knudsen, Karl, 85, 86, 89, **91**, 92–3
kura *see* cloaks

Lander, Joan, 195
Laverty, James, 221
Lee, Barbara, 56
Liddell, John W., 133
Liverpool, Mavis, 113–14
Lucas, Vinka, 226, 232, **236**, **236**, **237**, **238**
Lush family quilt, 39, **plates 7–8**
Lyttelton Orphanage, 121

McCahon, Colin, 212–13
McClunie, Jessie, 177
Macdonald, Alex, 53
McDonald, Clementine, 174–5, **175**
McDonald, James, 102–4
McGregor, Robert, 67
MacIntosh, Matthew, 53
McKenzie, John, 45
McKenzie, Thomas, 25
McKenzies Ltd, marching team, 191
McLaughlin, Daniel, 85, 86, 89, **91**, 92
McLean family, 72
MacPherson, Gary, 53
Mairehau High School, 56

Makoro, 24
mannequin parades *see* fashion parades
Māori clothing, 4–5; adoption of European styles, 14, 27; after urbanisation, 125–6, **126**; and mana, 23–7; impact of Europeans on, 70–1, 134; kūmara planting clothes, 24; traditional clothing, 5–7, 12–27, 71–5; whakapapa of, 95, 104–11; *see also* names of specific types of clothes
Māori Women's Welfare league, 125–6
marching girls, 9, 186–205; history of marching, 186–95; uniforms, 195–205
Marino, Santiago, 88, **88**, 89, **91**
Marsh, Mrs E., 137
masculinity: and clothes, 206, 211; *see also* femininity; men's clothing
Mason, Bruce, 204
Mather, Robert, 57
Mattar, Michael, 226–7
men's clothing, **6**, 62–4, 81, 114, **146**, **161**, **163**, **164**; *see also* kilts; masculinity; singlet, black; swimwear; waistcoats; wedding costume; women's clothing
Mercer, June, 231, 232
Methodist Church: and second-hand clothing, 127–8
Midhirst Spic-n-Span (marching team), **193**
Miet, Andrew, 104
Mika, Beatrice and Josephine, 105
Mildon, Emily, 9, 148–53, **149**
millinery, 140–1; in wartime, 172–3
Mills, John, sculpture by, 168, 185
Minhinnick, Gordon, **207**
Mitchell Kilt Hire, 51
moa skins: and Māori clothing, 15, 16
modernity: reflected in clothing, 155, 157–8, 204
Mohair Awards, 229
Munro, Jim, 61
Museum of New Zealand *see* Te Papa Tongarewa
museums: and clothing collections, 11, 75; eighteenth-century silk dresses in, 39; *see also* names of specific museums
Musgrave, Thomas, 77, 79

Napier Girls' High School, 54
Nekepapa, 25
Nelson, Peggy, 195
Nelson, Thomas, 132, **133**
New Zealand Army, Scottish units in, 47–9
New Zealand Gown of the Year, 224, 227
New Zealand Red Cross, transport driver, **184**
New Zealand Women's Land Service, 177, 182, **182**
Niblock, Ruth, 177–8
Nicholas, John Liddiard, 20
Nickson, Bev, 195
nudism, 157

Olsen, Emil Olaus, 142

Paenga, Rangi, 217
Palmerston North: development of shopping precinct, 135–43
Palmerston North Girls' High School, **56**
Papaioea *see* Palmerston North
Papanui High School, 54
Parry, W. E. (Bill), 191
Penberthy, Barbara, 68–70, 226, 237–9; *see also* Babs Radon (designer label)

Perry, Jane, 35
Peters, Jabez, 85
pipe bands: uniforms, 49–50, **50**
Pither, Olivia, 57
Pitt Rivers Museum, Oxford, **13**, 18, 98
poor: and clothing, 8, 113–26; *see also* second-hand clothing
Pōrutu, Ihaia, 25
Pōrutu, Ruhia, 25, **plate 12**
Pōrutu, Te Rira, 25
Pui, Bev, 195
Puke Ariki, 17
Puketapu-Hetet, Erenora, **99**
Pul, Michael, 86, 88, 89, **91**

quilts: Lush family heirloom, 39, **plates 7–8**

rabbit skins: in castaway clothing, 79
Rangi Ruru Girls' School, 55, **55**
Rapley, Yvonne, 173
rationing of clothing, 170–2
Rawahotana, 17
Raymond, Cherry, 70
Raynal, François, 77–8
Regnault, Claire, 70
Riccarton High School, 55
Ringatū religion, 108, **108**, **109**
Roberts, Albert, 84, 87, **88**, **91**, 93
Robertson, Peg, 174
Robinson Crusoe *see* Selkirk, Alexander
Rogers, Captain Woodes, 78
Ross, C. M. & Co., **139**, 142, 143, **147**, 148, **150**, 150
Ross, Charles, **139**, 140
Roy, Eric, 45
royalty: link with marching, 202–3
Rukutia, 23
Rutherford, Ernest, 45

St Hilda's Collegiate School, 54
St Joseph's Orphanage, Upper Hutt, **122**
St Mark's School, 55
St Michael's Church School, 55
school uniforms: compared with marching uniforms, 198; cost of, 123, 124–5; kilts and, 53–7; Māori children and, **126**
Scotch Kiwi Clothing, 53
Scott, Walter, 44
sea lion skins, 88, **89**
seal skins: in castaway clothing, 77, 79–81, **80**, **82**, **83**, 85–6, **87**, 87–8, **90**; in Māori clothing, 16
second-hand clothing, 126–31; *see also* poor; vintage clothing
Selkirk, Alexander ('Robinson Crusoe'), 78, 86
sewing machines, **3**, **113**, 139; *see also* home sewing
shearers: clothing of, 53, 212, **213**, 215–17, **216**, 218
shipwrecks: clothing of castaways, 8, 76–93
shoes *see* footwear
shopping, 8–9, 132–53; as recreation, 148, 152–3; *see also* consumerism
shops: as cogs of British colonial expansion, 133–5; discount sales, 143; in Palmerston North, 132, 135–43; mail-order services, 143–4; mannequin parades in, 147–8; second-hand clothing, 127–30, 142–3; window displays and interior design, 144–7; *see also* names of individual shops
silk: eighteenth-century, 29–31, 32–3, **33**, 35–7, **36**, 37, **plates 3–6**; re-used, 39, **plates 7–8**; stockings, 171–2, 185
Silver, Burton, 207, 210
Simpson, Joyce, 190, 204–5
singlet, black, 9, 11, 206–21; as women's wear, 218, 220; gays and, 221; in advertising, 212; in art, 212–3, **213**, **214**; Kiwi icon, 206, 211–13; on postage stamps, 212; urban wear, 218–9; use in comedy, 206–10
Skin Things, 231, 232
Slattery, Ned ('Shiner'), 117
Smither, Elizabeth, 130
Snelson, Louisa and George, 136
Snowden, Rita, 127–8
Spencer, Dr William, 64–6
sportswear, 206, 219; kilts as, 53; marching uniforms, 186–205; Scottish sports, 49, 51, **51**, **52**
Steele, John and Margaret, 239, 241
Steele, Patrick, 229
Steuart, Hew, 62–4
Stewart, J. T., 135
sunbathing, 156, 161–2
swaggers: and clothing, 115–17, **116**
swimming: as healthy exercise, 155–6, 162; as recreation, 158–9; *see also* sunbathing
swimwear, 9, 154–67; body image and, 163–7; costume bylaws, 156–9, **158**, 167; *see also* bikinis

Taharākau, 23
tailors: in Palmerston North, 137, 140–2
Tait, Davinia, 199, **199**
Taiwhakaea, 22
Tamango, 22
Tamanuiaraki, 23
Tamaterangi, 24
Tareha, 27
tartan, 42, 51–2, 53; choice for school uniforms, 54–5; codified, 45; in blankets traded with Māori, 43–4; in marching uniforms, 201–2; *see also* kilts
Tāwhaki, 24
Te Amai, Ramaka, 17
Te Angianga, 23
Te Awe Awe, Ereni, 26
Teer, James, 78–9, 81, 82, 84
Te Kanawa, Rangi, 73–4
Te Kira, 105
Temple of Fashion Costume Manufactory (Auckland), **2**
Te Oranga Reformatory, 121
Te Ore Ore Marae, 71
Te Panau, Kerei, **26**
Te Papa Tongarewa (Museum of New Zealand), clothing collections, 7, 114; collections of taonga, 94–6; eighteenth-century heirloom dresses, 28–9, 35, 38
Te Ratutonu, 25
Te Uremutu, Eruera, **101**
Thompson, Bessie, 66
Thompson, Charles, **151**
Thompson, Elizabeth (née Macauley), **151**
Thompson, Mildred, 66
Thomson, Anna, **55**
Timaru Balmoral (marching team), **202**
Tiniraupeka, Te Wharetoroa, 94, **97**, 98, 99, 102–4, 105–9, **106**, 110–11
Topeora, Rangi, 25

Toto, 16
Treaty of Waitangi, 25; clothing worn at, 25–7, **plate 12**
Tschepp, Maritza, 227, 229–30
Turi, 16

Uhia, 22
Underwood, George, 114
uniforms, 10–11; Air New Zealand, 236; feminisation of military uniforms, 186, 191–2, 198; gender issues, 179–85; kilts and, 45–9, 53–7; marching girls and, 9, 186–205; William Spencer's 18th Royal Irish Regiment tunic, 64–6, **65**; women and, 179–85, 188; *see also* school uniforms
Utiku, Rangi and Riria, 173, **174**

Victorian Heritage Festival, Oamaru, 112
vintage clothing, 130–1; *see also* second-hand clothing
Vivian, Harold, 146

waistcoats, 59; harakeke, 70–1, **plate 10**; Hew Steuart's, 62–4, **62**, **63**
Waitaki Girls' High School, 56
Waite, Edgar, 84
Waitere, Tene, 108
Walters, Henry, **88**, 89, **91**
Wanganui Highland Rifles, **47**, 48, **48**
Wapiti Handcrafts, 231, 232
Warnock, Kelly & Adkin, drapers, **140**
weaving, 14; of Māori cloaks, 20–1, 98–9, **99**
wedding costume, **151**, 228; as heirlooms, 66; for gays, 57–8; in wartime, 173–6, **174**, **175**; Scottish, 52–3

weka skins: in Māori clothing, 15–16
welfare state: and provision of clothing, 121–6; *see also* charitable aid; poor
Wellington City Mission, **127**, **129**
Wellington Sargettes (marching team), **187**, **194**
West, John, 231–2
Whakataupoti, 17
Wharepapa, 25–6
Windsor Primary School, 57
women: as upholders of civilisation, 81; in uniform, 177–85, 188; responsible for clothing provision, 79, 123–4; shopping and, 148–53; war work and, 180–1; *see also* femininity
Women's Auxiliary Air Force (WAAF), 178–9, 180, 181
Women's Auxiliary Army Corps (WAAC), 177–8, **179**, 180, 181–2, **183**
women's clothing, 7, 81, **155**, **160**, **164**, **166**; black singlet, 218, 220; in wartime, 9, 168–85; military uniforms, 177–85; worn by Emily Mildon, 9, 148–53; *see also* dresses; femininity; kilts; marching girls; men's clothing; swimwear; wedding costume
Women's War Service Auxiliary, 177, 198
Wood, W. T., **26**
Wood family, **26**
Woolworths (NZ) Ltd, marching team, 189, **189**, **190**
work clothes, 115–17, 142; black singlet as, 206, 211, 213–18, **220**; kilts as, 53; of women in wartime, 168–9, **182**
World of Wearable Art Museum, 229
World War II: marching girls during, 190–1; women's clothing during, 9, 168–85